Women, Power and the Economy

In the complex landscapes of multiple global crises, the book unfolds as a panoramic journey through the intricate pathways of women and power, weaving a tapestry that transcends crises and ushers in a transformative vision of a just world.

Against the backdrop of a patriarchal history steeped in autocratic power practices, the author urges us to recognize, understand and redefine power in its myriad forms for *collective feminist power practices*. With meticulous analysis, she unveils challenges posed by the patriarchal backlash, exposing the normalized male definitions of power and the societal structures that sustain pathological power relationships. The narrative of the book intertwines power, economy and patriarchy, laying bare the many traps for complicity with the patriarchal systems. The author advocates for a paradigm shift, emphasizing the role of female memories and genealogies as foundational elements for a *collective feminist practice*. Power, in this context, emerges not as a force for dominance but as the ability to make a positive impact, flourishing in the rich diversity of differences. The envisioned future is one where societies thrive on commons, planetary care, feminist economies and pluriversality. The narrative charts a course toward a feminist democracy, rooted in nurturing the planet and safeguarding future generations. Governance and networks stand as keystones in shaping these utopian landscapes, where pioneers and movements play vital roles in sculpting the contours of tomorrow.

The book offers practical tools for strengthening *collective feminist practices* that can restructure power pathologies. It unfolds as a captivating vista, where the echoes of the past harmonize with the aspirations of a feminist future.

Inca Petra Kuenkel is a transformation psychologist, systems scientist, university lecturer, visionary author and expert in change management and leadership. She is founder of the Collective Leadership Institute, member of the Club of Rome and the World Academy of Arts and Science.

'At a time of widespread despondency, this powerful book provides possibilities for hope. Emphasizing that patriarchal mindsets permeate all the central challenges of our times, it argues for the urgent need for a regenerative feminist paradigm of practice to move towards creating egalitarian and just societies that are in harmony with nature.'

Jayati Ghosh, *Professor of Economics, University of Massachusetts Amherst*

'*Women, Power and the Economy* connects feminist theory with actionable strategies for creating a balanced, just and regenerative partnership future for us all.'

Riane Eisler, *author of* The Chalice and the Blade

'As patriarchy, power and profit are re-gaining ground and destabilizing countries across the globe, *Women, Power and the Economy* offers another vision – one that weaves feminist wisdom and strategic insights on transformative change into a roadmap for building inclusive, life-serving civilizations. You don't need to be a feminist to understand that today's brand of patriarchy goes counter to deep human values and an understanding of 21st century challenges. The book shows how the application of different value-based transformational pathways is fundamental to meet those challenges.'

Sandrine Dixson-Declève, *Executive Chair of the Earth4All Initiative; co-author of* Earth For All: A Survival Guide for Humanity; *Honorary President of The Club of Rome*

Women, Power and the Economy

Collective Feminist Practice Can Transform the World

Inca Petra Kuenkel

Routledge
Taylor & Francis Group
LONDON AND NEW YORK

Designed cover image: Getty Images: AlonzoDesign

First published 2026
by Routledge
4 Park Square, Milton Park, Abingdon, Oxon OX14 4RN

and by Routledge
605 Third Avenue, New York, NY 10158

Routledge is an imprint of the Taylor & Francis Group, an informa business

British Library Cataloguing-in-Publication Data
A catalogue record for this book is available from the British Library

ISBN: 978-1-032-83346-0 (hbk)
ISBN: 978-1-032-80537-5 (pbk)
ISBN: 978-1-003-50888-5 (ebk)

DOI: 10.4324/9781003508885

Typeset in Goudy
by Newgen Publishing UK

To the women of the world past, present, and future – who have dared to dream, resist and reshape. This book is for our feminist ancestors who carved paths where none existed, for the voices that refused to be silenced and for the hands that built bridges of solidarity across cultures and generations. It is for those with the everyday acts of courage, the quiet revolutionaries and those building the collective power of women who stand up to patriarchy in all its forms – fighting not just for themselves, but for a world rooted in justice, care and dignity. With deep gratitude, I honor your resilience, your struggles and your unwavering determination to create a better future. This book is for all of you who shape the map of liberation, one act of defiance and hope at a time. May it encourage you to continue.

Table of Contents

Figures

About the Author

Inca Petra Kuenkel is a visionary scientific and non-fiction author specializing in sustainability transformations. As a leading expert on societal change, her work emphasizes partnership, dialogue and collaboration as catalysts for systemic progress. She founded and led the feminist-inspired Collective Leadership Institute for 17 years, pioneering frameworks for collective action and transformative leadership. Kuenkel is a distinguished member of the renowned think- and do-tank Club of Rome, where she served six years on its Executive Board, contributing to global thought leadership on ecological and social resilience. Additionally, she is a fellow of the World Academy of Art and Science, further solidifying her role as an advocate for integrating science, art and wisdom in addressing global challenges. Her impactful work bridges theory and practice, making her a prominent voice in sustainability and societal transformation dialogues.

Preface – Women are Shaping the Future of the World

Women, power and the economy are not just buzzwords in contemporary discussions, but rather the cornerstones of societies in transition and, moreover, of a world at the beginning of transformations which might go in different directions. In an era marked by significant technological and democratic advances as well as global interconnectedness, but also climate change and an outdated economic system that widens the gap between rich and poor, we face the challenge of a growing number of authoritarian regimes, the resurgence of wars, the undermining of democracy and the eroding of the constitutional state. Not surprisingly, there is an alarming increase in violence against women – within more peaceful societies in the domestic sphere, and in wars as the old tactic of dehumanizing the enemy through rape and torture. At the same time, we need to constructively deal with internal conflicts in feminist movements that are both testimony to the importance of acknowledging the difference among women and a symptom that is as old as patriarchy – divide and rule. Neither the growing patriarchal backlash nor the conflict among feminists is a new phenomenon. Whenever there is the abolishment of patriarchy on the horizon and advances are palpable towards egalitarian societies, the patterns have shifted and patriarchal thought systems struck back and manifested in societal structures, wars, exploitation and the degradation of civilization. Centuries of history are testimony of this. Can we change this trajectory?

Abolishing the patriarchal infrastructure, both mentally and physically at a global scale, is not an option, but an urgent necessity. It means not just the elimination of a dysfunctional order in certain areas such as equal rights, but the transition to a world in which men and women, people of all gender identities, can act on equal terms and relate to the non-human world with the kind of reverence that shows their capability of deep humanness. This transformation is the key to tackling the major challenges of our time, be it climate change, nature exploitation or social inequalities.

But what exactly are patriarchal thought systems? This invisible but powerful mental infrastructure holds the world in its grip without most people realizing it. Patriarchy manifests itself in a variety of forms, from subtly undermining women and people who do not fit the patriarchal norm to outright violence; from structures that keep women away from power positions to those that deliberately humiliate women. Patriarchy is easy to explain but difficult to grasp. It manifests itself in so many forms, ranging from subtle mental oppression to blatant physical brutality. But the fundamental principles have remained the same over centuries, if not millennia: Dominance, exploitation, aggression and oppression. Overcoming patriarchy requires not only a change in external structures, but also a change in internal beliefs and thought patterns.

But how can we overcome patriarchy? We must recognize the fundamental role of *collective feminist leadership*, which is based on the vision that women and people of all gender identities can shape the future together on equal terms. It's about resistance to the pervasiveness of a patriarchally coded world. It's also about recognition, respect and acceptance of diversity. And it's about dialogue and collaboration. This forms the core, the essence from which an immeasurable vitality and liveliness in societies arises. But to achieve this, we must overcome patriarchy as a structure and as a mindset. Because the so deeply ingrained forms of inequality, the non-acceptance of diversity, the lack of respect and the dominance of some people over others, need to be seen as what they are – human pathologies that require treatment. Patriarchy is a mental infrastructure of the past. This time of ours is of crucial importance. If we fail to abolish patriarchy, we will not be able to tackle the pressing problems of our time – be it climate change, exploitative economic structures or social inequalities. Because the central cause lies in the culture of dominance, be it of humans over nature, of men over women, of one region over others or of one skin color over another. Patriarchal mindsets permeate all of the global challenges of our time.

The road ahead is not an easy one. This book is therefore not just a collection of words; it's a path that I, as the architect of its narrative, have traversed, and it's one that awaits you, the reader. Like all journeys worth embarking on, this one is rich with unexpected encounters, leading us into uncharted territories of thought and action. Prepare to be challenged, inspired and maybe transformed.

My feminist journey of the past 40 years has seen despair and hope, successful and unsuccessful attempts to support female power ambition, realistic and unrealistic efforts to distribute my own power into the hands of other women. It has seen phases of powerlessness when I did not want to believe that even 50% women on a board could not result in shifting towards a feminist paradigm. There were times when I went underground with my feminist ambition, because there would have been no chances for a career or business success with an open feminist stance. At other times I doubted the possibility of feminist transformations when I was expelled from a feminist community, because of different thought and action, or when I realized that so many women just wanted to make peace with patriarchy. The road ahead is riddled with inconsistencies and serious dangers. Yet we need to take it.

Why do I call this book a journey? Because life itself is a journey, and within it, we find ourselves navigating through uncharted waters, often without a clear destination in sight. It's about embracing the unknown, being open to encounters and adventures, and learning from unexpected sources. Just as in life, this book will lead us to familiar places and unexpected detours, all with a deeper meaning waiting to be discovered. Writing it forced me to reflect on my feminist practice; reading it might challenge you to reconsider your feminist practice. Together, we might then improve our *collective feminist practice.* I believe it will be the most powerful path to transforming this world.

One of the hallmarks of a journey into uncharted territory is the ability to adapt and respond to what emerges along the way. Despite our best-laid plans, the course of our journey may shift unexpectedly, guiding us in new directions. So it will be with this book. We will navigate twists and turns, exploring diverse perspectives and uncovering hidden truths. This journey is an invitation to adventure, and I invite you to join me. Think of this book as your subtle compass, open to your individual adjustments and interpretations, guiding you through territories of thought and possibility, some old, some new, some surprising. Expect the unexpected, for within these pages lie profound insights and transformative experiences.

Why is this journey so important? Because we are at a pivotal moment in history, where the need for feminist transformations has never been more urgent and never more possible. Despite the despair we may feel when looking at the state of the world, the message on the horizon is clear: Patriarchy, with its deep-rooted pathologies, is coming to an end. It has held sway for far too long, shaping our societies and distorting our perceptions of human nature.

Over centuries and millennia, it showed its brutal face and does so today in some societies. In other societies it appears overcome on the surface, but undermines societal peace in both private and political realms, from domestic violence to right-wing populist movements. Its underlying paradigm of dominance, exploitation and competition has informed and still is informing our entire capitalist economy. But even in times when hopes grew towards the potential economic justice of communist or socialist societies, patriarchy returned in violent ways, showing its inherent disdain for the life of people and nature. The patriarchal mindset underscores the way we rape our planet, eroding the very source of life we stem from.

But it hasn't always been this way. Human nature is not inherently violent or oppressive; it is capable of collaboration, empathy and compassion. It knows how to take care of the planet. It is time to remember our true human history and stop believing the linear storyline of our men-driven human progress. What was once declared 'wild' in Western ignorance turns out to be most valuable Indigenous knowledge. What was once seen as 'irrational and emotional' in so-called rationality will become our pathway into life-serving societies. What was once seen as 'barbarian' may turn out to have been ancient societies that had much in common with modern sustainability movements, while the rational modern man turns out to be truly barbarian.

The time has come to envision a new paradigm – a *regenerative feminist civilization*. Feminism, in this context, is not about women ruling over men but about creating egalitarian, socially just societies that live in harmony with nature. It's about recognizing our interconnectedness and working together to build a better world for all. I am not advocating for false harmony or even surveilled societies. Inherent conflicts are and must be an inevitable aspect of human societies; however, our capacity lies in crafting civilizations that facilitate peaceful conflict resolution. This involves actively listening to each other's concerns, fostering spaces for collective intelligence to thrive and collaboratively working towards societal improvement that encompasses the needs of all individuals while preserving the environment. It's possible to adhere to principles of justice, fairness, equality and peace without advocating for superficial harmony. Dissent serves as the catalyst for innovation and learning, and it's through collective action that we can embrace this. Chaos is sometimes essential for growth and transformation; it propels us to elevate human capabilities. Therefore, it's not the presence of chaos, conflicts or disagreements that poses the challenge, but rather how we navigate them. The true question lies in our ability to cultivate societies where everyone is equipped to engage with disagreements, dissent and conflicts constructively, fostering a culture of continual learning and growth.

But overcoming patriarchy is no easy task. It requires us to confront our own complicity with the existing power structures and to challenge the deeply ingrained norms and beliefs that uphold them. Indeed, we need to embark on the long and arduous journey to *unlearn patriarchy*.[1] Women, in particular, must play a leading role in this transformation, as they have done throughout history in the fight against oppression and exploitation. Women play a crucial role in shaping a future civilization that has the central purpose of creating and maintaining a *Good Life for All*. It is time to bring women into power positions at scale. More precisely, it is time to bring feminist women into power positions at scale. Feminists are the pioneers for dismantling patriarchy as a structure, mindset and legitimation of actions. Why women, why feminists?

When I advocate for feminist and women-led transformations, I emphasize the vital role women must and will play in shaping the future. This is because men often exhibit a stronger complicity with existing power structures, finding affirmation in the norms of patriarchy that have become deeply ingrained and normalized. Many men perceive these structures as inherent to human nature, although some can see through the veil and realize their own captivity. It is evident that the outcomes of patriarchal systems – such as resource depletion, rampant capitalism, escalating conflicts, disregard for climate change and ecological balance, social inequalities, colonialism, racism and authoritarianism – are not desired by many men either. It's also important to recognize that complicity with patriarchy is not exclusive to men; there are women who uphold and benefit from these systems. Some women who attain power driven by ambition or by societal and geographical circumstances are often unaware of their perpetuation of patriarchal dominance over others. Understanding these mechanisms is crucial in fostering genuine transformation. Yet, men fundamentally gain from the masculine order, as it always offers opportunities for identification, particularly in times when traditional gender identities erode. Men are therefore even more unconscious in their complicity. They are more corruptible. It is even more difficult for them to distance themselves from patriarchal gains, although it is possible, and many men undoubtedly also aspire to the abolition of patriarchy.

I believe, not renovating, but dismantling patriarchy and inventing pathways into a regenerative civilization must be promoted by many more women, indeed by feminists. At the core of this effort should be a *feminist reference system* that establishes a new mental infrastructure, which then guides action, supports the legitimacy of a female and feminist ambition for power and leads to a new normality. The freedom and recognition of diversity, equality and respect are central elements of the paradigm shift we need to restore social, economic and ecological balance. Despite dissent and conflict, despite debate and mutual hostility, we need feminist collective action and mutual support based on a paradigm of future civilizations that care about the *Good Life for All.*

To understand what it would mean to be born into this new normal, imagine you lived in a global culture in which every girl deserves to be nurtured within a supportive framework, a symbolic structure that fosters her confidence and provides a sense of belonging. This framework would act like a mental support network she can rely on, establishing a climate where she inherently understands her worth and contribution to the world. Building such a reference system is not just crucial for women; it's fundamental for society as a whole. It is fundamental for everybody, women and men, in future civilizations. The new normal would serve as a foundational cornerstone, akin to a universal basic income, ensuring that every individual is empowered and validated.

Why should women save the world that has been taken on a destructive path by men? The answer sounds simple: Because nobody else will do in the way it is needed. Every attempt towards human betterment has been riddled with inherent attempts to *not* abolish patriarchy (or at least not entirely). Time is up now. For thousands of years life has asserted itself in and through us women. We have been giving this asset away to support patriarchal men, mindsets and structures. As Virginia Woolf elaborated the idea in her essay *A Room of One's Own*: Women have upheld mirrors that helped men to feel much greater than they were.[2] It is time to withdraw these mirrors from men and help women grow in their own image. Moreover, we should be confident in our capabilities for a more civilized future. Women, no matter where on this planet, are organizing life, in peace, in war, after wars, in cities, in the countryside, in companies, in politics.

Can we, for a change, withdraw our energy from supporting the patriarchy and focus our ability to foster life on women and their ambition to gain power and exercise this power in a responsible way? Can we use our skills, which have never left us throughout history, and direct them towards an emerging regenerative civilization?

This book is a call to action, a rallying cry for a collective feminist claim to power and social change. It's about reclaiming our humanity and forging a path towards a just and equitable future. So let us embark on this journey together, knowing that the destination may be uncertain but the rewards will be immeasurable.

Notes

1 The many facets can be discovered in Jaspers & Ryland (2022) and Jaspers et al. (2024).
2 See Woolf (1929).

References

Jaspers, L., & Ryland, N. (2022). *Unlearn Patriarchy*. Ullstein.

Jaspers, L., Ryland, N., & Horch, S. (2024). *Unlearn Patriarchy II*. Ullstein.

Woolf, V. (1929). *A Room of One's Own*. Hogarth Press.

Acknowledgments

A book like this takes shape long before the first word is written. This one began knocking on the door of my soul long before the idea of writing about women and power was fully formed. I can trace its origins back several decades, to a time when I was grappling with an unanswered question: Why do women relinquish their power to men who continuously erode the love that should be at the heart of world-making?

Since then, life has taken me to many corners of the world. I am deeply grateful for the privilege of encountering an incredible wealth of humanness – in Yemen, Zimbabwe, Laos, Colombia, Brazil, Germany, Namibia, Senegal, Mozambique, the United States, Vietnam, China, Argentina, Gambia, the Democratic Republic of Congo, India, Palestine, Egypt, Mali, Kenya, Lebanon, Tunisia, Thailand, Cambodia, Lesotho, Chile, and South Africa, the home of my heart.

Throughout my professional journey, a profound longing has accompanied me: The dream of an island where women rule with reverence for life, where I would feel safe and understood. A place where power is not a tool of domination but an obligation to serve people and the world. Yet the question of why women give away their power remained unresolved, lingering in the background as life unfolded, insights deepened and the rebel in me decided to act.

I envisioned creating such an island – not as a utopia, but as an institution that would embody the feminist values I see as essential for our collective future. Along this path, encounters, disagreements, challenges, disappointments and successes all shaped the content of this book. I am profoundly grateful for the conversations with my colleagues at the institute and with countless other women. Their insights gradually gave shape to the contours of this book, and their encouragement spurred me to turn it into a research and writing project.

As this journey unfolded, my encounters expanded. I rediscovered the continuity of feminist writing across centuries and geographies, and the enduring faithfulness of feminists to the vision of a different world. My deepest gratitude goes to all feminist world-makers – known and unknown, published and unpublished – for their dreams, expertise, longing, courage and unwavering commitment to creating feminist futures.

Introduction: The Urgency of a Feminist Practice of Power for a Vision of a Just World

Imagine you live in a country that looks quite different from those of today. Power, politically, economically as well as in all decision-making, is held by women. They lead and organize societal life, while men are responsible for the home and are supposed to stay in the family sphere. This means they are not supposed to show up in public and act as full-scale citizens. The country is peaceful and has been like this for as long as anybody can imagine. It has a harmonious landscape that looks like a garden, everything is protected and cared for. Buildings are constructed based on ecological criteria and agriculture is regenerative, only carried out with renewable energies. Ecological balance is lived and understood by everybody. This means, people only use electricity-powered machines, and always operate in harmony with the landscape. Cooking is done with solar energy and people move around in solar-powered flying cars. Women lead universities and conduct research on organic farming, nutrition and health. There is no military. There are no pandemics; everyone grows old and is committed to peaceful coexistence. A queen rules the country and the state creed is love and truth. Anyone who violates this must leave the country unless they regret the act. The reason men in this country were locked away is that women needed to prevent them from getting into mischief. They did not invent the reason for this danger, but acted out of experience. Every citizen knows the history and understands it should not be repeated. This learning how to best organize society came about long ago, when some people fled to this country from a dictatorial neighboring state that brutally suppressed people. The authoritarian ruler of this state demanded that the refugees be handed over, but the queen of this country refused. The neighboring ruler then declared war and invaded the country. Of course, all men in this fiercely attacked country were drafted into the army and fought bravely, but had no chance, because the enemy was too strong. When the enemy army was advancing dangerously, a council of wise women came together. They decided to save the country with collective intelligence and try out the plan a female university rector had suggested. To do this, all remaining men were asked to immediately withdraw into their houses. The university rector marched onto the battlefield with thousands of women. They were all focused on mentally redirecting the sunlight onto the enemy's army. No matter how advanced their weapons were, the aggressors could no longer stand the heat and light. So, they fled, leaving behind all their ammunition and weapons, which were burned by the concentrated heat of the sun. The country was never attacked again – and the men stayed in their houses forever.

I wonder what the comments column of your mind was remarking while you were reading this imagination. When did you start judging that we do not want a future simply turning around power relations between women and men? Or were you stumbling over the flying cars, which made it a utopian fairy tale, although, indeed, needing no roads would help our planet? Did you make a note that nothing was said about democracy? When did you feel reminded of today's male warlords and authoritarian rulers? Did you feel a secret wish to end all wars by redirecting sunlight?

Some of you may know the retelling of this story. It is a text from 1905 by a Bengali writer, Rokeya Hossain.[1] She was a feminist writer and a social worker. She fought for education for girls, and founded girls' schools and universities. 'Sultana's Dream' is the name of the short story. It is a utopia about a state she called Ladyland where women held public power. In the story, Sultana, an Indian woman, dreams that she wakes up in the middle of the night and is kidnapped into another world by a woman who she mistakes for her sister. In Ladyland, men have to stay at home and women have to deal with politics and shaping society.

There are four reasons why I start a book on women, power and the economy with the feminist utopian (not dystopian) story that has been imagined about 120 years ago, a timespan difficult to comprehend for our minds that are so locked in the present.

The *first* reason is that the story pushes us right into the topic of acknowledging that it may make a difference to our world, if women claim power at scale and together. Many women still believe we might shift the world toward peace and sustainability without claiming power collectively as women, and by always striving for fairness through balancing power equally with men. For now, stay with the story and consider that there might be an urgent need for women to indeed radically claim power, and that going back to balancing can be done much later.

The *second* reason is that the aggressive authoritarian ruler invading a country sounds so strangely familiar in our 21st century that it makes the story less utopian and more realistic. Even today, authoritarian men seem to find fertile ground and too much acclaim or obedience. We will see in the coming chapters how important it is that we understand the mechanisms of such power pathologies. It also hints to the consideration that the prospects of men not getting into mischief without radically abolishing patriarchy might be rather weak.

The *third* reason is that Rokeya stands with her story for millions of women who not only resisted patriarchy, but drafted a vision for a different future, in which women hold power. We will see in the chapters that follow whether these utopias that so many women sketched out are unrealistic dreams, achievable visions of future civilizations or memories of a distant past whose essence we urgently need to bring back into the present today.

The *fourth* reason is that I believe we need more positive utopias like the one from Rokeya that challenge our mind to go beyond our own comfort zone and to transgress the boundaries of our captured thinking. This is not about dreaming of the peaceful island that has once been existing somewhere and continues to inspire our longing. Only by consciously and collectively imagining what seems impossible today can we begin to build the future we want. It is time for female visionaries to take the stage, and for their unique perspectives on the future to be amplified, shared and widely discussed. Above all, we need to know these female visionaries of the past and the present.

Imagine, we could decide today to perceive the world with a different lens – like putting on a 3D glass. Imagine, we stepped out of our chronic longing for what I will call the *harmonious female island*, and we could suddenly see all these places in the world where women have been and are working towards an end to patriarchy in its variety of forms that come across as mental and structural order. Imagine if all these places – past and present – were suddenly illuminated. Picture looking at the globe, at a world map, and seeing them all lit up. Now, imagine if every place where women have nurtured ecological knowledge and cared for each other and the planet, ensuring life could continue, were also illuminated. The entire map would glow, so bright and full that you wouldn't see countries, let alone borders. There would be no space left for all the nonsense that happens in the world.

We know that patriarchy is a self-perpetuating mental and societal order, molded into similarly self-perpetuating social and economic structures. And yet: Both Indigenous peoples and quantum physics or even cognitive science tell us that reality changes depending on how we observe it. Currently, the world perceives itself through the lens of a patriarchal mental order – as if this were the only reality. Exclusively that. This filter renders the contributions of women invisible on the world map. They cannot be seen. We must make them visible. It is essential that we shift both our thinking and our perception. Here is the dilemma: When we only focus our awareness on fighting what is perpetuating patriarchy, we are at the same time unconsciously supporting it. There is nothing wrong with criticizing and challenging patriarchal structures. We must do so. But the point is not to renovate, tame or civilize the actual intrinsically barbaric patriarchal culture, but to abolish it. It is time to move beyond patriarchy.

So, what do I mean by patriarchy? Let me make an attempt at a simplified definition, knowing that there are as many connotations of patriarchal cultures as they are people on this planet.[2] *Patriarchy* is a social system that promotes male dominance and control over political, economic, social and cultural areas. It is based on a deeply rooted belief that men are superior and have the right to rule over women and other people they see as less important. This mindset has manifested itself for thousands of years in various forms around the world, leading to gender inequality, discrimination and oppression. It has created various social categories, such as gender, race, class, sexual orientation, religion and others, which are used as reasons for different forms of oppression that overlap and intersect in their effects. The patriarchal mental order can be seen in all social structures, from the economy and the exploitation of natural or human resources to authoritarian forms of state and government. Climate change, one of the greatest challenges of our time, can also be understood as a result of male dominance over resources, nature's ruthless exploitation and ignorance towards the planetary boundaries.

We can call patriarchy a *mental infrastructure* because it represents a deeply ingrained way of thinking, a cognitive framework that shapes how individuals and societies view gender, power and authority. This mental infrastructure legitimizes certain behaviors – such as male dominance and female subordination as a blueprint for various forms of power imbalances – by embedding them in the very fabric of everyday thought and decision-making. Over time, these power relations have been taken for granted, becoming seemingly natural or inevitable. At the same time, patriarchy functions as a *symbolic order*, a system of language and cultural symbols that structures how social relations and identities are produced, and what is considered valuable, powerful or legitimate.[3] This symbolic order not only reinforces male dominance but also exploits and humiliates those who do not conform to its open and subtle definitions of gender and power. Both concepts show how patriarchy operates on multiple levels: As an internalized mental framework and as a visible, structured system of cultural norms that perpetuates inequality and legitimized power imbalances.

We cannot really take a step towards a different future unless patriarchy as an arrangement of societies, as an arrangement of world society, as a spiritual agreement, and as an omnipresent *reference system* for action is overcome.

Only then is the path truly clear. Only then can we honestly talk about human evolution.

Advancements in gender equality and respect for gender identities are important stepping stones, but not more than that. For the radical shift required to abolish patriarchy globally, we need to understand its mechanisms, from its origins to its current forms, but we also need to gain distance in order to be able to envision a future like Rokeya and many other feminist visionaries did. We have to change our perception and focus on what is happening on the women's world map, on what would be the civilizational future of humanity. This is about amplifying these life-serving patterns of thoughts, actions and structures, strengthening them and focusing on them so that the perception of another reality, a possible future, can begin to create this other reality. A future with respect for the diversity in which women advance life on Earth under the best possible conditions, with reverence for the many identities that women live, that they have lived and that they could live in future. Imagine how powerful the world map of women can become, if women more outspokenly ascribe value to themselves and others, recognizing female authority in shaping the future on this planet. We will explore in some of the chapters how to make this counterworld, which is actually an existing reality, known so that all women would be able to see the world map and realize that it is no longer just islands, but the whole world. We will take this a step further and investigate ways of connecting what is still perceived by some as isolated islands of hope. We will explore how to develop common strategies across women of different geographies, and how a feminist-inspired and civilizational more advanced mental infrastructure could be manifested everywhere in the world. Not everywhere in the same way, because women, people, regions and experiences are different. Yet we need a mental infrastructure and a symbolic order, based on a *feminist reference system* with life-serving principles, which connects the ancient knowledge of women with women's expertise of today. We have to remember that it was once possible on this planet to live peacefully with each other and with all other living beings, to honor ourselves and everything else. This memory fuels our longing for a different world, for many worlds in one world. It gives us the strength to do what we must do, namely to rebuild the foundations on which our modern world stands. There is no other way if we want to get by without a collapse.

Sometimes consciously, sometimes unconsciously, sometimes hidden in pictures, in stories, in songs or unpublished texts, in poems, there is this female knowledge perpetuating about how to rebuild our civilizations. This knowledge has always survived somewhere in books, in the longings of women, in unpublished journals, deep in their soul. It needs to be revived and unearthed, uncovered and acknowledged. So many female and feminist visionaries had both memory and vision of different civilizations that deal with life on our planet in a cherishing way. This is what we need to see, recognize and preserve. Because only with recognition is there acknowledgment of female authority and only with acknowledgment is there the possibility of taking this past and present into the future of humanity. And nothing is more urgent than this at a time of global human development in which we, as a whole of humanity, can either destroy the current civilization or take a leap towards a next and better level of human evolution.

We have to re-learn to care. Every day. For each other and Mother Earth, whether we are in a corporate board position or in pediatric care. As feminists, we also have to revive and nurture our anger, gathering the angry spirits of so many women before us who have had enough of patriarchal dominance culture, but were too few to succeed. Many have been murdered, burned on the stake, or died in the real and in the metaphoric prisons of patriarchy. We have to honor their struggle. Every day.

In order to work towards peaceful civilizations that cherish people and planet, we need endurance and *collective feminist leadership*. Historically, notions of leadership have often been intertwined with traits traditionally associated with masculinity, such as goal clarity, perseverance and strength. These attributes have been defined as essential qualities for effective leadership, shaping perceptions of who is deemed fit to lead. On the backdrop of patriarchal thinking this reinforced entrenched gender norms. However, as we confront the complexities of overcoming patriarchy, it becomes increasingly apparent that such narrow definitions of leadership are inadequate for addressing the multifaceted challenges we face.

In today's complex and interconnected world, the pursuit of peaceful civilizations that prioritize the well-being of both people and the planet stands as a paramount imperative. Yet, achieving this ambitious goal necessitates a fundamental re-evaluation of traditional leadership paradigms and a reimagining of the qualities required to navigate the challenges of our time. Central to this endeavor is the recognition that working towards egalitarian, peaceful societies in harmony with nature demands not only individual resolve but also collective action guided by feminist principles: gender equality, intersectionality, inclusivity and diversity, empowerment, social justice and ecological restoration.

The call for *collective feminist leadership* emerges as a clarion call for change. It advocates for a paradigm shift away from hierarchical and patriarchal structures towards inclusive, equitable and participatory forms of governance. At its core, *collective feminist leadership* emphasizes collaboration, empathy and the amplification of diverse voices, recognizing the inherent value of each individual's perspective and experiences. *Collective feminist leadership* can become a catalyst for building peaceful civilizations.

Of course, ending patriarchy is no easy task. It is and has been a partly successful, partly unsuccessful marathon. It requires collective effort to overcome the patriarchal culture that we inhale with every breath. Education, raising awareness and promoting equality and gender justice are crucial steps on this path. Above all, women need to network and support each other in gaining power and influence. Can women abolish patriarchy on their own? No, of course not. But they can abandon their complicity with the patriarchy. This could inspire men to do the same.

There is an uncomfortable question that has been bothering my mind for decades. Is the current fragile state of the world a lack of willingness on the part of women to take responsibility? We need power. Do we want it? If history is our teacher, we know that many of our female predecessors had set out on this journey to power. We have to learn from them and find out which successes we can replicate and how we can prevent failure. Power is essential to our journey into the future, and we need to reclaim her. Learning to wield power without falling into abuse is an art that women, too, must master. To reject the desire and the need for power would mean refusing to grow up and to take responsibility. We would be deceiving ourselves when we reject power. Every woman has this deep urge for power, for shaping the world – unless the patriarchal conditions have driven this urge out of her. We need to see that exactly that urge may become the power of survival of humankind. Only if we acknowledge power as a necessity to influence the future, can we learn to control it and direct it towards positive impact. Yet, we need to dismantle an illusion. Power, even that which comes from women, is not always peaceful. This means that we must observe ourselves and others in the use of power. If our actions promote a *Good Life for All*, if they have a strengthening effect on women who in turn strengthen other women who will strengthen all other people, they may have a meaningful positive effect. This chain must never be broken. That is the art and that is the challenge.

Necessarily, women are ambivalent about power. Naturally, we have a disturbed relationship with power. This ambivalence invites us to adapt in advance to the expectations that have been placed on us as peaceful women for thousands of years. Hence, we tend to reject power precisely because we live in societies that historically have glorified the destructive side of male power in statutes and history books, in societies that subtly breathe the admiration for male heroes. We may even perpetuate a binary narrative by subconsciously labeling as 'good' what is metaphorically associated with Venus's energy – the loving, the reserved, the caring and the nurturing – while viewing as 'bad' what is linked to Mars's energy – the combative, the assertive, the forceful and the overwhelming. To change the world, we need both energies. Throughout history, women applied both energies to overcome patriarchy. We need a dynamic balance: within us, between us and in the way we convey ourselves into the world. If we refuse to acknowledge the full spectrum of power, we will act against each other by negatively judging women who are forceful. We may even label them as male. This then becomes a reason for disrespecting our different ways of changing the world, and instead devaluate each other. Nothing maintains patriarchy more than this mechanism. Yet it is time to reclaim power in a feminist definition.[4]

That's why the most important aspect in building our joined feminist impact is learning how to deal with power among women. We have to argue with each other to find the best possible pathways towards rebuilding the foundations for future civilizations, but we have to acknowledge each other's perspective and respect the different paths to female freedom. We need to engage in respectful discourse.

Yes, power needs control mechanisms. This insight is as old as humankind. There were checks and balance mechanisms in all ancient peaceful societies. Some of these mechanisms can still be traced in the governance systems of Indigenous people.[5] There are also well-developed governance systems in today's democratic societies, even though they might be far from ideal in keeping human power pathologies at bay. We may need to build additional systems of governance for power. We may need to find out how power among women was organized in our distant past and how we will organize it in future. There are no templates, no patent recipes, but there are opportunities to learn together from our predecessors and from today. If we lack the ambition to claim power and to define governance mechanisms for power, we undermine our potential feminist impact. The history of women is testimony to this. Then, patriarchy slaps us in the face and sends us back to the quiet places it intends for us.

Our ability to deal with equality, inequality and difference differently, even more constructively and productively, is an important step towards a changed female and feminist power practice, one in which power is understood as a shared power for a *Good Life for All*.[6] Recognizing inequality among women is a necessary tool in order to be able to identify where difference leads to injustice and where difference means enrichment. The future needs recognized diversity, as it is the source of wealth, life and vitality. Thousands of years of patriarchy demonstrate that injustice arises when differences are used to create and legitimize inequality. As women, even if we are committed to a better future, we often take part in this perfidious process of thinking and acting that turns people into 'others' and assigns them a subordinate, an unjustified role.

Even feminist research is riddled with these inconsistencies. This process of 'othering', which is so difficult for us to escape, has as many variations as there are people who grow up in a patriarchal culture.[7] The school of thought that unquestioningly assumes that it is human to turn difference into injustice is like an octopus whose arms reach everywhere. Openly and hiddenly they reach our minds, our indifference, our obliviousness. We need to know these connections and understand the dynamics between difference and injustice in order to draw future potential from women's diversity and work to overcome injustice. It will take centuries, perhaps millennia, and yet every recognition, every step, every action that advances the transformation of patriarchy into a humane civilization counts. Female freedom, female sovereignty, is the prerequisite for female and feminist agency. It can only grow with the diversity of women.

Female choice in shaping lives increases where women create relationships of mutual attribution of power and recognition. Both mean stepping out of the limited variations of ideas of power as hierarchy, position and influence. Power, freed from the patriarchal connotations we have grown accustomed to, means creating an impact toward a *Good Life for All*. Building this power collectively means cultivating reciprocal, meaningful relationships that respect difference. Differences of opinion, debates, directional discourses, contradictory solutions are just as important as dialogues, consensus-building or acceptance of dissent. In this way, a new construction of reality emerges that removes the ground from a patriarchal culture of dominance and thus expands the possibilities of assigning a *feminist reference system*, a *feminist symbolic order*, the place it deserves in the development of the world.

We are not starting from scratch in redefining power in a feminist way. In recent decades, feminist thought has challenged conventional notions of power, advocating for a paradigm shift towards a more inclusive and equitable approach to governance and social change.[8] At the heart of this movement lies a feminist practice of power – an ethos that seeks to dismantle patriarchal structures, amplify marginalized voices and cultivate collaborative decision-making processes. Central to the *feminist practice of power* is the recognition that traditional models of leadership often perpetuate inequalities and prioritize individual authority over collective well-being. Instead, feminists advocate for a more relational and participatory approach to power – one that values empathy, consensus-building and mutual respect.

At its core, feminist power rejects hierarchical structures in favor of horizontal and decentralized forms of governance. This entails creating spaces where all voices are heard and valued, regardless of gender, race, class or other social identifiers. By prioritizing diversity and inclusivity, feminist power challenges the monopoly of privileged groups and seeks to elevate marginalized perspectives. Rather than relying solely on individual activism or charismatic leadership, feminists recognize the strength of collective action and grassroots organizing. Through networks of support and mutual aid, individuals come together to challenge oppressive systems and work towards shared goals. Historically and today, a feminist power practice manifests in various ways, from grassroots movements and community organizing to policy advocacy and institutional reform.

If all this is already on the horizon, why then is this book important? Because this world needs *collective feminist transformation strategies* more than ever. We are all involved in the nitty-gritties of transformations. It is not surprising how exhausted we are by our daily struggle and how easy it is to become weary of the patriarchal way of things that continuously destroys what we constantly try to rename. As soon as we stop exhausted, normality, which is always patriarchal, rains down on us, crushes us and steals the words from our mouths. We can't help running into the traps laid out for us. We concentrate on claiming our share of patriarchal power, demand entry, organize participation and are satisfied when we succeed in getting a seat on the table. We may even declare our participation in patriarchal power structures a success. We allow ourselves to be celebrated and admired, as if we were really in power, and yet we might end up maintaining patriarchal power structures with our declared success. This is the paradox: **We need our participation in power structures to change patriarchal power structures**. Because there is no way out of this paradox, this book is a truthful company on this difficult journey. We need to honor our ambition to influence and become powerful, yet navigate the traps and join forces to shift the entire system. For this, it is important to embark on a journey into the differentiated reality behind the reality we all know. This book rests on a number of hypotheses that stem from observations, conversations, research and practice over the last decades.

The *first* hypothesis is that the current landscape of women's political and feminist transformation efforts still appears fragmented, which, to some extent, reflects the diversity among women, a diversity that is to be celebrated. However, this fragmentation also serves to uphold the existing patriarchal system, which systematically excludes women from collective power and stifles their agency in shaping societies and envisioning alternative futures. To address this, it is imperative to establish connections among women in power that embrace their differences while fostering a shared space for collective action, and between powerful feminist movements and women in institutional power positions. Imagine what difference it would make, if today's 1000 most powerful women in politics, business and civil society across the globe were connected and committed to a shared agenda for feminist transformations. We are far away from such a picture, but need to uphold its potential. Hence, there is a need to more deeply explore how *collective feminist power practices* could and should be advanced.

The *second* hypothesis follows this idea and suggests that there is a need to review feminist thought and feminist history regarding the concepts and the practicalities of *collective feminist power practices*. Has it been wishful thinking? Have good ideas got lost? Have certain practices been successful or abolished, because of lack of resonance?

The *third* hypothesis is that feminist transformations towards egalitarian societies and world transformations towards regenerative civilizations cannot and should not be separated. It suggests that the *Good Life for All* is impossible within a patriarchal order, and that gender equality alone does not help our civilization to survive. Overcoming patriarchy as a human pathology is paramount.

The *fourth* hypothesis is that, to move toward *collective feminist power practices*, we must confront our own entanglement in patterns that sustain patriarchal power. A key prerequisite for collective feminist action is shifting women's focus from seeking validation within the male symbolic order to fostering mutual support and empowerment. Without this shift, structural inequalities persist, hindering efforts to dismantle patriarchy. This transition must be intentional and visible, as reliance on male validation permeates various aspects of women's lives, including professional, political and social spheres. A conscious break from this pattern is essential to establish a *feminist reference system* for acknowledgment and claim to power. Breaking free from dependency on the male symbolic order requires deliberate efforts to challenge ingrained behaviors and thought patterns. This includes resisting the pull of male-dominated structures and nurturing alternative modes of recognition and affirmation based on women's experiences and values. We must confront our complicity and critically examine how we internalize and perpetuate patriarchal norms, even as we strive for change.

The *fifth* hypothesis is that for *collective feminist power practices* to achieve impact we need to co-create the feminist reference systems we need for personal and professional advancements so that they become a conscious alternative to the existing male-dominated reference systems. What do I mean with the term *reference system*? A reference system, in a broad sense, is a framework, a set of agreements or standards based on certain values, those in use or those espoused. Since the rise of patriarchy, most societies have been structured around a male-dominated reference system that has defined, in open and subtle ways, the position and possibilities for men and women in societies. We know through historic research that there were times – and in some areas there still are – where societies were structured around female reference systems. This might occur in certain matriarchal societies or in contexts where women have gained significant political or economic power. Reference systems permeate societies, influencing thinking and subsequent actions. Unless we deliberately revive or strengthen female reference systems and develop them into *feminist reference systems*, we are operating in our transformation efforts without a mental and factual support system. The establishment of *feminist reference systems* will and needs to be contextual, however, based on basic feminist principles. They can serve as the foundational framework for transformative efforts aimed at reshaping societal norms and structures. By prioritizing life-affirming values and substituting the existing male symbolic order, we pave the way for new civilizations rooted in equality and reverence for all forms of life.

At this stage I need to say something about my geographical experience and my professional expertise that made me arrive at the above hypotheses and write this book. My journey into feminist transformations began more than 40 years ago in Europe, when we – young and courageous protagonists of a thriving feminist movement – thought abolishing patriarchy would be a matter of decades, if not years. Future seemed to be on our side, despite the fact that many of us did not know about our feminist ancestors and some ignorantly looked down on the still oppressed women in what was then unfairly called the 'Third World'. My professional journey into sustainability transformations began more than 30 years ago. Both paths were always intertwined and kept me on my toes because I didn't want to give up believing that another world was possible. Both journeys have seen successes and failures, inspiration and discouragement, and above all, learning, reflection, reading, practice and learning again. When I departed on my sustainability transformation journey I wrote a book about feminist research in Africa. While I was living and working in Zimbabwe, I had the privilege of having access to a wealth of African scientific and experiential feminist texts (from Nigeria, Ghana, Zambia, Zimbabwe, Kenya, Malawi and South Africa), all gathered together in what was then called the Zimbabwean Women's Resource Centre. I was reading fierce criticism about the colonial approach of European and American feminist research approaches in Africa. It was an embarrassing eye-opener for me to realize that the feminist critics of androcentric mainstream research ended up as neocolonial Western feminist researchers in Africa making almost all the mistakes in their research about women in Africa that they accused male researchers of in other contexts. Western female researchers, with the best of all intention, replicated their limited view of the world in their research results. The only thing I could do was describe the paradox and give the African feminist researchers a voice. Yet, it did not free me from my own dilemma until I tried to follow the recommendations by my African feminist friends. Contextualize your own process of gaining insight, they demanded, and confront complexities without falling into the trap of simplifications. Reality, so they remarked, seldom fits into 'either/or' categories. 'As well as' is a more likely category that captures realities' complexities. Both recommendations influenced my life. I was born and bred in Germany, always struggling with a national identity I was not very fond of, lived and worked in Zimbabwe and South Africa for long, worked in organizational and societal transformation processes in many countries in the world in various sustainability topics, founded an institute based on feminist principles, developed a feminist-inspired change leadership methodology and have a deep reverence for the humanness that, combined with cultural difference, always emerges when one allows for real encounter. I must admit that I love this world and tend to see possibilities for bright futures. Hence, this book will name many dragons, will encourage reflection, but is guided by the thorough belief that a better future can be consciously co-created.

Part I: Recognizing Power Dynamics, explores the historical and contemporary intersections of women and power, focusing on how women can reclaim and reshape power structures for a just future. It recounts the often-overlooked stories of women's resistance to patriarchal systems, emphasizing the importance of these narratives in shaping *collective feminist power practices*. It emphasizes the need to realize how strongly feminists are connected with each other and their feminist ancestors. The section delves into the logic of patriarchal backlashes that we need to understand in order to help each other in countering autocratic regimes, which perpetuate regressive tendencies. Finally, it highlights the critical connection between patriarchy and global crises like climate change, arguing that a transformation towards more balanced power dynamics is essential for creating a sustainable and equitable world.[9]

Part II: Understanding Power Pathologies examines how patriarchal power structures have become deeply embedded in societal and economic systems, shaping the way power is understood and exercised. It begins by tracing the historical enforcement of patriarchal norms, revealing how these mechanisms became normalized and evolved into power pathologies that still influence today's societal and global dynamics. The section then explores how patriarchal power intertwines with economic systems like colonialism, communism, socialism and capitalism, highlighting the challenges in shifting economies toward more life-affirming purposes. Finally, it addresses the issue of complicity, showing how individuals, including women, unconsciously sustain patriarchal structures through ingrained norms and behaviors, and offering strategies for breaking this cycle.

Part III: Reclaiming Power in a Feminist Way, embarks on a journey toward fostering a feminist paradigm shift in power dynamics. The exploration of past and present matriarchal societies serves as an inspiration for constructing more equitable and inclusive power structures. The section emphasizes the importance of female genealogies, connecting historical legacies of female power with contemporary *collective feminist practice*. It advocates for a collective redefinition of power within the principles of feminism, celebrating the transformative impact of diversity. Encouraging women to embrace their agency, it underscores the need for women to assert their influence across various societal spheres. Finally, it presents a feminist approach for reclaiming power, positioning women as architects of future societies guided by principles of equality, inclusivity and collective well-being.

Part IV: Leading Feminist Transformations, inspires action, outlining how feminists can claim power and lead transformative change collectively. It advocates for a *feminist reference system*, suggesting a compass for *collective feminist power practices*, and encouraging a dual approach of both disobedience and collaboration to counter patriarchal systems. By embracing systems thinking, it promotes a new narrative of power rooted in interconnectedness. The section redefines leadership from a feminist perspective, showing how *collective feminist leadership* can fuel societal change. Finally, it highlights the critical role of feminist networks as the foundation for lasting change. These networks, both historical and contemporary, are shown as vital for fueling feminist transformations and advancing feminist futures.

Part V: Towards Feminist-oriented Civilizations, envisions a future where feminist principles guide societies toward justice, equality and a *Good Life for All*. It explores how feminist strategies can shape new ways of living that nurture both people and the planet. Drawing inspiration from Indigenous knowledge and sustainability movements, the section emphasizes a relational and systemic worldview as key to building ethical, life-enhancing societies. Feminist future civilizations are rooted in the concept of pluriversality, where multiple lived experiences coexist. It shows how feminist transformation strategies align with the creation of life-sustaining economies that prioritize shared resources and environmental care. By revitalizing the commons and rethinking the purpose of economies, these feminist-oriented approaches aim to build a world where everyone can thrive, grounded in democracy, sustainability and social well-being.

Throughout the text you will notice that I hardly quote men. The focus on women as reference is part of my feminist practice. Because we are only at the beginning of a feminist transformation, it is always more time-consuming to search for female writers. Many of them were visionaries, have been ignored and their narratives have been adopted by male writers. I have read many male authors that have inspired me and that I could cite but, in this book, at least to a large extent, I will not do so, because there are similarly many inspiring female authors. Searching for non-European and non-American women is even more time-consuming, because all these mechanisms of subtle, structural and outright exclusion are still in place. Yet, every female reference is a tiny step on the long road to transformation.

If the challenges posed by climate change and the rise of authoritarian regimes do not result in a fundamental change in consciousness, what else needs to happen for women to take the future of this planet into their own hands? We must create a network of relationships of feminist women who aspire to power positions and whose access to knowledge is diverse, whose differences are sacred to us because we respect each other in our differences. Because each of us is still wandering in exile in this world, in a world whose rules we did not make and which need to be changed, even if many of us, consciously or unconsciously, benefit from some of these rules.

I am confident we will change the world. A crucial practice is that we perceive reality different from the mainstream, and amplify the possibilities that arise. If we see the future in the present, we will discover new possibilities for action. The patriarchal mental order with all its cruel manifestations is a phase in the history of humanity that is nearing its end. If we look carefully, we notice that the end of patriarchy is already on the horizon. We have to accelerate this process.

Notes

1 Rokeya Sakhawat Hossain lived from 1880 to 1932. The story was originally published in English in the *Indian Ladies' Magazine* in 1905. It has been reprinted in 2005 as *Sultana's Dream; and Padmarag: Two feminist utopias by Rokeya Sakhawat Hossain*. See: Hossain (2005).
2 A deep and fascinating exploration and global journey into the origins of patriarchy can be found in Saini (2023).
3 Feminist philosophers have written extensively about the symbolic order: Luce Irigaray examines how language and cultural symbols buried female origins and created and reinforced patriarchal structures; see Irigaray (2012). Julia Kristeva discusses how the male symbolic order shapes identity and desire; see Kristeva (2024), originally published in 1984. Hélène Cixous critiques the patriarchal symbolic order and advocates for women to reclaim language; see Cixous (1976).
4 There are many attempts to do so. Examples are: Beard (2017); Arruzza et al. (2019). An interesting and historic Pan-African perspective can be found in Asiimire & Twinamatsiko (2021).
5 Without idealizing them, it is important to notice that there are many mechanisms to balance power in ancient and contemporary Indigenous communities that are

widely ignored by the modern world. Many have been destroyed through patriarchal colonialism. Examples can be found in Defriend & Cook (2024).
6 See Folbre (2020).
7 A fascinating journey of transforming the experience of *Othering* into strength can be found in Bezad (2023).
8 An inspiring and radical approach to community feminism and decolonizing feminism has been introduced by Adriana Guzmán (2014, September 17). In *International Feminism* Verónica Gago (2020) wrote a fascinating account of future feminist power possibilities. Sarah Ahmed's *Living a Feminist Life* (2019) shows how feminist theory can be lived in everyday practices, emphasizing resistance to patriarchal structures and the importance of collective feminist action.
9 The challenges in front of us are well described in: Steffen et al. (2018), The Club of Rome (2019), Lawrence et al. (2024).

References

Ahmed, S. (2019). *Living a Feminist Life*. Zubaan.

Arruzza, C., Bhattacharya, T., & Fraser, N. (2019). *Feminism for the 99%: A Manifesto.* Verso. https://www.amazon.com/Feminism-99-Nancy-Fraser/dp/1788734424

Asiimire, D., and Twinamatsiko, M. (2021). Pan African Feminist Perspectives Promoting Matriarchy. Women's Pre-Colonial Linguistic Power Perspectives, Power Loss and the Contemporary State of Affairs in Ankole Sub-Region. *Open Access Library Journal*, 8, 1–19. doi: 10.4236/oalib.1107870.

Beard, M. (2017). *Women & Power: A Manifesto*. Liveright Publishing Corporation, A Division Of W.W. Norton & Company.

Bezad, H. (2023). *Being Other. The Beauty and Power of Being an Outsider*. Dubai, UAE: The Dreamwork Collective.

Cixous, H. (1976). The Laugh of the Medusa. *Signs: Journal of Women in Culture and Society*, 1, 875–893.

Defriend, C., & Cook, C. (2024). Reawakening of Indigenous matriarchal systems: A feminist approach to organizational leadership. *Healthcare Management Forum*, *37*(3). https://doi.org/10.1177/08404704231210255

Folbre, N. (2020). Cooperation & Conflict in the Patriarchal Labyrinth. *Daedalus*, *149*(1), 198–212. https://www.jstor.org/stable/48563041

Gago, V. (2020). *Feminist International: How to Change Everything*. Verso.

Guzmán, A. (2024, September 17). Teach-In 15: Anti-Patriarchal community feminism. South Feminist Futures. https://southfeministfutures.org/teach-in-15-anti-patriarchal-community-feminism

Hossain, R.S. (2005). *Sultana's Dream; and Padmarag: Two Feminist Utopias*. Penguin New Delhi (India).

Irigaray, L. (2012). *In the Beginning She Was*. Bloomsbury.

Kristeva, J. (2024). *Revolution in Poetic Language*. Translated by Margaret Waller. New York: Columbia University Press.

Lawrence, M., Homer-Dixon, T., Janzwood, S., Rockstöm, J., Renn, O., & Donges, J.F. (2024). Global polycrisis: The causal mechanisms of crisis entanglement. *Global Sustainability*, 7:e6. doi:10.1017/sus.2024.1

Saini, A. (2023). *The Patriarchs: How Men Came to Rule*. Fourth Estate.

Steffen, W., Rockström, J., Richardson, K., Lenton, T.M., Folke, C., Liverman, D., Summerhayes, C.P., Barnosky, A.D., Cornell, S.E., Crucifix, M., Donges, J.F., Fetzer, I., Lade, S.J., Scheffer, M., Winkelmann., R. & Schellnhuber, H.J. (2018). Trajectories of the Earth System in the Anthropocene. *Proceedings of the National Academy of Sciences, 115*(33), 8252–8259. https://www.pnas.org/content/pnas/early/2018/08/07/1810141115.full.pdf

The Club of Rome (2019). *The Planetary Emergency Plan*. https://clubofrome.org/wp-content/uploads/2020/02/PlanetaryEmergencyPlan_CoR-4.pdf

Part I
Recognizing Power Dynamics

1
Women and Power – Writing a Different Story

This is an invitation to view history deliberately through a feminist lens. It's a conscious choice to re-examine the past with an awareness of the voices, struggles and contributions that have been marginalized or overlooked. It's human nature to select and interpret facts in ways that validate our beliefs and worldviews, but the challenge lies in understanding the broader implications of those choices. By using a feminist lens, we can reveal new dimensions of history, bringing to light narratives that have long been shadowed by dominant viewpoints.[1] Most explanations of the world have been tainted by patriarchal glasses. We have long viewed the world through a narrative that frames human evolution as progressing from primitive, barbaric cultures to civilized, economically developed and technologically advanced societies. Democracy is often seen as the final ingredient for securing a bright future, with Europe traditionally positioned at the forefront of this evolution. However, this view has been deeply challenged and eroded by its legacy of colonialism.

We know this dominant narrative is not true, not for Europe and certainly not for most of our world. But still, we breathe it in with education, at least in the Western world that is still transmitting this narrative that goes like this: The Neolithic turn from hunting and gathering to stationary agriculture has unfortunately, but unavoidably led to the rise of gender inequalities, defining the female space in all variations of care work and the male space in the public domain. Mankind was always cruel, at times barbaric, but the good side of it was that war gave rise to many inventions and technological developments to the benefit of humankind. This is still the case today, as we can see from space technologies and the internet that we are all dependent on. Competition is natural, as it selects the fittest, even though more and more men today hint to the fact that humankind might in fact be a cooperative species.[2] Thanks to great European men we remember the phase of enlightenment that has rescued us from barbaric cruelty, even though it was exactly the phase that made Europeans murder, enslave and rape uncounted numbers of people on other

DOI: 10.4324/9781003508885-2

continents that were called natives. But we have learned as a species, colonialism is not on the agenda anymore, even if imperialism still is. Economies follow a similar recipe all over the world with continuous growth being the basis for wealth creation. Unfortunately, wealth is monopolized by few almost everywhere. Increasingly, men emphasize that the ability to cooperate is the only prospect of survival for a future in climate change emergencies. Climate change we need to fight. Many wise men and some women warn that we have entered a stage of planetary emergency.[3]

This is an explicit encouragement to close this dominant and certainly annoying narrative like a window on your computer that you do not need for now. I am not suggesting you ignore what today is called the phase of *polycrises* that make the decline of our current civilization probable.[4] I deliberately invite you to courageously filter the complexity of the world and follow me on a journey through time and space. Let us discover a few known or unknown occurrences of the collective power of women. It is not about female heroines, but about the ability of women to get together, reclaim their power and make a difference for the future. I urge you not to judge these attempts according to today's criteria of impact projects. Rather, let us look at the world map of female self-determination as a continuous resistance against patriarchy with an open mind and heart, zoom into some of the successes and failures in an exemplary way and discover what we can learn for an individual and *collective feminist power practice*.

Looking at women's history can change our thinking about possible futures. It also allows us to better understand the present and future *potency* for regaining collective power. There has never been a century since patriarchy emerged and was enforced as a mental infrastructure and a way of organizing societal life, in which women did not resist their colonization, their restricted freedom and their loss of a different way of organizing societies. Even if it might have got lost in the cacophony of patriarchal human history writing and teaching, they did pass on their knowledge of other forms of societies to other women, in stories, songs, drawings, fairy tales, myths, rituals, books, articles and Instagram posts. They do so today.

The core of this knowledge is simple, but difficult to explain in our linear language. Because it has become a tacit knowledge that can, at times, hardly be brought to the surface of today's reality. It is almost like a hidden jewel somewhere in the soul that can't be named, a deep longing for a different world, a sense of homelessness in this world, an experience of an inner brokenness as if we constantly had to pretend to be someone different from who we really are. It is a silent insistence that the world is actually enchanted, even without spiritual rituals. At times, it is a longing for a fairy-tale island ruled by female priestesses that make sure everyone is happy. It may suddenly emerge for a brief moment as a deep confidence that another world is possible, before it gets severely attacked by the daily news. For some women, it is like a memory that refuses to fade, as if they felt a connection to the long chain of women that reaches across the globe millennia back into a world before this world.

In a nutshell, it is a knowledge about societies in which women had the freedom of choice about their lives, a world in which female collective power was natural, nature was enchanted, societies egalitarian and economies were serving the collective and individual well-being. It is the power of this memory that we can trace in the resistance of women against patriarchy.[5] It makes a significant difference to our collective future whether we can tap into a memory of collective female power or if we must assume that such power never existed and therefore needs to be created from scratch.

Don't we all long for a world where power didn't mean domination and where it wasn't socially acceptable to oppress others? Does this longing empower us, or does it turn us into dreamers who, while celebrating women's power through magical rituals on society's margins, avoid engaging with the patriarchal systems we seek to challenge? Do we have to surrender to the conditions of today's power rituals or will we rediscover the roots, the sources of our power as women, the origins of our abilities to give life, nourish life and take life away? Can we leap from the memory of the past into the future? Would the revolution begin?

Looking at the last 6000 years of human development, we have only lately scientifically rediscovered what many women at the fringes of our global world knew: That before patriarchy as the mainstream societal version, there were societies around the world that used a different, a female symbolic order. For Europe, Marija Gimbutas, an US archeologist and anthropologist born in Estonia, did ample research on what she called the *Civilization of the Goddess* in Old Europe, an area located between Ukraine and Bulgaria.[6] She referred to a prehistoric, Neolithic culture between approximately 6500 BCE and 3500 BCE. She claimed from the many archeological excavations she did that, back then, there was a thriving agricultural society that displayed no signs of war, had highly developed art and egalitarian societal structures. This culture had a strong female symbolic order and was organized around female strength and wisdom. Her research was severely contested, by men and also by some feminists. In different ways, both accused her of diverting from evidence-based science into interpretations of interconnections between artifacts that they considered inventions.[7] Yet by and large, her work has not only been rehabilitated, but acknowledged as a breakthrough in sketching out a different path of human development. Many female and feminist scholars followed her, added to her findings new ones and supported her or found similar historic interpretations. None of these researchers assumed that matriarchal societies have been the opposite of the emerging patriarchal societies. On the contrary, even though the sacredness of female fertility and nature's beauty as Mother Earth found its way into many artifacts and rituals celebrating the female, these seemed not to have been societies ruled by women dominating men. Yet, societal arrangements were fundamentally different from patriarchal modes of operation. Motherhood was not at all a constraint, female sexual freedom was the norm, gender identities more fluid, kids grew up in women's collectives also supported by men, and a variety of different arrangements between men and women regulated decision-making, economics and spiritual development.[8] Different from other regions in the world, Europe is the only continent where these ancient forms of societal arrangements have been totally erased or gone entirely underground. I mean this literally, because so many mythical European stories mention women who had to flee the emerging new patriarchal order and live under the Earth. However, we are not talking about mysticism here, even if much of the female knowledge has somehow survived in many country-sides, in the form of healing wisdom or knowledge about plants and planting. It may be hidden in myths, fairy tales and stories, lingering in places in landscapes that we could call sacred sites. But if you decided to travel through Europe on foot, you would find old healing knowledge among women across all countries, and you would be surprised how closely knit the network of ancient sacred sites is that can be traced back to societies which honored the female. Yet, they are not signposted as of matriarchal descent and there are only a few history books that attempt to make a connection between these sacred sites and ancient female knowledge.[9] Hardly any other continent has eradicated women's historical cultures so thoroughly, researched them so little and remembered them with so much fear. Just a few centuries ago, women's knowledge was brutally destroyed in the witch hunts that lasted in Europe over the centuries from about 1490 to 1775, killing between hundreds of thousands and millions of women (estimated).[10] In Europe, this was a systematic destruction of women's self-confidence, knowledge and collective power. The history of the witch hunt as an institutionalized mass murder has never been appropriately examined by the Christian churches whose power structures initiated it, implemented it and benefitted. It became the foundation for the establishment of law and order throughout Europe.[11] Even though the women's movement in the 1980s tried to turn this historic burden around by positively identifying themselves as witches, the brutal tortures and murders left their scars in the psyche of women until today.[12] There is this deep psychological fear many European women live with, contributing to female insecurity, causing a tendency to conform to patriarchal norms. It is this subtle fear of being denounced, identified, fought against and persecuted for a certain knowledge, a different world view, a different way of thinking or being, for healing powers or for simply not matching the mainstream. Above all, for being a feminist. But more so, it is the mistrust towards other women, because the system of denunciation during the witch hunts was so perfidious that you could never know who had betrayed you. Women may have tried to rescue themselves by denouncing other women.

Do European women actually know how thoroughly the memories of strong female cultures have been driven away from them? Are we aware how colonized our minds still are? Is the memory of female collective power much more difficult to pick up than on other continents? Is there a deeply rooted envy for the powerful continuation of collective female power on other continents?

In an opening speech for the 2019 Buenos Aires Book Fair the Argentinian-Brazilian anthropologist and philosopher Rita Segato spoke about the power of disobedience. She suggested that Europe is lonely and isolated because it looks in narcissistic reflection only on its own achievements, lacking a true mirror of the vibrant and beautiful world out there.[13]

In many regions of the Global South[14], different societal arrangements honoring the female or living gender parity have in adapted ways survived until today – even if scattered and endangered – among Indigenous people and nations as well as modern societies. A whole body of literature has emerged that suggests a different explanation of world development, one in which female identities shaped societies and future development in a powerful way. This does not mean dreaming of the happy island. It isn't about imagining a utopian past or idealizing a distant era. It's about uncovering the historical evidence and inherent reality of collectively powerful women throughout history. Today we know that between Morocco and South Africa alone there were proven to be 13 matriarchal societal structures that still vaguely exist, albeit adjusted to the modern world, and also a number of strong queendoms.[15] The latter did not necessarily mean peaceful societies, as the feminist Cameroonian author Leonora Miano explains.[16] Not much different from European history, women warriors and cruel queens who did enslave women and men, torturing and killing their own people, were also part of the African development before colonization. But peaceful matriarchal societal structures also existed throughout Africa alongside warlike tribes.[17] Over centuries the matriarchal societies had fled increasingly aggressive peoples and monotheistic religions such as Islam to west and south and had established new empires through assimilation, marriage and trade. Many integrated the elements of patriarchal structures or fully adjusted to the newly emerging patriarchal societal structure, so that only elements of previous societal forms survived. In her research the historian Heide Göttner-Abendroth suggests that there are 15 such matriarchies or rudimentary matriarchal structures also in Asia, 14 in Australia and Oceania, and 20 in North and Latin America.[18] What Marija Gimbutas suggested for the demise of the old matriarchal Europe seems to apply globally. Peaceful societies fled warlike tribes, tried to establish new societies in difficult-to-access areas, surrendered to take-overs and adjusted their customs.

There is a lot that we still do not know, but what the ancient science historian Adrienne Mayor in her research about the Greek 'Amazons' stories suggests may also be true for other regions: Biased research expectations in archeology have often overlooked women because they did not expect them.[19] The archeological findings of Scythian graves, a tribe living in southern Russia at the time of Greek history writing and the Hellenic state, contained battle-scarred skeletons of women, buried with weapons and horses. Bio-archeological methods reveal that armed females represent a significant portion of cemetery populations on the steppes, challenging previous perceptions that these warriors in the graves must have been men. The steppes harbored Scythian warrior cultures with a gender parity unprecedented in ancient Hellenic societies. In Greek mythology, the lines between myth and reality blurred, leading to the identification of the independent women of Scythia as 'Amazons'. Recent archeological and linguistic findings provide insights into the factual basis underlying Greek Amazon myths. These discoveries bridge the gap between modern understanding and ancient Greek perceptions. Their fascination with rumors of warlike nomadic societies, where women could attain renown through martial prowess, fueled a proliferation of mythic narratives. These stories portrayed bold, resourceful women warriors as equals to men, inhabiting the fringes of the known world, engaging in legendary conflicts with the greatest Greek heroes.[20] According to Mayor, the persistent presence of warrior women across a vast geographical range for over a millennium indicates a historical reality that extends from the western Black Sea to northern China.

These discoveries are reshaping scholarly interpretations of the role of women in ancient societies. While Marija Gimbutas suggested that the peaceful matriarchal societies of the Old Europe have been besieged and subjugated by warlike horse-riding tribes coming from the Russian and Central Asian steppes between 6000 and 2000 BCE[21], Adrienne Mayor shows that these very tribes had towards 500 BCE at least one-third women warriors who fought either alongside men or in female groups.[22]

We cannot know if Old Europe was besieged and subjugated by male and female warriors from the Russian steppes, or if the female warriors of Scythia were late descendants of matriarchal intermingling societies, living and defending the remnants of their female culture of strength and independence, adjusting to warlike societies and reclaiming their freedom and power. But the research shows that women over millennia claimed their power in shaping European and Asian societies.

Let us travel across the ocean to the Latin American continent. The Amazon River, which everyone knows of today, because of its tremendous role in preserving our climate and biodiversity, received its name from what was long considered the fairy tale originating from Greece that now turns out to be reality – strong warrior women. Stories of fighting women, both alongside men and independently, have been passed down among Indigenous peoples, particularly during resistance against Spanish colonization. The legend of the Amazons, independent warrior women who founded their own societies with thriving cities and without men, is connected with the Latin America ancient and contemporary Arawak culture.[23]

The matriarchal culture of the Arawak in Latin America holds significant importance due to its endurance and influence across vast regions. Originating from ancient agricultural societies, the Arawak's culture is intertwined with the earliest civilizations of the Americas, showcasing remarkable similarities with pre-Incan cultures in Colombia and Bolivia around 500 AD, with roots in even more ancient cultures such as the Valdivia culture in Ecuador from around 3000 to 1500 BCE.[24] Their geographical spread, from Latin America to the Caribbean and beyond, demonstrates their extensive cultural influence. Matrilineal and matrilocal social structures defined their communities, with women holding substantial power within clans and households. This matriarchal system persisted despite external pressures coming from warrior tribes pushing the Arawak towards the east and north. They fled aggressive, neighboring tribes, such as the Caribs and the Tupi, who were superior to them in arms.[25]

Some of them settled on the Antilles Islands. When Columbus arrived there in 1492, it marked the beginning of a series of terrorizing calamities for them: Diseases, enslavement, cultural devastation and genocide. The first Indigenous people he encountered were the Arawaks who inhabited the islands of the Greater and Lesser Antilles. Despite having a highly developed culture on these islands, they were brutally enslaved. Within decades the population was decimated by the rampant spread of smallpox, with estimates suggesting that by 1535, out of six million Indigenous people, only 500 remained on the entire island.[26] Yet, Columbus and other colonizers encountered resistance. He was fought not only by men, but by many warrior women, which surprised the Spanish so much that they made detailed accounts of this phenomenon.[27] While these women may have initially fought alongside their male counterparts, an ancient legend recorded in Guayana presents a different narrative. According to this tale, there existed a small, independent Amazonian territory on a mysterious island called Matenino (Tobago), near Trinidad, not too far away from the mouth of the Amazon. The legend says women migrated there without men, living as skilled warriors in great prosperity, adorned in beautiful garments and magnificent armor. This legend, also known in the Antilles, suggests the presence of warrior women predating the arrival of the Spaniards, forming independent, male-less societies. It is essential to distinguish these Amazonian women clearly from the more commonly encountered female combatants fighting alongside men, to understand the sociocultural significance of these female warrior societies. Why did they become warriors, if they originated from the peaceful matriarchal culture of the Awarak?

These Amazonians were not only protagonists in legends. In 1542, an expedition of Spanish conquerors exploring the river, which is still named Amazonas, encountered the female warriors near the mouth of the Rio Negro. They described them as large, fair-skinned (probably painted), muscular women, wielding bows and arrows with great strength. Their territory was large, but actually hidden in inaccessible areas, probably the mountains on the Rio Negro and at the source of the Orinoco.[28] It comprised wealthy settlements, described as stone cities with gates and streets. We do not know how true these accounts are or how much they are born of the fantasy of men, but they span centuries. They depict the Amazonians as culturally advanced, city-building women, possessing precious metals, elaborate garments and advanced domestic technologies such as pottery, typical of matriarchal cultures. It was said that the Amazonians occasionally declared war on neighboring tribes, capturing their men after victory to impregnate themselves. Male offspring were either killed or returned to their fathers, while daughters were raised ceremoniously and trained in the art of combat.

Were these women descendants of peaceful matriarchal cultures who adopted the warrior culture out of necessity? Did they cultivate warlike skills and use them to their own advantage? Did they learn early enough and different from the peaceful societies of the Old Europe that they needed to revert to weapons and fighting in order to resist patriarchal domestication and colonization? Did they learn to maintain their societal foundations and expand and control their territory out of necessity? We don't know. But there is enough evidence that they existed.

In the last century, in the region of the vast islands at the mouth of the Amazon, archeologists discovered an ancient urban civilization. This society practiced corn cultivation, crafted advanced ceramics, constructed large clan dwellings atop artificial hills and produced goddess figurines, mirroring the characteristics of early agrarian cultures led by women on the west coast of Latin America (such as the Valdivia and subsequent cultures).[29] This, again, shows that, long ago, women on the American continents claimed their collective power and resisted patriarchy and colonization.

Let us embark on a journey to the west coast of Africa. The Portuguese colonization was neither less brutal nor less disastrous for Indigenous people than the Spanish colonization of Latin America. The Bijagos Archipelago is located off the coast of Guinea Bissau. Diverse ethnic groups inhabited different islands, resulting in a rich cultural tapestry. The culture was and is matriarchal. Women played pivotal roles in land cultivation, house construction and food gathering, with the autonomy to select their husbands. But the culture was also warlike, as men engaged in boat construction and raids on coastal settlements. Bijagos also engaged in the slave trade, selling captives to European traders, albeit largely avoiding enslavement themselves due to their islands' isolation and their rebellious culture. The people of Bijago still pay reverence to their famous queen and high priestess Okinka Pampa Kanyimpa. She died in 1930 at the age of over 100 and successfully led her people's resistance against colonization by the Portuguese. As a result, the islands were largely spared the brutal effects of colonial power compared to the mainland, although the Portuguese finally occupied the islands in 1936.[30] Following her father Bankajapa's reign, she assumed leadership of the islands and was asked in 1910 by her people to resist the Portuguese with armed forces, safeguard their ancestors and preserve their matriarchal traditions. During this period, Portugal sought to occupy the Bijago Archipelago to bolster its territorial claims in Africa, aiming to establish trade ports and enhance the economy for Portuguese settlers. Leonora Miano narrates the story in this way: Bright enough to assess the low chances of the poorly equipped Bijago inhabitants, Okinka Pampa considered a different tactic to resist the Portuguese. She allowed them to land on the shores, but convinced them not to advance inland where the settlements of the Bijagos were located. In turn, the Portuguese received food and other goods. Surprisingly, the colonizers obeyed. Leonora Miano suggests that Okinka Pampa used more than her smartness, but also her spiritual power. It is said that she eventually negotiated a peace treaty with the Portuguese authorities, while simultaneously instituting reforms that advanced women's rights and abolished slavery. Even today, the matriarchal traditions on the Bijago Archipelago continue, including a form of democracy that may sound strange. Problems are discussed among men and women separately, then together at length, until the three queens make the final decision. Settlements are still situated inland on the islands. Agricultural land is collectively owned and uninhabited islands are considered sacred and communal territory, prohibiting permanent settlement but allowing for cultivation. Their special matriarchal feature of societal organization makes them a destination for tourists, film-makers and women who seek inspiration. For global citizens the lifestyle of these about 33,000 people would look poor and we do not know how happy or unhappy their citizens are, but they seem to have empowered women towards strong self-confidence that is used to claim power.

Let us travel back to Europe. While Okinka Pampa was busy strengthening female power and peacefully resisting the Portuguese colonization, the male-led and male-dominated European nations decided to enter into World War I in 1914. We know the outcomes from history books. It resulted in widespread trauma and human atrocities with approximately 8.5 million soldiers and 13 million civilians perishing. Four patriarchal imperial dynasties collapsed in Austria, Germany, Russia and the Ottoman Empire. The extensive movement of soldiers and refugees contributed to the global dissemination of the 'Spanish' flu pandemic in 1918 and 1919, with another 20–25 million people dying. Territories in Europe were redistributed among the victorious allied patriarchal powers. Upheaval in Russia saw the Bolsheviks coming to a different, but still patriarchal authority. The patriarchal United States emerged as a new world power. Nationalism in patriarchal central and eastern Europe grew, laying the groundwork for the subsequent global conflict in World War II.

In the midst of the madness of World War I, about 1200 women met for a women's peace congress in 1915 in The Hague. Initiated by a group of feminist activists such as the German Anita Augspurg and her partner Lida Heymann and the Dutch feminist Aletta Jacobs, these women worked tirelessly to get feminists from Europe and the United States, including those from the nations at war, together. Because the United States was at that stage still neutral, the American feminist Jane Addams was therefore asked to lead the conference. The patriarchal governments did their best to prevent women from attending. Some countries did not issue passports; the Americans were stopped midway because the English Channel was closed due to the war, which also prevented British women from going.[31]

Feminists knew each other – they were internationally networked in the fight for women's rights and particularly for their right to vote and stand for parliament. But they also had disputes, disconnects and were not at all united. However, despite the war and the disunity among the feminist movements, courageous visionaries planned this women's peace conference. In an article published in a feminist journal in Germany in 1914, Lida Heymann laid down the intention that inspired her and others to make the impossible possible – a women's peace conference in the midst of war. She insisted that the women were not infected by the hatred of nations, but instead that their acknowledgment of people as people, no matter which nation they belonged to, had not diminished.[32] In another article in 1915 in the same journal she anticipated the visionary results of the conference: 'There will always be villains, fraudsters, thieves, murderers, etc. in international politics. Why don't we protect ourselves from them through international law, through international judgments: why don't we force them under the law and make them harmless to the peoples?'[33] This question remains still unanswered today, more than 100 years later.

Some of the outcomes had been previously mentioned by the male-dominated peace conference in 1899 that had also seen women's demonstrations against increasing armament of all nations, but no final resolution in that regard had been decided. The outcome of the women's peace congress was truly revolutionary. Even though it has shifted into obliviousness for many international politicians, male and female, the Women's Peace Congress of 1915 in The Hague marked a pivotal moment in the history of international peace advocacy. Among the key resolutions adopted during the congress were calls for the immediate cessation of hostilities and diplomatic negotiations; the establishment of a permanent peace tribunal capable of arbitrating disputes between nations; disarmament and arms control; economic sanctions for nations which occupy foreign nations; the recognition of rape and mass rape as war crimes; the promotion of diplomacy and negotiation for peaceful conflict resolutions; recognition of women's role in peacebuilding and their formal inclusion in formal peace processes and decision-making bodies.[34] These demands found their ways much later into the Charter of the United Nations, the establishment of the International Criminal Court or the founding of the World Trade Organization.[35] The conference also laid the groundwork for the establishment of the Women's International League for Peace and Freedom, which still exists today.[36] The gathering made clear that a commitment to international cooperation and peaceful conflict resolution is linked to the advancement of women's rights as essential components of lasting peace.

We all know that in 1915, the collective power of women was not strong enough to prevent the disaster of World War I or the pathological development towards World War II with even more unspeakable atrocities. Though the women's peace congress's immediate impact may have been limited, it laid the visionary groundwork for subsequent efforts in the pursuit of peace and gender equality on the global stage. What is important for us here is that the women claimed collective female and feminist power, no matter how they were seen by the global crowd of patriarchal rulers.

Let us assume that the few examples mentioned here are just a tiny fraction on the world map of visionary female revolutionaries against patriarchal domination. Imagine how our societies would look, if not only these few, but all stories globally were compiled and became part of standard history lessons at school. From our short journey through time and geographies we have seen that female forms of claiming collective power are different. They are contextual and historically determined by their possibilities. Yet, we have also seen that they require vision, enormous courage and perseverance, even if nobody will say thank you or issue an award. Claiming power as a female collective is a huge risk. It may succeed or fail. But it is necessary for the future of human civilization. In order for this to become gradually more realistic, we need to write this different story, the history that has never been in the forefront of collective human memory. It needs to be told from preschool to university, everywhere in the world.

A lot has happened in the culture of remembrance. There are feminist archives around the world. The more feminists work in the media, the more courageous women get featured in media. Are we doing ok against the trend of erasing women as shapers of the future faster than they can be drawn into the history books? I think we can still improve, not just because we should honor women who were brave. We have to perceive the infinite chain, the world map, on which we too are just one dot among billions of dots. Because all of these courageous women, who claim female collective power, hold a small piece of the memory of a world before this world, in which women were one thing above all: Free. They all hold a mosaic piece in their hands that will crumble in their grave-yards if we don't begin to see it. That is why this chapter is dedicated to the inextricable connection between our ability to remember and our ability to work toward future civilizations in which we will do one thing above all else: nurture life.

Major insights for *collective feminist power practices* from a glimpse into herstory:

1. It is important to realize that the female fight for self-determination and against patriarchal domination and colonization is at least 6000 years old and has never stopped.
2. We must learn to think not just in the present, not just in recent history, but in time spans of thousands of years to strengthen our certainty and confidence that patriarchy can be ended by collective effort.
3. We need to collect and teach the many stories of women in resistance to patriarchy and sharpen our eyes to how and where this resistance took place or continues to take place.
4. We must notice the invisible thread that connects us to all women before us who have longed for egalitarian, peaceful societies and all those who will come after us.
5. We need to recognize from women's stories that there is not one form of female or feminist collective power practice, but many different ways to restore women's freedom.
6. We need to understand how exactly women have built collective power and impacted the course of history, no matter if they succeeded or failed, were made invisible or got erased from historic accounts. Under the difficult conditions of patriarchy, failure should never be seen as defeat.

Notes

1 A brilliant overview of what feminisms look like across centuries can be found in Delap (2021).
2 A widely read example is Bregman (2020).
3 The *Planetary Emergency Plan* by the Club of Rome (2019) describes key policy levers to address the cross-cutting challenges of climate change, biodiversity loss and human health and well-being. A widely read article among scientists elaborating the dangerous trajectories of the world is Steffen et al. (2018).
4 See Lawrence et al. (2024).
5 For example, Nancy Folbre (2020) highlights how patriarchy skews cooperation, often marginalizing women, but she emphasizes the collective power of women to challenge and transform these systems for greater equality.
6 Marija Gimbutas, see Gimbutas (2001, 1991). She portrayed Old Europe as a matristic, peaceful and egalitarian society, challenging the dominant androcentric views in archeology.
7 Gimbutas' later ideas, suggesting a coherent story of women's collective power – not supremacy – were criticized by other archeologists for being ideologically driven and lacking academic rigor. In the late 1980s and 1990s, criticism of her work intensified, leading a divided feminist movement partly to join the criticism and partly to view it as a coordinated effort to undermine Gimbutas' academic reputation. She rejected claims of ideological bias in her work, asserting that her gynocentric interpretation was driven by the archeological evidence itself, and that her research was simply sound archeology. An elaborate account of Gimbutas' work and its criticism can be found in Navickaitė (2022).
8 For an extensive review of features of matriarchal societies of the past in Europe and West-Asia, see Göttner-Abendroth (2019).
9 See Göttner-Abendroth (2014).
10 Eighty to 90% of the people killed in this period as witches or heretics were women. The numbers of women killed in Europe vary from 40,000 to 1 million; the majority of brutal tortures and killings took place in Germany, Austria and Switzerland. See Wisselinck (1986).
11 Wisselinck (1986).
12 Silvia Federici compares the European witch hunts to modern forms of violence specifically targeting women, interpreting it as a phenomenon linked to capitalist enclosures under globalization. See Federici (2004).
13 See Segato (2019).
14 When I use the term Global South, I suggest that every time you read it, you turn the world map around and subsequently see a tiny Europe and the not-too-large United States. We need to keep in mind, as Sylvia Tamale suggests, that the Global South is, in terms of population and space, the majority world.
15 See for example Amadiume (2001, 2015) and Göttner-Abendroth & Smith (2008).
16 Miano (2022).

17 See Göttner-Abendroth and Smith (2008).
18 See Göttner-Abendroth (2021, 2022).
19 See Mayor (2016).
20 Mayor (2016).
21 See Gimbutas (2001).
22 See Mayor (2016).
23 See Göttner-Abendroth (2022, p.20 Kindle Version).
24 Göttner-Abendroth (2022 p.21).
25 Göttner-Abendroth (2022 p.30).
26 See Rouse (1963).
27 Göttner-Abendroth (2022, p.30ff).
28 Göttner-Abendroth (2022, p.30ff).
29 See Roosevelt (1991, 1994).
30 See Miano (2022).
31 See Dünnebier and Scheu (2002).
32 Dünnebier and Scheu (2002 p. 217).
33 Dünnebier and Scheu (2002 p. 219).
34 Lunz (2023).
35 Allen (2007).
36 See: https://www.wilpf.org

References

Allen, A.T. (2007). *Women in Twentieth-Century Europe*. Basingstoke and New York: Palgrave Macmillan.

Amadiume, I. (2001). *Re-inventing Africa: Matriarchy, Religion, and Culture*. London; New York: Zed Books.

Amadiume, I. (Ed.). (2015). *Male Daughters, Female Husbands: Gender and Sex in an African Society*. Zed Books Ltd.

Bregman, R. (2020). *Humankind: A New History*. Little, Brown.

Club of Rome. (2019). Planetary emergence plan: Securing a New Deal for people, nature and climate. https://clubofrome.org/wp-content/uploads/2020/02/PlanetaryEmergencyPlan_CoR-4.pdf

Delap, L. (2021). *Feminisms: A Global History*. Pelican Books.

Dünnebier, A., & Scheu, U. (2002). *Die Rebellion ist eine Frau. Anita Augspurg und Lida G. Heymann – Das schillerndste Paar der Frauenbewegung*. Heinrich Hugendubel.

Federici, S. (2004). *Caliban and the Witch: Women, the Body and Primitive Accumulation*. Autonomedia.

Folbre, N. (2020). Manifold exploitations: Toward an intersectional political economy. *Review of Social Economy*, *78*(4), 451–472. https://doi.org/10.1080/00346764.2020.1798493

Gimbutas, M. (1991). *The Civilization of the Goddess: The World of Old Europe*. Edited by Joan Marler. San Francisco, CA: Harper Collins.

Gimbutas, M. (2001). *The Living Goddesses*. University of California Press.

Göttner-Abendroth, H. (2014). *Matriarchale Landschaftsmythologie: Von der Ostsee bis Süddeutschland*. Kohlhammer.

Göttner-Abendroth, H. (2019). *Geschichte matriarchaler Gesellschaften und Entstehung des Patriarchats: Band III: Westasien und Europa (Das Matriarchat, III, Band 3)*. Kohlhammer.

Göttner-Abendroth, H. (2021). *Matriarchale Gesellschaften der Gegenwart: Band I: Ostasien, Indonesien, Pazifischer Raum (Das Matriarchat, I)*. Kohlhammer.

Göttner-Abendroth, H. (2022). *Matriarchale Gesellschaften der Gegenwart: Band II: Amerika, Indien, Afrika (Das Matriarchat, II, Band 3)*. Kohlhammer Verlag.

Göttner-Abendroth, H., & Smith K.P. (2008). Matriarchies as Societies of Peace. *Off Our Backs*, *38*(1), 49–52.

Lawrence, M., Homer-Dixon, T., Janzwood, S., Rockstöm, J., Renn, O., & Donges, J. (2024). *Global Sustainability*, 7e6. https://doi.org/10.1017/sus.2024.1

Lunz, K. (2023). *The Future of Foreign Policy Is Feminist*. John Wiley & Sons.

Mayor, A. (2016). *The Amazons: Lives and Legends of Warrior Women across the Ancient World*. Princeton University Press.

Miano, L. (2022). *Sisterhood*. Aufbau Digital.

Navickaitė, R. (2022). *Marija Gimbutas: Transnational Biography, Feminist Reception and the Controversy of Goddess Archeology*. Taylor & Francis.

Roosevelt, A.C. (1991). *Moundbuilders of the Amazon: Geophysical Archaeology on Marajo Island*. Academic Press.

Roosevelt, A.C. (1994) (Ed.). *Amazonian Indians from Prehistory to the Present: Anthropological Perspectives*. University of Arizona Press.

Rouse, I. (1963). The Arawak. In: *Handbook of South American Indians*, Vol. 4. New York Cooper Square Publications, pp. 517–519.

Segato, R. (2019). *Rede zur Eröffnung der Buchmesse in Buenos Aires Die Kraft des Ungehors a ms Rita Segato*. Rosa-Luxemburg-Foundation. https://www.rosalux.de/fileadmin/rls_uploads/pdfs/Ausland/Lateinamerika/discursoRitaSegatoSinCortes.pdf

Steffen, W., Rockström, J., Richardson, K., Lenton, T.M., Folke, C., Liverman, D., Summerhayes, C.P., Barnosky, A.D., Cornell, S.E., Crucifix, M., Donges, J.F., Fetzer, I., Lade, S.J., Scheffer, M., Winkelmann., R. & Schellnhuber, H.J. (2018).

Trajectories of the Earth System in the Anthropocene. *Proceedings of the National Academy of Sciences*, *115*(33), 8252–8259, https://www.pnas.org/content/pnas/early/2018/08/07/1810141115.full.pdf

Wisselinck, E. (1986). *Hexen. Warum wir so wenig von ihrer Geschichte erfahren und was davon noch falsch ist*. Frauenoffensive.

2
Patriarchy Strikes Back – Backlash and Tendencies Towards Authoritarian Regimes

Imagine we had a global archive of female and feminist documents, meticulously ordered since ancient times, that recounted not only the acts of famous women, but every woman's writing, thoughts, letters, poems, drawings, stories, paintings, theater plays and posts over time in all possible languages. Precisely, over a long time. Centuries, millennia. Imagine an artificial intelligence able to capture the content of the archive and attempt a preliminary analysis. There would be waves of courage, followed by waves of despondency, evident in the documents. These shifts would ripple through the archive's shelves in a temporal sequence. Periods of discouragement would coincide with arguments among women and feminists, which might appear arbitrary or erratic. At times, fierce disagreements would arise on topics such as the choice of terminology, whether sex work is a profession or a crime, whether motherhood is a burden or a blessing, whether women should collaborate with men or distance themselves, and whether they should remain peaceful or become warriors. It would become clear that phases of courageous political writing by women would be followed by phases in which attention would no longer be focused on external changes, but on their own internal development. There would be times when the lyrics would lose their clarity and sharpness. Then there would be turning points. Sudden outbreaks of fury towards the impossibility of changing the world would show up in the documents. Anger would rise like a wave that calls women to destroy the very power which fuels a patriarchal system designed to feed on the violence against women. As if in response to such turning points, there would be more and more courageous texts, sometimes downright visionary documents.

What if the rhythm we would discover between despondency and courage, between hopelessness and vision, was an indirect reflection of the phases of societal development that move between advancements towards egalitarian societies and regression towards androcentric power paradigms? It is unfortunate that such an archive does not exist, although feminists in many countries

DOI: 10.4324/9781003508885-3

have gone out of their way to archive the voices of women, pay reverence to ancestral thoughts and encourage women to learn from past and present.[1]

To this day, patriarchy has persisted against all odds, even when the signs point to its demise, which, unless we collectively act otherwise and return to live in harmony with nature and each other, will be the demise of our civilization, as some of the Indigenous peoples predicted. In 1973, at a young age, I had the privilege of visiting a Hopi reservation – a dream come true for me, as I had always been fascinated by the Hopi Nation of North America and their rich cultural traditions as a child. I was shocked at the poor conditions people lived in, which spurred my own lay research into the processes and effects of their colonization and marginalization. I can't remember why, but we came across an old man who introduced himself as 'White Bear'. He began to explain to us what he called the 'four worlds of the Hopi'. I sat down late that evening, took my journal and wrote down what I remembered, and which I could not believe as it sounded like a fairy tale or a fantasy. We live, I recall him explaining, in the fourth world, which is predicted to end in a huge fire unless humanity chooses to reconnect with the wholeness of creation in a harmonious way. The only people to survive would be those who have an intimate and loving relationship with Mother Earth.[2]

Today, the effects of climate change are forcing many people in the world to realize that the Hopi prophecy may hold some truth. With global warming, fires are already destroying homes and claiming lives, and will continue to do so in the future, making some areas uninhabitable and leading to increasing migration. Why do we need to understand these future scenarios? We must recognize that climate change is not just an unfortunate side effect of industrial activity that can be solved with technological advancements, but a pervasive consequence of human misbehavior that is now palpable everywhere. We need to understand scientific insights as much as Indigenous people's ability to see what we don't see, to look at the reality behind our superficial reality. So that one day we can change this trajectory, so that one day we will be able to break out of the inevitable dynamics of evolutionary destruction that is always combined with patriarchal retention of power.

We stand at a critical juncture in the history of humankind, where our inability to coexist peacefully and nurture our planet and ourselves has dire consequences. This is not mere happenstance; it follows a logical pattern that is asking for our understanding. Climate change and patriarchal power structures are directly connected. Failure to grasp this logic will inevitably lead to a future with more wars, authoritarian states, environmental disasters, human rights abuses and ecocide.

Femicide and misogyny have always been both precursors to and integral components of rituals of power abuse. From the psychology of oppression, we know that acts of humiliation, torture and violence serve to transfer power from the victim to the perpetrator. One might even argue that those consumed by their own weaknesses seek to appropriate the victim's life force – its innate power – at any cost. With every tortured confession, agonizing cry, act of rape or killing, power shifts from the persecuted to the persecutors, fueling their dominance and sustaining their control.[3] From a psychological perspective, such acts are not merely human disorders but manifestations of severe pathologies. Yet, most societies have failed to identify power pathologies as aberrations of human behavior. The repercussions are dire for everybody, but in particular for women: most societies do not negatively sanction an upsurge in violence against women, or widespread sexism. They hardly notice the brutalization of language, the mechanisms that make women invisible and discredit them, or the perpetuation of rituals of subjugation. Too few people understand that these regressive societal trajectories ultimately culminate in warfare, the epitome of male pathology, stripping men and women of their humanity and reducing many women to mere objects that become victims of rape and mass atrocities.[4]

Yet, in their quest to gain power by eliminating human spirit or human life, the perpetrators unwittingly obliterate the very knowledge that could carry us as humankind into a different future. The wise women – those in the story of Rokeya, those reigning Old Europe or those giving advice to Okinka Pampa on the Bijago islands did not question what holds the world together at its core; they knew it instinctively – the primal urge to live well which is reflected in the human ability to care. It is time we reclaim this wisdom, resist the forces of oppression and restore balance to our world before it's too late.

The two German feminists Lida Heymann and Anita Ausgburg, among others working to make the aforementioned women's peace conference in 1915 happen, did not stop their activism after World War I ended.[5] They engaged internationally, wrote about unscrupulous economic imperialism and tirelessly argued against the upcoming Nazi mentality in Germany. Not surprisingly, they found themselves on the death list of the Nazis. In 1933, when Hitler seized power, and established a regime of terror within months, they were on a holiday abroad. Urged by feminist friends who had already fled Germany for fear of detainment, they did not return home. The Nazis seized their entire wealth and properties in Germany so that they became destitute refugees in Switzerland. It was their international network through the Women's League that helped them through. But even though they were both over the age of 70, they did not stop naming the culprits. With her incredible ability for strategic foresight, Lida Heymann wrote a flaming article in the journal *Pax International* in 1933, arguing that those who would 'let fascism take its course are depriving themselves of freedom' and 'allow themselves to be driven into the next Holocaust with their hands tied and their mouth stuffed.'[6] They also did not stop engaging in diplomacy. Together with their feminist friend Gertrud Baer, who had also fled Nazi Germany, and later on moved to the United States, they gathered facts and figures about the growing armament of Germany and predicted the war which, at that time, most European leaders thought would not happen. Instead, the leaders assumed the women were exaggerating. In 1935 Heymann wrote another article in *Pax International*, naming the Nazi pogroms against the Jews, the torture, the terror and the concentration camps, and accused the other European nations' appeasement policies of complicity with the Nazi terror as their economic involvement with Germany strengthened the totalitarian regime.[7] She even gave up her pacifist attitude, suggesting in 1936 that Nazi Germany should be reacted to by military means instead of appeasement and negotiations with Hitler. In 1941, when World War II, which she had been predicting, was raging about Europe, she wrote that 'the violent methods of fascism and National Socialism can no longer be overcome today through pacifist means… [they] can only be destroyed by means that impress the violent enactors of fascism and nationalism and that can only be violence.'[8]

Why do I dwell on the story of this feminist and visionary couple? The two women are just one example of collective feminist activism that has moved the world forward, even though they were not able to reap the rewards within their lifetime. There are millions of these examples in women's history. The more we know about them, the braver we can become in our strategies towards counteracting patriarchal backlash. Understanding these stories can help building the *collective feminist power practice* we need to predict and counteract patriarchal backlash. From this particular example we can learn how patriarchal backlash and the logic of war are closely interconnected. This connection must be observed and named. Can it be counteracted early enough? Can it be prevented without resorting to violence? This is open for debate and feminists would produce contradicting answers. Lida Heymann and Anita Augspurg started off as true pacifists – until Nazi Germany showed its horrific face. Of course, not only women or feminists fought against fascism. Many courageous people took up the fight and many paid with their lives. However, and for the purpose of this book, we need to look at fascism as the most brutal form of a patriarchal backlash and understand how patriarchy and fascism are intrinsically linked.

At the start of the 20th century, the international women's movement aimed for more than surface-level progress, seeking peace and equality. Yet, patriarchy reasserted itself, continuing its destructive path. The women's peace conference in 1915 symbolized both success and failure, marking the beginning of a lasting patriarchal backlash. Despite a vibrant feminist and androgynous culture in Europe after World War I[9], the rise of new gender possibilities collapsed with World War II. Feminism only regained strength between 1970 and 2000, and much of the earlier movement was erased from history. While we may hope such a backlash won't repeat, recent developments suggest otherwise.

The global landscape in the third decade of the 21st century is witnessing a concerning trend towards right-wing ideology and the rise of authoritarian states. This change reflects a complex interplay of socio-political factors. Uncertain and endangered futures, economic fears and cultural changes lead to uncertainty, which populist, right-wing movements and 'bad state actors' take advantage of. Nationalist, populist and often authoritarian narratives resonate not only in Europe but around the world.[10] Climate change and foreseeable transformation processes contribute to uncertainty and lead to a loss of trust in traditional political institutions. Many people have the impression that the established political parties in democracies are disconnected from their needs and concerns. This prepares the ground for actors who promise decisive action and simple solutions. At the same time, these same actors use social media including hybrid war methodologies to further fuel fears, such as threats to national identity or security and prosperity. They are often supported by authoritarian state actors that have an interest in promoting their ideology and destabilizing democracies.[11] In addition, neoliberal economic policy leads to an increase in the wealth gap and fears of social decline lead to resentment and insecurity. Again, right-wing actors take advantage of such grievances by scapegoating marginalized groups such as immigrants, refugees and minorities while offering simplistic solutions and promising economic recovery. Most often they also target women and feminists. Social media is used to amplify right-wing narratives and facilitate the spread of disinformation.[12] This paves the way for online echo chambers, which are in turn reinforced by algorithms. Prejudice reinforces pre-existing beliefs and creates fertile ground for the spread of extremist ideologies and conspiracy theories, which in turn undermine democratic values and institutions. These right-wing and authoritarian tendencies are intertwined with a patriarchal backlash. What do I mean by that?

A *patriarchal backlash* is a regressive response by individuals and institutions rooted in patriarchal systems to challenges posed by women, feminists and intersectional movements seeking to abolish outdated gender roles and power dynamics.[13] Such a backlash can have a variety of manifestations that depend on the forms of society, the culture or the state of development. But it typically occurs when there are movements, initiatives or structural changes aimed at advancing gender equality, gender fluidity, women's rights and economic empowerment, and when there is a decline in male shares of power over societal structures. The form backlashes take can be subtle or explicit, mildly oppressive or outrightly violent depending on the context, culture and societal settings.

In its mild manifestations, the backlash unfolds gradually, characterized by the insidious brutalization of language and the proliferation of violent imagery in literature, film and theater. Women are increasingly depicted as weak or subjected to violence, strong women and particularly feminists are fought and defeated, not unlike the tales about the Amazons in Hellenic Greece, which had a proliferation of horrific stories that always ended in defeating or killing Amazons brutally.[14] Often militarization, both by state and by private actors as well as by criminals, and increasing armament go hand in hand with the escalation of aggression. Violence against women intensifies in the private sphere, coupled with a systematic discreditation of women in public positions of power, unless they confer with the male power structures. A broad shift towards right-wing ideology is another indicator, with feminists and feminism explicitly targeted.[15] When the backlash grows, violence against women reaches alarming levels, while feminists face widespread discreditation and dismissal. Women's rights are either declared achieved enough or deemed unnecessary, as society clamors for the return of strong male figures. The call for a strong man gains momentum, often accompanied by an escalation in military spending and narratives that justify military interventions.

The principles of advanced patriarchal backlashes have remained the same over millennia and centuries: Violence, terror, rape, enclosure, assimilation, appropriation, exploitation and war. All this hits not only women, but everyone who does not fit, is considered useless or not valid, poses a threat to the dominant system or resists the mainstream. Has humanity learned something during the last millennia? Yes, but not enough.

The in-depth investigations by numerous female and some male scientists lead to a disastrous conclusion: Over the past centuries, whenever social values associated with the feminine have gained prominence or were on the rise, when women took to the stage and the call for fundamental systemic change was heard by many, proponents of the patriarchal order rallied to defend it.[16] These protagonists often had, and still have, the faces of individual men, but it goes beyond a few men acting irrationally. The patriarchal backlash is lived at structural and individual levels at the same time. The system asserts itself.

Denis Mukwege, the medical doctor and recipient of the Nobel Peace Prize from the Democratic Republic of Congo, has dedicated his life to treating women who have endured the horrors of rape and sexual mutilation in times of armed conflict. In his book, *The Power of Women* (*La force des femmes*), he asserts that the core of male violence stems from the patriarchal framework that molds societal standards, economic structures, family dynamics and political decisions.[17] This system, he argues, perpetuates a culture of masculinity that conditions men toward aggression and dominance. He also highlights that this is not an African phenomenon, but a pattern to be found around the globe. As an example, he mentions the absence of any rape convictions during the Nuremberg trials in Germany after the end of World War II.[18] This shocking societal failure to address rape as a weapon of war is not surprising, but evidence of a profound lack of understanding of the connection between war, war crimes and reinforced patriarchy.

While the specific manifestations of patriarchal backlash may vary, the underlying patterns have remained consistent across time and regions. Anyone who looks at the witch hunts in Europe, the reactions to the women's movement in the 19th century, the suppression of free-spirited thinking in the 1920s in Europe and around the world, the social discrediting of women described negatively as emancipated women or man-haters in the early years of the 21st century, the increase in violence against women and femicides in Latin America, Asia and Europe, or the recent elections in the United States, is able to see the same patterns. When patriarchy strikes back, the reins of male dominance are being tightened. The call for the strong man becomes loud, and shockingly also from women who are blind to the effects that they themselves will have to feel.

In her book *The Chalice and the Blade*, the futurist and system scientist Riane Eisler shows that social regression and misogyny are always the preparation for more violent forms of patriarchal backlashes.[19] Wars, she says, can be predicted, not only as a conclusion based on armament and military maneuvers, or failures of peace diplomacy and economic cooperation. They can be predicted, because they are part of a systems dynamic that shifts societal patterns into evolutionary androcentric regression. What follows are new eras of oppression and repression paving the way for the next war.[20] Every war, then, brutalizes people and takes their attention away from societal progress. It legitimizes domination even more, celebrates weapons production, and justifies destruction and loss of lives. Human beings become disposable. It is a set-back of the evolutionary process of humanity. Are there no ways out?

We may believe we've advanced with better legal systems, international courts, stronger networks and global solidarity among women and feminists. Social media can instantly document and mobilize people, but it can also be misused by patriarchal forces. It's crucial to analyze the mechanisms driving patriarchal backlash, which are often linked to authoritarianism, neoliberalism or rising fascism. I encourage you to uncover as many such methods as possible in your context, your country.

One of the early stages of patriarchal backlash is legal and policy change. Rolling back laws or policies that promote gender equality or protect women's rights is a method that is even very popular in democracies. Women's reproductive rights are and always have been the primary point of attack. An example of collective feminist action to counteract such a patriarchal backlash is Poland, a country with a restrictive abortion law. The Constitutional Tribunal, whose judges had largely been appointed by the then ruling extreme conservative Law and Justice party, declared in 2020 abortion even due to fetal abnormalities unconstitutional. This decision severely limited access to legal abortion in Poland, sparking widespread feminist protests across the country and drawing criticism from international human rights organizations. Already in 2016, the *All-Poland Women's Strike (OSK)* was formed to organize protests opposing proposed stricter abortion laws, mobilizing 100,000 people across 143 locations in the country. They collaborated with Argentinian activists from the Ni Una Menos movement, and initiated the International Women's Strike, involving women from 28 countries.[21] In 2023 this specific form of patriarchal backlash was halted. The women's protests were crucial for the political change in the elections in Poland in 2023, a decisive step in re-strengthening the country's democracy. One of the leaders of the All-Poland Women's Strike, Katarzyna Kotula, even became Minister of Equality in the new left-oriented government.[22] These are the milder versions of legal means towards strengthening patriarchy. The heavyweights also using legal means are the Taliban in Afghanistan. After they seized power again in 2021, their interpretation of the Sharia law has resulted in banning girls from attending school beyond a certain age, forcing women professionals out of work and restricting their freedom of movement.[23]

Another mechanism is more subtle, and less dependent on state actors, but also functions effectively. We could call it a social and cultural backlash, which works through subtly or openly influencing social norms. The aim is the reinforcement of patriarchal gender norms by perpetuating stereotypes and, above all, marginalizing if not criminalizing LGBTQ individuals. This can be seen in media representations that portray women as submissive, men as dominant and both confined to traditional roles. Conservative religious teachings or right-extremist ideologies may propagate the belief that non-heteronormative relationships are immoral, contributing to the stigmatization of individuals and their exclusion from societal acceptance. This has an effect on others, who become afraid of living differently, or even think their adaptation to patriarchal norms is their voluntary choice. In times when many countries in the world have legalized same-sex marriages and have strong LGBTQ communities, this backlash may sound outdated. But it isn't necessarily, because the mechanisms are subtle and can therefore swing in a different direction when they are supported by right-wing parties gaining strength. Or they can be outrightly brutal by criminalizing people who support the LGBTQ movement, such as in 2024 in Russia where a law has been passed that makes such an engagement a terrorist act and where people have been detained.[24] Patriarchal backlash, authoritarian states and fierce discrimination against non-traditional gender identities are closely linked. A highlighted form of backlash is increased violence and harassment against women. The 2023 World Population Report notes that South Africa and Brazil lead in violence against women, including sexual violence and homicide, followed by Russia and Mexico.[25] Even in countries with lower risks, like Canada and Scandinavia, there's no fully safe place for women. UN Women reported a shadow pandemic during COVID-19, with violence against women rising from 243 million to 736 million victims globally.[26]

A well-known mechanism of backlash that has received much attention from feminists over decades is reviving the economic disadvantage of women. While efforts over the decades aimed to reduce this, such as integrating women into the labor market, promoting women into parliament[27] or introducing quotas for female leadership, silent backlashes often persist, leaving women to struggle individually. Every country has different strategies for issues such as non-equal pay or state-supported child care. Yet, again, backlash can go unnoticed or be difficult to address, often because women struggle individually. The case of German reunification illustrates this: In the former socialist East, women were fully integrated into the labor market and many held high-status jobs, while West Germany reinforced traditional gender roles, following the American narrative of happy housewives, and thus limiting women's professional opportunities. After reunification, female representation in fields like computer science in the former East dropped from 50–60% to just 20%.[28] While it may have seemed like an individual misfortune, this was actually the result of a systemic issue: A complex, detrimental combination of necessary economic transformation and the long-established male dominance in computer science in Western Germany.

Also, backlashes in the form of harassment of women or feminists can take forms that do not get captured in statistics and are less obvious to societal development. They are not less dangerous. Many female politicians and women in influential public or institutional roles become targets of subtle, hard-to-detect campaigns. The common tactic, often but not always employed by men, involves scrutinizing something these women have published or done that can be used to undermine their professionalism. This is then turned into a public smear campaign or a criminal complaint aimed at damaging their reputation. These women often step back, withdraw into private life or give up their activities. It is difficult for those who are not involved to recognize whether the accusations are unreasonable or have any truth. These women are often alone with their experiences and it is only the frequency with which this has happened in recent years that suggests that this is a backlash that has a certain logic.[29] More visible is this form of backlash in the hatred against feminists on social media. This also happens in Western democracies that would love to be seen as advanced in women's rights, openness to fluid gender identities and support of women in power positions. The backlash works in the media as a reactionary counter-movement undermining the rise of female power. This is supplemented by misogynistic rhetoric in politics. Conservative and right-wing verbal assaults on women become normalized. But it got tremendously brutal in recent years on TikTok, YouTube or other social media. Fantasies of violence against women have huge numbers of followers. As we know from feminist research over time, the fantasies become real and are followed by brutalization of societies, paving the way for even worse atrocities such as wars.

There is a debate over whether patriarchal backlash comes and goes in waves. If we had the women's archive I asked you at the beginning of this chapter to imagine, we would certainly have the evidence over time spans of centuries and millennia. Back in 1991, at the height of the then wave of feminist movements, the American feminist journalist and author Susan Faludi described in her book *Backlash – The Undeclared War Against American Women* in a detailed way the mechanisms that attacked and undermined feminist achievements when, for example, misogynistic myths and bad images about working women in the United States flooded the public.[30] In another more recent book on backlash tendencies, published in 2023, the German journalist Susanne Kaiser suggests that we must realize an increasing divergence: The more women occupy positions of power in politics, companies and civil society organizations, and the more they act as influencers on social media platforms, the more fierce reactions can be expected. What manifests in the private domain as domestic violence and femicides, manifests in the public domain as stalking, sexual assault, hate speech, death threats or discreditation campaigns.[31]

The question is: Can we counteract the many manifestations of patriarchal backlash by *collective feminist power practices*? The women's strike approach in Poland has been one of the encouraging examples. To patriarchal backlash applies what is valid for right-extremist and fascist developments: Notice it early enough and collectively resist the beginnings. We could say: Feminists, seize collective power early enough in many different ways. And no, it cannot only be feminists, it can not only be women in order to have the effect we wish to see. But let us first get inspired by practices that have happened or are already happening, not judging their effectiveness or success.

Let us journey to the continent where centuries back, the Amazons insisted on their female power in a large inaccessible territory and also women today take collective action against patriarchal institutional violence and femicides. On November 20 in the year 2019, a feminist performance entitled 'Un violador en tu camino' ('A rapist on your path') was performed together with 40 women by the women's collective Las Tesis in the Chilean city of Valparaíso. Blindfolded women pointed their index finger at an imaginary perpetrator and shouted through the streets: You are the rapist!

The members of a trans-inclusive, intersectional feminist arts collective, Sibilla Sotomayor Van Rysseghem, Daffne Valdés Vargas, Lea Cáceres and Paula Cometa, translated elements of feminist theory into visual and linguistic performance. They took up approaches from the aforementioned Rita Segato as well as the Italian-American and Marxist-feminist scientist Silvia Federici. Violence against women is clearly stated as a systemic pattern in the performance. This is about rape and femicide, especially about institutionalized sexual violence against women by police, government officials and other systems of state power. A few days later the performance was repeated in Santiago de Chile. The video of the performance went viral. Feminist groups from several other countries asked if they could use the song, replicate the performance and adjust it to their context. First, women in other countries on the continent took up the demonstrative display. Within weeks to months the performances spread all over the world. It was performed in London, Berlin, Paris, Madrid, Barcelona, Tel Aviv, New Delhi, Tokyo, Beirut, Istanbul, Mexico City, Caracas, Lima, Buenos Aires, Karachi, but also in the Andes, in African countries, in Russia and in India. It resonated with so many women because it was a global outcry against patriarchal societal systems in which violence against women not only arises from an individual perpetrator, but is inherent in the social arrangement of these societies. Feminists around the world made socially legitimized male dominance and power pathologies visible in street performances.[32]

The collective Las Tesis became so famous within weeks that they could hardly keep up with press requests and inquiries. Because of global access to social media, something that was locally anchored and intended to act as a critique of Chilean society reached the entire world. The performance not only gave a strong impulse to political protests in Chile at that time, but also spurred feminist research on the prospects of feminist collective action, and the role of social media in mobilizing such collective action and in the growing transnational feminism.[33] There is a lot to learn from Latin American feminists and their courage to address patriarchy and patriarchal backlash.

Not all use arts, not all use peaceful means. In 2019 the government of Mexico slashed funding for women's shelters. Activists criticized this, saying that two decades of work in support of women was endangered.[34] Despite the surge in femicides at the beginning of the pandemic in 2020, many women's institutions again saw serious reductions in state funding. Millions demonstrated against gender-based violence. The anger about the increasing number of femicides in Mexico and the low level of legal prosecution of perpetrators spurred the formation of a radical feminist group – the feminist bloque negro. In observing this development, Patricia Olamendi Torres, a professor and the Director of the Justice and Human Rights Training Institute in Mexico, explains this as an almost logical reaction to the impossible situation of violence against women in Mexico, even if it shakes up the image of peaceful women. It is the only way they get heard and acknowledged, she said.[35] The members of the bloque negro wear black clothing and always cover their faces so that they cannot be identified by the authorities. Some of them are direct or indirect victims of violence, some relatives of victims of feminicide, others women's rights activists. The Mexican group was inspired by the so-called radical black bloc who took to the streets in Berlin and other European cities in the 1980s using improvised weapons to fight against the police with helmets and shields in order to create what they consider autonomous space, such as occupying empty houses. The Mexican women did something similar. They occupied a building and created a space for women and their children who had become victims of violence against women. In the physical space they created women could recover, and feel free again and supported by a community of women with similar experience. They get trained in self-defense and organize their communal living together with democratic decision-making. *Violence until violence against women ends* is one of the mottos of the feminist bloque negro, although the rule is to only use violence against objects. The exception is the police as, in their view, they represent the violent state system. It feels uneasy to see the masked women of the bloque negro, but are we entitled to judge their conclusion that only violence and creating fear among perpetrators will help end violence?

There are many other places in the world where women got seriously furious because their lives were threatened, or their power and freedom curtailed. Let us shift time and geography and look at a counteraction that can also be understood as a fight against patriarchal backlash. In 1929, at the height of the global economic regression, a conflict arose in the town of Aba in the south-east of Nigeria. For the people living in the area, it was remembered as the war of the women. Colonial occupation worked, as in many other places, by strengthening or installing local male rulers who functioned as an extension of the colonial administration. One of them aimed to introduce, alongside the local poll tax, a new tax on poultry owned by women. Women held considerable power in the local markets and were usually financially independent. They got so angry with the prospect of yet another tax that they rallied together and marched towards the city of Aba. The tax would have endangered the survival of their businesses. Up to 25,000 women participated in the demonstrations against the local courts, freed detained people and damaged the colonial administration and the English bank, which they plundered. They revived a traditional form of protest that had been used in the past within their communities whenever the political authority of women had been curtailed or endangered by men. Leonora Miano, in her book *Sisterhood*, explains that the metaphoric translation of this form of protest is 'sitting on a man' or 'making war on a man'.[36] In order to call men to order they would organize a strike or a boycott and gather at the man's place and dance, offend his virility in songs, damage the house or beat the man up. The tax issue became an opportunity to stand up against the colonial system. The protest was successful regarding the tax – its introduction was withdrawn. But when the uprising did not end, the British colonial power hit back brutally. Many women died; some villages were burned in the attempt to reinforce patriarchal rules. Yet, some success was achieved. The British opened up to integrate local customs into their colonial administration.

These examples show that resistance to patriarchal backlash is manifold, it can be peaceful or violent. Let us for now not judge whether one or the other is the right path, but notice that collective female and feminist action is and has been a way of resisting patriarchal power backlashes. What all the examples in this chapter show is that counteracting patriarchal backlash cannot be successful without such collective action. Individually, women cannot withstand the forces of androcentric regression, not even if they hold important economic or political power positions. We will see in later chapters how crucial the role of collaboration is among women in power, which is still rare, among feminist activists across countries, and between grassroot movements and women in power. The examples also speak of the interconnectedness between women's issues and other societal issues, such as economic disparities, right-wing developments, colonial heritages, racial injustices and environmental concerns.

Recognizing and naming patriarchy and its backlash, both historic and contemporary, has been a significant achievement of the women's movement.[37] While we have analyzed its mechanisms and devised countless strategies to resist it, disagreements over approaches have often divided us. Patriarchal backlash, however, targets women individually while operating as a systemic societal structure. Therefore, it can only be effectively challenged and overcome through collective action.

If we imagine the female and feminist archive I mentioned at the beginning of this chapter being analyzed by artificial intelligence, I believe it would reveal waves of disagreements among feminists that coincide with the early beginnings of patriarchal backlashes. There is a method to the madness that we need to become aware of. The way patriarchal backlash becomes effective is similar to the many ways in history that oppressors have tried to make the oppressed docile, and it has been elaborated by many: Spread dissent among the oppressed and see what happens. Usually this takes on a dynamic by itself that can hardly be traced back to its origins. It might escape the simple cause and effect logic, but history shows that mutual discreditation, women divided and fighting each other create the perfect backdrop for patriarchal backlash. Leonora Miano is right when she advocates for a better dialogue between women who respect each other in their place and on their journey, exactly the way they are, with their experiences, their longings, their anger – and as true sisters.[38]

It is time to end mutual discreditation and, instead, celebrate our arguments and let each other stand constructively with our differences and our different opinions. It's time to look at the bigger goal. We don't all have to do the same thing, or aim for the same thing. What unites us, however, is the desire for future civilizations in their egalitarian, peaceful and regenerative manifestation, civilizations that give women every opportunity to develop their potential, that give all people freedom and take caring for life on this planet seriously. If we want to claim power as feminists, we need to look at the bigger picture of current world developments.

Major insights for *collective feminist power practices* from patriarchal backlash and women's counteraction:

1. It's crucial to realize that the current resurgence of patriarchal backlash is connected to historical patterns that span centuries, if not millennia, as repeated androcentric societal regression.
2. We must recognize that patriarchal backlash comes in multiple – subtle and severe – forms that are intertwined. Despite overarching similar patterns, the manifestations are contextual. It is important to identify these different manifestations and understand their connections.
3. It is important to stay aware that patriarchal backlash in its subtle as well as violent manifestations hits women and marginalized people individually, but it is a societal phenomenon that can only be addressed collectively.
4. Patriarchal regressions typically feature male protagonists, who embody and celebrate power imbalances. While it is crucial to pinpoint individual actors, we must comprehend the structural dynamics driving patriarchal backlash.

5. We need to give room to our justified anger, understand the various forms of counteraction or even prevention of patriarchal backlash across the globe, historically and contemporary, in order to learn together for future strategies.
6. We need to upgrade feminist networking locally, regionally and worldwide for mutual support, coordinated strategies and collective action. As feminists, we need to anticipate backlash proactively and share strategies to counteract it effectively.

Notes

1 A good source offering an overview of feminist archives can be found on the following website: https://fla-network.com/directory/international. For an interesting article elaborating feminist archiving in the 1970s see Samer (2014).
2 Only much later did I realize that he must have been the co-author of *The Book of The Hopi*, see White Bear and Waters (1963). While the prophecy in the book is less disastrous, my journal from 1973 speaks of the destruction by fire.
3 Hardly anything can be found in research about this transfer of energy, although it is an important aspect of understanding the act of torture as a human pathology. My understanding is derived from the many conversations I have with a dear friend who was part of the South African Truth and Reconciliation Commission.
4 I have tried to capture the patriarchal mechanisms of this process in a contribution to the Club of Rome publication: *Peace in the Anthropocene*. See Kuenkel (2024).
5 A detailed account of the life and work of this feminist lesbian and activist couple can be found in Dünnebier and Scheu (2002).
6 Dünnebier and Scheu (2002 p. 296ff, translation by the author).
7 Dünnebier and Scheu (2002 p. 297).
8 Dünnebier and Scheu (2002 p. 230).
9 The city of Berlin was a stunning example of the changing role of women – it was even called 'the city of women' with feminist and often androgyn activists in arts and culture, many of them Jewish. With the rise of Nazism and antisemitism their thriving contribution to society came to a sudden end. See also: Schönfeld (2022 pp. 1897–1908).
10 Particularly interesting here is the brilliant analysis of the Indian-born social anthropologist and rector of the European University in Vienne, Shalina Randeria, who coined the term *soft authoritarianism*. A good summary of her thesis can be found in an interview with her, see Selzer & Plote (2021). A more scientific account of the concept can be found in Adam et al. (2024).
11 An overview concerning the European situation can be found in: Lonardo (2024).
12 Today, this is supported by artificial intelligence, which can produce false realities in picture that are impossible to reveal for laypersons.
13 Many feminists have described both the origins and features of patriarchal backlash, even if not all of them used the exact term. Here is a small selection: In *The Undeclared War Against American Women* Susan Faludi (1991) investigates how

the media, politics and cultural forces reacted against the feminist advances of the 1970s. In *Gender Trouble* Judith Butler (2006) talks about societal attempts to reinforce binary gender norms. Throughout her writings, including *Feminism Is for Everybody* bell hooks (2000) addresses patriarchal resistance to feminist goals intersecting with race and class. In *Right-Wing Women* (1983) Andrea Dworkin wrote about how male-dominated systems retaliate against women's liberation movements. In the famous *Women, Race, & Class*, Angela Davis (1983) explores how historical patriarchal backlashes have worked to suppress both feminist and anti-racist movements. In her book *Backlash: Die neue Gewalt gegen Frauen* ('Backlash: The New Violence Against Women'), Susanne Kaiser (2023) examines how patriarchal forces respond to feminist progress in the age of social media, populism and far-right movements.

14 See Mayor (2016 p. 31, Kindle Version).

15 This was very obvious in Germany in 2022 with the ridiculing of gender-sensitive language that has been introduced in newspapers, radios and TV. The follow-on step of patriarchal backlash is under way: In some federal states, gender-sensitive language has already been banned.

16 See Faludi (1991), Banet-Weiser (2018) and Kaiser (2022).

17 Mukwege (2022).

18 Mukwege (2022 p. 240).

19 See Eisler (2011).

20 Personal conversation with Riane Eisler.

21 In 2020, Klementyna Suchanow, a key figure in OSK, published a book in polish, with the (translated) title 'This is War', documenting the origins of the OSK and the International Women's Strike. See Suchanow (2020).

22 See https://www.gov.pl/web/primeminister/katarzyna-kotula

23 See Qazizada (2024).

24 See: https://www.hrw.org/news/2023/11/30/russia-supreme-court-bans-lgbt-movement-extremist

25 See the *World Population Review*: https://worldpopulationreview.com/country-rankings/most-dangerous-countries-for-women, and *The Women, Peace and Security Index* of the George Town Institute, https://giwps.georgetown.edu/the-index

26 See UN Women Statistics, accessible at: https://www.unwomen.org/en/news/in-focus/in-focus-gender-equality-in-covid-19-response/violence-against-women-during-covid-19

27 Although an authoritarian state, in 2024, Rwanda tops the list: slightly above 60% of members of the parliament are women, and more than a third of the ministerial positions are held by women.

28 See Schinzel (2007).

29 Personal conversations.

30 See Faludi (1991).

31 See Kaiser (2023).

32 Liinason (2024).

33 A fascinating account and proposal for collective feminist action can be found in Gago (2020).

34 See: https://www.theguardian.com/world/2019/mar/05/mexico-funding-cuts-womens-shelters-domestic-violence
35 See a courageous documentation on the TV channel ARTE: https://www.youtube.com/watch?v=_OgdhJSzH1k
36 See Miano (2022 p. 194).
37 This ranges across decades from Daly (1990) to Saini (2023).
38 Miano (2022).

References

Adam, J., Flader, U., Steinhauer, H., & Randeria, S. (2024). Soft authoritarian lawfare. Threats to democracy from within. In: Lonardo, L. (2024). *Addressing Hybrid Threats*. Edward Elgar, p. 130–148.

Banet-Weiser, S. (2018). *Empowered. Popular Feminism and Popular Misogyny*. Durham: Duke University Press.

Butler, J. (2006). *Gender Trouble. Feminism and the Subversion of Identity*. Routledge.

Daly, M. (1990). *Gyn/Ecology: The Metaethics of Radical Feminism*. Beacon Press.

Davis, A. (1983). *Women, Race, & Class*. Vintage.

Dünnebier, A., & Scheu, U. (2002). *Die Rebellion ist eine Frau. Anita Augspurg und Lida G. Heymann – Das schillerndste Paar der Frauenbewegung*. Heinrich Hugendubel.

Dworkin, A. (1983). *Right-Wing Women*. The Women's Press.

Eisler, R. (2011). *The Chalice and the Blade: Our History, Our Future*. Harper Collins.

Faludi, S. (1991). *Backlash. The Undeclared War Against American Women*. Crown Publishing Group.

Gago, V. (2020). *Feminist International: How to Change Everything*. Verso.

hooks, bell. (2000). *Feminism Is for Everybody*. South End Press.

Kaiser, S. (2023). *Backlash: Die neue Gewalt gegen Frauen*. Tropen.

Kuenkel, P. (2024). Beyond patriarchal paradigms: Reimaging peace. In: *Club of Rome. Enduring Peace in the Anthropocene*, pp. 18–23. https://www.clubofrome.org/wp-content/uploads/2024/05/Enduring_peace_in_the_Anthropocene.pdf

Liinason, M. (2024). The performance of protest: Las Tesis and the newfeminist radicality at the conjunction of digital spaces and the streets. *Feminist Media Studies*, *24*(3), 430–447, https://doi.org/10.1080/14680777.2023.2200472. Open Access. https://www.tandfonline.com/doi/epdf/10.1080/14680777.2023.2200472?needAccess=true

Lonardo, L. (2024). *Addressing Hybrid Threats*. Edward Elgar Publishing.

Mayor, A. (2016). *The Amazons: Lives and Legends of Warrior Women across the Ancient World*. Princeton University Press.

Miano, L. (2022). *Sisterhood*. Aufbau Digital.

Mukwege, D. (2022). *The Power of Women. A Doctor's Journey to Health and Healing*. Flatiron Books.

Qazizada, M. (2024, February 8). *Impacts of the Taliban's Ban on Women's Work and Education*. Devpolicy Blog from the Development Policy Centre. https://devpolicy.org/impacts-of-the-talibans-ban-on-womens-work-and-education-20240209

Saini, A. (2023). *The Patriarchs: How Men Came to Rule*. Fourth Estate.

Samer, R. (2014, June). Revising 'Re-vision': Documenting 1970s Feminisms and the Queer Potentiality of Digital Feminist Archives. *Ada: A Journal of Gender, New Media, and Technology*, 5, https://scholarsbank.uoregon.edu/items/691e215e-e26c-4167-af63-23df9f271113

Schinzel, B. (2007). Informatik und Geschlechtergerechtigkeit in Deutschland – Annäherungen. In: Leicht-Scholten, C. (Ed.): *Gender and Science. Perspektiven in den Natur- und Ingenieurwissenschaften*, Bielefeld: transcript Verlag, 2007, pp. 127–146. https://doi.org/10.1515/9783839406748-008

Schönfeld, C. (2022). Women in the City: Berlin (1900–1933). In: Tambling, J. (ed) *The Palgrave Encyclopedia of Urban Literary Studies*, pp 1897–1908. Cham: Palgrave Macmillan. https://doi.org/10.1007/978-3-319-62419-8_197

Selzer, C., & Plote, B. (2021, September). *Soft Authoritarianism: An Interview with Shalina Randeria*. Up2date.uni-Bremen.de. https://up2date.uni-bremen.de/en/article/soft-authoritarianism

Suchanow, K. (2020). *To jest wojna. Kobiety, fundamentaliści i nowe średniowiecze*. Agora. https://kulturalnysklep.pl/product-pol-61525-To-jest-wojna-Kobiety-fundamentalisci-i-nowe-sredniowiecze.html

White Bear, O., & Waters, F. (1963). *Book of The Hopi*. New York: Viking Press.

3
Transformation to a World in Balance of Power – Our Only Chance

If we project the features of patriarchal backlash into the future, combine it with the rising tendencies towards authoritarian regimes, add social disparities as a result of an untamed neoliberal capitalism, complement it with the widespread consequences of the climate crisis coupled with biodiversity loss – we are heading for total disaster. The word families describing what we could call death-driven societies sound like this: Femicides, crimes, catastrophes, consumerism, climate change, violence, genocides, monopolies of power, mass manipulation, murders, wars, coercion, decomposition, destruction, and so on. The ancient great goddess, or a therapist for planetary health, would shake her head and announce the result of the patient's thorough anamnesis: A serious psychopathological phenomenon of a culture characterized by a longing for death. This refers, she would explain, to an inherent addiction to destruction, an urge to blindly drag others into disaster with short-term gains or false happiness in the medium term, a deep-rooted ignorance of life. She would try to identify the cause of the psychopathological disorder. This, she would declare, is what happens when the male principle occupies the world and makes the female principle a willing slave. It can only go wrong. The danger she would warn about: Essentially an organized collective suicide.

Here, in the middle of the third decade of the 21st century, we as humanity are at crossroads. If we are willing to listen to climate scientists, then we know that we may have less than a decade to work together to care for our planet and our shared humanity as quickly and as intensely as possible so that we can reduce the consequences of man-made global warming to a tolerable level. Those who advocate for a different future, including many women, are more present than ever at the international climate conferences, but we know it is not enough, we know that the political processes are not fast enough to prevent the catastrophic effects of global warming: More storms, more flooding, more earthquakes, more severe weather events, more forest fires, more droughts, more destitute people, more migration, more undermining of democracies,

DOI: 10.4324/9781003508885-4

more challenges to govern states. It's like Gaia has been watching long enough to get really angry. That's why we must do more than we have ever done to claim power for the future of this world, knowing that we may only be a small group of women, yet, connected to so many other groups of women (and many men). We will change this world. We will bring together the building blocks of future civilizations that value life on this planet and allow women – indeed, all people – to be free.

Let us, for the moment, escape the horrific trajectory and jump a few decades, maybe a few centuries, maybe a millennium into the future. People in this future civilization begin to smile when history books mention previous civilizations, because they are not able to imagine how the awareness of human interconnectedness with one another and with the planet could ever have been missing from the consciousness of humanity. They have all learned at school that at the end of a second decade in the 21st century we humans had to learn to come to terms with our planet. It was a century, so tell the history books, in which it wasn't clear whether humanity would forfeit its own civilization or find its way back into an intimate friendship with the land that bore their feet. In this future civilization, everybody gets taught that once upon a time humanity found itself at crossroads. Centuries of heedless exploitation of the planet's resources and a continuous pushing back of the power of women, the wisdom of Indigenous peoples and the collective intelligence of many had serious repercussions that were difficult to handle. However, amid the challenges, a new vision emerged. It grew like a weed that was pulled out at times, because it annoyed those in power, but the vision was stronger. It grew inexorably, rooted in sustainability, equity and a profound respect for the delicate balance of the Earth's systems. It became the foundation for societies that began to operate according to some basic rules. History books also remind pupils of an autistic 16-year-old girl who refused to go to school on Fridays and instead, went on strike for the climate; a girl who had by no means remained alone, but had inspired young people all over the world to demand their future, many of them girls. Citizens of these future societies are glad that women saved the world because they finally claimed the power that was legitimately theirs.

In these societies that have emerged, the *first rule* is deeply anchored into collective consciousness: Renewable resources are cherished as the lifeblood of civilization, but their use is governed by a sacred principle – using them not faster than they can regenerate. Forests, bogs and meadows are revered as the lungs of the planet, carefully managed to ensure their continual renewal. Farmers are stewards of ecosystems. Crops are cultivated in a manner that nourishes the soil rather than depleting it. Healthy food is accessible for everybody.

The *second rule* relates to products and consumption. It is obligatory for every product to undergo rigorous scrutiny to ensure that it does not burden the environment beyond its capacity to cleanse and renew. Companies only have a license to operate when they pass the scrutiny. Waste is not an inevitable byproduct but seen as a design flaw that would be rectified through innovation. Societies are beacons of waste-free living, which includes biodegradable materials and closed-loop manufacturing processes.

The *third rule* that is carefully observed is that non-renewable resources stay where they are. People make jokes about the stupidity of previous civilizations that used such resources as the backbone of industrial progress. They have long since been replaced by renewable substitutes invented by the ingenuity of women and men, ensuring that material use is evenly renewable. Of course, solar panels adorn every rooftop, making sure energy production disturbs landscapes as little as possible while harnessing the boundless energy of the sun. Wind turbines are carefully arranged in the landscape and in smaller versions on rooftops wherever efficient. Farmers, ordinary citizens, small and large companies, municipalities and administrations, simply everybody is a clean energy producer and distributor.

When the global crisis of climate change occurred, which everybody is regularly reminded of through historic documentation, the activists and protagonists of the transformation to regenerative societies knew that more was needed than a technical change. Societies were rebuilt in different ways, because people had realized that it was the social fabric that needed to change in order to create a foundation for the societies of the future. A re-evaluation of humanity's place in the grand tapestry of life was done at a global scale, bringing in knowledge and collective intelligence from everywhere. The era that had begun with the crises long ago had been called the *Anthropocene*, a phase in humankind's development when the impact of human civilization had started to alter the conditions of the planet.[1] What was seen as a challenge then was turned into an opportunity. The *fourth rule* therefore refers to societies' commitment to a combination of education, gender-fluid family planning and future responsibility, ensuring that the population remains in harmony with the planet's carrying capacity. People love children and see them as messengers of a future that everyone cares about. Cities are vibrant hubs of innovation, culture, urban gardening, biodiversity and social life. Cities and rural regions work hand in hand to create optimal living conditions.

The *fifth rule* underscores the importance of governance systems, social justice and a fair distribution of power in shaping societies. Democratic institutions flourish, although they constantly evolve by integrating feedback from citizens. Everybody feels responsible to safeguard the planet for future generations and collaboratively engages in making sure institutions deliver. Equity is the fundamental principle for economies and woven into the fabric of these societies. Access to resources, opportunities and decision-making is ensured for everybody.

The *sixth rule*, which emerged from looking back at past undesirable developments, refers to the fact that gender, cultural characteristics or skin color really no longer play a role in societal arrangements. A wide variety of lifestyles, gender identities and sexual orientations are respected and encouraged. Nobody would dare to derive either advantages or claims to power from their gender identity, their skin color or their place of birth.

This vision of how future societies could operate is not my invention, but an illustrated version of what the system scientist Donella Meadows suggested in 1972 as co-author of the Report to the Club of Rome *The Limits to Growth* for a stabilized world.[2] I took the liberty of adding the sixth rule. Donella Meadows, bright and young at that time, worked with four hard-core men (also bright and young) on a scientific systems dynamics modelling of scenarios between 'business as usual', which meant just carrying on with the human nonsense of unlimited economic growth, scenarios that included the potential invention of advanced technologies for reduction in pollution, increase in agricultural yields and resource efficiency, and finally the scenario called 'stabilized world' that would require the above rules. This scenario, in addition to the technical advancements, assumed that globally, societal priorities would change, and that this would translate into policies and subsequent different human behavior. It was the only scenario in which declines in civilizational well-being could be avoided.

The publication was novel at the time and almost a revolutionary breakthrough in shifting thinking, at least in many Western parts of the world. The book became a bestseller, and many people globally, certainly not only in Europe and the United States, were inspired, sometimes very personally: Scientists, teachers, activists, communities, farmers, biologists, ecologists. It encouraged people to see a more environmentally and socially friendly future as necessary and feasible. But the book also received strong criticism, from scientists who contested the appropriateness and validity of the systems dynamics model used, the data input or the conclusions. Not surprisingly, the majority of critics were men, scientists and, above all, economists. Indeed, mostly neoliberal oriented protagonists in economic and political power structures, including the media, were pivotal in organizing society's ignorance of the political report's findings and recommendations. Instead, the rise of neoliberal capitalism was consolidated. Economic growth became both an addiction and an obligation for every nation, every business, every government. Any attempts towards fast enough transformations to regenerative and just societies were slowed down or halted altogether. It is not that scientific criticism is not important as a method to improve research. But what happened was a discreditation campaign of the report's findings which, in the context of this book, I dare to interpret as part of a patriarchal backlash. It had the typical effect: While in the beginning some powerful politicians acknowledged that the report's findings should be considered in policy-making, more and more decision-makers distanced themselves from the message – and went down the scenario route of slightly adjusted 'business as usual'. In terms of the actual development of the world, with climate change and biodiversity loss, they have won.

In 2020, the Dutch econometrician, sustainability researcher and women's rights activist Gaya Herrington published a comparison of empirical world data towards the second decade of the 21st century with the modelling scenarios of the original *Limits to Growth* report.[3] She concluded that a scenario mix of 'business as usual' and 'comprehensive technologies' was most consistent with current data. The world had decided, whether consciously or out of habit, to go down this route that is now leading us into serious danger. The more promising scenario, a 'stabilized world', that would have required the paradigm shift, was the least consistent with current world data. It had not been taken seriously as a possible option.

Since the publication of *The Limits to Growth* the world has become more complex, technology has made great advances, many societies have advanced social progress, environmental legislation has been passed, but the underlying trend has remained the same: We still treat natural resources as if they were infinite, we are losing ice at the poles and many species, we have dangerously polluted the oceans and significantly destabilized the climate. Economic growth, measured by gross national product, became the increasingly unquestioned measure of progress, as if it were the only trustworthy promise of human development. Despite increasing corporate commitment to social and environmental issues, the decisive shift in humanity's approach to its future has not occurred – trends have not changed to the extent required.

Donella Meadows was a true visionary, but I doubt she would have called herself a feminist, although her vision was pretty much how a feminist society could look, at least with the added rule six. It would be a world where humanity had learned to tread lightly upon the Earth, guided by principles of *collective stewardship* and foresight informed by *collective intelligence*. It was a vision that would revere planet Earth as much as humanity, and where the carrying capacity of the planet would be no barrier but a pathway to a more sustainable, equitable and thriving future. Yet, Donella Meadows might have been oblivious to the deeply ingrained patriarchal power structures that would inevitably hit back.

However, with regard to the necessary changes in social values, the book, along with many other similar pleas, provided an important impetus for a paradigm shift that is absolutely necessary, if we want to advance human evolution in a more meaningful way.

Much has been happening to promote a paradigm shift, a change in thinking about what our collective human responsibility is in the era of the Anthropocene, but we have not yet reached what is called by scientists the 'social tipping points' that would lead to an entirely different behavior at scale.[4] What has been made scientifically clear and substantiated by world data, can be experienced by a growing number of citizens: We are or have been approaching the 'climate tipping points' that may propel us further into what some scientists call 'the Hothouse Earth'.[5]

Let us explore the word 'we' in the last sentence. A better understanding of collectivity is crucial for our future, but the word as such can, at times, disguise reality. What the great goddess or the planetary therapist identified as a tendency towards collective suicide is a fair diagnosis, but it needs to be unpacked. This will take us into a dangerous jungle, much more life-threatening than the one to which the Amazons of ancient Latin America flew in order to build their own female empire, probably for good reasons. The jungle we will be entering now is a jungle of power, extremely well networked, difficult to find a path through, even if a huge collective of women was equipped with sharp machetes. Let us start with climate change. It is not caused by everybody, nor does it hit everybody in the same way.[6]

Greenhouse gas emissions (GHG), the biggest contributor to global warming, increased between 1990 and 2019 by 50%.[7] The energy sector, which includes the generation of electricity and heat, energy use at consumer level, transportation, manufacturing and construction, contributed around 76% of emissions in 2019. This was followed by industrialized agriculture, disastrous waste management like landfills, offshore drilling and fracking, deforestation, overfishing and melting permafrost.[8] Methane emissions from industry and agriculture also play an important role, but next to agriculture and land-use change (more precisely: urbanization and loss of biospheres), GHG emissions from fossil fuels have won the game over time. The statistics are clear and known. They are on the agenda every year at the international climate change conferences, the Conference of the Parties (COP). The last two saw vague mentions of a vague goal of vaguely ending the era of fossil fuel use. Too-strong interconnected powers made sure no radical changes would occur. The conglomeration of power includes the governments of some countries, the global fossil fuel and car industry, and the huge number of individual consumers, not only in highly industrialized countries, but around the world, who need their fossil fuel cars to survive and run their businesses. Despite this extraordinary concentration of power, the global shift in mindset and the implementation of effective government policies on climate action have at least ensured that, since 2013, emissions from the energy sector – though still increasing – are rising at a significantly slower pace. This is not the case for industrialized agriculture. Its emissions grew in the same period by 16%, the contribution of waste by almost 20% and industrial emissions by a skyrocketing 203%.[9] It has been repeated one million times: If we want to avoid the worst climate impact, we need to revise the upwards trend in all sectors and rapidly decrease GHG emissions to net zero by 2050. Many countries are committed to such a goal, there are even industries that have committed themselves to net zero by then, and there are many consumers who start making different decisions, but without a true collective commitment by everybody in the world, particularly those who hold the grip on the money-making fossil fuel industry, the pathways of the many will be negatively influenced by the few. Women get increasingly active and demand a seat at the table of the yearly COP meetings, but the decision-maker composition and outcomes of the meetings confirm that the power held by fossil fuel promotors is still in full swing.[10]

This pattern, where the few determine the paths of the many, recurs throughout history. It has, at its core, the term 'inequality' that must sound familiar to us as we are trying to come to terms with the features of patriarchy. Injustice and inequality have been the most dominant features of patriarchal societies for thousands of years. They have played out in exploitation, in slavery, in colonialism, made only a slight detour in communism and socialism (without truly abolishing male dominance patterns), in order to resurge in different, sometimes more disguised ways in capitalism. They got even more strengthened in neoliberal capitalism, although it promised more equal and democratic societies that would get many people out of poverty – and for some this promise came true. They set out on new flights of fancy towards data and surveillance capitalism and a finance system that feeds the wealthy, those who are able to make more money with more money.[11] I am not saying women are not part of this game of the few, but men are certainly in the majority. Overly wealthy women surely exist and their share has increased, but they hold around 13% of the billionaires' total wealth, so we can say that even at this high end, wealth is male.[12] But still, the behavior of the few determining the paths of the many is a deeply patriarchal feature, even if a few women climb the ladder towards extreme wealth. Between 2020 and 2023 the five wealthiest men in the world doubled their wealth to 869 billion USD.[13] In the same period, more than half of humankind, the 60% poor and lower income earners, lost 20 million USD.[14] In 2023 global corporations increased their profits by more than 50%. Of course, some of the wealthiest men give returns by investing or funding sustainability.[15] But this money comes, as all development aid does, with strings attached and the worldview of the funder. In principle it is a good idea that the rich give back to the world. In fact, this is a principle that had prevailed in many societies, sometimes rudimentary. But do we need to let social disparities get out of hand first, in order to then expect the overly rich to pay for damages and restore what should not have been destroyed?

Let us get back to GHG emissions, which have begun to alter the lives of everybody on this planet in the form of climate change. In a 2023 report on the connection between climate change and inequality, Oxfam, an international advocacy organization, produced stark figures. They calculated that the richest 1% of humanity produces more carbon emissions than the poorest 66%.[16] Yet, the consequences of climate change are roughly the other way around. Less industrialized countries, often with a severe colonial heritage – and, within these countries, vulnerable communities, in which most often women organize survival – feel the consequences of climate change most: Floods, droughts, destroyed possibilities for subsistence farming, loss of business and income opportunities. Although disasters as a result of extreme weather events hit many people, including in wealthier countries now, we know that those who are already marginalized or live in poverty are disproportionately affected. Their limited access to resources and insurance, plus inadequate infrastructure, or absence of financial resilience, make it much more difficult for these communities to adapt to, or even recover from climate-related disasters. The Oxfam study came up with very clear numerical material. We do have an elite group in the world, composed of roughly 77 million people out of the roughly 8 billion world population (hence approximately 1%), that determines the paths of all of us. Not surprisingly, the majority of them resides in the Global North.

The recipes for the transformative shifts we need are variations of the rules Donella Meadows suggested. None of these rules is illogical, outrageous, unrealistic or impossible. On the contrary, all her original five rules are so self-evident that the question arises: How could we create structures and systems that deliberately ignore them? How could anybody have assumed they would not harm life, the planet and people by ignoring them? Is the paradigm shift Donella Meadows was hoping for, already under way?

From a feminist perspective, the element of care for planet and people runs through all five rules (plus the sixth) and has been advocated for by feminist writers, economists, systems scientists, transformation experts and policy advocates for decades. Among them are, for example, Maria Mies and Vandana Shiva, who argued in their book *Ecofeminism* and many other publications long ago that patriarchal structures and capitalist systems intertwine and perpetuate a combination of exploitation of women and nature.[17] There are many female and feminist authors who have begun to name the dragon – an outdated neo-liberal capitalist economic system that destroys people and planet in its effects – whose thoughts we will pick up in later chapters. We could argue that the failure to adopt the above rules, which should have long been standard practice for every government and business, reflects a historic pathology and a persistent feature of the patriarchal system. It is fed by a mindset of unlimited extraction, unlimited growth and monopolizing power at the expense of others (women, people, nature, minorities, the poor etc.). It is important to remember that patriarchy is not simply unjust by organizing societies so that more than 50% of the population are seen as less capable of shaping the future; it is a system of fundamentally legitimizing extraction of people and nature. *Collective stewardship* of thriving futures calls for abolishing the outdated patriarchal worldview of the past, embracing a holistic vision for the future and addressing the present, so that caring for life becomes everyone's daily responsibility. But stewarding thriving futures also requires us to make choices. Which technological, social and societal achievements can we integrate into a thriving feminist future? Which structures, rules, laws and governance systems are useful, and which need to be amended? Which of the memories of our global past before patriarchy became the dominant form of society do we need to unearth, cherish and revive? What can be integrated into a modernity that begins to see that reality is infinitely broader, deeper and much more pluriverse than the current industrial worldview suggests? How can we begin to understand and appreciate wealth as our common heritage, not numbers displayed in currencies?

The 2022 report to the Club of Rome titled *Earth For All* is, among others, co-authored by two women, the then Club of Rome co-president and Belgian climate activist Sandrine Dixson-Declève and the Indian feminist economist Jayati Ghosh. It suggests two updated scenarios and describes them in imagined lives of girls. The 'too little to late' scenario says we are trying hard, but not hard enough by far; the 'giant leap scenario' urges us to take the planetary emergency situation seriously and transform the world. It therefore calls for quickly and proactively moving towards turning points.[18] The five most important turning points that the report calls for include overcoming poverty, sustainable food production, green energy, equality and distributive justice as well as women's empowerment. The 'too little too late' scenario warns urgently that social disparities and the extreme gaps in prosperity combined with climate change will possibly make countries ungovernable. The patriarchal backlash towards right-wing nationality mentalities can be seen as harbingers of this development.

We know what to do. All the knowledge we need is already in the world. But unless the paradigm shift really happens, we treat our global collective consciousness like the oceans into which we discharge wastewater and in which we let fish die in plastic nets. We confuse our consciousness with the recycling bin, as if there wasn't a complicated process between a leftover piece of shrink-wrapped tofu and an empty basmati rice cone, for which some people do things we wouldn't like to do. Instead of cultivating our reverence for our planet, we let mad guys sweep the ocean floor, a treasure trove of incredible life and biodiversity, with robots to catch manganese nodules so we can use rare earths for wind turbines and electric cars. The best possible technical solutions will lead to new threats, if the patriarchal mindsets do not shift.

There are signs on the road that suggest that this century is the beginning of a process to rehabilitate life on this planet. It is the beginning of the development and establishment of a symbolic, yes, a feminist order that is dedicated to preserving the fascination of life in all its forms, in all its diversity, in all its interconnectedness, in all its liveliness. Because isn't that our job as humanity? Aren't we actually capable of sustaining life?

The hierarchical narrative of power as dominance and subordination as a model for constructing reality has not only become morally and ethically obsolete, but it also practically does not take us into the future. In the history of humanity, asymmetrical relationships and the power pathologies that build up on them, be it between genders, cultures, geographies, knowledge or individual and social prosperity, have always resulted in enrichment for the benefit of the few – to the detriment of the many. That's why we can and must no longer allow outdated narratives about power to go unchallenged. In order to abolish outdated power narratives, we need to name them as pathologies. We need to understand better, how these patriarchal pathologies emerged, how they survive and how they get reinforced.

Major insights for *collective feminist power practices* from the emerging transformation agenda towards a world in balance of power:

1. The trajectories of current world development look scary, unless there is a decisive and collective paradigm shift and proactive collective turnaround.
2. The current state of the world is intertwined with the historical and contemporary development of patriarchy, resulting in mutually reinforcing cycles. Examples include climate change, resource depletion and economic disparity.
3. Patriarchal history has always seen an imbalance of power. The current formats of this imbalance that play out at global scale are: A financial system out of control that feeds the wealthy; a globalized neoliberal capitalist economy that sees tremendous corporate gains; and a lifestyle of the few (and the industrialized nations) that creates a threat for the many.

4. The knowledge on what we can and must do as world society, is already available. A lot of this knowledge is held by women visionaries and experts – in many countries, at the local level, in subsistence farming and in Indigenous communities, but also at all other levels of societies, in science, academia, technology, social change, policy or business.
5. There is a noticeable global shift towards embracing a new paradigm of planetary care, offering various approaches ranging from technical solutions and economic paradigm shifts to fostering a culture of care. Women around the world are pivotal in driving this new paradigm forward in movements and exemplary actions.
6. There's a lack of awareness in the sustainability movement regarding the underlying issue of patriarchal power pathologies and therefore a need for a *collective feminist practice* of power.

Notes

1 A fascinating article that spurred a lot of scientific discourse and laid the ground for the spread of the term *Anthropocene* can be found in Crutzen (2002).

2 The rules described in the book use a more technical language: 1. Renewable resources should be used not faster than they can regenerate. 2. Pollution and wastes shall not be put into the environment faster than the environment can recycle them or render them harmless. 3. Nonrenewable resources shall not be used at all and renewable substitutes should be developed. 4. The human population and the physical capital plant have to be kept at levels low enough to allow the first 3 conditions to be met. 5. The previous 4 conditions have to be met through processes that are democratic and equitable enough that people will stand for them. See Meadows et al. (1972).

3 Herrington (2021).

4 The Polish-German social scientist Ilona Otto is one of the researchers on and promoter of the idea of possible social tipping points that, if we foster them, could help towards the necessary transformations. See Otto (2020).

5 See Steffen et al. (2018).

6 See Klein (2014).

7 These figures refer to a scientific article by Chancel (2022).

8 An easily understandable list of contributors to global warming can be found here: https://www.humanrightscareers.com/issues/causes-of-global-warming; and a good overview of number crunching is available here: https://www.sustainabilitybynumbers.com/p/global-warming-contributions

9 The World Resource Institute has created an interesting and interactive map of the world's top emitters of greenhouse gases, accessible here: https://www.wri.org/insights/interactive-chart-shows-changes-worlds-top-10-emitters.

10 Among many feminist actors, the organization SheChangesClimate, a global network of activists, is advocating for a strong female share in leadership and

decision-making at the COP meetings. For more information, see: https://www.shechangesclimate.org

11 The UK-based feminist think tank the Women's Budget Group has published a readable overview of the current flaws of the global financial system. See: Hopkins and Bürgisser (2020).

12 Forbes regularly publishes about the most wealthy. See the results from 2023 here: https://www.forbes.com/sites/samanthakroontje/2024/04/02/the-richest-women-in-the-world-francoise_bettencourt-meyers-taylor-swift-alice-walton-2024/#

13 Who they are stays more or less the same. Among the 10 wealthiest there is usually an up and down on the hit list without much change of names. The five on top include, Bernard Arnault (Louis Vitton among others), Jeff Bezos (Amazon), Elon Musk (Space X and Tesla), Mark Zuckerberg (Facebook) and Bill Gates (ex-Microsoft).

14 Oxfam published a report in 2024 highlighting the horrendously increasing wealth gap. See Oxfam International (2024), accessible at: https://www.oxfam.de/system/files/documents/bp-inequality-inc-150124-eng.pdf. Another informative source is Piketty et al. (2022).

15 An example is Amazon CEO Bezos' Earth Fund. He pledged $1 billion for climate action and landscape restoration. See more here: https://www.bezosearthfund.org/news-and-insights/bezos-earth-fund-announces-22-million-locally-led-restoration-africa. As good as this sounds, there is heavy criticism of a strategy of funding that furthers inequality by mainly funding the already large international and white- and Western-dominated NGOs.

16 See Oxfam (2023, November 20).

17 See Shiva and Mies (1993).

18 See Dixson-Declève et al. (2022).

References

Chancel, L. (2022). Global carbon inequality over 1990–2019. *Nature Sustainability*, 5(5), 1–8. https://doi.org/10.1038/s41893-022-00955-z

Crutzen, P.J. (2002). Geology of mankind: The Anthropocene. *Nature*, *415*(6867), 23–23.

Dixson-Declève, S., Gaffney, O., Ghosh, J., Randers, J., Rockström, J., & Stoknes, P.E. (2022). *Earth For All: A Survival Guide for Humanity*. A report to the Club of Rome (2022), fifty years after *The Limits of Growth* (1972). New Society Publishers.

Herrington, G. (2021). Update to limits to growth: Comparing the world3 model with empirical data. *Journal for Industrial Ecology*, *25*(3), June 2021, 614–626, https://doi.org/10.1111/jiec.13084

Hopkins, E., & Bürgisser, E. (2020). Rethinking the global financial system for gender-equal economies. Womens Budget Group. https://www.wbg.org.uk/wp-content/uploads/2024/04/Rethinking-the-global-financial-system-for-gender-equal-economies.pdf

Klein, N. (2014). *This Changes Everything: Capitalism vs. the Climate*. Vintage Canada.

Meadows, D., Meadows, D., Randers, J., & Behrens, W. (1972). *The Limits to Growth: A Report for the Club of Rome's Project on the Predicament of Mankind*. London: Earth Island Limited.

Otto, I.M., Donges, J.F., Cremades, R., Bhowmik, A., Hewitt, R.J., Lucht, W., Rockström, J., Allerberger, F., McCaffrey, M., Doe, S.S.P., Lenferna, A., Morán, N., van Vuuren, D.P., & Schellnhuber, H.J. (2020). Social tipping dynamics for stabilizing Earth's climate by 2050. *Proceedings of the National Academy of Sciences, 117*(5), 2354–2365. https://doi.org/10.1073/pnas.1900577117

Oxfam. (2023, November 20). *Climate Equality: A Planet for the 99%*. Oxfam Policy & Practice. https://policy-practice.oxfam.org/resources/climate-equality-a-planet-for-the-99-621551

Oxfam International. (2024). INEQUALITY INC: How corporate power divides our world and the need for a new era of public action. Briefing Paper. https://oxfamilibrary.openrepository.com/bitstream/handle/10546/621583/bp-inequality-inc-150124-en.pdf

Piketty, T., Saez, E., Zucman, G., Duflo, E., & Banerjee, A. (2022). World Inequality Report 2022. World Inequality Lab. https://wir2022.wid.world/www-site/uploads/2023/03/D_FINAL_WIL_RIM_RAPPORT_2303.pdf

Shiva, V., & Mies, M. (1993). *Ecofeminism*. Zed Books.

Steffen, W., Rockström, J., Richardson, K., Lenton, T.M., Folke, C., Liverman, D., Summerhayes, C.P., Barnosky, A.D., Cornell, S.E., Crucifix, M., Donges, J.F., Fetzer, I., Lade, S.J., Scheffer, M., Winkelmann, R., & Schellnhuber, H.J. (2018). Trajectories of the Earth System in the Anthropocene. *Proceedings of the National Academy of Sciences, 115*(33), 8252–8259. https://doi.org/10.1073/pnas.1810141115

Part II
Understanding Power Pathologies

4
The Enforcement of Patriarchal Structures – How Power Pathologies Became Normal

Different connotations of the concept of power extend throughout human history and in the past few hundred years many men and a few women have tried to define and explain it. Not surprisingly these definitions are the result of lived realities of power and a tacit agreement that coercion and dominance are normal parts of the power game, as if this was a natural phenomenon. We typically associate the term power with something negative, or – on the contrary and depending on our intention – with something desirable. Often, when we think of power, the first thoughts that come to mind are the pathologies that arise when power is either misused or, at least, not used for the good of all. The term causes ambivalences: We need power and we detest it. Both our human history and the current world show us that power abuse in politics leads to oppression, autocratic states, conflicts or wars and predictably brings suffering and grief to countless people. We are also familiar with patterns of abuse of power in the domestic sphere, but also in business, when managers enrich themselves, act unethically or unfairly eliminate the competition. We know of corporations that abuse their power when they exploit people and resources, or avoid tax. We may note that these negative power phenomena were and are predominantly, although not exclusively, manifested by men. This raises the question of whether ideas of heroic masculinity and abuse of power are linked, or whether our social structures make men more vulnerable to the abuse of power. Yes, they are linked and yes, they do offer men more opportunities to identify with male heroes enacting power abuse. Yet, for a livable and sustainable future, for the feminist vision of egalitarian, regenerative and just societies to come true, we need power, probably a lot of collective power and influence, to steward the fate of our planet into a much more desirable direction. At the same time, we certainly don't need the continuation of power pathologies in the form of dominance.

We need a different concept of power, one in which power is understood as both responsibility and creative potential. *Power*, in a *feminist* version, is

DOI: 10.4324/9781003508885-6

the capability to collectively shape a future that creates a *Good Life for All*. We could term it neutrally as the realization power of future egalitarian and thriving societies. The current version of a realization power is in the hands of the few – they are many, but compared with the world population a few – to the detriment of the larger part of the world population, as the previous chapters asserted. This means that power pathologies drive the world's development and the numerous and laudable attempts to shift the paradigm into collective responsibility for the future have not yet yielded the intended results.

One such attempt to turn things around was the development of global goals. The 17 sustainability development goals (SDGs) published by the United Nations in 2015 are certainly an indicator that the paradigm shift is actually really under way.[1] For the first time in human history, humanity has agreed on common goals that can guide our future. They provide a detailed framework for public, private and civil society actors worldwide to implement significant and transformative change towards just, equitable and ecologically sound societies. The SDGs aim to create a more prosperous, fair and sustainable world for all, in which people and nature can thrive, and all genders are treated equally. They focus on globally and locally challenging issues such as, among others, mitigating and adapting to climate change, environmental restoration, secure and healthy food, gender equality, clean water and sanitation, renewable energy, fair employment, sustainable human settlements or regenerative consumption and production patterns. This could give us hope, because the SDGs were created through an arduous negotiation process of comprehensive intergovernmental agreements resulting from extensive consultations with different interest groups, including civil society and Indigenous communities. These goals are truly global, apply to all countries and show that the world is an interconnected place that all people need to care about. Many scientists severely criticized the goals, not necessarily because they disliked the idea of inspiring a collective care for humanity and the planet. They contested whether it would be feasible to implement them without overstepping the planetary boundaries; they argued that their interconnections had not been worked out adequately; and they gave evidence that certain factors had not been taken into account. These experts might be right in their criticism, but what they probably underestimate was the inspiration and guiding power of these goals – they inspire a small city in Guatemala to work towards a more sustainable living as much as people working in a regenerative farming project in Mongolia. Their treasure lies in the global thinking that emerged as a result of them. If Donella Meadows could have experienced the advent of the SDGs, she might have seen the first signs on the road that her vision for a paradigm shift was coming true. And yes, there is progress. The SDGs increased the global awareness of climate change, put the topic of an interconnected humanity and our joined responsibility for the future of our world on the agenda of politics, cities and companies. This does not mean that all actors act accordingly, but that there are more and more people, ordinary citizens as well as managers, who demand different actions and want to shape the future through transformation processes – innovatively, together and responsibly. Is the world ready for a shift in the conception of power? From heroic, individual and pathological to collective and responsible?

The patriarchal backlash described in Chapter 2 speaks a different language. Power pathologies are re-emerging everywhere, so much so that we may get lost and desperate while searching for the good versions of power. For the development of *collective feminist power practices*, it is crucial to recognize the early signs of a global paradigm shift in the right direction as well as the persistent global phenomenon of patriarchal power pathologies – their forms, mechanisms, traps and seductions. Understanding dominance as a form of power pathology is essential, as it has been normalized for millennia. Only by identifying the many manifestations of these pathologies can we avoid them and construct a new narrative of power. This will enable us to foster the emergence of feminist network structures necessary to dismantle patriarchal power dynamics while building new structures of power. Yet, without meticulously observing patriarchy's mechanisms of power assertion, we risk becoming part of its dynamics – either as victims or as agents. At worst, we feel powerless. Hence, *collective feminist power practices* depend on the capacity to understand these power pathologies.

As we have seen in Chapter 1, there is ample research showing that there have been societies in which women held collective power, and there are such societies today, even if they are rare. Women were in leadership positions for thousands of years, before patriarchy became the dominant mode of organizing societies.[2] That's how we would describe it today, even though the term stewardship may be a better fit for their function. The agricultural revolution of the Neolithic area began more than 10,000 years ago. Back then, technological advancements served the betterment of living standards. People, some authors say, predominantly women, invented agricultural tools, furniture and city planning. Thriving arts decorated houses, palaces and streets. The invention of weaving and tailoring gave rise to creative garments. These societies were not at all perfect, but social power seems to have meant responsibility for the good of all, inspired by sacred feminine goddesses seen as the creative force behind all life. As we have seen, there was a societal paradigm shift, manifesting over the course of a few thousand years. Men increasingly asserted power and held public positions, and the societal cultures in which women had the say were pushed into the background. They assimilated into the emerging new models of social dominance that featured men as superior. All sorts of hierarchical patterns of organizing societies became the new normal, abolishing the lived reality of more or less egalitarian and peaceful collective living. This trend was exacerbated by the establishment of asymmetric relationships such as the subordination of women, slavery, violence etc. Surely, some women, even if they were in the minority, adopted the cruel new paradigm and became brutal queens. Female power pathologies have been documented in many areas of the world. Hence, it is not just about women or men in power, but about the arrangement of societies that gives rise to power pathologies.

When wars and violence became the prime modus operandi to secure territories and economic profits, there was resistance to this paradigm shift, as we have seen in Chapter 1. The previous, most often peaceful and egalitarian matriarchal, cultures had to flee and look for new areas, surrender or adapt to the new customs. But even those that found a holy island, on which they could perpetuate their peaceful traditional way of living, experienced a degradation of their cultural achievements, and at some point, were overwhelmed by the rising new patriarchal order, most often brutally.[3]

Patriarchy as a way of organizing societies has been reigning for such a long time that facts and figures about the origins of patriarchal systems are difficult to establish and get mingled with assumptions and hypothesis. There is a scientific assumption that the change in these societies towards patriarchy might have been caused by effects of climate change: In the steppes in central Asia, heat waves may have led to food crises, which led to hierarchization of societies, to a strengthening of male roles, militarization and ultimately to migration and war.[4] These tribes could be seen as migrants of climate change effects as they moved further west in search of more habitable areas. For Europe, Gimbutas suggested that, in three waves over a few millennia, the more warlike tribes coming from the central Asian steppes occupied and subjugated societies in the Old Europe that had been much more peaceful and egalitarian. For Latin America, the pressure of patriarchy seems to have come via the Pacific Ocean, pushing matriarchal cultures further north. For Africa, the displacement of matriarchal cultures seems to have taken place from north-east to west and south.[5]

What is most irritating in the search for an answer to the 'why' of the patriarchal paradigm shift is how little historical and contemporary research deals in depth with ancient and contemporary peaceful societies and with the reasons for the radical change towards hierarchy and dominance, the law of the strongest, as well as war and oppression.[6] As if this assumption of previously peaceful and egalitarian collective living with strong roles for women either was an unimportant peripheral idea, or did not fit with the self-image of science. At best it was declared a fairy tale only feminists would love. Could there be anything more important in our times of planetary emergency, the resurgence of authoritarian regimes and wars, than to understand what these ancient and contemporary peaceful societies got right? When and why did the construct of reality change? Why did women give up power? In which labyrinth of thoughts did they get lost while men took the wheel of the world? I can hardly believe that there is no answer to these questions that every child would need to learn at school, because it is the most crucial question in the development of humanity at this stage. And yes, it makes a huge difference for our present global challenges, if we can draw at least some wisdom from peaceful human societies and understand why humanity was captured by pathologies of a strange nature.

For now, let us confirm that there is this mental and physical infrastructure called patriarchal dominance that we are exposed to from birth and that we learn to consider normal. In this infrastructure, the principle of war, the mentally or physically violent victory of one over the other, is legitimized as the basic model of social assertion. Dominance and submission are a consistent pattern – between people, as well as between people and nature. This includes everything that supports this paradigm, such as language, behavior or structures. It is riddled with struggle and competition. The law of the strongest applies. Everything we have created, human rights, legal systems, democracies, social systems, environmental regulations, is there to limit, contain, tame, somehow civilize this seemingly natural, and sometimes barbarian, human nature – the right of the strongest – as if this and only this were the origin of human societies. It is a misleading tale. Patriarchy has been a detour in human evolution and it is time we get back on track.

Let's consider the possibility that archeologists and historians who state the existence of peaceful egalitarian societies worldwide before the advent of patriarchy, and in some areas until today, are right. They describe these societies as fairly egalitarian, worshipping nature and goddesses in different ways. These societies had vibrant arts and culture, and held a deep appreciation for life. This period of humankind's evolution purportedly lasted for an extended period in human history on a global scale.

We must acknowledge that what have often been termed 'primitive' societies – some of which have preserved aspects of their cultures to this day – are remnants and reminders of a time before patriarchy began its global ascension. How difficult it must have been to shift from peaceful, egalitarian societies to warlike, dominance-driven cultures. This transformation required violence and brutality to break the hearts and minds of people, but it also needed other means to establish an absurd narrative of evaluative differentiation: Between sexes, skin colors, cultures and socioeconomic classes. This narrative legitimized the domination of some over others. The paradigm shift created a structurally and mentally entrenched dominant culture, one that claimed as 'natural' what was not natural at all – superordination and subordination. So successful was this shift that the patriarchal symbolic order continues to prevail, though to varying degrees, across all societies. It manifests itself in the minds of people and in institutional structures as a male-oriented reference system. Order, many people still think, requires male rule. If women get into power, which is seen as legitimate in modern societies, they need to adjust to this reference system. Far too many people still believe in this narrative, which justifies unfair discrimination between people, creates social inequalities and worsens our partnership with the intelligence of the non-human and natural world. As we have seen, our economic system is based on this completely outdated paradigm of seizure of power, with an addiction to growth and an exploitation mentality. People, animals and nature, in this paradigm, only play a role if they can be used as capital to create value. Astonishingly, this tremendous shift in world view, in how collective living should be organized, which occurred a few millennia before our times, worked without social media, without internet trolls, without the media monopolies we know today. Let us identify a few mechanisms that made the paradigm shift towards patriarchal societies work. It is important to understand them as manifestations of patriarchal power pathologies, because most of them are still operating today. Identifying their different manifestations and impacts is important for developing *collective feminist power practices*.

The *first* and most obvious mechanism to introduce and maintain a patriarchal order of societal living is **coercion**. There are as many forms of coercion as there are and have been attempts to establish or ascertain patriarchy as a dominance culture. But usually, coercion requires a variety of measures such as violence, murder, rape, enslavement, detainment and forced work. Marija Gimbutas traces this mechanism back to the waves of territorial expansions and occupation that she assumes happened between approximately 4000 BCE and 2000 BCE in the Old Europe.[7] But we have seen that similar mechanisms were used, probably much later, in the displacement and overmolding of the ancient matriarchal cultures of Latin America and Africa. Since then, this kind of enforcement of a new paradigm of patriarchal hierarchical order has filled history books, so much that even today pupils may think this enforcement is actually human nature and the way things are and will forever be. The coercion mechanism is not over. It saw its resurgence in the two world wars in the 20th century; it shows its ugly face in the crushing of the democratic movements in Myanmar and Belarus, the civil wars in Sudan and Yemen, the atrocities of the Boko Haram in West Africa, the Russian invasion of the Ukraine and the horrendous military conflicts in the Middle East, just to name these few examples. Coercion happens in many countries with autocratic regimes. It happened brutally in the slashing of demonstrations in the aftermath of the death of Jina Mahsa Amini in Iran. The examples could fill libraries. Coercion also has advanced forms such as systems of denunciation like those in the former German Democratic Republic, those during the witch hunt in the dark Middle Ages in Europe, or, what appears as a 'mild' version, the surveillance systems in modern China. What we need to realize is that **without coercion the patriarchal order could not emerge, and cannot be maintained and revived**. Coercion is patriarchy's most important means of power. Its targets are not only women, by far, but male dominance became the blueprint for other forms of oppression. For the feminist paradigm shift we need to know that this mechanism will not be given up quickly, as it is patriarchy's last resort.

The *second* mechanism to reinforce a patriarchal order of societal living is **institutionalization**. This may sound strange as we think of the emerging patriarchy a few thousand years back. But throughout human history, power was held in structure, and subsequently in institutions, societal and religious. The way such institutions operated might have been entirely different from today, but the principles are the same. Societal power is yielded through institutional arrangements. Long ago this might have been the introduction of castes, layers of hierarchies in societies, patrilinear heritage, land ownership, a ruling class, hierarchical societal layers, spiritual rituals or functions, and many more. The feminist historian Gerda Lerner concluded in her book *The Creation of Patriarchy* that, for example in Mesopotamia, the subordination of women was institutionalized by men taking over the temples, and developing a warrior culture. Finally, they emerged as kings, taking over from female sovereignty.[8] Of course, such developments take decades, centuries and even millennia. But these **institutionalized arrangements become a kind of guarantee that the established order will continue to exist, even beyond the lives of individual people**. There is something long-term about institutions. Even if they evolve, they will not radically change their purpose. If we look at institutions of today that reinforce a patriarchal, most often neocolonial order, then we find them everywhere, from the World Bank to private banks, from global corporations to small-scale enterprises. Institutions carry power that cannot easily be abolished. We need to know this for a feminist paradigm shift. **Institutions**, even if we think they may become agile and engage in organizational learning, **are the gatekeepers of an established order**. When we want to rearrange societal living, we need power in institutions. Yet, the dismantling of patriarchal institutions is an enormous challenge, and the building of feminist, egalitarian, peaceful structures and institutions is a mammoth task. The dream of future peaceful civilizations, however, cannot only be built on self-organized movements. We need to re-invent organizations and structures that are fit for purpose, meaning they must be capable of carrying a new paradigm and a new concept of power.

The *third* mechanism to reinforce a patriarchal order of societal living is **gaslighting.** I am deliberately using this rather modern term, because it so profoundly captures the core element of this mechanism. The term 'gaslighting' is used when someone consciously and deliberately alters and ultimately shatters another person's self-perception. This happens through lies, attributions, distortions, fabricated allegations, manipulations and insinuations. Its purpose is to change the thinking and finally the belief system of a person in order to gain power over the person.[9] The mechanism of **gaslighting has worked on a collective scale in the establishment and the maintenance of a patriarchal order** and it must have been hard work. Moving women from a lived experience as powerful agents in egalitarian societies, and as representatives of the life force once worshipped as great goddesses, to a state of subordination required more than mere coercion and institutionalization. The hard work was meticulously done. Over centuries and millennia, the goddesses were replaced by male gods, leading in the established monotheistic religions to the one and only male god with no further possibilities for women to relate to their life-giving properties. The entire narrative of creation was rewritten, some of it evidenced in religious texts.[10] Around the world we find ancient creation myths which relate to a female goddess representing the force that life originated from. Yet, many of these myths were pushed into the background. The Greek threw out women from the pantheon and made sure male gods held the reins. The monotheistic religions, particularly the bible, even managed to turn ancient knowledge and life-giving properties around and create a pretty unrealistic story. A male god created the universe as well as the human beings Adam and Eve. Of course, Eve is so potentially evil that she would have to remind all women of her potentially dangerous character, which legitimized their subordination. Mary had a virgin birth as the mother of Jesus and subsequently had a diminishing importance as it was her son who united and led Christians. We can go around the world: the gaslighting did not stop at entirely unrealistic and fantasized stories that served the purpose of taking the inert power of women away and making them humbly accept their fate. We already mentioned the institutionalized gaslighting that was part of the witch hunt in Europe. Today, this still works in many countries. We should not think the mechanism has been totally abolished in our modern and democratic societies. It simply works in a much more subtle way. There are ample examples that undermine female self-confidence in democratic societies or ensure that feminists would not declare themselves feminists. This ranges from subtle remarks regarding the irrelevance of female contributions to not citing the scientific work of feminists or rendering it unnecessary to have at least 50% women in governments or on corporate boards. When we want to work towards the realization of a new paradigm for egalitarian regenerative societies, we need to be mindful of this gaslighting mechanism that plays out in a subtle but powerful way. And no, we would not want to adopt it as a strategy for a feminist transformation; however, we need to counteract it and strengthen the narrative of women's not only inert, but outspoken, power as a prerequisite and necessity to change the world.

The *fourth* mechanism is the well-known tactic of **divide and rule**. It has worked very well in the history of patriarchy, helping to maintain power, and still does so today. It is a mechanism that has been applied not only to women, but to all forms of hierarchy and oppression. The strategy is simple: The ruling group sows discord and disunity among those that should stay in a subordinate position. This creates divisions among the oppressed, and causes different factions to emerge that then are pitted against each other. This prevents any forms of potentially dangerous unified uprising against the authorities. We know that there are many ways of fostering mistrust among women, creating envy and sowing stories such as mare biting as typical female behavior. If we remember the Greek stories that described the free-spirited Amazons as brutal women that finally needed to be overwhelmed by men, we must assume that the depiction of the Amazons as horror figures was intended to prevent Greek women from finding solidarity with them. This also works today in the description of feminists as man-haters, or in the way women need to behave in order to be accepted in male-dominated board rooms. **The patriarchal mechanism of divide and rule serves to maintain power without much effort, because the target groups often do the actual work themselves**. Weakening the opposition has been successful throughout history. The divisions in the feminist movements, today and historically, can be interpreted as successes of this mechanism. Not that discourse is not important, but we need to distinguish between necessary disputes and actions that disunite and mutually disempower. Whenever women argue or devalue each other, we first have to think about this mechanism, which works even if we cannot see any connection to patriarchal power. Because the history of the oppression of women, as well as the oppression of other marginalized groups, teaches us one thing: Once mistrust and arguments have spread, they take on a life of their own. Divide and rule is a perfidious mechanism, because it is so difficult to distinguish from important debate. Even worse, one specific aspect of the divide and rule mechanism for maintaining patriarchal power is **selective empowerment**, which works by granting limited power or privileges to certain groups, if they comply with patriarchal rules and gender norms. Maria Lugones describes this in her concept of 'coloniality of gender' – how gender arrangements of Indigenous communities have been distorted.[11] Also in colonial Africa men were authorized to enforce new rules on behalf of the colonial masters.[12] It was very similar in Europe with the implementation of capitalism, which early on promised men economic participation by forcing women out of the economy.[13] The strategies of selective empowerment are subtle and often hardly distinguishable from genuine empowerment. They can manifest as economic opportunities, political positions, the elevation of a social status or the creation of a moral or factual hierarchy among those that should not rise to power. As feminists we may all know the dilemma of aspiring to power positions in order to yield our influence, and the pitfalls that occur when we fall into the trap of behaving according to male rules (which are often generalized as the only possible rules) in a position of influence. If we want to succeed in feminist transformations, we need to stay alert to the many creative forms of the *divide and rule* mechanism. We need women in power positions in politics, NGOs and businesses, but we do not need *selective empowerment* of women; instead, we need collective re-powerment.

The mechanisms above show how important it is to focus awareness and attention on the mechanisms of the continuous enforcement of patriarchy. It's never only about men and women; the mechanisms work best in intersectionality, where layers of different reasons for discrimination or oppression are enacted to keep the patriarchal order and make the different mechanisms work together. Men are trapped in this as much as women, but overall, they tend to be better off in this system and are certainly more validated.

Mechanisms to enforce or reinforce the patriarchal order use power in a pathological way and create an open or tacit societal consensus that it is ok to do so. Let us look at how power gets conceptualized and what the difference is that female voices suggest. Power as a social construct has been described, analyzed and interpreted by many philosophers, anthropologists and sociologists. Most of them were male. Probably one of the most famous definitions of power in Europe, which legitimized the above-mentioned four mechanisms for reinforcing patriarchy, colonization as well as authoritarian regimes, came from Max Weber. For him, power was always a form of enforcing one's own will (or that of a group) against the will of others.[14] We could say that this is actually describing a human pathology: It paves the way for justifying violence or manipulation.

Human history has shown that power as persuasion and manipulation, or assertion of interests, does not exclude violence. Power and influence, according to the above description of Max Weber, leads to the nature-destroying and human-degrading systems of dominance. The massive exploitation of natural resources is also based on this narrative, as is the colonial oppression of many peoples, the legitimization of economic monopolization and, last but not least, the shark mentality that has prevailed in the capitalist economy – grow or disappear. In the age of digitalization, when algorithms read our most secret wishes, cyber-attacks are increasing and election results are being manipulated, this power pathology is often something that is not directly perceptible: It can work in the background, influencing our thoughts and actions, or work subtly as so-called silent power. The above mechanisms reveal the intertwined strategies of open and silent power.

For *collective feminist power practices* that aim at feminist transformations towards a *Good Life for All*, we won't get far with male-centered definitions of power. We may agree that the future emerges collectively on the continuum between power, impact and influence. Yet, it makes a huge difference for future-making when realization power emerges collectively as a result of dialogue and negotiation processes. Hence, we have to look for other explanations for the concept of power. Power needs a feminist narrative.

There are interesting and well-known female protagonists of a different narrative of power, of whom I would like to mention three: Hannah Arendt, Riane Eisler and Mary Beard.[15] Their conceptualization of power provides us with useful ideas for *collective feminist power practices*. One of the best-known critics of the conventional definitions of power, as mentioned above, is Hannah Arendt, a political scientist and journalist who lived from 1906 to 1975. As a woman and a Jew, she experienced pronounced pathologies of power, specifically the unleashed terror of the Nazi regime, which forced her to flee Germany. These experiences shaped her work, in which she suggests a difference between power and violence. She states that in order to be effective, realization power requires resonance and relationality – this means some form of agreement between people about its effect. Violence, in her opinion, begins where this agreement no longer exists and, instead, an attempt is made to maintain power as an end in itself. This becomes the starting point for power pathologies, such as domination, terror and institutionalized brutality, and totalitarian ruling based on the spread of fear. In her understanding, power, if exercised in agreement and relationality, does not necessarily have to slide into the pathological realm. It is in its essence neutral, namely something that a person or a group does not simply possess, but rather something situational. She sees it as a potentiality that manifests through attribution; hence, it arises from perception and action in the relationship between people. According to Hannah Arendt, power refers to the human capacity to unite with others and act in collaboration with them. Power in this sense is based on relationships and therefore requires communication processes. It must resonate with people in order to be effective. If it doesn't do that or no longer does that, it loses its potentiality. It dissolves or, as described above, mutates into tyranny. In her view, the perceived fear of losing power is an important component in the pathologization of power into violence and domination.

The systems scientist Riane Eisler, born in Austria in 1931, similar to Hannah Arendt, fled the Nazi regime as a child with her mother and lives today in the United States. Growing up in the slums of Havana, she began to draw a connection early on between the structures that produce poverty and those that produce terror. In her case, too, the attempt to understand how such structures arise and reproduce themselves again and again led to interdisciplinary research that produced a holistic approach to addressing power issues. In her cultural transformation theory, she distinguishes between two fundamentally different narratives of power that shape societies and become the basic model of their organization. One is the dominance narrative, for which she chose the *blade* as a symbol. It thrives on enforcement, superiority and subordination, just as described in the mechanisms of patriarchal enforcement above. Destruction of life and the living – in the form of nature as well as people – is to a certain extent sanctioned as normal in this narrative. The other is the partnership narrative, for which she chose the *chalice* as a symbol. It thrives on consensus, cooperation, commitment and diversity. Preservation of life and vitality are the focus here. Symmetrical relationships are the norm. She suggests that the partnership narrative of power must become mainstream, if humanity wants to survive.

Also, the historian Mary Beard challenges us to rethink power, to reconceptualize it as something communal, something that values people in advancing the future in mutual support. Power, she reminds us, is not a static possession. It is a process of action leading to empowerment, and requires the ability to be effective together, in cooperation and complementarity. Not everyone has to be the same, be equally strong, equally knowledgeable or equally visionary. However, power as a manifestation of *collective feminist leadership* is built on communicative resonance and it must be both mandated and legitimated.

For *collective feminist power practices*, these conceptualizations of power are encouraging, as they align around a few aspects. The *first* aspect is the understanding that power arises through communication – i.e., it is attributed to people or groups of people who are able to build resonance. These can, for example, be visions for the future, value systems or expert solutions. Power arises through the attribution of power and this can be **mutual empowerment in an egalitarian partnership approach**. The *second* aspect is the recognition that **power arises through collective agreements** – i.e., as a result of cooperation, dialogue and negotiation between people. Only this establishes the legitimacy of power. Ideally, this is the way modern constitutional states and democracies function. People grant other people power, but can also withdraw legitimacy. For the latter, procedures and control mechanisms must be in place. The *third* aspect is that, if power is relational, **an essential element of preventing power pathologies is checks and balances** – also known in the political and business sectors as the separation of powers. Realization power as an ability to create the future requires mechanisms that uncover pathological tendencies and prevent them from becoming established and expanding.

For *collective feminist power practices*, we can embrace power as something that thrives through communication, cooperation and mutual support. When we recognize power as relational and grounded in collective agreements, we not only create a more just and egalitarian future, but we also ensure that power remains accountable. With checks and balances in place, we can prevent power pathologies and nurture the ability to build a future that reflects the values of equity and shared strength. From this and from female-connoted definitions of power, we must derive the foundations for a concept of power that will be useful for future feminist-inspired societies.[16]

The power of patriarchy can be dismantled. This statement will guide our further journey, no matter how unrealistic it might seem to you at this stage of human history. Yet, patriarchy contributes to its own disintegration. We will preserve some of its useful fruits and make them available for the future. We will, even if it will take a long time, step by step repair the incredible damage it has caused. This will take centuries. Maybe thousands of years. Nonetheless, in order to move forward collectively, we must strengthen and spread precisely this narrative: **Patriarchy is a *human* and evolutionary *pathology*, and by no means normal human behavior.** This must be stated clearly at every opportunity. Pathologies need treatment, particularly this one, as it has become harmful for people, societies and the planet.

Major insights for *collective feminist power practices* from the enforcement of patriarchal societal structures and female-inspired power definitions:

1. We must understand the historical enforcement of patriarchy as a long road to a new normal that has never been natural, and see how the maintenance of patriarchy continues.
2. We need to keep an awareness of the four mechanisms – coercion, institutionalization, gaslighting and divide and rule – in order to mutually alert us to the many manifestations of contemporary patriarchal reinforcements.
3. We must name the male-oriented practices of power in the form of domination clearly as a human pathology that can only survive when it is sanctioned by societies with the continuous repetition of misleading tales.
4. We need to unmask these misleading tales in their many variations and must recognize the pathologies of human behavior in male-defined concepts of power, which are still recognized as normal today.
5. We need to understand what feminist power can be, namely the collective shaping of the future towards a *Good Life for All*.
6. From this and from female-connoted definitions of power, we must derive the foundations for a concept of power that will be useful for future feminist societies.

Notes

1 An overview of the global goals and the history of their development can be found here: https://sdgs.un.org/goals. In 2024 additionally, the Pact for the Future was agreed: see United Nations (2024).
2 Gerda Lerner argued that the rise of patriarchy was linked to early agricultural societies, the development of private property and class structures, where men increasingly dominated women in both the domestic and public spheres; see Lerner (1987).
3 Riane Eisler describes how the Island of Crete in Greece defended their relatively egalitarian society longer than other areas in Europe, until finally it was also subjected to the patriarchal paradigm; see Eisler (2011).
4 See Gimbutas (1991).
5 Göttner-Abendroth (2017).
6 A compilation of thoughts and approaches to Feminist Peace research can be found in Wibben et al. (2019).
7 See Gimbutas (1989).
8 See Lerner (1987); also Saini (2023).
9 Its effect can be culturally biased, as Elena Ruíz describes. See Ruíz (2020).
10 Riane Eisler (2011) gives examples of this for the Christian religion.
11 Maria Lugones' concept of 'coloniality of gender' is a critical framework that challenges the Eurocentric, patriarchal systems imposed during colonization, showing how these structures constructed rigid, hierarchical gender norms that continue to oppress marginalized groups. Lugones (2016).
12 Miano (2022).
13 Federici (2004).
14 See Weber (1985).
15 See Arendt (1969), Eisler (2011), Beard (2017).
16 For further inspiring deliberations on power and feminist transformations, see Batliwala (2019, 2015).

References

Arendt, H. (1969). *On Violence*. Stellar Classics.

Batliwala, S. (2015). *Engaging with Empowerment*. Women Unlimited.

Batliwala, S. (2019). *All About Power: Understanding Social Power and Power Structures*. CREA. https://creaworld.org/wp-content/uploads/2020/07/All-About-Power.pdf

Beard, M. (2017). *Women & Power: A Manifesto*. Liveright Publishing Corporation, A Division Of W.W. Norton & Company.

Eisler, R. (2011). *The Chalice and the Blade: Our History, Our Future*. Harper Collins.

Federici, S. (2004). *Caliban and the Witch: Women, the Body and Primitive Accumulation*. Autonomedia.

Gimbutas, M. (1989). *The Language of the Goddess*. San Francisco, CA: Harper and Row.

Gimbutas, M. (1991). *The Civilization of the Goddess: The World of Old Europe*. Edited by Joan Marler. San Francisco, CA: Harper Collins.

Göttner-Abendroth, H. (2017). Matriarchal studies: Past debates and new foundations. *Asian Journal of Women's Studies*, *23*(1): 2–6. doi:10.1080/12259276.2017.1283843.

Lerner, G. (1987). *The Creation of Patriarchy*. Oxford University Press.

Lugones, M. (2016). The Coloniality of Gender. In: *The Palgrave Handbook of Gender and Development*. Palgrave Macmillan, pp. 13–33.

Miano, L. (2022). *Sisterhood*. Aufbau Digital.

Ruíz, E. (2020). Cultural gaslighting. *Hypatia*, *35*(4), 687–713. https://doi.org/10.1017/hyp.2020.33

Saini, A. (2023). *The Patriarchs: How Men Came to Rule*. Fourth Estate.

United Nations. (2024). Summit of the future outcome documents: Pact for the future, global digital compact and declaration on future generations. https://www.un.org/en/summit-of-the-future/pact-for-the-future. Available at: https://www.un.org/sites/un2.un.org/files/sotf-pact_for_the_future_adopted.pdf

Weber, M. (1985). *Wirtschaft und Gesellschaft. Grundriss der verstehenden Soziologie*. Tübingen: Mohr Verlag.

Wibben, A.T.R., Confortini, C.C., Roohi, S., Aharoni, S.B., Vastapuu, L., & Vaittinen, T. (2018). Collective Discussion: Piecing-Up Feminist Peace Research. *International Political Sociology*, *13*(1), 86–107. https://doi.org/10.1093/ips/oly034

5
Colonialism, Communism, Socialism, Capitalism – The Intertwining of Patriarchal Power and the Economy

Let us assume that the utopia which Rokeya Hossain designed in 1905 and the vision that Donella Meadows laid out before us in 1972 hint to possible futures in the evolution of humankind and the planet that can inspire us to change the current self-destructive trajectories and build a feminist future inspired by the *Good Life for All*. Every step that we would like to take in such a direction would inevitably need to include the re-design of our currently outdated economic system, so that it stops draining vitality from the planet and people in favor of a privileged few, and instead regenerates and maintains our social and ecological life support systems. Patriarchy as a mental infrastructure normalizes supremacy in all its different and intersecting forms, taking rac*ial* and male supremacy as a starting point, followed by wealth supremacy. As a system of power, it has shaped not only cultural and political structures but also economic systems. How to overcome this is a question with a complicated answer, but there are signs on the road that it would not be impossible to find answers, if we put our collective intelligence to use. Inspiring approaches for future economies are lining up.[1] Many of these concepts have been invented or are driven by women or explicitly feminists. We will dive deeper into their potential in Part V of this book.

Extraction and accumulation have been the basis of economies worldwide for centuries, if not millennia, and are still widely adopted almost everywhere in the world. All economic models of our patriarchal past are based on the exploitation of women, nature and the 'other'.[2] The latter was always contextually defined, but usually it meant marginalized people. This applies to capitalism and colonialism but partly also to communism and socialism. Because the history of capitalism in all its variation is longer and it is the currently most dominant version of economies, we will first look deeper into its ways of manifesting. The patriarchal power pathologies of **coercion, institutionalization, gaslighting**

DOI: 10.4324/9781003508885-7

and divide and rule, including **selective empowerment**, have played a significant role in establishing the imbalances of past and contemporary economic systems. *Historically, they have been used in colonialism and* they are structurally embedded in *neo-colonialism*, in our globalized markets and nationalized governments. They keep the economic system running as it was and as it is, and make it extremely difficult for future-looking actors, men, women and feminists to get a handle on the transformative changes required towards life-serving future economies. Economic power pathologies safeguard the status quo. Power, in this case economic power, is created, maintained and reinforced.

Many feminist scholars have analyzed how capitalism exploits and weaponizes[3] the bodies, unpaid labor, reproductive power and caregiving roles of women and marginalized people. They show how capitalist economies, historically and today, only work with the racialized exploitation of women, oppressed communities and natural resources, reinforcing social inequities. This includes the seizure of Indigenous lands and legitimizes environmental destruction. Feminist scholars *such as* ***Silvia Federici*** argue that the colonization of women's labor, nature and territories was fundamental to the initial accumulation of capital.[4] They therefore emphasize the importance of dismantling both economic and patriarchal structures that perpetuate inequality and unsustainable growth. **Vandana Shiva** has long critiqued the extractive economic model, describing how the exploitation of nature and women are intertwined. In her book *Staying Alive: Women, Ecology, and Development*, she argues that neoliberal capitalism treats both ecosystems and women's labor as resources to be exploited for profit, often depleting them beyond recovery.[5] **Chandra Talpade Mohanty** examines how global capitalist practices impact women in the Global South. In her work on feminist decolonization, she critiques the ways in which the patriarchal growth model perpetuates both gender and economic inequalities, often overshadowing women's contributions to their communities.[6] **Bina Agarwal** critiques the exclusion of women and marginalized communities from decision-making about land and natural resources. In her work on *Gender and Green Governance*, Agarwal shows how patriarchal and capitalist systems prevent equitable access to resources, perpetuating both environmental degradation and social inequality.[7] **Verónica Gago**, in her work *Neoliberalism from Below*, explores how neoliberal policies impact women, particularly those in informal and precarious labor sectors, showing how these systems exploit both labor and natural resources.[8] **Ariel Salleh** argues that capitalism's focus on profit maximization leads to unsustainable industrial practices and climate change, disproportionately affecting women and Indigenous populations who rely on nature for survival, highlighting the need for ecofeminism to address the exploitation of both women and nature.[9] **Mercedes D'Alessandro**, in *Economía Feminista*, argues that the growth imperative reinforces gender, class and racial inequalities, as economic systems extract value from the bodies and labor of women, especially those in the Global South.[10]

Power imbalances and unequal access to resources are central to both neoliberal capitalism and patriarchy. Despite efforts toward renewable energy, sustainable value chains and circular business models, today's economies remain extractive. Flawed tax systems and global finance concentrate wealth and power in the hands of a few, reinforcing gender, class, geographic and racial hierarchies. Feminist economists challenge these structures, advocating for models that prioritize ecological balance and social equity over endless growth.[11] Patriarchal economic power strategies have persisted for centuries, despite changes in actors, policies and forms. Many of these power dynamics have become normalized and socially accepted, making them seem like inherent, unchangeable parts of economics. However, by unmasking them, we can better understand their impact, which is a crucial first step toward feminist transformation.

The *first* patriarchal strategy to secure economic power, both historically and today, is **capitalist enclosure** – the control of access to resources. Focusing on natural resources like land, water and minerals, we see a pattern: While ancient and Indigenous societies emphasized the commons, capitalism and colonialism target commonly owned land as 'unowned' land.[12] From the expropriation of Irish farmers in the 17th century to the displacement of Latin American communities for lithium mining in 2022, the process is consistent. Capitalist enclosure identifies resources for profit, followed by legal or political moves that dispossess marginalized communities. Resources are privatized, either seized or bought, and turned into commodities. The profits rarely benefit the affected communities, while the environmental and social consequences – soil degradation, deforestation, pollution and growing inequality – are widespread. Despite resistance and environmental laws, this practice persists, often seen as necessary for 'economic progress'.

Monopolizing resource control is another hallmark of capitalist enclosure, concentrating power among a few actors. This system was central to colonialism and is evident in industries like fossil fuels and land grabbing around the world today. The exploitation of people as 'human capital' follows similar patterns, with slavery abolished but forced labor and poor conditions still prevalent. The latest form of capitalist enclosure is data mining, where personal data is extracted, privatized and commodified for profit.

Resisting enclosure means challenging patriarchal and economic power, advocating for equitable resource management and promoting sustainable, just alternatives. Activists, especially in the Global South, fight against this system. Vandana Shiva, for example, has led the fight against the enclosure of seeds, battling corporations like Monsanto, which has been accused of human rights violations and promoting unsustainable farming practices.[13] Does gender play a role? Yes. While men have historically driven resource control, the negative effects disproportionately impact women, especially in marginalized communities.

The *second* patriarchal strategy to secure economic power is **wealth concentration**, following directly from capitalist enclosure.[14] Neoliberal economics has allowed a small elite – mainly men – to amass immense resources and shape the lives of many. In 2024, the top eight wealthiest people in the world were all men, whose fortunes depend on global support and dependence.[15] Their methods of wealth accumulation are more subtle than in previous eras, often appearing to have public consent. From Bernard Arnault's luxury goods empire to Jeff Bezos' Amazon dominance and Elon Musk's electric cars for the wealthy, these men have created vast systems of dependence. Mark Zuckerberg has made the world addicted to Facebook, while Larry Page's Google is nearly inescapable, both profiting from data mining and overconsumption. Bill Gates' software, Warren Buffet's investments and Larry Ellison's Oracle have similarly cornered markets, extracting wealth from global consumers. What makes this power pathology insidious is its widespread acceptance and even admiration. These men are often seen as heroes, their wealth a mark of brilliance, reinforcing a narrative that celebrates individual success while ignoring structural inequality. Wealth concentration is not just an individual pathology, but a collective one, often linked to specific countries or regions. Historical examples, such as the wealth of European cities built on colonial exploitation, or the United States' post-war dominance, illustrate this.

The 2022 Global Inequality Report highlights stark disparities: North America's average wealth is 390% of the world average, while Sub-Saharan Africa's is just 17%. Europe follows at 230%, and East Asia at 142%, while the other regions are around 40–50%.[16] Wealth concentration leads to deep inequality and distributive injustice, particularly harming women and marginalized communities. In wealthier countries, some women benefit from selective empowerment but, globally, women bear the brunt of poverty. Wealth concentration feeds itself, driving materialism, corruption and resource overconsumption. Despite a brief period of increasing economic distributive justice in Europe between 1950 and 1980, neoliberal policies have since widened the gap between rich and poor, reinforcing patriarchal power structures that disadvantage women and marginalized people most.[17] Looking at the world as a whole, half of the population today accounts for around 2% of global wealth – i.e., a tiny piece of the global cake. More than 75% of the cake is shared by the richest 10% of the world's population. Adding the inherent dynamics of financial markets, wealth increases where it already exists, and is hardly distributed among the entire population.[18] Collectively, women, throughout the inequality phenomenon, take the larger share of poverty, even though women in wealthier countries in general and some women in poorer countries benefit from their **selective *economic* empowerment**. Wealth concentration is a broadly sanctioned and perfectly organized patriarchal power pathology that takes away the life chances of many women and men, yet, in addition to other economic and culturally embedded patriarchal structures, disadvantages women and marginalized people even more.

The *third* patriarchal strategy to secure economic power is **policy and regulatory capture**. This occurs when governmental or regulatory bodies, meant to serve the public interest, are heavily influenced by powerful interest groups, often tied to concentrated wealth. Such influence leads to policies and regulations that favor these groups at the expense of public welfare. Corporations, often led by men, excel at this tactic, known as **corporate capture**, which undermines human rights and environmental protection.[19] It includes manipulating communities, influencing courts and policies, revolving-door employment between public and private sectors, shaping public opinion through campaigns, and funding biased research. The tobacco industry's manipulation in the United States during the latter half of the 20th century, despite evidence of smoking's health risks, is a classic example. It used marketing, public relations and lobbying to block regulations and weaken public health efforts.[20] This strategy is not limited to any one country and has evolved into what is now called state capture, where corruption plays a central role. State capture involves government officials, companies or wealthy individuals manipulating laws and policies for their benefit, often with disastrous impacts on climate change, social justice and inequality.[21]

A notable example to counteract state capture is the 2023 campaign by the Association for Women's Rights in Development (AWID) before the UN Climate Change Conference (COP) in Dubai, highlighting how policy capture undermines global climate action.[22] Despite civil society efforts, corporate and petrostate interests have often triumphed, worsening planetary crises that disproportionately affect women. While women also participate in these corrupt practices, men dominate the landscape. Whether led by men or women, capture is a patriarchal pathology that prioritizes short-term profits over long-term sustainability and justice. Civil society organizations continue to fight against this through transparency, accountability and independent regulatory processes, but the battle remains a David vs. Goliath struggle.

The *fourth* patriarchal strategy to secure economic power is **reproductive enclosure**. Like the capitalist enclosure of land, it involves the appropriation of women's reproductive capacities, vital for sustaining societies. Feminist theorist

Silvia Federici describes this as foundational to capitalist accumulation, where men's labor became economically valued, while women's reproductive labor – child-rearing, caregiving, domestic work – was deemed unproductive and invisible.[23] This division fueled vast economic gains by assigning reproductive work to women without remuneration. Reproductive enclosure persists today, despite feminist struggles. Globally, women continue to shoulder the majority of unpaid or underpaid caregiving and domestic tasks, as seen in health, education and child-care sectors. The Global Gender Gap Report looks at 146 countries. The global average gap in 2023 stands at 68.4%, with the most gender-equal country being Ireland with 91.5%, but many, even countries claiming to be advanced, far below such a high percentage.[24] Reproductive enclosure also includes control over women's bodies, such as restrictive reproductive policies, forced sterilizations or coerced childbirth. From Afghanistan's exclusion of women from education to Germany's tax laws that incentivize women to stay home, reproductive enclosure is entrenched in societal and institutional structures worldwide. Despite progress, these patriarchal strategies remain deeply rooted in modern society, limiting women's autonomy and economic *power*.

The *fifth* patriarchal strategy to secure economic power is the **commodification of nature**. Though often framed as a solution to climate change and biodiversity loss, it stems from the same mechanisms of capitalist enclosure that prioritize profit over people and ecosystems. Commodification turns nature into 'natural capital', assigning monetary value to ecosystems, such as clean air or carbon sequestration, to justify their exploitation within a capitalist framework. While initially intended to protect nature by highlighting its value, this approach reinforces the view that nature only has worth if it serves human needs. The hope was and still is that, in a monetized world, putting monetary value on nature would help conserve and restore it as well as inform better decision-making processes regarding land use, conservation and resource management. The promotors of the concept of 'ecosystem services' argue that it has the potential to realign the modern separation of people and nature, especially in the Western world, and improves understanding of the complex interactions between ecosystems and human societies.[25] Others warn that using an economic metaphor such as services exacerbates the already exploitative relationship between economic actors and nature. The financialization of nature – through carbon markets, biodiversity offsetting or environmental investing – takes this further by integrating nature into financial markets, turning ecosystems into tradable assets. This may at first sound like a good solution that beats capitalist enclosure with its own means of profit-making, but the financialization of nature raises serious concerns about the potential for speculative behavior, inequitable distribution of benefits, land grabbing, dispossession of local communities and the prioritization of financial returns over environmental and social goals.[26] It leads to land grabs, local dispossession and prioritizing profit over environmental and social well-being. This phenomenon, known as 'green grabbing', echoes historical capitalist and colonial land appropriation, but now with environmental concerns as the justification.[27] While it may appear like a new solution, it is rooted in patriarchal exploitation of both nature and marginalized communities, particularly women.

The above strategies to ensure economic power in capitalist economic systems appear overwhelming. Looking at them from a bird's eye perspective can make us feel desperate, particularly as, in addition to the strategies for ensuring economic power, the patriarchal power pathologies of coercion, institutionalization, gaslighting and divide and rule keep the system running in a literally well-oiled manner. Yet, around the world, there is a growing movement to shift our economic system, and there is fierce resistance to oiling the economic machine. Particularly in the Global South, where the effects of the pathologies are felt in a much more tangible way, there are ample networks, collective action groups, policy advocates, local and some international NGOs constantly naming, fighting and criticizing the way economic power is seized, maintained and expanded. Such resistance is, of course, not new. The criticism of capitalist accumulation is and has historically been the foundation for creating different types of economies and societal arrangements such as communism and socialism. Let us briefly look at how both variations of attempts to change the economic system relate to patriarchal power pathologies and the above strategies to secure economic power.

Socialism and communism share several common principles and objectives, despite being distinct ideologies with differences in their approaches and historical manifestations. Both socialism and communism aim to overcome the fundamental inequalities and injustices inherent in capitalist economies, rightly arguing that capitalism fosters exploitation, alienation and inequality through wealth concentration. Both advocate for alternative economic systems that prioritize social welfare, economic justice and collective ownership of resources. As forms of rearranging societies and economic systems they have a number of elements in common that are important for our search for feminist transformation strategies. In theory they are both committed to social justice. Their ideologies are built on the emancipation of marginalized and oppressed groups. Originally, they sought to challenge systems of domination, exploitation and discrimination. Historically, gender equality was or is an integral part of their respective ideologies, but especially in communism it used to be seen, not too long ago, as a so-called secondary contradiction. This means, the liberation of women was secondary to the liberation of the working class. It meant that the intrinsic relationship between patriarchy and domination has been neglected and ignored. Friedrich Engels' historic deliberations on *The Origin of the Family, Private Property and the State* led him to an assumption that never came true: He suggested that the invention of private property caused the suppression of women and that, once private property was abolished, there would be gender equality.[28] Indeed, some communist and socialist societies tended to have stronger gender parity in the professional sphere. This included a state-driven collectivization of child care so that women would be free to join the workforce. This did give a lot of hope to women and showed that gender stereotypes could partly be overcome within a generation by asserting a different narrative. Yet, Maria Mies analyzed, in 1989, the disappointments of women after communist or socialist revolutions in, for example, China, Cuba, Tanzania and Vietnam.[29] Women were recruited for liberation and drawn into the respective armies or military wings of parties. They had strong roles defending their countries or resisting occupation, Apartheid or capitalist enclosure. In many cases they constituted the majority of the workforce in industry and held many leadership positions. Yet, after wars or revolutions and despite progressive constitutions on gender equality, a well-organized patriarchal backlash removed women from political and economic leadership positions, opening these positions for men. Gradually, the strategies of reproductive enclosure took hold again. Women were often idealized as symbols of national unity and self-sacrifice, while gradually being re-confined to traditional roles as wives, mothers and caregivers.[30] Patriarchy reinforced its societal stronghold. The role of women in liberation struggles was obscured by the idealization of founding fathers, most of them male heroes: Lenin, Mao, Stalin, Castro, Mugabe, Ho Chi Minh and others. Yet, each of them used coercion and institutionalization in the form of violence to stay in power.

Communism and socialism share the vision of classless societies with equal opportunities and access to resources for everyone. Theoretically, they laudably prioritize the well-being of society as a whole over individual profit or accumulation of wealth, and there might be a lot to learn from the attempts to include access to healthcare, education, housing and employment for all members of society. Yet, the reality of especially communist societies emerged as a huge patriarchal backlash, in which we can recognize the power pathologies – coercion, institutionalization, gaslighting and divide and rule. The regimes were often motivated by a fear of social upheaval, which led them to suppress dissenting voices and alternative political movements. Any challenges to the status quo and the prescribed ideology were perceived as a threat to the regime's authority and control. Accelerated state control, repression, systems of mutual denunciation were installed that could assert the ruling party's patriarchal dominance. Even the divide and rule pathology worked, when no independent women's organizations were allowed, but instead women had to form their organizations as part of the ruling party's structures.

Authoritarian regimes have historically been a feature of socialist and communist countries, although we know that they can exist in capitalist societies, too. The rise of authoritarian tendencies or governments can also be observed, as we have seen before, in democracies. Not always, but predominantly male authoritarian rulers gradually distort seemingly democratic procedures, undermine the constitutional state or introduce the rule by law, instead of the rule of law. This leads to asserting patriarchal power features.

In principle, communist and socialist ideologies would reject any forms of capitalist enclosure. Conceptually, they aspire to create a more just, equitable and to some extent democratic world where the needs of all people are met and where social hierarchies based on class, race, gender or other factors are dismantled. This is still the appeal of left-wing ideas today, which for many who want a different, a just and, yes, a feminist future, is an important clue to how societies could be organized differently. But without the abolition of patriarchy as the blueprint for domination the aspired social change has, so far, contradicted its original intentions. Historic reality revealed itself as just a modified version of patriarchal dominance and patriarchal power pathologies.[31]

In addition, many socialist and communist countries focused on rapid industrialization to achieve economic development. Environmental concerns were often pushed so much into the background that this had severe negative effects not only on ecosystems, but also on the population. The construction of heavy industries, mines and power plants resulted in pollution, deforestation, habitat destruction and health challenges. Natural resources got exploited with ignorance towards the environment and the health of people. In effect, this was and is quite similar to the effects of capitalist enclosure and the commodification of nature in capitalist societies.[32] The collectivization of agricultural production at scale led to harmful practices, no different from the industrialization of agriculture in capitalist societies. This enclosure of access to natural resources had a different face, but followed the same underlying patriarchal logic of the exploitation of nature. Hence, a fundamental disdain for people and nature, a deeply patriarchal pathology, is an element that male-led authoritarian communist regimes and capitalist corporations have in common. It reminds us of the interconnectedness of misogynies and nature exploitation Susan Griffin wrote about.[33] Anger, rising from millennia of domination, would certainly be justified. Humankind learned and is still learning the hard way: With patriarchal power pathologies still too often unquestioned and unexplored, the best of all intentions, brought forward with perseverance and institutionalized in societal structures, but void of the fundamental paradigm shift needed, can lead to even more patriarchal domination.

As we have seen, the patriarchal foundation of asymmetrical relationships – whether between individuals or between humans and nature – and the notion of power as coercion, both mental and physical, including manipulation, has deep historical roots. This worldview has fostered a sense of legitimacy and assumed authority over the shaping of the future, as though it were not merely a mental construct that could be changed, but rather the sole and unquestionable premise of humanity. We all recognize this truth: Addressing the deeply entrenched patriarchal power structures and their strategies to secure economic dominance demands nothing less than a full-scale systemic transformation. Fragmented resistance or isolated reforms will not suffice. Taming the capitalist enclosures through moral appeals or market mechanisms is inadequate. Civilizing the pathologies of patriarchal power with laws and democratic procedures alone will not dismantle the root of the problem. We must confront these forces with bold, radical change that reshapes the very foundations of power, economy and society – anything less is complicit in their continued survival.

Pathways toward life-serving economies and societies – those that prioritize the well-being of people and the planet – demand not only dedicated feminist strategies but also broad, unwavering collaboration and a deep commitment to real transformation. Feminists alone cannot shoulder this burden, but history has shown us one undeniable truth: Without abolishing patriarchy as both a mental framework and a concrete infrastructure, even the noblest of intentions will inevitably trigger a patriarchal backlash, reinforcing power pathologies. Therefore, dismantling patriarchal power structures is not merely important – it is imperative. It must be the central thread woven into every future-oriented *economic* transformation strategy, whether fostering inclusive governance, promoting gender equality and social justice, or building a narrative of hope for life-serving economies.

Yet we must confront the harsh reality: The pathological power strategies have been devastatingly effective. What we can learn from them is this: Feminist transformation strategies must be just as bold, creative and multifaceted. They must challenge power on all fronts and be deeply interconnected, working together like a living, breathing organism capable of overturning the entrenched systems that thrive on exploitation and inequality. Anything less will fail to bring about the transformative change our world so urgently needs.

While a small, privileged minority – including some women – benefits from the global patriarchal pathologies that secure economic power, the vast majority of the global population, particularly in the Global South, is suffering from their destructive manifestations. Individuals and organizations across the world are resisting these harmful dynamics, challenging the status quo. But resistance alone is not enough. What is equally vital is the growing discourse around alternative futures – possibilities that are most vividly emerging from the Global South. These conversations are happening in grassroots networks, agricultural communities, civil society organizations, feminist circles, networked Indigenous nations, political arenas and government agencies. Even within corporations, albeit to a lesser extent, we see sparks of this transformative dialogue.

Furthermore, complex frameworks of laws and enforcement mechanisms have been put in place to mitigate these *economic* power pathologies, achieving some success in curbing their most immediate effects. However, still too many people believe that perpetuating an outdated economic system is inevitable, and many admire those individuals that hold disproportionate power. Some idolize them, some benefit from their actions on a smaller scale and many passively accept these behaviors as the inevitable rules of the game. Patriarchal power structures, especially those rooted in economic systems, thrive on this mix of active support and tacit complicity.

In the next chapter, we will therefore delve deeper into the dynamics of complicity – how patriarchal power remains alive not just through force, but through everyday choices, beliefs and systems we continue to uphold. Understanding these layers of complicity is essential to dismantling them. Only when we uncover the mechanisms of our own involvement in sustaining this broken system can we truly begin to transform it. Radical change starts with recognizing how deeply we are all embedded in this outdated infrastructure and how we must, collectively, choose a different path forward.

Major insights for *collective feminist power practices* from the close intertwining of patriarchal power pathologies and economic systems:

1. Many people today see the economy as something simply given, something that just happens, and in which the participation of women must be strengthened. Yet, we must stay aware of the intertwining of any economic system with patriarchal power dynamics and pathologies.
2. Let us stay alert to the idea that even new economic approaches that intend to center the purpose of economies on life-serving and well-being of people and planet need to be examined regarding their potential to reaffirm patriarchal power pathologies.
3. We need to realize that all economic models of the past, no matter whether capitalism, communism, socialism or neoliberal capitalism, are informed by and based on variations of the patriarchal power pathologies: Coercion, institutionalization, gaslighting and divide and rule.
4. We need to stay aware that all economic systems have so far been built on the exploitation of women, nature and the 'other', while the latter was contextually defined, but usually included marginalized communities.

5. We need to understand that capitalism, including neo-capitalism, secures economic power through patriarchal and pathological strategies: Capitalist enclosure, wealth concentration, policy and regulatory capture, reproductive enclosure and the commodification of nature. If we want to counteract these patriarchal economic power strategies, we need to develop creative, manifold and interconnected feminist transformation strategies.
6. Socialism and communism aimed at eliminating injustice and accumulation of wealth for the few, but despite some good intentions and partly practice of gender equality they did not abolish patriarchy. On the contrary, many such societies became authoritarian regimes and saw a resurgence of patriarchal power pathologies. If we want to pick up good ideas from left-wing conceptual thought, we need to be alert to any potential for deeply ingrained patriarchal backlashes.

Notes

1 An overview of approaches can be found in Kuenkel (2022) and will be explored in Part V of this book.
2 See Merchant (1980), Griffin (2016).
3 The term *weaponizing women's bodies* refers to the practice of using women's bodies as tools or symbols to assert control, exert power, achieve political, social or cultural goals and reinforce patriarchal power structures. It can manifest in various forms, such as **sexual violence**, **reproductive control**, **cultural and religious norms** or **objectification in media**. Women's bodies become battlegrounds for larger struggles related to power, control and oppression. The weaponization reinforces systems of inequality and devalues women's autonomy.
4 See Federici (2004).
5 Shiva (2016) and Shiva & Mies (1993).
6 Mohanty (2003).
7 Agarwal (2013).
8 Gago & Mezzadra (2017).
9 Salleh (2017).
10 D'Allessandro (2018).
11 See the feminist economist Jayati Gosh (Gosh, 2024).
12 Communism had similar strategies, even though the land did not move into private ownership.
13 See Shiva (2016) and Ellis-Petersen (2023, April 28).
14 See Kelly (2023).
15 An example of a list of the wealthiest can be found here: https://www.forbesindia.com/article/explainers/top-10-richest-people-world/85541/1
16 Piketty et al. (2022).

17 Between the years 1950 and 1980, distributive justice through progressive taxation increased within countries in Europe, partly as a result of policies that aimed at balancing social and economic needs. During this time, the gap between high- and low-income earners narrowed, although the gender gap only slightly narrowed, see: Morgan & Neef (2020).
18 Piketty et al. (2022).
19 For a brief and informative introduction to corporate capture see: https://www.escr-net.org/resources/manifestations-of-corporate-capture
20 Hertel-Fernandez (2019).
21 Chipkin et al. (2018), Smith & Lee (2018).
22 See: https://www.awid.org/news-and-analysis/laughing-face-corporate-capture-feminist-perspective
23 Federici (2004).
24 World Economic Forum (2023, June 20).
25 A thorough analysis of critique and supporting arguments of the 'ecosystem services' concept is well summarized in: Schröter et al. (2014).
26 A brief introduction into the topic can be found in Friends of the Earth (2024).
27 See Fairhead et al. (2012).
28 See Engels (2010) and critique of his concepts in Carver (1985).
29 Mies (2022).
30 Mies (2022 p. 257).
31 A heart-breaking example is Nicaragua, poignantly described in Giaconda Bellis book: *The country under my skin: A memoir of love and war* (Belli 2003).
32 A review of the environmental impact oft he UDSSR can be found in: Feshbach & Friendly (1992).
33 See Griffin (2016).

References

Agarwal, B. (2013). *Gender and Green Governance: The Political Economy of Women's Presence within and beyond Community Forestry*. Oxford University Press.

Belli, G. (2003). *The Country under my Skin: A Memoir of Love and War*. Anchor Books.

Carver, T. (1985). Engels' feminism. *History of Political Thought*, 6(3), 479–489. https://www.jstor.org/stable/26212414

Chipkin, I., Swilling, M., Friedenstein, H., Peter, C., Prins, N., Mzusiki, Q., Mondi, L., Duma, S., Buthelezi, M., & Bhorat, H. (2018). *Shadow State: The Politics of State Capture*. Wits University Press.

D'Allessandro (2018). *Economía feminista: Las mujeres, el trabajo y el amor*. Ediciones B.

Ellis-Petersen, H. (2023, April 28). Fighting giants: eco-activist Vandana Shiva on her battle against GM multinationals. *The Guardian*. https://www.theguardian.com/global-development/2023/apr/28/fighting-giants-eco-activist-vandana-shiva-on-her-battle-against-gm-multinationals

Engels, F. (2010). *The Origin of the Family, Private Property and the State*. Penguin UK.

Fairhead, J., Leach, M., & Scoones, I. (2012). Green Grabbing: A new appropriation of nature? *The Journal of Peasant Studies*, *39*(2), 237–261. https://doi.org/10.1080/03066150.2012.671770

Federici, S. (2004). *Caliban and the Witch: Women, the Body and Primitive Accumulation*. Autonomedia.

Feshbach, M., & Friendly, A. (1992). *Ecocide in the US: Health and Nature Under Siege*. Basicbooks.

Friends of the Earth. (2024). *Financialisation of Nature*. https://www.foei.org/what-we-do/forests-and-biodiversity/financialisation-of-nature

Friends of The Earth International. (2024, October 21). The biodiversity mirage. https://www.foei.org/publication/biodiversity-offsetting-crediting-report

Gago, V. (2017). *Neoliberalism From Below: Popular Pragmatics and Baroque Economies*. Duke University Press.

Gago, V., & Mezzadra, S. (2017). A critique of the extractive operations of capital: Toward an expanded concept of extractivism. *Rethinking Marxism*, *29*(4), 574–591, DOI: 10.1080/08935696.2017.1417087, https://doi.org/10.1080/08935696.2017.1417087

Gosh, J. (2024). Why and how economics must change. *Finance and Development Magazine*. IMF. https://www.imf.org/en/Publications/fandd/issues/2024/03/Symposium-Why-and-how-economics-must-change-Jayati-Ghosh

Griffin, S. (2016). *Woman and Nature: The Roaring Inside Her*. Counterpoint.

Hertel-Fernandez, A. (2019). *State Capture: How Conservative Activists, Big Businesses, and Wealthy Donors Reshaped the American States and the Nation*. New York, NY: Oxford University Press.

Kelly, M. (2023). *Wealth Supremacy: How the Extractive Economy and the Biased Rules of Capitalism Drive Today's Crises*. Berrett-Koehler Publishers.

Kuenkel, P. (2022). Collective stewardship towards life economies. In: Kuenkel, P., Ragnarsdottir, K.V. (eds) *Transformation Literacy*. Cham: Springer. https://doi.org/10.1007/978-3-030-93254-1_21

Merchant, C. (1980). *The Death of Nature: Women, Ecology, and the Scientific Revolution*. Harperone. (Original work published 1980).

Mies, M. (2022). *Patriarchy and Accumulation on a World Scale: Women in the International Division of Labour*. Bloomsbury Academic.

Mohanty, C.T. (2003). *Feminism Without Borders: Decolonizing Theory, Practicing Solidarity*. Duke University Press.

Morgan, M., & Neef, T. (2020). What's new about income inequality in Europe (1980–2019)? World Inequality Lab – Issue Brief 2020/04 November 2020. https://wid.world/document/whats-new-about-income-inequality-in-europe-1980-2019

Piketty, T., Saez, E., Zucman, G., Duflo, E., & Banerjee, A. (2022). World Inequality Report 2022. World Inequality Lab. https://wir2022.wid.world/www-site/uploads/2023/03/D_FINAL_WIL_RIM_RAPPORT_2303.pdf

Salleh, A. (2017). *Ecofeminism as Politics: Nature, Marx and the Postmodern*. Zed Books; 2nd Edition.

Schröter, M., van der Zanden, E.H., van Oudenhoven, A.P.E., Remme, R.P., Serna-Chavez, H.M., de Groot, R.S., & Opdam, P. (2014). Ecosystem services as a contested concept: A synthesis of critique and counter-arguments. *Conservation Letters*, *7*(6), 514–523. https://doi.org/10.1111/conl.12091

Shiva, V. (2016). *Staying Alive: Women, Ecology, and Development*. North Atlantic Books.

Shiva, V., & Mies, M. (1993). *Ecofeminism*. Zed Books.

Smith, J., & Lee, K. (2018). From colonisation to globalisation: A history of state capture by the tobacco industry in Malawi. *Review of African Political Economy*, 45(156), 186–202. https://doi.org/10.1080/03056244.2018.1431213

World Economic Forum. (2023, June 20). Global Gender Gap Report 2023. https://www.weforum.org/publications/global-gender-gap-report-2023/in-full/benchmarking-gender-gaps-2023

6
Complicity with Patriarchy – How We Keep the System Running

Given the previous two chapters, we may realize that patriarchal power pathologies are still pervasive, outrightly brutal in some areas of the world, more subtly persistent in other areas of the world. They show contextually different faces, and intersect in the process of othering with gender, race, class, religious and cultural differences. Across historic and geographical contexts, the four patriarchal power pathologies *coercion*, *institutionalization*, *gaslighting* and *divide and rule* still work. Wars are the most extreme manifestation of patriarchal power pathologies. Although we are still far from abolishing patriarchy and can observe clear trends of patriarchal backlash, there is overall progress toward greater gender equality and increased access to power for women. Despite rising violence against women and a global shift toward authoritarianism, women's rights and their presence in institutional leadership roles are expanding. Notably, the number of female heads of state has significantly increased, especially in democratic nations, between 1960 and 2022.[1] Usually they were pretty lonely and hardly ever followed a female head of state or prime minister, which hints at an interesting pattern. Most often, men follow men, but women do not follow women.[2]

Yet, did any of the female heads of state did have an explicitly feminist agenda? Would they have been elected, if so? Mary Robinson, the former president of Ireland, is the co-founder of a project that supports women in climate action. She explicitly calls for women to lead transformations. She heavily criticized the lack of women among the heads of state present at the 27th COP in Egypt's Sharm El-Sheikh, and demands women be among the decision-makers at all levels.[3] She has also been one of the co-founders of the *World Council for Women Leaders*, a network of members composed of present and past female heads of governments or female heads of state.[4] Mia Mottley has been prime minister of Barbados since 2018 with a strong agenda on restructuring climate finance towards global justice, but no explicit feminist agenda.[5] The German Angela Merkel served as chancellor for 16 years. She would never declare a feminist

DOI: 10.4324/9781003508885-8

agenda, but in fact she supported many other women and mediated their path to power.[6] During her term in office between 2019 and 2023, the Finnish prime minister Sanna Marin clearly pursued goals such as gender equality, climate mitigation and fighting sexism, without explicitly naming it a feminist stance.[7] She led a Five-Party-Coalition of women party heads, which is certainly rare in history and an interesting view into possible futures, in which women in power collaborate across different interest groups. Given the analysis of the previous chapters, it is not surprising that in 2023, Sanna Marin was defeated in the elections, and Finland, since then, has a conservative coalition including a right-wing party. Must we assume this was a well-organized patriarchal backlash disguised in the democratic formation of people's opinions? Iceland seems to have a better strategy – female prime ministers follow female prime ministers. In December 2024 the newly elected prime minister Kristrun Frostadottir formed a coalition with two other parties, all led by women.[8] At the same time Iceland's president is also female. May the ancient longing come true, that female leadership can be more easily restored on islands?

Historically, the global share of women in parliament has increased substantially, from 11.3% in 1995 to 26.5% in 2023, with substantial differences by region: The Americas with an average increase from 12.7% in 1995 to 34.9% in 2023, and Europe with an increase from 13.2% in 1995 to 31% in 2023, are frontrunners. Yet, if we look at individual countries, Rwanda is the frontrunner with around 60% women in parliament, followed by Finland, Cuba, Nicaragua, Mexico, New Zealand, Iceland, Costa Rica, South Africa and Bolivia.[9] These countries usually had a steady increase in female parliamentarians over a long time. Many other countries linger at around 30–45% women in parliament, but there are also countries – not surprisingly those with authoritarian governments such as Russia, Iran or China, or those with a patriarchal stronghold on society like Japan, India or Brazil – where the percentage drops below 25% or even below 10%.[10]

Few women in institutional power have an explicitly feminist agenda, can afford to pursue one or see themselves as part of a global movement to abolish patriarchy. What does participation in power mean within a patriarchal system? Can women in such roles shift the paradigm of patriarchal domination, or does assimilation inevitably occur? When do they become susceptible to complicity with patriarchy and lose the spirit of revolution? Can patriarchal systems be transformed from within, or is the risk of succumbing to their seductions – or becoming victims of backlash – too great?

These questions have accompanied feminist movements across the waves. Feminist strategies aim not to reform but to abolish patriarchy, yet women – especially feminists – must navigate the challenge of holding power without reinforcing the very structures that sustain patriarchy.

We face a difficult dilemma: We need at least 50% women in institutional power positions, ideally 50% feminists, in order to gradually shift patriarchal power structures. Rokeya Hossain would have suggested 100%. Yet, history has shown that women in institutional power positions do not necessarily contribute to feminist transformations. Every woman in power does, in so far as she becomes a role model for other women and shows that female power is possible and can be normal. Society gets used to women in power. This contribution should not be underestimated. Acting as a woman in power in an explicitly feminist way rarely happens, but it does happen, often as a surprise to society. The German Foreign Minister Annalena Baerbock and the German Minister for International Cooperation Svenja Schulze – both in power in their positions since 2021 – jointly presented a Feminist Foreign Policy and a Feminist Development Policy Strategy to the general public in 2022, which achieved positive resonance, but of course, also belittling commentaries.[11] Examples of Feminist Foreign Policy can be seen in countries like France, Sweden, Mexico and Chile, with recent efforts emerging at the EU level.[12] Though these remain a minority, they signal future possibilities. Currently, openly feminist leaders are rare in political or corporate power. Many women in decision-making roles either avoid a feminist stance, fear being associated with it or are constrained by their circumstances. Some are discouraged by patriarchal backlash, while others simply adapt to the prevailing system.

We clearly need more feminists in influential positions within patriarchal structures, and more importantly, a network of connected feminists. Presently, many of the outspoken feminists are found in academia, NGOs, activist organizations, the arts, philanthropy, impact investing and authorship, or they maintain private feminist views separate from their public persona. While this grassroots influence is not to be underestimated, it highlights the dilemma: Feminists in power risk either conforming to patriarchal structures or being ousted for resisting them. To address this dilemma and shift patriarchal power from within, we must acknowledge how women – including feminists – sometimes participate in upholding these structures.[13] It's a difficult path, but by exposing complicity with patriarchy, we can begin to unravel the invisible forces that seem to separate feminists from power. What do I mean by complicity?

In the context of this book and for the aim of understanding the possibilities for feminist transformations, the term *complicity* is used to describe our *individual and collective unconscious support* for the maintenance of the patriarchy. As the American feminist philosopher Alison Jaggar described it, 'one of the most important questions confronting all feminist theorists…[is] why women who are, after all, a majority in most populations, so often seem to submit to or even collude with their own subordination'.[14]

The most extreme examples in Europe today are women who, benefiting from the opportunities created by feminist equality movements, now lead political parties that promote populist right-wing or even far-right agendas, driving patriarchal backlash. Examples are Marine le Pen in France, heading the Front National (FN) in France; Pia Kjaersgaard, leader of the Dansk Folkeparti (Danish Peoples' Party, DF); Giorgia Meloni, heading the post-fascist party Fratelli d'Italia (Brothers of Italy) and acting as prime minister of Italy in a center-right coalition since 2022; Siv Jensen, leader of the Norwegian Fremskrittparti (Progress Party, FrP): or Alice Weidel, co-leader of the right-extremist party Alternative for Germany (AFD).[15] Is the prominence of women in strongly patriarchal political parties an unintended consequence of century-long feminist fights for gender equality that has gone astray?

There is a growing feminist research literature on the phenomenon of complicity of women with oppressive patriarchal patterns. Feminists are not completely exempt from this. The most known work on this began in the 1990s in the United States with unmasking the role of white feminists in male-dominated systems that, consciously or unconsciously, contributed to upholding power structures alienating and disempowering People of Color.[16] Equally important is the earlier work of African feminist scholars who, in the 1980s, critiqued the approach of European and American feminist researchers in Africa. These Western scholars often replicated patriarchal patterns by generalizing about the 'African Woman', stripping African women of their diverse identities, contexts and histories.[17] Their work revealed how, despite good intentions, Western feminist researchers contributed to the victimization of African women by turning them into research objects rather than recognizing them as active agents and authorities on their own realities. Whether consciously or not, these researchers reinforced images of African women shaped by their privileged research positions and Western worldview. More recently, in her book *Decolonization and Afrofeminism*, the Ugandan academic and human rights activist Sylvia Tamale critiques Western feminism for its narrow focus on *gender equality*, arguing that it often overlooks the legacies of colonialism, racism and economic exploitation that Western women take part in.[18] She advocates for reclaiming Indigenous knowledge and practices that promoted *gender balance* before colonialism imposed patriarchal systems.

It was the realization of the many forms of complicity with power structures that led to the emergence of the term *intersectionality*, and finally *intersectional feminism*, making space for the voices, the knowledge and the world interpretations of women experiencing overlapping forms of patriarchal oppression. The American law professor Kimberlé Crenshaw crafted the term in 1989, using it as a lens to see how different forms of inequality in law cases and in societies operate together and exacerbate each other.[19] She conceptually captured a phenomenon that she acknowledged women before her had hinted at, such as the Black Liberation Activist Anna J. Cooper in the 19th century and the American philosopher and political activist Angela Davis.[20] The term is today widely used as it makes different forms of discrimination and their intertwining more conscious: e.g., gender, race, age, socioeconomic status or class, educational status, physical or mental disabilities, sexual identities, religious orientation, cultural geographies or ethnicity. The acknowledgment of intersectionality in the feminist community has opened possibilities to make complicity with discriminatory power structures more conscious.

The concept of complicity is complex, shaped by habits, personal experiences, social relations, societal narratives and structures as well as collective and individual aspirations to claim power. In building a *collective feminist power practice*, the focus should not be on complicity as active and intentional participation in wrongdoing, which is well covered by moral and legal frameworks. Instead, we are concerned with *tacit complicity* – subtle, often invisible complicity with patriarchal structures. This form of complicity is rarely recognized as problematic by those involved; they act this way because it's familiar, normalized or beneficial, or they unconsciously follow ingrained behaviors. Recognizing these patterns among men, women and feminists allows us to help one another avoid the traps of complicity. This isn't about blaming or finger-pointing but about seeing what we may have overlooked and using that awareness as a foundation for a new *collective feminist practice*.

Let us remember that the fourth perfidious patriarchal power pathology is *divide and rule*, with the special mechanism of *selective empowerment*. It works with the obliviousness of the willing supporters of patriarchal patterns, because they are offered or gain a certain portion of power. Hence, power and open or tacit complicity are inextricably linked. In order to understand this linkage, let us first look at power in a different, more psychological way.

Power emerges from the perception of how energy flows. When power is attributed to individuals or institutions, collective consciousness amplifies it, creating a snowball effect. Where power is perceived, power is also attributed. This process has a reinforcing effect. This dynamic is not just the strategy of social media influencers but also of charismatic leaders and brutal dictators. The continual reinforcement solidifies the perceived power, which is then maintained and protected by institutional structures. Attention is the fuel that transfers energy to power. When focused on an individual, it heightens their sense of self-importance and influence. Those seen as powerful become magnets, attracting others who hope to share in that power. There's an unconscious belief that proximity to power equals opportunity, and admiration, obedience and devotion further reinforce this dynamic. However, power weakens when attention is withdrawn and attribution is refused – a fear central to authoritarian rulers. Hannah Arendt highlighted this, showing how power turns to violence when it must be upheld at any cost, as seen in the historical context of Nazi Germany.[21] In relation to the four patriarchal power pathologies, we can identify that in order to uphold power, in highly patriarchal and authoritarian societies, the mechanism of *institutionalization* increasingly shifts toward *coercion*, with *gaslighting* used as propaganda to legitimize that *coercion*. In more liberal patriarchies, power is maintained primarily through *gaslighting* and the *divide and rule* tactic.

Without these power pathologies, we can conceptualize power neutrally as *'realization' power* – a form of individual and collective future-making that has an impact on many people, small scale or large scale. We have learned from female definitions of power that it is a relational concept, emerging in communication. Hannah Arendt suggests this relationality leads to power as an agreement between people, hence a collective process, and is directed towards a collective purpose. Ideally, this is a good purpose. Let us unpack this.

If any of us ran around a neighboring city claiming power, no one would take us seriously – some might even laugh. Simply claiming power doesn't mean you have it; people must attribute power to you for it to be real. They need to grant the authority that comes with a position of power. There are many ways to convince, urge or force people to grant authority, but two mechanisms are key. First, you must capture attention by being convincing and charismatic, or using force. Second, you need to occupy a position within an institutional structure that structurally conveys power. Typically, power is attributed when both factors are present. Thus, power is deeply connected to human attention, perception and institutional structures. We can see power as a form of energy concentration that becomes a tangible force for organizing relationships. Because power is inherently attributed, securing this attribution is the basis for organizing institutions. They hold power and exercise authority. Without such acknowledgment of authority, power remains dormant, and cannot manifest its influence. Whether for benevolent or malevolent purposes, this fundamental rule persists: Where attention goes, power grows, and where power grows, attention goes. We are all human: Where we perceive power, our attention gravitates. This has worked throughout history in our patriarchal societies, but is important to consider for feminist futures and a *collective feminist power practice*. This becomes most evident when we examine social media. While social media platforms function as free tools, ostensibly designed for human-to-human connection, their operation is driven by what is known as the *attention economy* – a concept in information management that treats people's attention as a scarce and marketable commodity. Competition for attention in order to sell it for advertising (or manipulation) has led to the development of creative tools: Algorithms, personalized content, focus on visual content, gamification, fear of missing out alerts, or social validation. Users are encouraged to act in a way that will gain them followers, in competition with other users. Those with more followers get more attention: People attribute power of influence to them, give them more attention and thus grow their influence. People who cannot compete in the game lose out and can only become followers. Power attributed to individuals can also turn into collective power, as people gather around the messages influential users convey, spread the messages and organize action: For good or for bad. Social media has transformed the way people communicate, organize and mobilize collective power. It offers new opportunities for connectivity and activism. Yet, we know the inherent dangers: Echo chambers, disinformation, polarization, manipulation, intimidation, lack of accountability. It can also be used for the patriarchal pathology of *coercion* in the form of surveillance. Social media offers an interesting example of how power structures are created, how existing ones can be dismantled or reinforced, and how attention can be manipulated or harnessed for collective action.

As we have seen in the previous chapter, developing such social media technologies to organize the attention of people towards perceived power has created some of the wealthiest, most powerful men in the world, who can hardly be held accountable for the effects they create. Yet, social media are only the easy-to-understand example of managing attention and power attribution. Attention, of course, does not exist in a vacuum in societies. Beyond the digital or virtual world, organizing attention to power is solidified and maintained through factual institutional structures. I have described *institutionalization* as a patriarchal power pathology in so far as past and current institutions have been built and maintained to keep patriarchy running and reinforce male reference systems. Their purpose is to hold institutional *realization power*, so that this power is consolidated over a long period of time. The power of a social media influencers can vanish within days; the power of institutions is enduring.

This is important to note, acknowledge and observe when we intend to step into organizing power for feminist transformations. We need more feminist institutions that are powerful; we need to become part of the power of existing patriarchal institutions in order to shift them; and we need to use social media for organizing collective power. Yet, we need to stay alert at every step that we move into potentially dangerous traps of complicity. By using social media, we become complicit with the very patriarchal industry that thrives on the *attention economy* and is built on domination versus exclusion. We need to hold positions of power in institutions – whether in academia, politics, corporations or civil society organizations – but by entering these spaces, we inevitably adhere to the very rules that sustain the patriarchal structures we seek to dismantle. There's no way to avoid complicity entirely, except by navigating these traps consciously, supporting one another in minimizing them, and developing strategies to disrupt patriarchal institutions from both within and outside.

In her book *Complaint*, the British-Australian feminist scholar Sarah Ahmed explores how to break away from complicity with institutional cultures by using collective strategies among women to lodge complaints.[22] She offers inspiring ideas for complaint collectives, who can work together through the difficult process of disrupting, challenging and holding accountable patriarchal power within institutions. Toward the end of her book, she shares a powerful account by a group of women who jointly confronted an academic institution where sexual harassment and abuse of power had been normalized. For years, women in the department developed individual strategies to cope with harassment or the consequences of refusing complicity. Each had their own experience of living with the fallout of either complicity or resistance within a toxic culture. The collective acknowledges that their story of unity is intertwined with moments of resistance, even in silence amid harassment that left them feeling isolated. Through ongoing conversations, they began to bridge their disconnection and strengthen their collective. When the situation became unbearable, they reached a turning point: Realizing they needed to challenge the toxic culture to protect future female students and employees from similar despair. The women came together to draft an anonymous report detailing sexual harassment and abuse of power within the academic department, aiming to expose the institution's complicity in perpetuating this harmful culture.[23]

What stands out in this story is the silent, organized disconnection among women, which is key to how patriarchal cultures secure complicity, stifle collective action and preserve power structures. Patriarchal organizational culture invites complicity by preventing *collective feminist practice* and thus maintaining patriarchal power systems. Women who see, experience or name patriarchal pathologies are usually lonely. The danger is that when they speak up, they become outcasts. It is this disconnection among women that we must overcome by all means when we want to help each other out of complicity. As we have seen from the above example, institutional power protects the powerful, through normalizing the abuse of power. To see this and name this collectively is a decisive step out of complicity.[24]

Patriarchy is a power structure securing continuous attention flow to the many manifestations of male reference systems, and within these systems to protagonists, men and women, who maintain the system. This gets rewarded. Exceptions prove the rule. As Sarah Ahmed elaborates poignantly in her other book *Living a Feminist Life*, disturbing this power game by naming it, by pointing out the many situations where the system of power reaffirms itself, is arduous work.[25] The feminist killjoys, as she calls them, usually do not get rewarded, moreover; they get scolded, accused and excluded. They get blackmailed, if not detained. They become the problems. They dare to name the dragons and disrupt the tacit complicity that men and women have with ingrained patriarchal modes of behavior and thinking. They become targets of gaslighting, as Sarah Ahmed summarizes it: 'Feminists are always looking for problems. As if these problems did not exist before you addressed them; as if the act of naming them would make them exist.'[26]

Uncovering complicity with patriarchal thought and action is uncomfortable. It causes awkward situations for oneself and others. We tend to avoid this. It makes people unhappy and they might direct their unhappiness towards us, both men and women. Yet, we know it is our daily job, if we want to work towards feminist transformations. But even as the most committed feminist we walk into traps, are surrounded by circumstances that seem to control us, need to avoid risks or see no other possibilities than colluding with what we actually want to abolish. Moreover, we might really not notice our own and others' complicity. It helps to remember the many women before us who did take the risk, were courageous or oblivious to the dangers of disrupting patriarchal power structures.

The more we observe, the more we know, the more we can counteract *tacit complicity*. The most important aspect is to take this as an opportunity to observe ourselves and others in the many variations of support for the patriarchy that we actually aim to abolish. Some of these forms may be hard to overcome; others we may be able to reflect on and change; some we may be able to name so that they lose their tacit impact. It is important to understand our own often unconscious collusion with patriarchal structures, narratives and power pathologies. It is equally important to empower ourselves to observe the *tacit complicity* of others so that we do not fall into the same trap. To advance a *collective feminist power practice* we need to understand the mechanisms of power attribution as much as those of *tacit complicity* with power. Yet, let us suspend judgment, because we are not infallible. What we observe as patriarchal power pathologies might come around as tacit power dynamics among women or among feminists.

I render this uncovering essential for a feminist collective power practice. Only then can we make different decisions, name the dragons and change actions. Observation precedes insight, and insight is the mother of change. *Tacit complicity* is a mental trap of patriarchy that men fall prey to, but also women, when they stay disconnected, keep each other from power, undermine each other or ensure that the main, hence often the male, reference system remains intact. The effects keep women away from power and isolate them when they do attain it.

The following is a collection of acts of tacit complicity that I have observed and experienced over many years, often discussed with like-minded friends and feminists. These acts subtly contribute to upholding or reinstating patriarchal power structures. This collection stems from my personal journey, leadership experience, strategic work in international and local transformation projects, and participation in influential global networks. While I have encountered various cultures through my work, this list is framed by my European upbringing. It is incomplete and serves as an invitation for you to create your own list, which may differ based on your background and context. I encourage you to seek out your own observations of complicity and discuss them with fellow feminists. Although some examples I will use are fictional, they reflect real experiences.

The *first* form of tacit complicity with patriarchal power pathologies is the **perpetuation of women's exclusion**, a phenomenon with countless variations. Consider the common scenario of a management or board meeting where women are in the minority. It's not uncommon for a woman to make an important contribution, only for the next speaker to ignore her input and continue with his statement. If a man later repeats her suggestion, it is suddenly accepted, often with support from others, while no one acknowledges the original idea came from a woman. She stays silent to avoid appearing ego-driven, and other women in the room follow suit, not wanting to disrupt the consensus. Next time you experience a similar situation, step in, name the dragon, preferably in a rational and descriptive way and congratulate the woman for being the originator of the contribution or suggestion. The more women consciously engage in this practice, the less they need to resort to the common female pathologies of demanding attention. Because unsurprisingly, women often develop various strategies to counteract exclusion and attract the attention of men, who are typically seen as decision-makers. These strategies may include becoming a 'drama queen', playing the victim, adopting a domineering approach, speaking seductively or acting as moral accusers.

But what if the same happens at scale in a much more structural way – for example, in knowledge production? I have a friend working in an honorable academic institution, a declared feminist. When I suggested she publish a book on feminist strategies for sustainability transformations, her immediate reaction was: No, you can't do this, nobody will read it, because they will think this is only about women's issues. Yet, many male philosophers have explained the world to us, developed theories and formed schools of thought that endured over centuries and are still considered today. They dared to talk about the whole of humankind, not the male half. Few female philosophers have done this in the same way and reached similar fame. Hannah Arendt was one of them. Have there really been so few female philosophers? Did they not get published? Or have their publications been ignored? Or did people think men can ponder about humankind, while women only ponder about women's issues that are secondary to humankind's evolution?

There is an interesting process we can observe in female and feminist knowledge production: Men usually come from a place of knowing, while many women come from a place of exploring. The consequence is ignorance towards women's knowledge production. This can be obliviousness towards women's research work or deliberate refusal. It is simply declared non-existent. If it shows up anyway, the next stage is arrogance. It is belittled as biased or unscientific, too intuitive, or downgraded, because it may not have been produced in one of the elite knowledge factories. If the female knowledge still persists, it is declared irrelevant. There might be a good point in it, but it cannot be generalized; or it lacks validity. If the female knowledge still persists and can't be ignored, declared invalid or irrelevant, it gets appropriated by men and its content is taken into mainstream knowledge without making reference to its origins. Important aspects of the original knowledge production are eliminated. This certainly happened to many female and feminist researchers who researched the role of egalitarian and peaceful societies in the Neolithic era. It was declared too intuitive, not scientifically grounded, then judged as the exception to the rule of a belligerent human (not male) nature. More recently there are increasing numbers of male authors writing about the new insight that humankind may actually have been and can be a cooperative species.[27] It happened to early ecofeminists' writings, of which many aspects have been taken up by sustainability activists, change agents and scientists with hardly any reference to the earlier work. Are women complicit in perpetuating this? Yes, they are. There is feminist literature belittling feminist research about egalitarian societies in the Neolithic age.[28] There is a belittling of ecofeminist writings. Many female authors, sometimes even feminists, quote men rather than women, maybe because it is simply more work to find female sources, or maybe because they attribute authority to men, justifying it with special expertise. But the female expertise exists. We can dare to be biased. I encourage you to do the minimum and take Sarah Ahmed and Riane Eisler as good examples: Sarah Ahmed makes her feminist practice explicit by mentioning that she will not cite *White* men; Riane Eisler has a huge body of footnotes that give credit to many female and feminist authors, of which many have been forgotten.[29]

The *second* form of tacit complicity with patriarchal power pathologies is **male-biased power attribution.** Most of us have been raised in patriarchal societies where power, expertise, knowledge, authority and experience are predominantly expected from men. While we've become increasingly aware of mansplaining, and remind or sometimes even embarrass men in their assumption of knowing, we must also recognize more subtle dynamics at play in institutions that operate according to male reference systems.[30] Male-biased power attribution reinforces gendered expectations, with power and authority disproportionately ascribed to men, while women are often marginalized or underestimated. In professional settings, men are generally assumed to possess leadership qualities by default, while women face skepticism or heightened scrutiny when asserting their expertise. Are women complicit in this? Yes. Women also contribute to it by referencing male colleagues' contributions more frequently or downplaying their own achievements to avoid appearing overly assertive. As power is attributed to men, women may gravitate toward them, seeking opportunities to share in that power. Additionally, women may unconsciously reinforce stereotypical expectations of femininity by valuing communal harmony over individual assertiveness. Conversely, in male-dominated environments, women often adapt to prevailing norms to navigate their careers, conforming to masculine leadership styles to gain acceptance and recognition within the existing power hierarchy.

There are other surprising variations of tacit complicity with male-biased power attributions. Women in power positions often surround themselves by men, as if creating male followers was a safer way of securing power than having female followers. They feel more protected by men. Once the female power position has been safely installed, men become willing followers, while women may only be ambivalent followers of women in power, and are subsequently dropped by women in power. There is only one way out of these variations of tacit complicity: It is a decisive and courageous strategy towards female-biased power attribution. Still, to a large extent, in most of our societies power is mediated by men. To change this would be one of the most important goals of *collective feminist power practices*. Deliberately granting authority to women and doing this individually and collectively, is an essential strategy. This is happening, but not enough, not strategically enough and not collectively enough. In the different waves of feminist movements, many feminists have suggested ways to strengthen these strategies. We will look into them in more details in the coming chapters.

The *third* form of *tacit complicity* with patriarchal power pathologies is **devaluation of female power or expertise.** Have you ever come across the following experience: A woman in a political power position, an influential female author or a credible female university professor is suddenly in the news or targeted with criticism in social media. It may look like a campaign against this woman, but you do not know, because you don't know her personally. The aspects that are brought to bear may be unfair behavior in professional settings, unprofessional decision-making in politics, a compromising video from her private life, allegations of corruption or fraud, or any other accusations that go viral in media. It is difficult for you to judge whether there is any truth in the accusations. The woman voluntarily steps down, is removed from her post and after a while she has disappeared into private life or a different career. I am not saying that all public criticism of women in positions of power is wrong. But I urge you to be alert to very common, yet insidious strategies of patriarchal backlash with the aim to undermine the authority, credibility and contributions of women in positions of influence. Are women complicit in this? Yes.

Public campaigns and smear tactics deployed against women in power or influential women are a tactic that is often supported by women, or at least they withdraw support from the woman in question. They find it difficult to keep the confidence in the woman. While men who are the target of campaigns fall into a network of supporters who quickly provide them with an alternative position, women usually fall deep. I know of several feminist friends who took years to recover from such campaigns. Of course, there are milder forms of undermining women's credibility, leadership and legitimacy through tactics such as character assassination, concerted efforts to discredit their expertise, downplaying their achievements or marginalizing their contributions. They have milder effects, but also contribute to loss of self-esteem, insecurity and above all isolation.

Discreditation campaigns also happen among feminists. Social media technologies do invite us to easily transition from necessary discourse to disrespectful discreditation. I wish, as feminists, we would not fall into this trap that makes patriarchal power structures happily smile, because those who are pitted against each other are less dangerous to the system. Fragmented feminists will have less impact on feminist transformations. Critical discourse is as important as fierce debate about different feminist positions. We need both to take place in a respectful way. Yet, we need a form of mutual acknowledgment of a person as a person, a way of criticizing the other woman with a different opinion that still leaves her whole as a person in her contextual place. This must become part of a *collective feminist power practice*.

The *fourth* form of tacit complicity with patriarchal power pathologies is **female or feminist disconnect**. We remember, fragmentation among women or feminists is the aim of the *divide and rule power pathology*. It manifests in different forms: Mistrust among women towards each other; doubts about or experience with lacking female solidarity; suspicion of male-oriented allyship; and isolation of women. In the face of patriarchal backlash or sexual harassment, women often find themselves isolated and unsupported, struggling to recognize allies within their own gender. The female and feminist disconnect is very apparent in countries that claim to be advancing gender equality, but have no traditional culture of female circles that exist historically as a way of societally sanctioned female togetherness apart from men. Have you ever been in a decision-making group, such as a board, with nearly 50% women, yet witnessed mistrust among female members and their alliances with influential men, and disconnected or even hostile relationships between women? These patterns are challenging to change. Often, the level of mistrust is so severe that it becomes impossible to foster connections, engage in pre-discussions on issues or cultivate mutual acknowledgment, confidence and respect for diverse perspectives. At times, even suggesting that women connect separately to navigate and counteract patriarchal dynamics is met with resistance. Unfortunately, men often emerge as the winners in these situations. There seems to be an unspoken rule against forming connections among women, as if such solidarity is morally questionable and could lead to manipulation in decision-making. This reflects an internalization of the patriarchal narrative that women must be rivals and adversaries, or the belief that gender is irrelevant in a decision-making group.

Tacit disconnection can take even more subtle forms. I recently read an article about a feminist event. The feminist writer began by explaining that the event was particularly good, because there was no typical moral finger-pointing feminism. What was the point of this subtle distancing and from whom? Why did she have the need to strengthen the narrative that feminists are usually finger-pointing? We should be mindful of creating fragmentation among feminists and feminist movements. We know how quickly in feminist spaces differing perspectives and priorities can lead to internal divisions and infighting. We know how many women hesitate to align themselves with a feminist cause for fear of being labeled, although we should believe bell hooks in her plea that 'feminism is for everyone'.[31]

As mentioned, discourse and debate are of utmost importance and should be the preparation for dialogue, not for dividing feminists. We need to negotiate pathways into the future without diminishing each other's value. It weakens access to power, individually and collectively. Only if we recognize the many overt and covert mechanisms of patriarchal power pathologies that we may be tacitly complicit with, can we build a *collective feminist power practice*.

Major insights for *collective feminist power practices* from the different forms of complicity with patriarchy as a way of keeping the system running:

1. Complicity with patriarchal thinking and patriarchal structure is a significant mechanism that upholds patriarchal power structures and keeps women away from power.

2. We need to uncover and name male complicity with power pathologies. It helps if this done by collectives of women rather than individually.
3. We need to understand power as organized flow of attention and notice more consciously in what ways power gets attributed predominantly to men.
4. For a *collective feminist power practice*, we need to develop strategies to counteract the normalized power attribution to men and establish female forms of acknowledging authority among women and feminists.
5. It helps if we all become more conscious about our own and other women's forms of tacit complicity with patriarchal power structures. This is not about blaming or finger-pointing at each other, but about helping us to mutually liberate each other from patriarchal power traps.
6. It is also important that we overcome the ingrained disconnection among women and develop a *collective feminist practice* that fosters discourse and debate, yet respectfully acknowledges difference without diminishing each other's credibility.

Notes

1 UN Women (2023, March 7).
2 Exceptions do exist: After her election victory in 1990, Mary Robinson became the first female president in Ireland. Mary McAleese followed her in 1997.
3 United Nations (2022, November 15).
4 See: https://www.councilwomenworldleaders.org. A regular update of female heads of state/government and ministers can be found in UN Women (2024).
5 She initiated the Bridgetown Initiative, a political agenda to reform the global financial architecture. For a feminist critique, see Bigda (2023, June 21).
6 See Merkel (2024).
7 See Abend (2020).
8 See Reuters (2024, December 3).
9 See: Inter-Parliamentary Union (IPU) (2023).
10 Herre (2024).
11 See: Auswärtiges Amt (2023, March 1) and The Ministry for Economic Cooperation and Development (BMZ). (2023, March 1).
12 Lunz (2023).
13 A good overview of the issue can be found in Knowles (2022).
14 See: Jaggar (1983, p. 149).
15 Meret & Siim. (2017).
16 Monteverde (2017).
17 Künkel (1995).
18 Tamale (2020).
19 Crenshaw at al. (1995).

20 See IWDA (2018, November 8).
21 See Arendt (1969).
22 Ahmed (2021).
23 Ahmed (2021 p. 264).
24 Interesting research shows how the #MeToo campaign spurred attention and awareness about sexual harassment and violence. See: Kaufman et al. (2021).
25 Ahmed (2017).
26 Ahmed (2017 p. 60).
27 See for example: Bregman (2020), Lent (2021).
28 See Saini (2023).
29 See Ahmed (2017) and Eisler (2011).
30 See Solnit (2014).
31 hooks (2000).

References

Abend, L. (2020). Finland's Sanna Marin, the world's youngest female head of government, wants equality, not celebrity. Time.com. https://time.com/collection/davos-2020/5764097/sanna-marin-finland-equality

Ahmed, S. (2017). *Living a Feminist Life*. Duke University Press.

Ahmed, S. (2021). *Complaint!* Duke University Press.

Arendt, H. (1969). *On Violence*. Stellar Classics.

Auswärtiges Amt. (2023, March 1). Guidelines for Feminist Foreign Policy: A foreign policy for all. German Federal Foreign Office. https://www.auswaertiges-amt.de/en/aussenpolitik/themen/ffp-guidelines/2585074

Bigda, L. (2023, June 21). *Unpacking the Bridgetown Initiative: A Systemic Feminist Analysis & Critique*. WEDO. https://wedo.org/unpacking-the-bridgetown-initiative-a-systemic-feminist-analysis-critique

Bregman, R. (2020). *Humankind: A New History*. Little, Brown.

Crenshaw, K., Gotanda, N., Peller, G., & Thomas, K. (1995). *Critical Race Theory: The Key Writings That Formed the Movement*. The New Press.

Eisler, R. (2011). *The Chalice and the Blade: Our History, Our Future*. Harper Collins.

Herre, B. (2024). Women have made major advances in politics – but the world is still far from equal. Our World in Data. https://ourworldindata.org/women-political-advances

hooks, bell. (2000). *Feminism Is for Everybody*. South End Press.

Inter-Parliamentary Union (IPU). (2023). Women in parliament 2022. https://www.ipu.org/resources/publications/reports/2023-03/women-in-parliament-2022

IWDA. (2018, November 8). What does intersectional feminism actually mean? https://iwda.org.au/what-does-intersectional-feminism-actually-mean

Jaggar, A. (1983). *Feminist Politics and Human Nature*. Sussex, England: Harvester.

Kaufman, M.R., Dey, D., Crainiceanu, C., & Dredze, M. (2021). #MeToo and Google inquiries into sexual violence: A hashtag campaign can sustain information seeking. *Journal of Interpersonal Violence*, 36(19–20), 088626051986819. https://doi.org/10.1177/0886260519868197

Knowles, C. (2022, December). Beyond adaptive preferences – Women's complicity in their own subordination. *European Journal of Philosophy*, 30(4).

Künkel (1995). *Die Mühen der Differenz: Frauenforschung in Afrika südlich der Sahara*. Breitenbach.

Lent, J. (2021). *Patterning Instinct: A Cultural History of Humanity's Search for Meaning*. Prometheus.

Lunz, K. (2023). *The Future of Foreign Policy Is Feminist*. John Wiley & Sons.

Meret, S., & Siim, B. (2017, June 8). A Janus-faced feminism: Gender in women-led right-wing populist parties. Paper presented at European Conference on Gender & Politics. https://www.researchgate.net/publication/332703804_A_Janus-faced_feminism_Gender_in_women-led_right-wing_populist_parties

Merkel, A. (2024). *Freedom*. Pan Macmillan.

Monteverde, G. (2017). Navigating Complicity in Contemporary Feminist Discourse. In: *Exploring Complicity: Concept, Cases and Critique*, edited by Afxentis Afxentiou et al., Rowman and Littlefield, pp. 99–118.

Reuters. (2024, December 3). Leader of Iceland's Social Democrats invited to form new government. *Reuters*. https://www.reuters.com/world/europe/iceland-president-asks-leader-social-democrats-form-government-ruv-reports-2024-12-03

Saini, A. (2023). *The Patriarchs: How Men Came to Rule*. Fourth Estate.

Solnit, R. (2014). *Men Explain Things To Me*. Haymarket Books.

Tamale, S. (2020). *Decolonization and Afro-feminism*. Daraja Press.

The Ministry for Economic Cooperation and Development (BMZ). (2023, March 1). Feminist development policy. https://www.bmz.de/en/issues/feminist-development-policy

UN Women. (2023, March 7). Women in power in 2023: New data shows progress but wide regional gaps. https://www.unwomen.org/en/news-stories/press-release/2023/03/women-in-power-in-2023-new-data-shows-progress-but-wide-regional-gaps

UN Women. (2024, October 2). Facts and figures: Leadership and political participation. https://www.unwomen.org/en/what-we-do/leadership-and-political-participation/facts-and-figures

United Nations. (2022, November 15). Mary Robinson: We need transformative decisions. https://www.un.org/en/climatechange/voices-from-cop27/mary-robinson

Part III
Reclaiming Power in a Feminist Way

7
The Recollection of Knowledge – What We Can Learn from Past and Present Matriarchies

If we ponder the previous chapters' deliberations on patriarchal power pathologies and women's (including our own) complicity with upholding patriarchal structures and mechanisms, the underlying power dynamics begin to reveal their fatal course. We realize: Perceived power receives attention, which supports more power generation. If power is held predominantly by men; if power in societal and institutional contexts is mainly mediated by men; if power is exerted within a male reference system and sanctioned according to male definitions, complicity with patriarchal power structures is almost unavoidable. However regrettable it may seem, it becomes understandable why women seeking power and influence, while entangled in patriarchal complicity, often don't support one another. Within a patriarchal framework, supporting other women can be seen as aligning with the 'weak' or those perceived as lacking power. Protecting or fighting for the weak and marginalized is an important human trait, actually a survival trait for the human race and a cornerstone of egalitarian societies. Many women do have this sweet spot of caring for those that are pushed into the background. Without this deeply human side our patriarchal civilization would not have survived until now. Yet, in the power dynamics described in the previous chapters, it does not come as a surprise that this caring role, which is so important for human societies, is neglected, ignored and undervalued.

The desire for power under these conditions pushes women to adapt to male-centric power structures. If they aren't conscious of this dynamic, they risk being drawn toward the type of authority that is attributed to men. In today's world, participating in power often means reinforcing male dominance. For women to truly support each other in their pursuit of power, they must recognize these underlying forces and intentionally resist being shaped by them. Understanding the female dynamics of attention to power under patriarchal circumstances is crucial.

If female power is rare and those few women in power act either like men or at least within a male-defined reference system, power attention continues

DOI: 10.4324/9781003508885-10

to go to men. In patriarchal thinking, being a woman often carries negative connotations, even if subtly in modern societies. Within the current male-dominated framework of power, identifying with women rarely equates to identifying with power. When these mental structures are deeply ingrained in consciousness, it creates a logic in which women compete for validation and appreciation by men, because men are generally perceived as having more power. We could argue that today, in the 21st century, there are already so many women in power positions, and there have been so many female political leaders and heads of state that by now the consciousness must have shifted from perceiving female power as an exception to seeing it as a normality. We could further argue that, particularly in corporations, there has been a shift towards acknowledging female leadership styles as decisively different and more suitable for the health of an organization. Soft skills, as the human and caring element in leadership is often called, have become an essential element of leadership development for men and women. But the underlying current of power transfer to men remains intact. What would happen if women began to see each other as genuinely powerful, pay attention to each other's power and enact this perception so that it shifts reality? Would this be a pathway to shifting the rules of the patriarchal game?

The dream is not new, but in a number of feminist utopia, changing the rules of the game was only envisaged as possible with clear separation from men. Accompanying the emergence of feminist movements was the vision of powerful women who organize women-only societies and economics differently, according to a reference system that some may call female, others simply call life-serving. Rokeya Hossain's utopia of *Ladyland* was one among many.[1] In her future vision no men could disturb the clear rationality of life- and society-serving female leadership. They were locked way. In Charlotte Perkins Gilman's novel *Herland*, written in 1915, published as a book only in 1979, a female society lives in an isolated area in Latin America and is composed entirely of women.[2] They have been cut off from the rest of the world for a long time as a result of a natural disaster through which all men died. With no men living among them, women develop a harmonious community guided by a spirit of cooperation and mutual respect, free from conflict, crime and inequality. Education is highly valued, mental faculties are cherished, intellectual pursuits encouraged and everybody is dedicated to continuous learning. Knowledge and wisdom are valued highly. Motherhood is rendered important in order to secure the future of the community. It happens through parthenogenesis. No men are needed. *Herland* describes a society in which resources are shared, and decision-making is consensus-driven. The women exhibit a strong sense of solidarity and collective responsibility for the well-being of their community.[3]

In Sally Miller Gearhart's novel *The Wanderground – Stories of the Hill Women*, published in 1978, a collective of women flee from the male-dominated cities, and take refuge in nature in a secluded, all-female community in the wilderness.[4] Their intention is to live in harmony with each other and nature. The women are endowed with psychic abilities of telepathy as means of communication as well as the capability of mentally lifting and moving heavy objects. Unlike the other two utopias, there is still a connection to the dystopic world of patriarchy, in which conditions for women worsen. There is increased control of women in cities, their lives become even more endangered and men are encroaching into borderlands, making the separate world of women more fragile.

If we travel centuries back, we can find a fiction of a female society in Christine de Pizan's *The Book of the City of Ladies*, written in 1405, in which she redefines the concept of lady as a woman of noble spirit rather than social status.[5] In the attempt to challenge the prevailing misogynistic culture of her time she counteracts harmful stereotypes about women by inviting a whole range of present and ancestral women into the city of ladies. Her female advisor *Lady Reason* helps her to build protective walls against the men's influence and shows how the female power of intellect and rationality dismantles patriarchal narratives and recognizes the inherent worth of women. Her second advisor, *Lady Rectitude*, helps her to construct the houses of the city and fill them with virtuous women of diverse backgrounds. She highlights women's capacity for prophecy, chastity and devotion, and their important contributions throughout history. Her third advisor, *Lady Justice*, helps to equip the city and convince the women to defend it against slander. She urges them to uphold their integrity and reputation. With the allegory of the city, Christine de Pizan built a utopian space, in which women honor and empower each other through simply knowing and understanding the legacy of high-spirited women throughout history.

These are just four out of presumably millions of utopias that women have been writing or thinking about. If we had the aforementioned meticulously kept archive of forgotten female manuscripts that would reach back for millennia, we would find many dreams of a different world constructed by women – separate from men – hidden in pictures and stories. Is the separation from men a prerequisite for female power lived within a female reference system? Or are these utopias a reaction to the continuous intrusions of patriarchy and, like the Amazons in the jungle of the world's most mysterious river, a different society could only survive in a protected space? Were these utopias imaginations of a dreamed future civilization or unearthed memories of a distant past, in which another civilizational arrangement was built on the power of women?

These questions are important for our endeavor toward a *collective feminist power practice*, yet they cannot be answered with any certainty. What we learn from the utopias is that lived female power and the establishment of a female reference system might require some kind of protection from patriarchal power pathologies. The existence of societies grounded in female power has often been called a myth. But, as mentioned before, there is ample research that could remove the veils and turn the myths into knowledge about different forms of societal arrangements that are relevant for our future. Most importantly, this knowledge about female power shaping societies in a peaceful way has survived until today. It resiliently encroaches into the patriarchal space. The traces of these different forms of civilizational fragments, which not only feature women as a source of power, but also have a different way of relating to life in its complexity and diversity, have always survived somehow and somewhere throughout the last thousands of years. They show up in utopian stories, in music, in painting, in female activism, in Indigenous communities, in feminist circles. For a *collective feminist power practice*, it is important that we sharpen our perception so that we see and acknowledge this scattered knowledge. Because only with recognition is there acknowledgment, and only with acknowledgment is there the possibility of taking elements of this past and present into the future of humanity. Above all, the more we see the fragments of female power practices, the more we realize their connection.

We can recognize a globality that once existed thousands of years ago as it does today, and thus we can see through this global tapestry of alternative pasts into possible futures. This can inspire us to add a new notion to the many efforts towards peaceful, ecologically sound and socially just development efforts that evenly spread throughout the globe. Digitalization is helping us uncover this knowledge, these attitudes to life, this very mentality of life-serving purposes. It encourages us to believe that the consciousness of humankind may indeed shift, despite the increasing number of wars, and the mounting crises that are not always dealt with in a humane way.

However, I believe we need to go a step further and expose today's world to a knowledge that is as old as the civilizational endeavor of humankind. Imagine a critical mass of people begin to render and name patriarchy in its manifold variations a pathology that has brought, despite technical and social advancements, a continuation of destruction: Enslavement, wars, rape, the climate crises, social and economic injustice. Imagine a critical mass of people in the world knew, because they have been taught, that societies existed that had a better way of dealing with crises, conflicts and challenges. Nothing is more urgent at this time of human evolution than realizing that humankind was once capable of living in societal arrangements inspired by female power without wars. Indeed, as many historic accounts show, these societies were built on happiness, because happiness and vitality were so central to their civilizations.[6] If we look at the history of humanity from the perspective of the survival of fragments of these civilizations, we begin to analyze religious, political, social and economic developments in a completely different way. Yet, we have more than fragments of the past. Many foundations of these past civilizations have survived, albeit adjusted to the patriarchal mainstream, in the form of female-oriented societies on islands or in remote areas. They exist today, often devalued as poor communities that are seen as having an outdated and strangely different lifestyle: The Mosuo in China, the Minangkabau in Indonesia, the Khasi in India, the Lovedu in South Africa, the Bemba in Zambia, the Akan in Ghana, the Bijago in Guinea-Bissao, the Kuna in Panama and Colombia, the Zapotec in Mexico, and many more.[7] These societies are different in lifestyle, customs, organization, governance and belief systems. What they have in common is that women enjoy high social status and that power in the hands of women is normal. If we created a world map, we would understand the wealth of knowledge that still exists about powerful women.

Yet, it is important to note that such societies seldom have or had female-only communities. The female-only communities seem to have emerged in protection from men who exerted patriarchal power or have become the utopian dreams in resistance to the patriarchy. As we have seen, patriarchy becoming the dominant mode of organizing societies did not happen within centuries – it has emerged slowly, more violently in some areas than others, with fierce resistance by people who wanted to continue their matriarchal culture, with surrender to necessities in some places, with welcoming integration in others. Neither can we assume that there was a universal form of societal arrangements in the form of female-oriented societies across the globe. People, cultures and contexts were different back then as they are today.

The science journalist Angela Saini, in her book *The Patriarchs*, explores these different lived realities of female-oriented or female-powered societies in the past and in the present.[8] None of them was or is the longed-for paradise that can model humankind's future. But all of them hold a piece of a puzzle that could help us make sense of a feminist future beyond patriarchy. Angela Saini distinguishes, as many others do, between *matrilineal* societies, in which descent is traced through the female line and property is inherited by female descendants; *matrilocal* societies, in which men move into the women's clan or home after marriage; and *matrifocal* societies, in which women are the head of the family. Yet, in many communities or societies, past and present, in which female power was highly acknowledged, these differentiations may blur. Some display all of them, others under certain circumstances some of the features, still others may have only kept rituals, customs, values and habits, yet on the surface they may look like patriarchal societies. Riane Eisler has coined the term *gylany* for societies in which the sexes were balanced in equality and linked in a cooperative way, but not hierarchically ranked in superiority and subordination, which is typical of patriarchal societies.[9] The philosopher and scientist Heide Göttner-Abendroth dedicated her lifework to the study of ancient and contemporary non-patriarchal societies across the globe. She advocates using *matriarchy* as an overarching term to describe societal arrangements that demonstrate balance between the sexes, with female spiritual and economic power being central. Her reasoning seeks to reclaim and reframe the concept, moving away from the common misconception that matriarchies are a mirror image of patriarchy, where women dominate men. She argues that, tracing the term back to its Greek roots, it more accurately means 'in the beginning the mothers.'[10] Research on matriarchal societies shows no evidence of women dominating men as in patriarchal systems, but it does show that women often held decision-making and economic power, and were vital to the survival of these societies. For the purposes of this book, I will follow the recommendation to use *matriarchy* and *matriarchal* as terms describing societies or elements within them that demonstrate gender parity, peaceful conflict resolution, social equality, reverence for nature, and the centrality of female power.

I render the continuous feminist discourse on such societal arrangements important. A lot has been unearthed, but the exploration of diverse cultures and civilizations where women held central roles in governance, decision-making and social organization should not end. On the contrary, I encourage you to journey into the historic matriarchies and matriarchal fragments of your own cultural context. Because it will shift your perception from the patriarchal concealment of female power and the separateness of women's reality, indeed their loneliness, towards the presence of female strength and power that persists even in the most difficult circumstances. Matriarchal worldviews are part of our everyday life, often secretly, sometimes buried under the rubble of crises and atrocities, but nonetheless living. For a *collective feminist power practice*, we must tune in to this hidden layer of reality – like an undertone that continues to resonate and demands our attention. The moment we begin to listen to this undertone, it is suddenly everywhere. Our task is to make it sound loud again, so that, one day, it will override the sounds of patriarchy. This encompasses our ability to discern matriarchal moments, structures, events and patterns. By actively attending to these elements of our reality, we infuse our worldly encounters with different interpretations, thereby reinforcing and nurturing this alternate worldview. It changes our view of reality, like putting on a new lens that sees through the fiction of patriarchy. It enables us to see the pathological power that comes from that fiction, and to penetrate the surface in a way that makes us feel a different kind power – if we connect with timeless female knowledge from around the globe. We must collect and redefine this power. This is not about dreaming, but about gaining strength in believing in and constructing possible futures. It is the prerequisite for claiming and building power in a feminist way.

Here is just a tiny example. I currently live in northern Germany – a landscape that has been formed by the ice age. The rocks that travelled far from the north of Europe settled roaringly in the midst of the melting ice that formed hills, valleys and as many crystal-clear lakes as you may want to enjoy swimming in. In the past centuries human desire for wood as a resource for glass production led to deforestation, intelligent insight empowered reforestation, while later socialist, today capitalist, industrial agriculture took and takes a toll on the resilience of the ecosystems, although the area is declared a nature park. Climate change lets the groundwater drop, endangers the forests and makes the lakes shrink in such a gradual way that most people still do not notice the threat. Within these landscapes lie thousands of burial sites, impossible to plough because of the rocks. Hence around the pebbles and rocks nature could partly regenerate and so the fields and meadows are sprinkled with these tiny extra hills, which are a nuisance for farmers, but which lie confidently in the landscape and offer refuge for everything that wants to survive the chemistry of agriculture. Of course, some of these sites have been researched, they have been declared burial sites from the bronze age. But why would people scatter these sites in the landscape with such an enormous effort and in such an incredible number? I wandered many times through the landscape, discovered that the views from some of the burial sites were breathtaking in relation to the hills and the lakes, and that almost all sites were within sight of each other. It was the deep dive into the matriarchal culture that, in a distant past between 7000 and 4000 years ago had spread throughout Europe, that let me begin to see a different landscape. Among others, it is Heide Göttner Abendrot who suggests that people in matriarchal societies were able to *read* landscapes, as she calls it.[11] What she means is that they were able to recognize certain patterns in landscapes and, above all, perceive energy patterns. In their life-affirming culture they did what they could to reinforce these energy patterns through the way they laid out paths, roads, cities, houses and burial sites. Most importantly the latter were sacred sites that empowered people to communicate throughout the landscape over long distances. Through the creation of these energy points, the energetic potential that was already in the landscape was strengthened in order to further support the communities living in these landscapes. The readings helped me see the landscape in a different way. Suddenly, there was a logic to the order of what appeared as cultural interventions into the landscape. Unlike our modern interventions with buildings and roads, these sacred sites functioned as part of a language of the landscape that we today cannot understand anymore. Interestingly, the Christian churches, built a few millennia later, turned out to be constructed on these artificial hills with stunning views.

Matriarchal cultures and worldviews in Europe have gone underground, but they do exist. In most other parts of the world, these cultures survived so that their social arrangements, their economic organization and their way of organizing gender relations can be scientifically analyzed even today. Yet, given the above plea to look at knowledge production not only in scientific terms, there is much more to matriarchal worldviews than the detailed account of certain practices. I could probably only begin to understand the landscape of the nature park in northern Germany because I had lived in Zimbabwe for years, a country with both Shona and Ndebele people having an extremely close relationship with the landscapes. Hills have spirits, rocks, too, and rivers. Living in the countryside meant harsh conditions compared to modern lifestyles in the city, but it also meant being embedded – as a person and collectively – in an enchanted, spirited landscape that required relating and communicating. Some may consider this romantic nonsense, yet, far beyond a few esoteric Westerners, it is the daily reality of many people in the world. They hold a form of knowledge that may be crucial for our future.

You may consider this not scientific evidence of the landscaping influence of previous civilizations that had a different relationship to the surrounding nature than modern men. The intertwining of observations, research into artifacts from matriarchal societies and intuitive knowledge would not match contemporary scientific standards. But does it need to? A lot of female-held knowledge around the world is produced in the space between experiential insights, observable facts, retold stories, information passed down through generations and modern scientific analysis. I am convinced that feminist transformations need to be built on these different forms of knowledge, in acknowledgment of their validity.

The individual discovery of matriarchal patterns, traditions or stories is infinitely important. But it is of limited use to us collectively, because it may only reinforce our individual sense of longing and homelessness in the patriarchal world. The connection to a matriarchal worldview requires structure, so that it becomes a collective memory and part of our everyday knowledge, beyond myths and beyond esoteric rituals. With diversity of knowledge production in mind, let us therefore uncover the lessons embedded in the fabric of past and present matriarchies in a more systematic way. How did and do matriarchal societies organize power and governance, resolve conflicts, cultivate social cohesion and secure wealth?

As mentioned, matriarchal societies of past and present display as much variety and complexity as there are geographical contexts and historic or cultural developments, resistance to patriarchal influences or forced reshaping by our modern world. But in order to understand the wealth of knowledge, let us look at overarching social patterns and principles of matriarchal societal arrangements. Let us highlight what we may learn for feminist transformations and *collective feminist power practices*.[12] Let us also note where we can find similar existing or emerging patterns and principles in our contemporary societies, or where we have difficulty being inspired by the principles. As in all societies, social, economic, cultural and political levels intertwine. But for the purpose of structure, let us look at each of these levels separately.

For the **social fabric**, kinship is the most important element in matriarchal societies. As the basis for social structures, it shapes communal living arrangements. The social organizing unit is the clan, which, depending on the form of matriarchal tradition, includes matrilineal (inheritance traced exclusively through the female line) and matrifocal (men move for marriages into the clan of the woman) arrangements. Clans are usually composed of multiple generations, while primarily women live together. There is one, sometimes several clan mothers, plus their daughters and granddaughters, along with related men such as brothers, sons and grandsons. Despite many variations, across all these societies, generally women hold significant power of disposition over the goods of the clan. This particularly includes the power to control the sources of nourishment: Land, agricultural products and food. Male–female relationships, often called marriages, although they do not resemble our contemporary forms of legal marriages, serve as a means to connect clans within the broader community. Mutual marriages between members of different clans are common practice to foster inter-clan relationships. Paternity is not emphasized; even if biological fatherhood is known, it is rather disregarded. The practice is that men assume the task of social fatherhood towards the children of their sisters. Some matriarchal societies practice what is called the visiting marriage, where husbands spend nights with their wives in neighboring clan-houses but return to their maternal home at dawn. Sexual freedom for both genders is positively sanctioned, a sequence of changing partners over a lifetime normal. Children belong to the mother's clan; hence it is the mother's bloodline that counts. Women are usually physically strong and trained. In some of these societies gender roles can be fluid, men can assume mothering roles or women live in close relationships with women. Through the marriage customs and communal living in clans, nobody stays alone, is isolated from the community or not cared for. Within villages or towns, all are interconnected either by birth or through marriage, forming a cohesive network of kinship ties. The overall social fabric is like an *interconnected network of kinship clans*: Horizontal, non-hierarchical and to a large degree egalitarian, with acknowledgment of the clan mother(s) as natural authority.

The **economic structures** of matriarchal societies are deeply influenced by their social fabric centered around clans. Traditionally, matriarchal societies are based on subsistence agriculture. This ranges from gardening to land cultivation to sophisticated irrigation systems in more urbanized cultures. Technological invention was throughout history part of these societies – examples are weaving, pottery and metalworks. Matriarchal economies operate without private property. Hence, there are no territorial claims, but a system of usage rights over the land and resources. The guiding principle is the understanding that Mother Earth's abundance is shared among all people as gifts, not possessions. Over time economies became more complex, and there are many variations of allocation of tasks between the genders, but overall women hold significant power over agricultural goods, trading, herding products, hunting pray, fishing yields and handicraft products. Female economic power resembles the generosity of Mother Nature. The matriarchs within the clans, and wealthier clans within societies, distribute goods equally among clan members for their sustenance and protection. There are differences in wealth, but societal rules prevent accumulation and exploitation. Land and houses are owned collectively by the clan, with women serving as guardians and distributors of essential goods. These are distributed based on kinship lines and marriage patterns, preventing accumulation by any individual or group and reinforcing principles of reciprocity. Fostering a culture of sharing and giving is common practice. For example, at seasonal festivals, more affluent clans host the entire village, giving away their goods as gifts, ensuring that no one remains in poverty. Caring for all, ensuring no one loses out, is deeply embedded in economic practices, leading to different forms of mutual support and preventing competition for goods. Ensuring economic distributive justice is an important element maintaining a balance in the community.

Political decision-making in matriarchal societies is also deeply rooted in kinship clan structures. Forms of governance vary depending on the context, the degree of matriarchal organization and the exposure to the patriarchal world. But guiding principles are achieving consensus and ensuring equality in the sense of listening to different voices. Within the closer clan community, e.g., within the house, both women and men participate in a form of council meetings to discuss domestic matters, sometimes separately. Everybody in the household is included, and the principle remains that decisions are reached through consensus. At the village level, representatives of each of the clans, mostly chosen by the matriarchs, gather in the form of village councils to deal with all issues that concern the village. In some societies, brothers and sons are chosen for this role, which is usually the role of a go-between, and not that of a decision-maker.[13] Also decisions at the village level are achieved by consensus, so that no clan can dominate the process. This can be time-consuming, as the representatives may need to go back to their clans, discuss the matter again, and come back to the village council. Similarly, at a regional level, representatives from all villages come together in the form of regional council meetings. They exchange decisions made at the village level, and coordinate any actions. Again, representatives' function is to convey information. The decision-making power remains at the village and at the clan level. We can consider this a *decentralized approach to governance* that prevents the accumulation of political power and ensures that decisions reflect the collective will of the community. There is no ruling class, nothing similar to our modern representative democracies, and instead strong inclusivity. The system may not always be ideal, but in principle it ensures that minority voices are not marginalized, but instead integrated into the decision-making process, even if this may take time. Political decision-making takes place through decentralized governance, reflecting the attitude that diversity in opinions enriches the quality of decisions, and that *consensus-building decision-making* takes the society as whole into a peaceful future. Dialogue, negotiation and conflict resolution are prioritized.

The **cultural environment** of matriarchal societies is rich and complex. It is contextualized and embedded in the particular surroundings of nature, landscape and weather patterns. Based on their specific historic traditions and experiences, belief systems, rites, myths and spiritual customs develop in conjunction with the underlying principles of reverence for life and Mother Earth. For many the concept of rebirth in a concrete sense is central to their belief system: Individuals are reincarnated within their own clan through the women of their lineage. This belief underscores the profound respect accorded to women, because they are seen as the givers of rebirth, ensuring the perpetuation of the clan. Many of these societies are experiential scientists in the sense of detailed observations of the natural world, where herbs for healing grow and cycles of growth, decay and renewal become a foundation for understanding life. Celestial phenomena, such as the rising and setting of stars, the sun and the moon, are meticulously observed and understood as part of the cosmic cycle of creation and destruction that influences the lives of the individual as much as the society. Many matriarchal societies have creation myths featuring goddesses or Earth Mothers of various kinds. The matriarchal worldview is a systemic approach without any dualistic thinking that would, for example, separate the spirit from nature or the society from nature. Human existence is perceived as intimately connected to the cycles of nature, devoid of rigid distinctions between good and evil. Life and death are seen as integral parts of the cosmic order, with each phase necessary and meaningful in its own time. Male and female beings are seen as complementary, fluid and dynamic cosmic polarities, each possessing inherent value and significance. Cultural practices ensure the veneration of ancestors, honoring the *sacredness of Earth and the cosmos* and subsequently the ritualization of daily tasks.

While reading these analytic descriptions of female-oriented societal arrangements, what did your comments column say? Did you feel the urge to scientifically question the existence of matriarchies? Or did you think this is too much wishful thinking in a too ideal description of peaceful societies? Or did you feel attracted and, if possible, would want to live in such a society? Or, on the contrary, did you feel repelled by a feeling of constriction, thinking how it would have been to grow up in such a society?

As mentioned at the beginning of this chapter, I am not suggesting we recreate matriarchal societies, but I believe we need to know their essence and principles, because they hold a knowledge that is paramount for our future. Moreover, they remind us that in some places today and once upon a time, the paradigm of how we as humans relate to the planet Earth (notice that many people would not dare to say Mother Earth anymore) and each other was different, and it is time for a shift in global consciousness that picks up at least some of these principles. Donella Meadows would be happy to know; so would be Rokeya Hossain. Many elements of matriarchal societies have been part and parcel of scientific development of the past hundred years, have been declared discoveries in modern organizational development, have become principles of transformation processes and have inspired the sustainability movement: Dialogue and consensus-building, good governance, protection of nature, social responsibility, network building and collaboration. Moreover, feminists have experimented with elements of matriarchal societies today and for centuries. What I am suggesting is that the wisdom of matriarchal societal arrangements has been buried and rebirthed, assimilated, appropriated and utilized. It lives on, even though hardly anybody recognizes it. Let us unpack this with a few examples, while I encourage you to put on the matriarchal lens and find many more examples in your social settings.

Let us start with the *social fabric* and the *political decision-making*. While the term 'clan' may evoke negative connotations because it reminds us of today's clan crime in strongly patriarchal societies, we need to acknowledge that kinship communities are a human form of organizing, who belongs and who not, that is as old as humankind. Where there are no communities of belonging and mutual care, societies deteriorate. Where they become too rigid in building boundaries, societies degenerate into conflict. What we learn from matriarchal societies is *balance*. This means belonging, inclusivity with rules, yet also exchange, permeable boundaries through dialogue and relationships, as well as the realization that every community needs to negotiate its vitality with other communities. In that way, matriarchal societies seem to be up to date with systems theory. The evolutional biologist Elizabeth Sahtouris suggests that systems thrive in *mutual consistency*, a term describing the worked-out balance between systems, subsystems and the larger whole through dialogue and negotiation.[14] This takes place between the needs and identity of the smaller whole and the needs and the identity of the larger whole. Relative autonomy is constantly negotiated within the larger whole. This process, as the systems scientist and environmental activist Joanna Macy says, shows the system's intelligence.[15] The openness to dialogue makes a system more vulnerable, but also more able to adapt to changes and learn. Power in such a system is distributed and decentralized, which is an important feature for the much-needed sustainability transformations. If we think that the consensus-building process between the communities of belonging sounds arduous for our fast-paced time, we need to notice that it has found its way into many contemporary settings, not perfectly modelled after matriarchies, yet discernably different from hierarchical patriarchal social structures. We find fragments in efforts towards the de-hierarchization of organizational structures, from learning organizations to consensus-building forms such as holacracy or sociocracy, both forms of decentralized management and organizational governance, built on equality, responsibility and self-organization. We find the fragments in multi-stakeholder dialogues that exist in all major sustainability efforts as inclusive and consensus-building processes. We can find elements in our democracies, or in modern citizen assemblies, and we can recognize remnants in corporations picking up traditional forms of dialogue that are most known on the African continent.[16] None of the protagonists of these approaches, most of them men, would make the connection to matriarchal societies, but present these advancements as entirely new. As feminists, we should make the connection.

Let us continue with *economic structures* and the *cultural environment*. We have looked at the destructive effects of patriarchal pathologies in securing economic power for men and the wealthy. Matriarchal societies may have wealth difference, but according to their paradigm of ensuring a *Good Life for All*, they have developed a variety of measures to distribute wealth. Hence, the belief that the community thrives if all of its members are cared for is deeply embedded in the thinking of matriarchal societies. This also extends to the non-human world. We know that in patriarchy, most prominent in the Western world, the neoliberal paradigm pertains in which everybody is responsible for their own individual wealth creation. It is a cornerstone for all societal arrangements, and for many this sounds much more attractive than the collective matriarchal responsibilities. Some sub-Saharan cultures still know the practice of human interconnectedness, expressed in different terms, but most known as *Ubuntu*, a Zulu word often translated as 'I am, because you are.'[17] It is not just seen as a philosophical concept, but the capability of people to live in acknowledgment of the interconnectedness of humankind and nature. This can also mean that as you grow your wealth, you are responsible for giving the benefits to your kinship community. African friends of mine complain that its neoliberal and patriarchal distortion leads to strange excesses: Men, sometimes women, use every leeway to gather money, not shying away from corruption, in order to make large gifts to their kinship communities. This, in turn, raises their status and power.

We have seen that the caring for all, in principle, was anchored in socialist movements, albeit never fully realized in socialist states under the circumstances of patriarchy. It also did and does exist in capitalist societies as a measure to avoid letting societies deteriorate into chaos. Social security measures and progressive tax systems are, particularly in social market economies, a way to ensure a minimum of wealth distribution. Hence, the underlying principle of wealth distribution, economic distributive justice and caring for all has – often in distorted fragments – survived throughout history. We have learned that reviving this paradigm is more important than ever for our future, as the widening gap between rich and poor, between countries, but also within countries is a recipe for disaster.[18]

But matriarchal societies, in all their varieties, have another aspect of the emerging paradigm shift. It is the *purpose of economies* that is directed towards the well-being of individuals *and* the community, while at the same time using, worshipping and serving nature. In view of today's facts that patriarchal pathologies lead to environmental destruction, the climate crises, wealth and income gaps and increasing military conflicts, redefining the purpose of economies and connecting it with a healthy nature is more than urgent. Many scattered fragments of a paradigm shift already exist: The sustainability movement, sustainable agriculture movements, new economic concepts such as the sharing economy, the care economy, the solidarity economy, the well-being economy, the feminist economy. We'll dive deeper into this in Part V of this book.

Matriarchal societies hold a crucial essence of what we need for transforming into a future that ensures a *Good Life for All*. Many women and feminists know this, stay connected to the matriarchal paradigm, promote, support and listen to women from Indigenous nations and communities in order to amplify the paradigms that can help us into the future. Some create intentional communities, in which it is possible to live such values in protected spaces. Others may be repelled by the perceived rigidness of such communities. We do not all need to take the same path. But for organizing feminist transformations and developing a feminist practice of power, it is important to acknowledge the possibilities that exist in matriarchal paradigms, observe their often-distorted remnants in our current societies and notice the global paradigm shift that is already under way, still scattered, too weak, but nonetheless existent.

Major insights for *collective feminist power practices* from the recollection of knowledge about past and present matriarchies:

1. We should consider that women, over the course of history and today, hold substantial knowledge about non-patriarchal and intelligent ways of organizing societies. This is evident both in feminist utopia and in the research into contemporary and ancient matriarchal societies.
2. We know that the existence of ancient egalitarian, peaceful societal arrangements built on female power has long been contested and declared a myth, even by feminists. However, ample research shows that a variety of societal arrangements with strong female power and gender parity must have existed in the past and still exist today in many areas of the world.
3. Unearthing the essence across different forms of matriarchies reveals interesting patterns, such as interconnected networks of kinship clans, economic distributive justice, decentralized consensus-building decision-making, sacredness of Earth and the cosmos.
4. By understanding these cross-cutting principles and paradigms, we may draw insights for organizing a *collective feminist power practice* while avoiding patriarchal power pathologies.
5. Diving deeper into ancient and contemporary knowledge of matriarchal societal arrangements also helps us shift and strengthen our perception: We notice how these principles have survived as knowledge and practice fragments throughout herstory and begin to emerge as building blocks of future societal arrangements.
6. We do not want to simply copy and paste ancient and contemporary matriarchal societal arrangements into a feminist future, but use female and feminist knowledge building to recreate a new normal: The possibility of peaceful, egalitarian societies that live within our planetary boundaries.

Notes

1 Hossain (2005).
2 Perkins Gilman (1979).
3 See Donaldson (1989).
4 Miller Gearhart (2002).
5 De Pizan (1999).

6 Riane Eisler in her book *The Chalice and the Blade* elaborated this using the example of the gynocritic societies of Crete in Greece which survived on the island for much longer than in other areas in Europe. See Eisler (2011).
7 Göttner-Abendroth (2022).
8 See Saini (2023).
9 Eisler (1981).
10 Göttner-Abendroth (2017), also supported by Reeves Sanday (1998).
11 Göttner-Abendroth (2014).
12 The insights are derived from various sources. Among them are Amadiume (1987), Eisler (2011), Reeves Sanday (1998), Göttner-Abendroth (2017, 2019, 2022).
13 This fact often led anthropologists to assume that men were in governance and decision-making roles, because they arrived with their biased patriarchal thinking.
14 Sahtouris (2000 p. 23).
15 Macy (2021).
16 One example is the Lekgotla, a way of governance practiced by traditional societies in the Southern African region. It is a forum for open communication and decision-making with the participation of usually all adult members of a community. The approach has been taken up in leadership development by De Liefde (2007).
17 Sylvia Tamale (2020) hints to the fact that across African cultures there are different terms, but they all refer to a similar understanding.
18 See Dixson-Declève (2022).

References

Amadiume, I. (1987). *African Matriarchal Foundations: The Igbo Case*. London: Karnak House.

de Liefde, W. (2007). *Lekgotla: The Art of Leadership Through Dialogue*. Jacana Media.

de Pizan, C. (1999). *The Book of the City of Ladies*. Penguin UK. Written in 1405.

Dixson-Declève, S., Gaffney, O., Ghosh, J., Randers, J., Rockström, J., & Stoknes, P.E. (2022). *Earth For All: A Survival Guide for Humanity*. A report to the Club of Rome. New Society Publishers.

Donaldson, L.E. (1989). The eve of de-struction: Charlotte Perkins Gilman and the feminist recreation of paradise. *Women's Studies*, *16*(3–4), 373–387. https://doi.org/10.1080/00497878.1989.9978776

Eisler, R. (1981). Gylany: The balanced future. *Futures*, *13*(6), 499–507. https://doi.org/10.1016/0016-3287(81)90105-1

Eisler, R. (2011). *The Chalice and the Blade: Our History, Our Future*. Harper Collins.

Goettner-Abendroth, H. (2017). Matriarchal studies: Past debates and new foundations. *Asian Journal of Women's Studies*, *23*(1), 2–6. https://doi.org/10.1080/12259276.2017.1283843

Göttner-Abendroth, H. (2014). *Matriarchale Landschaftsmythologie: Von der Ostsee bis Süddeutschland*. Kohlhammer

Göttner-Abendroth, H. (2019). *Geschichte matriarchaler Gesellschaften und Entstehung des Patriarchats: Band III: Westasien und Europa* (Das Matriarchat, III, Band 3). Kohlhammer.

Göttner-Abendroth, H. (2022). *Matriarchale Gesellschaften der Gegenwart: Band II: Amerika, Indien, Afrika* (Das Matriarchat, II, Band 3). Kohlhammer Verlag.

Hossain, R.S. (2005). *Sultana's Dream; and Padmarag: Two Feminist Utopias*. Penguin New Delhi (India).

Macy, J. (2021). *World as Lover, World as Self: 30th Anniversary Edition*. Parallax Press.

Miller Gearhart, S. (2002). *Wanderground*. Spinsters Ink. Written in 1979.

Perkins Gilman, C. (1979). *Herland*. Pantheon. Written in 1915.

Reeves Sanday, P. (1998). Matriarchy as a Sociocultural Form: An Old Debate in a New Light. https://web.sas.upenn.edu/psanday/articles/selected-articles/matriarchy-as-a-sociocultural-form-an-old-debate-in-a-new-light. Paper presented at the 16th congress of the Indo-Pacific Prehistoric Association, Melaka, Malaysia, 1–7 July.

Sahtouris, E. (2000). *Earthdance: Living Systems in Evolution*. Iuniverse.com, Inc.

Saini, A. (2023). *The Patriarchs: How Men Came to Rule*. Fourth Estate.

Tamale, S. (2020). *Decolonization and Afro-Feminism: An Afro-Feminist-Legal Critique*. Daraja Press.

8
Female Genealogies – Why Female Power and Female Freedom are Intrinsically Linked

An interesting article was published in November 2020 in the *Proceedings of the National Academy of Sciences* (*PNAS*), a highly acclaimed American science journal. The researchers wanted to find out whether, in the matriarchal Mosuo society of China, the fact that women had much greater autonomy had an impact on the health of men and women.[1] The findings suggest that this is positively the case. Because the wider Mosuo communities know both matrilineal and patrilineal factions, a comparison was possible. It is globally researched that women tend to have a longer life span, but also a higher morbidity. While some researchers ascribe this purely to biology, it has been shown that health outcomes are intricately intertwined with social and cultural contexts. This, of course, includes gender norms that determine autonomy, resource distribution and social support systems. In order to test the hypothesis that female-centric gender norms mitigate health disparities between genders, the researchers analyzed gender differences in inflammation and hypertension in both matrilineal and patrilineal Mosuo communities. Notably, the generally assumed and observed gender-based health disparities were reversed in the matriarchal Mosuo societies. The researchers found a marked improvement in women's health without detrimental effects on men. In the matriarchal community, there was less hypertension and less chronic inflammation among women, while for men it was similar to the patrilinear communities.

One single medical study in one matriarchal society cannot be generalized, but the findings underscore that women's autonomy may significantly contribute to preventing their susceptibility to chronic diseases. In a non-scientific way, we would suggest the matriarchally organized women in the Mosuo societies were happier. We can dare to assume that they feel healthily free.

The Mosuo on China's Yunnan and Sichuan regions neighboring Tibet have been so much researched and visited that we can assume the external effects are changing the matriarchal culture. Different practices emerge as a result of exposure to the modern world, but for a long time the matriarchal communities

DOI: 10.4324/9781003508885-11

have been relatively isolated. This enabled them in the past to maintain distinctive cultural practices characterized by many feminist authors undoubtedly as matriarchies.[2] As is typical in matriarchal kinship clans, children inherit their mother's family name and reside with them throughout their lives. Household affairs, including financial decisions, are overseen by matriarchs, typically the grandmothers. Inheritance passes from mother to daughter. They practice the aforementioned visiting marriage. The practice is a form of serial monogamy, sometimes long term, but it can be ended any time if one or both partners decide so. It looks as if this is a way of avoiding gender conflicts and unattainable expectation. Women, unlike in many modern patriarchal societies, are not isolated. They do have their kinship relationships, which seem to support their self-confidence. Motherhood is rendered important. Children that result from the visiting marriages belong to and are raised in the mother's family, supported by their mother's sisters and brothers, so that paternal roles are assumed by many. They may know their fathers and pay respectful visits, but biological fatherhood does not mean parenting responsibilities. Social and kinship parenting keeps children nurtured and with ample possibilities to identify with female or male relatives: Mothers, aunts, uncles, grandmothers. There is no so-called nuclear family, as we have known it from Western societies since the beginning of industrialization. Men in matriarchal Mosuo communities do have some political influence, albeit less than women. The latter own and inherit property. Despite awareness of alternative societal structures elsewhere, Mosuo men usually express contentment with the matriarchal societal arrangements. Thus, while acknowledging the changes that are already happening, it seems that the matriarchy that has been more or less maintained over 2000 years has enabled women to enjoy significant autonomy and freedom, more so than in many other regions dominated by patriarchies. Is there an atmosphere of female kinship belonging that boosts happiness for women, makes motherhood easy and avoids unnecessary conflicts with male lovers?

Matriarchies are societies centered around maternal principles, encompassing caregiving, nurturing, mutual support and conflict resolution through negotiation. These values extend to all individuals, regardless of gender or parental status. Their aim is to ensure, and we would today say optimize, collective well-being. Thus, in matriarchies, motherhood evolves from a biological reality into motherliness as the cultural archetype of the society, extending to nature's capacity to create and feed life in all its forms of vitality. Women's connection to this life-giving force becomes the reference system around which these societies are organized.

I have not placed strong emphasis on this feature of *motherhood* as the core of a female reference system in the previous chapters, for a particular reason. Motherhood, in contemporary feminism, is a contentious topic. While the principle of motherhood seems to empower women in matriarchies, the confinements of it are at the center of upholding patriarchy; it is the patriarchal narrative for women's calling and destiny; it is the foundation for constructing patrilineal power structures; it is the reason for confining women to the domestic sphere. Motherhood is the short summary of women's unpaid jobs, their perceived closeness to nature and their reduction to biology. No wonder, women around the world have borne children, yet tried in many creative ways to escape the patriarchal consequences of motherhood. For good reasons, feminists do not want to be reduced to their biology and their potential to give birth. Yet, what if motherhood and female freedom were intrinsically linked? Because this is the conundrum: Redefining motherhood may need to become an essential element to move towards female freedom. Here the difficulties start. Let us unpack this.

But before we do this, I encourage you, particularly if you grew up or live in a Western context, drop for the time being any of your ideas about contemporary motherhood. Drop your criticism towards the women you perceive as overly motherly. Drop your bad conscience over not having a child. Drop any memory of either a loving or conflictual relationship with your mother. Drop your feeling of guilt, if you are or have been a working mother with too little time for your kids. Let us disconnect the term motherhood from any images of the so-called nuclear family that has conquered the world: Father, mother, child. Let us for now not get seduced by its variations: Father, father, child; or mother, mother, child; and not argue about the statistic reality of single mothers; less so single fathers.

The *nuclear family* is a very recent development in human history, even in Europe, from which its spread over the world as astonishing reality stems. The nuclear family is and always has been tied to a patriarchal and capitalist culture. Radically spoken, even if it may offend many people, the nuclear family is a product of patriarchal pathologies and capitalist strategies for economic power. For good reasons, it removes the focus on kinship of the extended family of sisters, brothers, grandparents, nieces, nephews, aunts and uncles that is still prevalent in so many cultures of the Global South. The social construct of the nuclear family, in psychological and practical arrangements, is much easier to keep under patriarchal control than the complexity of extended kinship communities.

The nuclear family model as a patriarchal stronghold is even orchestrated in cultures that display value system very different from Western societies. The Chinese culture, which traditionally saw the subordination of women to their fathers, then their husband, and later their sons in patrilineal clans, has kept a number of cultural elements that could be traced back to matriarchal origins or at least resemble some of the principles. For example, unlike the individualistic culture of the West, it has a strong emphasis on collective well-being. Man Fang, a Chinese psychotherapist and public policy scholar, mentions three elements of Chinese culture that remind us of the foundational principles of matriarchies.[3] The first is the urge for harmony with the result of consensus-building processes, based on the Confucian philosophy, in which the ethics of self and humanity is integrated with that of the family, the state and finally the world. The second is a strongly relational family-oriented ethical and behavioral reference system, in which the *We* is more important than the *I*. The individual is perceived as contextually embedded and interconnected in society in nature. The third is the primacy of the heart as the emotional ability of people to sense what we would call in systems theory a field of interaction. This enables people to sense what the collective needs are rather than just pushing their interests through. All three intertwine in the complex reality, are volatile in modern societal development and remain ambiguous for the individual. Yet, at the household level, the *nuclear family* has been and is the dominant mode of living.[4] Societies are changing, including the Chinese, but it is not surprising that China does not sanction the kind of female freedom and kinship organization of the Mosuo. For the Chinese government, the visiting marriages of the Mosuo that allow women and men low-conflict and long-term relationships are not culturally acceptable and are considered promiscuous.

For the European region, Silvia Federici meticulously analyzed the pivotal role that the cultural establishment of the *nuclear family* played in building and sustaining the social arrangements of capitalist societies.[5] It emerged at the beginning of industrialization in the 19th century as a social construction that ensured men as the primary labor force of capitalist industries would be nurtured and catered to by women within the household without any monetary compensation. The patriarchal and capitalist conflicts have been and still are lived out in the *nuclear family*. Violence and abuse against women and children as a means of subordination were the logical consequence. Despite the questionable functionality of the *nuclear family*, societal norms exerted moral influence and pressure on people to pursue the model in what is supposed to be a monogamous relationship for women, while for men promiscuity was and is culturally sanctioned. Later on, the relationship model developed its own dynamic and was societally romanticized as finding the lover of your life that should fulfill all expectations around partnership, parenting and soul-companionship. The *nuclear family* as a social construction has not supported female freedom, neither in its heteronormative nor in its same-sex variation. We know the current statistics of divorce and sequential monogamies of temporary life partners.[6]

In the early Soviet era, at the beginning of the 20th century, the communist and feminist revolutionary and later diplomat Alexandra Kollontaï wanted to free women from the domestic burdens of *nuclear families*.[7] She strongly advocated for women's sexual freedom, communal living and the equitable distribution of domestic labor between genders. In her view the establishment of community-based support services such as nurseries, communal kitchens and neighborhood laundry facilities was needed to empower women's contribution to political and economic societal development. Her vocal and courageous influence cannot be underestimated. Socialist countries have laid the basis for what is in many countries today the norm of partly public-financed child-care options or domestic work. Yet, austerity measures in some countries and the absence of extended family care options lead to increased reliance on the self-organization of the *nuclear family*. With all good intentions and support programs of advanced democratic governments, and acknowledgment of the economic advancements for women, attempts to overcome inequality while keeping the social construction of the *nuclear family* have not yet led to female freedom. Maybe, today, there is more hope for female freedom in the various complex settings of divorced couples, new relationships, children moving between biological and social fathers or mothers, almost like a network of loose kinship communities that require a lot of organization, but offer at least new options for women's freedom and children's options to identify with different parental figures, not only the biological mother or father. It seems that female freedom in modern capitalist or socialist societies definitely requires us to overcome the outdated notion of the *nuclear family* as the core of society, and a mix of delegation and sharing of motherhood.

Women in power delegate the work of child care – wealthy women, too. Other women in power decide against motherhood. The employment of domestic workers that take care of children is much more common in the Global South, including for the less affluent. In many of these countries there are as many single mothers as elsewhere, but employed child-care or extended family options are more accessible.

We face a paradox: We can run away from the female power to give birth and we can't run away from it. For *collective feminist power practices*, we need to move beyond the paradox and find innovative exits. This calls for creative variety, tolerated complexity and normative fluidity. Strategies to solve the conundrum of female freedom and motherhood may change contextually, repeatedly and unexpectedly.

Let us accompany the Nigerian ethnologist Ifi Amadiume on a journey to regions in Africa where women did and do live motherhood and female freedom between matriarchal traditions, and patriarchal as well as capitalist realities. We may draw important inspiration from the creative complexity for possible feminist futures. Ifi Amadiume's life work has focused on matriarchal cultures as relational and interconnected social interactions and female power within, superficially, by many perceived as patriarchal cultures. Her studies of matriarchal social and cultural constructions of sex and gender began in the Igbo village of Nnobi in Anambra State in south-eastern Nigeria.[8] Her extensive research has allowed us to discover complex forms of gender complementarity and cooperation in the matricentric principles of some African societies. She argues that many issues of gender equity were imported with colonialism and monotheistic religions, whereas ancient African matriarchies and their contemporary remnants had and still have powerful women as social leaders, wealthy business women as well as female prophets and spirit mediums, all highly recognized societal functions. In these societies, motherhood and female freedom seemed to be less of a contradiction. Usually, the work of mothering is shared as a collective activity in an extended family, mainly by women, but often also men. Grandmothers, aunts and siblings in everyday mothering are what we would call co-mothers. The most important point for our discussion is that the social construct is different from the many ways of organizing motherhood in a *nuclear family*. While in the latter, others – paid child-minders, publicly financed child care or aunts, grandmothers or uncles – step in almost as an exception and in order to relieve women from what is still societally and morally expected from them as biological mother, in many traditional and contemporary societies in Africa biological motherhood is less important. The bonds of belonging of the child are with the kinship community as collective social parenting. Children know they have many mothers, women and men, which can be seen as boosting their self-esteem and their option to choose bonding relationships. The West African proverb, it takes a village to raise a child, captures the essence of a world in which the responsibility of motherhood is taken up collectively. Western societies are flooded with research about the crucial bonding of biological mothers (not fathers) for the cognitive development of the child in the early years of child development.[9] Must we assume that many African children have a hampered cognitive development? Or, can we detect the scientific underscoring of biological mother–child bonding as a Western, capitalist and patriarchal narrative? Love and care must be reliable, but not necessarily come from the biological mother and father.

In pre-colonial Africa, women across various regions had powerful roles in subsistence production, farming, trading and commerce. Female economic wealth was reflected in cultural and political power. Ifi Amadiume notes that despite the disempowering influence of patriarchy, colonialism and capitalism, female solidarity groups, rooted in kinship, marriage and family, endured partly until today. Kinship arrangements were flexibly and contextually different, yet displayed an enormous creativity. Social practices showed gender-allocated tasks, but in flexible, inclusive and complementary ways. Same-sex marriages were possible, and a variety of different roles existed such as male mother, female father, male daughter and female husband.[10] Does this remind us of contemporary patchwork families, child adoption and same-sex partnerships with children?

The strange ideal of the *nuclear family* has also travelled to Africa. Many African women have adopted the European monogamous and *nuclear family* norms, but the practice of kinship obligations persists, serving as vital support networks during challenging experiences like divorce or widowhood. Yet, the remnants of the matriarchal structures embedded within African communities helps us understand that **powerful leadership roles assumed by women are intrinsically linked to the cultivation of female solidarity and communal responsibility for mothering**. Complex familial arrangements can function not only as a safety net for children, but as empowering support networks for women claiming power.

For the development of *collective feminist power practices*, it is important that we do not get trapped by patriarchal pathologies. It is not motherhood as such that contradicts female freedom, but the moral expectations deeply ingrained in the social construction of the *nuclear family*. Female freedom requires a release from these expectations towards motherhood. It requires choice. This undeniably includes full reproductive rights for women: Not having children or deciding for an abortion within a set period. More women will choose to claim power for feminist transformations if there are creative, complex and gender-fluid ways of raising children collectively with love and care.

However, motherhood as a female capacity and potential has more meanings than giving birth or mothering children. The social arrangements of matriarchies teach us that beyond the collective upbringing of children, motherhood, or more specifically motherliness, was a guiding principle of the philosophy and belief systems guiding societies.[11] The societal reference system centered around the life-giving properties of nature and women, literally and metaphorically. Yet, the birth rates, particularly at the time of highly developed matriarchies, were relatively stable, presumably because reproductive rights were in the hands of women with accountability to societal well-being.[12] Female power was natural and not questioned. Understandably, the global transformation to patriarchy with a male and hierarchical reference system as the standard for societal organization must have come across, for many people, as artificial and against what could be observed as nature. Hence, the fierce resistance to patriarchal take-overs is not surprising, nor is the overt assimilation to the new rules with covert underground continuation of female-powered spheres that still exist in so many cultures, most prominently in the Global South. There is a logic to why many matriarchies survived with mixed strategies such as keeping the kinship system with powerful women, but authorizing men to deal with the political spheres. People, not only women, found many creative ways of ensuring that power was not concentrated in the hands of what emerged as new rulers. Ifi Amadiume's account of kinship systems, organizing motherhood and female solidarity communities in many African countries, shows some of these creative variations. These are important inspirations, because, if we look at Europe, it is the structural undermining of female solidarity as a pathway to power and women's identity as naturally powerful that has made it possible for the patriarchal *divide and rule* pathology to be so tremendously successful.

Silvia Federici and many other researchers have explored how the aforementioned witch hunts in Europe broke any bonds of female solidarity by pitting women against each other. It became a prerequisite and blueprint for patriarchal societal organization.[13] The German theologist Christa Mulack shows how the establishment of the father as owner and ruler of the family required control mechanisms, because he could never be sure to be the biological father.[14] The enforcement of patrilocality and patrilineal descent also destroyed the bond of female ancestry, when mother–daughter relationships deteriorated, because the new rule devalued female children and made it a must to give birth to male heirs. It socially and economically disempowered women, uprooted them from the collective power of their kinship, created all kinds of distortions of motherhood and deprived women of the opportunity to identify with female power.

In today's world, it is understandable that the patriarchal narrative which defines women as motherly and still subtly confines them based on such a narrative in a subordinate role, does not make motherliness, motherhood or mothering a particularly attractive concept for achieving the female freedom we need for *collective feminist power practices*. But as feminists highlighted in the 20th century: What is societally delegated into the private sphere of the nuclear family is actually highly political. We have to unravel and push back the many patriarchal encroachments on female power and disentangle the emotional confusion around motherhood, motherliness, femininity, the capability to give birth, female ancestry, female solidarity and female freedom.

The dream of female freedom is probably as old as patriarchy. But what exactly is female freedom and how can it be organized without recreating traditional matriarchies?

Let us travel geographically to Milan in Italy and a few decades back in time. The Libreria della Donne di Milano is the oldest women's bookstore in Italy. It is also the name of a feminist philosophical women's collective founded in

1975. Among the founders was the art historian and philosopher Luisa Muraro. The collective was part of a global feminist movement to create institutions that allowed spaces for women, feminist discourse and possibilities to publish and to read specifically feminist literature. Today, the bookstore has nearly 8000 curated works by feminist writers, mainly in Italian, creating a powerful women-only space that encourages us to read and hear the power of women's voices. It cannot be the global archive of unpublished manuscripts that I suggested before, but for a certain geographical space, it is a convincing genealogy of feminist culture. One of the most famous books the collective produced, in 1987, is about how female freedom can emerge. It is written by 35 female authors who are mentioned at the beginning of the book, but have no separate sections. They truly wrote this as a collective of women, a practice that has become more common for feminist collectives in the 21st century. The original title in Italian, translated into English, would read *Don't Think You Have Rights – The Generation of Female Freedom in the Idea and Events of a Collective of Women.*[15] At a time when women across the Western world demanded equal rights as the focus of the feminist struggle, the collective of women took a different road. They argued that female freedom requires acknowledgment that women experience the world differently, and that merely gaining women's rights within the patriarchal system would not lead to female freedom.[16]

The collective insisted on female difference as a source of power and as a foundation for a *collective feminist power practice*. Female freedom, in their view, cannot be realized in women's equality with men within the existing patriarchal reference system. They suggested that the struggle for recognition within the framework of a male symbolic order, which had been created for men's needs, would distort women's potential for power. Instead, they proposed that female freedom arises when women build and maintain meaningful relationships with one another, attributing power and authority to each other. This meant creating feminist standards and frameworks for a female symbolic order, a *feminist reference system*, that would give orientation for women through political action, reflection and open debates. Without referring to the global history of matriarchies, they rendered women's search for symbolic reference points embodied by women a very old longing, suggesting that for female freedom the relationships with other women require care, because they saw them as an irreplaceable source of personal strength, intellectual originality and social integration.

The book has been heavily debated, mainly in Europe, because it reminds us that participation in patriarchal power options is participation in a performance of power that is based on a culture of dominance. The Italian collective named the dilemma. As we saw in the chapter on complicity, participation in power structures without dismantling the foundations of patriarchy always means injustice towards those who cannot or should not participate in the same way. The *divide and rule* pathologies are hard to escape. It may be difficult to digest, but **participating in power without deconstructing patriarchy means strengthening it**. Where participation in power becomes social privilege that others do not have and which is neither reflected, criticized nor changed, complicity with the patriarchal culture of dominance is the unwanted effect. Hence, in the search for female freedom and *collective feminist power practices*, we encounter another paradox. We need to fight for equal rights, for equal representation of women in power structures to move towards female freedom. Yet, female freedom, indeed female sovereignty, is not realized by achieving equality as an adaptation of women to the power structures and to the symbolic order of patriarchy. It is not achieved in the successful struggle for recognition within the limited constructs which patriarchal societies allow for female identities.

The Italian collective of feminists therefore suggested that female freedom, hence, the possibility of choosing how to shape one's life and society, grows where women step out of the limiting ideas of power as hierarchy, position and influence. Instead, they need to cultivate reciprocal, meaningful relationships that respect their difference. The collective created the Italian term *affidamento* to describe the conscious and proactive practice of attributing positive female authority. It involves a dynamic in which one woman places trust (affidamento) in another, recognizing her as a figure of authority or wisdom, and through this relationship, both women cultivate their own sense of identity, strength and power. The concept of *affidamento* is key to rethinking power as something shared and relational, rooted in female connection. For the Italian collective, the psychological and factual encroachment of patriarchy into female spaces of power would diminish if woman univocally derived their source of value from other women. They assume that a female and probably feminist frame of reference would emerge if women's meaning of existence as well as access to power were mediated by women. In their view, women must become the source of social authority, the source of social and economic existence, and also accept being judged by female, not by male, standards. Focusing on equality only, the Italians predicted in 1987, will inevitably produce waves between seeming liberalizations of patriarchy and patriarchal backlashes.

This is important to consider, even if we can't stop fighting for equality and justice. We need the struggle for women's rights in order to enhance female freedom and access to power, yet the political practice of *affidamento* may show us a pathway out of the jungle of complicity and help derive very concrete strategies for *collective feminist power practices*.

There is one interesting turn that the Italian collectives' reflective practice processes arrived at. They talk about the so-called *autonomous or symbolic mother*. They use this term to symbolically recognize mothers, but at the same time escape patriarchal definitions of motherhood. Under the conditions of patriarchy, they note, the relationship between women and their biological mothers is structurally and symbolically distorted. Yet, in order to become free, women need to reinstate this relationship. The price of a woman's freedom, they say, is to pay a symbolic debt back to the woman who gave birth to her, the human being who made life possible for her. If they can't, for any reason, do this with their biological mother, they need to do this symbolically with the greater mother, hence metaphorically with other women they relate to. They courageously challenge us by saying that women's insecurity is a vast abyss despite abundant encouragement, largely stemming from an unwillingness or inability to acknowledge the symbolic debt to one's own or the generalized mother. In their view, recognizing this bond between women is the cornerstone of female freedom. **Every act of gratitude, they say, between women holds more significance for female liberation than any movement devoid of such appreciation.**[17]

These are challenging thoughts, because they hint at an element that may be essential for *collective feminist power practices*: Gratitude as an amplifier of female power. The inspiring assumption is that if women experience life, solidarity, love, knowledge or encouragement with gratitude towards the origin of the support, they will be able to access an inexhaustible source of self-worth. Hence, the empowerment of women doesn't simply come from their participation in male-dominated spaces or from asserting demands upon patriarchal power structures. Instead, it stems from a fundamental exchange where women acknowledge each other's existence, thereby affirming their collective power as females.[18] Doesn't this remind us of the many fragments of our female ancestry? Could we amplify and project it into the future? One of the founders of the Italian collective, Luisa Muraro, suggests that the value of history depends on whether female excellence is recognized and acknowledged. She encourages us not to judge female excellence, but to grant female excellence the authority to judge.[19]

The strengthening of female power within patriarchal systems only comes about when we remember our ancestry and the power of female knowledge rationally and intuitively, emotionally, subjectively and objectively. We need to remind ourselves that, in principle, as women, we are not homeless, but undividedly strong, fluid and flexible on the polarity between male and female possibilities as we freely choose. Yet, we have to name and redefine the many options of being female, while recognizing and unmasking the limited definitions of femininity patriarchy grants us. As Luisa Muraro says, life is continuous through us. Deciding to provide life, give birth and nourish life is a primordial female ability, an enormous power. Should we give it away to patriarchally organized reproductive technologies? I suggest no, even though reproductive technologies can enhance female freedom of choice, and will certainly be an element of feminist-oriented societies. For now, we need to acknowledge that we can draw strength from the potential power of giving life without reducing ourselves to our biology. Because, from this connection to life arises a way of approaching transformations that we must take with us from the matriarchal past into a feminist future. **Women are powerful per se and in and of themselves.** Only if we grant ourselves this inherent access to power can we transform the world. This rational and intuitive knowledge helps us assemble the building blocks we need for future civilizations. The rest, I won't hide it, is hard work and the road will be rocky, and not only because patriarchy is extremely persistent. The road ahead requires all of us to have confidence, build our willingness to deal with ignorance and uncertainty in a friendly manner, and strengthen our ability to listen to one another. We need to enjoy diversity, if we want to create future civilizations in which women are free, hence, in which people are free. Yet, the world map that emerges from women's memories and present actions will be moving and growing constantly as we begin to notice its power and potency. It will come alive in the best sense of the word. We will shout at each other and proclaim the future feminist republic until we realize that it will not be one, but many different ones. We will argue about the forms of future civilizations and about the ways to get there.[20] This discourse is already part of the future.

But something will be different: Because when women remember and acknowledge the power of female genealogies, they will listen to each other and not, as they learned under patriarchy, silence each other. Because when they remember, they will be strong enough to hear other dreams, other hopes, other longings. If we are able to extend our memory to a few thousand years back, and if we are able to touch the hearts of the chain of freedom-seeking ancestresses that lead to the present, we will also be able to envisage a future in which happiness, female freedom and female power are at the core of societies. When we listen carefully, a new sound will emerge that will vibrate peacefully in dissonance. This will be the first step into the freedom of the future, the first step into the foundation of future civilizations.

Major insights for *collective feminist power practices* from female genealogies:

1. The strengthening of female power under the conditions of patriarchy only comes about when we remember female ancestry and the power of female knowledge rationally and intuitively, emotionally, subjectively and objectively.

2. Female freedom requires a release from patriarchal and capitalist expectations towards motherhood. It requires choice. This undeniably includes full reproductive rights for women. More women will choose to claim power for feminist transformations if there are creative, complex and gender-fluid ways of raising children collectively with love and care.
3. The empowerment of women doesn't only come from their participation in male-dominated spaces or from asserting demands of patriarchal power structures. Instead, it stems from a fundamental exchange where women acknowledge each other's existence, thereby affirming their collective, yet differentiated, identity anywhere on the polarity of gender-fluid choices.
4. With our female potential to create life, we are intimately connected to the tremendous vitality of the forces of life. From this connection to life arises a way of approaching transformations that we must take with us from the matriarchal past into a feminist future.
5. For a *collective feminist power practice*, we need to remember that women, per se and in and of themselves, are powerful. Only if we grant ourselves this potency, the inherent access to power, can we transform the world.
6. Every act of gratitude between women is an amplifier of female liberation and female power. If women experience life, solidarity, love, knowledge or encouragement with gratitude towards the origin of the support, they will be able to access an inexhaustible source of self-worth.

Notes

1 See Reynolds et al. (2020).
2 See Gao & Tassone (2021).
3 See Fang (2022).
4 Hu & Peng (2015).
5 Federici (2004).
6 See Ortiz-Ospina & Roser (2020).
7 See Kollontaï (1977). It must be noted that despite her strong feminist stance, in her later years, she supported Stalin despite his brutal and authoritarian rule.
8 Amadiume (1998, 2015, 2024).
9 For an example see Joas & Möhler (2021).
10 See Amadiume (2015).
11 Göttner-Abendroth (2013).
12 This has, for example, been shown for the Mosuo society, in China; see Johnson & Zhang (1991).
13 Federici (2004); Wisselinck (1986).
14 Mulack (2006).
15 Translation by the author. In Italian: *Non credere di avere dei diritti, La generazione della libertà femminile nell'idea e nelle vicende di un gruppo di donne*. The German

translation of the book in 1988 chose the title (translated in English) *How Female Freedom emerges – a New Political Practice*. Unfortunately, the book is not available in English. The German version: Libreria della donne di Milano (1991).

16 It would be an interesting journey to explore the connections between the Italian feminist philosophers' approach and the criticism of Sylvia Tamale about the focus of western feminists on gender equality. See Tamale (2020).

17 See Libreria della donne di Milano (1991, p. 156).

18 Libreria della donne di Milano (1991, p. 169).

19 See Muraro (2019).

20 An exploration of female transformation approaches can be found in Kuenkel & Ragnarsdottir (2022).

References

Amadiume, I. (1998). *Re–Inventing African Matriarchy, Religion and Culture*. London & New York: Zed Books Ltd.

Amadiume, I. (Ed.). (2015). *Male Daughters, Female Husbands: Gender and Sex in an African Society*. Zed Books Ltd.

Amadiume, I. (Ed.). (2024). *African Possibilities*. Bloomsbury Publishing.

Fang, M. (2022). Chinese cultural treasures as contributions to a mindset of interconnectedness for global transformations. In: Künkel, P., & Ragnarsdottir, K.V. *Transformation Literacy: Pathways to Regenerative Civilizations*. Springer EBooks, 75–89. https://doi.org/10.1007/978-3-030-93254-1_6.

Federici, S. (2004). *Caliban and the Witch: Women, the Body and Primitive Accumulation*. Autonomedia.

Gao, Z., & Tassone, B. (2021). Feminist interpretations of the Mosuo society of China. *European Journal of Humanities & Social Sciences*, *5*(3). https://doi.org/10.29013/EJHSS-21-5-3-12

Göttner-Abendroth, H. (2013). *Matriarchal Societies: Studies on Indigenous Cultures Across the Globe*. Peter Lang.

Hu, Z., & Peng, X. (2015). Household changes in contemporary China: An analysis based on the four recent censuses. *The Journal of Chinese Sociology*, *2*(1). https://doi.org/10.1186/s40711-015-0011-0

Joas, J., & Möhler, E. (2021). Maternal bonding in early infancy predicts childrens' social competences in preschool age. *Frontiers in Psychiatry*, *12*. https://doi.org/10.3389/fpsyt.2021.687535

Johnson, N.E., & Zhang, K.-T. (1991). Matriarchy, polyandry, and fertility amongst the Mosuos in China. *Journal of Biosocial Science*, *23*(4), 499–505. https://doi.org/10.1017/s0021932000019593

Kollontaï, A. (1977). *Selected Writings of Alexandra Kollontai*. Translated by Alix Holt. Norton.

Kuenkel, P., & Ragnarsdottir, K.V. (2022). *Transformation Literacy: Pathways to Regenerative Civilizations*. Springer.

Libreria della donne di Milano. (1991). *Wie weibliche Freiheit entsteht: Eine neue politische Praxis*. Orlanda Frauenverlag.

Mulack, C. (2006). *Die Wurzeln weiblicher Macht: Frauen erkennen ihre Stärke*. Pomaska-Brand.

Muraro, L. (2019). *Vom Glück, eine Frau zu sein*. Christel Göttert Verlag.

Ortiz-Ospina, E., & Roser, M. (2020). Marriages and Divorces. *Our World in Data, 1*(1). https://ourworldindata.org/marriages-and-divorces

Reynolds, A.Z., Wander, K., Sum, C.-Y., Su, M., Thompson, M.E., Hooper, P.L., Li, H., Shenk, M.K., Starkweather, K.E., Blumenfield, T., & Mattison, S.M. (2020). Matriliny reverses gender disparities in inflammation and hypertension among the Mosuo of China. *Proceedings of the National Academy of Sciences, 117*(48), 30324–30327. https://doi.org/10.1073/pnas.2014403117

Tamale, S. (2020). *Decolonization and Afro-Feminism: An Afro-Feminist-Legal Critique*. Daraja Press.

Wisselinck, E. (1986). *Hexen. Warum wir so wenig von ihrer Geschichte erfahren und was davon noch falsch ist*. Frauenoffensive.

9
Redefining Power for Feminist Transformations – Women as Architects of Our Future Societies

We have seen in the previous chapters that feminist transformation efforts are relentless endeavors often overshadowed by the noise of the context-dependent status quo of patriarchy. At times the efforts dry up or become weak because of exhaustion or because of complacency with successes; at other times, they become immersed in the urgent and necessary collaborative endeavors to fight for human rights in general, to resist threats to democracy or to find solutions to today's sustainability challenges such as climate change and biodiversity loss. Feminist struggles bloom again and rise to become collective when patriarchal resurgence or backlashes are on the horizon. Yet, within these meandering efforts lie the seeds of profound and transformative change, waiting to be noticed and acknowledged by women (and, of course, men). The journey towards rebuilding patriarchal societal structures into feminist-inspired structures seems to be never-ending. It requires a vigilant eye and a commitment to continuous struggle, for what may seem self-evident today is the culmination of tireless work by generations of women. Yet, achieved progress in female freedom and sovereignty in one country, in one region, does not mean that the work is done. On the contrary, the danger is that we get seduced by participating in patriarchal power structures, stop working actively for feminist transformations, or benefit from power dynamics that disadvantage other women.

Complicity with patriarchy is and will be a constant threat we cannot avoid, but which we need to collectively observe and name. We must bear with ourselves when we are exhausted in the process of dismantling, even more so disarming, the patriarchy, while we do not yet exactly know where we are heading to, given the challenging global developments. We may not yet know what feminist-inspired future civilizations will look like. Moreover,

DOI: 10.4324/9781003508885-12

our commitment to such feminist futures is challenged by the many subtle and open invitations to give up on changing patriarchy and choose to maintain it in a slightly liberalized version. We remember that the laudable global efforts of socialist movements to overcome capitalist exploitation patterns often rendered patriarchal domination as a secondary problem that would disappear once socialist societies had been established. But it did not, and often, these seemingly progressive societal arrangements fell back into patriarchal power pathologies. We know that the global effort to economically empower women that is at the forefront of the Sustainable Development Goals, the fight for appropriate female representation on corporate boards or for adequate representation of women in political decision-making positions are extremely important. Yet they do not necessarily change patriarchal conditions, nor do they shift neoliberal patterns of exploitation, under which most societies and economies operate. We have seen that the memory of a world that came far before this world of ours, in which female power informed the reference system of societal arrangements, helps us gain the confidence that a different future will be possible. This is particularly relevant when we learn how many remnants and creative variations of female sovereignty and collective power still exist at the fringes of our modern society, and how they are openly or also clandestinely embedded in the cracks of patriarchal societies. The more we notice and acknowledge the diversity of past and present practices of female sovereignty and power, the more they can inspire us to expand and grow *collective feminist power practices*.

We also know that, in order to avoid falling prey to the prevalent patriarchal reference systems still permeating all of our societies, we need to build a deliberate system of appreciation, acknowledgment, gratitude and mutual support among women. Female freedom – a foundation for feminist-inspired civilizations – requires us to break the rules and undermine the patriarchal reference system by deliberately attributing power, value and authority to women. This calls for a solid dedication to the development of a *feminist reference system* that might become a seed for building a new operating system for humanity on this planet. The Italian feminist philosophers remind us to mediate power through women and not stay dependent for power and authority on patriarchal protagonists and institutions. If we do, we are co-creators of the destructive trajectories that we now so massively try to hold in the global sustainability movement. But even this movement is dominated by men. The Italians suggested that the only way out, and the only pathway towards merging our freedom and our necessity to transform this world, is a radical relatedness to women. Only this, they assumed, will ultimately open the pathways to feminist-inspired civilizations that cherish the freedom of all, partner with nature, regenerate life on Earth and honor the wisdom of evolution.

Yet, how do we deal with the vast difference among women – indeed, among feminists? How do we deal with hatred between women, between feminists? How do we handle the indifference towards the intersectionality of patterns of dominance? How do we deal with the spots of ignorance towards privileges? Can we grant authority to women, to feminists, whose opinions or approaches we do not share? How do we deal respectfully with opposing views on matters we care about without falling prey to the successful *divide and rule* pathology of patriarchy?

The practice of difference among women, and feminists, is an art we need to master. It is a necessary filter to identify where difference means inequality in the sense of injustice and where difference means diversity. Diversity is enriching when it is respected and celebrated. It can be based on knowledge, expertise, age, geography, experiences, culture and much more. We know that life operates with utmost diversity as a foundation for vitality. The human future needs us to understand that diversity is wealth. But difference can also arise from injustice, which always refers to the inappropriate and involuntary restriction of opportunities to live a self-determined life. It is a constant invitation to reflect and name. We need to know these connections and recognize the dynamics between diversity and injustice in order to draw future potential from women's difference and work to overcome injustice. Consciously or unconsciously perpetuating global power structures contradicts even the best of intentions of feminist transformations. The first step is naming the issues.

Among those who named these issues early on was the Indian-born gender and sociology scientist Chandra Talpade Mohanty when she published her influential critique of the hegemonies of Western feminism in 1984.[1] She then pointed out a crucial aspect: Not being aware of hegemonies and privilege, of homogenization and generalizations about 'other women' is a form of exercising power and perpetuating, if not strengthening injustice. It is a form of complicity. Scientifically (or politically) defining the reality of others without contextualizing one's own viewpoint revives the patriarchal pathology of making objects out of subjects. In her later work, Mohanty reminds us that feminist solidarity cannot become powerful without a concerted effort to decolonize knowledge, question the hegemony of Western thoughts and structures, and dismantle an unjust economic system.[2] Feminist transformation efforts cannot assume a unified 'sisterhood', but need to look at tangible power differentials and disparities.[3] We need to face the complexities of today's world. Mohanty's invitation to reorientate feminism has opened new avenues of engagement. A lot has happened in the decades since her groundbreaking publication, but the decolonization of knowledge and scholarship still has a lot of ground to cover. Hegemonies are not over. What was at the time of Mohanty's publication still called the 'Third World' is now called the 'Global South'; as a matter of fact, it is the 'Majority World' – in terms of geographies and population, but also in terms of the power and the variety of feminist movements. Even though we may only be at the beginnings of the beginnings of shifting global power structures, the past decades have not only brought the concepts of feminist decolonization and intersectionality to the forefront, but also their presence in debates, discourses, conferences and publications. More importantly, they have started to become part of *collective feminist power practices*.

Decolonial feminism emerged as an approach that builds upon the activism, scholarship, insights and lived realities of feminists from the Global South.[4] It seeks to challenge and dismantle systems of oppression and marginalization rooted in colonial legacies. At its core, it recognizes that the struggles for gender equality, female sovereignty and decolonization are deeply interconnected, and one cannot be achieved without the other. Moreover, it reveals a worldview that may feel familiar even to those in the West who have resisted mainstream narratives of progress and development. This perspective embraces ambiguity and interconnectedness – between people, and between people and nature. It acknowledges uncertainties and contradictions and reflects a lived reality that navigates between Indigenous cultural traditions and contemporary modernity. An author collective of women from Brazil, the Philippines and India captures poignantly that decolonization is an ongoing 'process of peeling away of the layers of imposed identity conferred by the colonizers, rejecting the stories offered, and a general ripping off the veils of illusion created by malicious omissions and elisions to design palatable chronicles of progress, development, and the white saviour model'.[5]

Feminist decolonization also entails interrogating and deconstructing the Eurocentric, or broader, Western views that have shaped feminist theory and practice without protagonists contextualizing their knowledge production. It does not make such knowledge production less important, but it justifiably challenges its validity for women in the Global South. Feminist decolonization paves the way for multiple ways of understanding the world, which is opening a window into feminist futures. But it is not necessarily only a conceptual approach; on the contrary, it encompasses a range of actions, from grassroots organizing and advocacy for land rights, to academic research, cultural activism and insisting on bringing Indigenous knowledge and perspectives into policy-making and decision-making processes. In this process intersectionality emerges as a guiding principle, reminding us that female freedom cannot be achieved through a singular lens. It demands a recognition of the intersecting forces of oppression and privilege.

Collective feminist power practices require us to look at feminist decolonization as an invitation to continuously reflect power imbalances and sources of power.

This will inevitably lead to disagreements, debates over directional discourses and contradictory solutions, which we need to learn to happily enjoy. They are just as important as dialogues and consensus finding. When I lived and worked in Zimbabwe, I often facilitated strategy workshops together with a Zimbabwean colleague. On one journey to a place deep in the countryside she explained to me in her polite and story-based Shona way that 'we' Europeans needed to learn that in the lived realities of her country there was always a solution, but never only one, and that the typical 'either–or' mentality of white people would silently receive a response as a lived 'and or both'. Trust the process, she would often say, when I was nervous about outcomes.

Our ability to suspend judgment, enjoy ambivalence, embrace uncertainty and reject mutually excluding options may become a pathway to the resilience we need for feminist transformations. **We must forge a new narrative of power, one rooted in a *feminist reference system*, where power serves life and nurtures the vitality of people and the planet.** This requires a radical shift in perspective, challenging entrenched notions of authority and embracing the diversity of human experience. At the heart of this transformation lies the idea of female sovereignty as the right of women to shape their destinies free from the power pathologies of patriarchy. It acknowledges interdependence and transcends individual autonomy to encompass collective empowerment. Yet, what we have learned from the past decades of feminist movements is that patriarchal pathologies manifest differently depending on geography as well as cultural and historic contexts. Equally, the spaces for female freedom are different and diverse, eluding any generalized and fixed description. Societies with structures in place for female emancipation and gender equality may perpetuate misogynist cultures in a subtle, yet highly effective way. Societies with outright misogynist structures in place may have sanctioned spaces of female freedom that can be highly empowering.

Collective feminist power practices require iterative learning so that at some point in the future structures for female freedom match cultures for female freedom and match respective institutions. Ultimately, our pursuit of feminist transformations is a testament to the resilience of the human spirit and is intricately intertwined with the vision of future civilizations. We are on a relentless journey towards a world that works for 100% of humanity and the planet. As we navigate the complexities of power and privilege, let us try to approximate a working definition of power as part of a *collective feminist power practice*.

Feminist power is essentially a collective vehicle for transformative impact towards a *Good Life for All*. It requires the individual and collective capacity to collaboratively shape current and future societies through a synergy of strength, strategy, communication and mutual support, and it includes

agreed-upon checks and balances. Such a conception of power emphasizes resonance among diverse voices and experiences, fostering inclusive leadership and transformative action aimed at dismantling oppressive systems while promoting equality and justice in what can be described as a feminist ecosystem of transformative efforts.

However, a crucial aspect is often overlooked in the feminist claim for power: The need for structures that support and sustain feminist power. While patriarchal institutions often hinder transformation, history shows that both ancient and modern matriarchal societies have used power structures – life-affirming and inclusive – that balanced individual and collective well-being. Therefore, feminist power requires its own structures and institutions, testing new models and learning from matriarchal practices as well as from contemporary feminist movements, especially in the Global South. This requires establishing autonomous feminist structures in the form of institutions, or integrating feminist approaches within existing institutions. This gradual process of feminist institutionalization must be grounded in collaboration, transparency and collective leadership, ensuring that power is distributed rather than concentrated. Such structures must be flexible and adaptive, supporting decision-making processes that value dialogue, consensus-building and care. Rather than perpetuating hierarchies, it is about cultivating networks of accountability and cooperation, encouraging a dynamic balance between autonomy and interdependence.

Despite the strategic need to consolidate power in autonomous feminist institutions, the claim to power is both an individual and a collective practice. This will inevitably involve the participation of women and feminists in existing patriarchal structures and institutions, even if the numerous traps that invite us to become accomplices of patriarchy are waiting for us there. Yet, we should not devalue women's efforts to engage in existing forms of power, such as political and institutional power, or the power of language, meaning and science. Instead, the practical challenge ahead of us is how we can embed women in these patriarchal power structures in a network of feminist support helping them to avoid conforming to the patriarchal system. We know the ideal: Women should be able to utilize power within these structures to transform the structures, while inspired by and committed to a *feminist reference system*. This requires creative forms of collaboration within a framework for *collective feminist power practices* that helps navigate the complexities and challenges of feminist transformations.

Ideally, this would help us connect with different ways of thinking, stay in tune with life, the world and each other, and safeguard us against the corruption often associated with power. We know, ultimately, power should always be wielded in service of life, but what constitutes being beneficial to life must be constantly collectively reevaluated and redefined. We also know that *collective feminist power practices* are happening all the time, but the more we recognize their impact, the more we can amplify and strengthen them. It's essential to share approaches and outcomes, acknowledging them as power practices from which we can learn and grow.

The former Prime Minister of Australia, Julia Gillard, became famous for her powerful 'misogyny speech' that she delivered in the Australian parliament in 2012.[6] While the media reacted negatively, the video went viral, and inspired many women to stand up and speak up against sexism and misogyny, create songs, poems and videos. Her 15-minute parliamentary speech that she did not let anybody interrupt despite many loud hecklings is worth watching for the clarity, the calm anger and the incredible power she attributed to herself. She stood up for millions of women who had gone through similar misogynistic attacks and waves of sexism. It was not a preplanned speech, but a spontaneous and extremely strong reaction to the constant sexism which she had to endure from the opposition throughout her term in office. She claimed the power for herself as an individual that was already hers as Prime Minister, but in an unexpected form that meant that her courage and clarity had an impact far beyond herself.

In claiming feminist power collectively, individual courage to claim power intertwines with collaborative efforts and complex alliances. Achieving female sovereignty often requires structural changes within patriarchal systems, such as legal or institutional reforms. Argentina offers a powerful example, having legalized abortion in 2020 – a hard-won victory for reproductive freedom that many women around the world still seek.[7] This marked a major shift from the restrictive 1921 Criminal Code, now allowing abortion on demand up to 14 weeks and beyond in cases of rape or health risks, with mandatory free provision in public healthcare.

The success of this movement is rooted in Argentina's rich history of feminist mobilization and strategic alliances since the 1970s. Women's organizations held regular strategy meetings to build solidarity and coordinate action. Despite setbacks from strong religious opposition and politicians fearing electoral loss, feminists forged multi-party coalitions and tirelessly advocated within their parties to push for reproductive rights. Street demonstrations, often linked with anti-femicide campaigns, helped shift public opinion and emboldened lawmakers. Although a 2018 attempt to pass the bill failed, the societal view on abortion had already shifted. Following the election of a pro-choice president in 2019, feminist activists ramped up pressure, maintaining momentum with campaigns, performances and strengthened political alliances. When the bill was finally passed in 2020, it marked a milestone in the fight for women's reproductive rights.[8]

Claiming power often requires creating safe spaces for women. Umoja village, in Kenya's Samburu County, is a powerful testament to the resilience of women who did just that. Founded in 1990 by 15 women as the Umoja Uaso Women's Group, they created an autonomous, women-only village, supporting themselves through economic activities.[9] The initiative was sparked by Rebecca Lolosoli, who, after being beaten for teaching women about their rights, planned a community where women could be safe. Samburu culture is known for forced marriages, polygamy and female genital mutilation. Umoja's founders, many of them victims of rape, sought refuge from this system. A 2003 Amnesty International report exposed the rape of over 1000 Samburu women by British soldiers between 1965 and 2001.[10] Umoja has since become a sanctuary for survivors of violence, as well as young girls fleeing forced marriages or female genital mutilation. More than a village, Umoja symbolizes empowerment and solidarity. Its women support each other, raise children in safety and earn a living through crafts and tourism. Although they are led by a matriarch, decisions are made collectively, ensuring every voice is heard. This governance model challenges the patriarchal structures of surrounding communities. Despite facing threats from men, the women have persevered, transforming Umoja into a thriving, self-sustaining community that attracts global visitors. Umoja stands as a reminder that solidarity and resilience can lead to female empowerment, even in the face of adversity.

These three examples are just a tiny fraction of the many occasions in which women and feminists claim power, individually and collectively. As different as they are in context and process, they stand for important elements in the process of claiming feminist power.

The *first* inevitable element in the process of claiming feminist power is **disrupting the system**. Julia Gillard, already powerful in her role as prime minister, acted in a way nobody expected from her. Rebecca Lolosoli with her female friends rearranged living conditions for women. The Argentinian feminist movement took to the streets until the perception of abortion changed.

The *second* element in the process of claiming feminist power is **strategic collaboration and networking** across different feminist groups, individuals and organizations. This is most obvious in the case of Argentina, where over many years feminist activists and organizations regularly met to discuss and coordinate joint strategies.[11]

The *third* element in the process of claiming feminist power is **creating safe and empowering spaces** for women, the ground on which visions and ambitions for the future can grow, and mutual attribution of power can emerge. These spaces are like protected islands of the future. They harbor possibilities and lay the ground for collective action. Throughout herstory, safe spaces have been vital components of the feminist movement, offering sanctuaries where women can express themselves, seek support and advocate for their rights without fear of judgment or harm. They have certainly never been free from debates, conflicts, disagreements, disappointments or exclusive tendencies, but they are the ideal opportunity to practice what the future needs: Mutual respect for difference, joint learning and the development of expertise.

The *fourth* element in the process of claiming feminist power is **organizing the system**, which was most obvious in the arduous, yet very strategic path towards legalizing abortion in Argentina. It means understanding the institutional, political and societal context of an issue extremely well and strategically creating alliances between movements and feminist protagonists in institutions.

The *fifth* element in claiming feminist power is **self-attribution of power** as a prerequisite of **mutual attribution of power** among women. In the examples this is most obvious in Julia Gillard's misogyny speech and in Rebecca Lolosoli's decision to create a women-only village. We may not notice this element in the example from Argentina, because the claiming of power took place over such a long time, by so many different women. Yet, the attribution of power is always both an individual and a collective process. Individually, it may arrive at a moment, when anger is turned into power, or the inspiration of other women's claiming of power may initiate self-attribution of power. Yet, a lasting transformative effect happens when the self-attribution of power empowers other women, too, or leads to a collective self-attribution of power. This is the fertile ground for feminist transformations.

The American feminist philosopher and human rights activists Barbara Starrett suggested decades ago that under patriarchal conditions, we cannot get rid of the power exercised over us without claiming power ourselves.[12] She urged us to remember that patriarchies actually operate with *female* power, namely the power women unconsciously transfer to a male-dominated system, hence the power women do not claim for their own visions of the future. If only a fraction of women decided to withdraw their power from patriarchal systems and claimed power for their own and other women's future, she assumed, the tipping point for feminist transformations would quickly be reached. Power, she said, is always directional. Like energy, it cannot disappear – it can only be transformed. This means that claiming feminist power will always reduce the amount of patriarchal power. Is this what patriarchal protagonists energetically feel? Does this lead in open and subtle way to patriarchal backlash? In a way, yes. It seems unavoidable. Because energetic and practical resistance is to be expected from protagonists of patriarchy, it is especially important that we understand as much as possible about transformation processes at scale. Our claim for power must be embedded in sophisticated strategies.

There are important aspects to consider for feminist transformation strategies from the emerging research about transformative societal change processes. When we talk about *systems transformations*, the term captures the following characteristics:[13]

- An innovative approach towards changing thinking and actions that includes changes in power structures and relationships.
- Long-term radical, yet short- and medium-term incremental change in the way societies and international relations are organized.
- The gradual rebuilding of structures and institutions towards better functionality for the well-being of humanity and the planet.
- A collaborative and co-creative process of collective learning with multiple different stakeholders aiming at increasing the vitality of people and the planet.

All of these characteristics also apply to feminist transformations with the particular focus of taking female freedom and female sovereignty as a condition and starting point for a *Good Life for All*. This hints to a crucial realization: Claiming power for feminist transformations needs to be radical to disrupt the system, yet it also needs to become structurally embedded in societies. The more connected feminist power claims become, the more will incremental change steps aggregate to systems change, even though this might only happen over a long period of time. Hence, **large-scale transformations are the result of different, yet connected feminist actions at scale**. This can only to a certain degree be coordinated, but networks, knowledge exchange, transnational collaborative structures and digital communication play an important role in scale.

Feminist transformations can, in the long run, only be successful if their various different manifestations are integrated in societal narratives as much as in societal structures, presumably in a step-by-step fashion. The law of legalizing abortion is an exemplary important example, even if one issue in one country looks small in relation to the immense global need for feminist transformations. Laws can change again, but once a fraction of female freedom is anchored in the legal system, and societies get used to the respective practice, it takes tremendous effort to change it. We need to firmly anchor feminist aspects in processes and systems. Only in this way will these efforts be sustainable.

Will this not lead to feminist assimilation of patriarchal systems, procedures and institutions? Yes, the danger is always present. Is a revolutionary approach to abolishing patriarchy hopeless or impossible? We do need revolutionary approaches to feminist power claims that disrupt the patriarchal system. Radical approaches are always the predecessor of a change in narratives. But as with all revolutions, the peaceful ones have the greatest chance of surviving and not returning to forms of domination. We need to build strategic connections and alliances between movements, campaigns and women in institutions and power structures. The present global, and still patriarchal, system with all its procedures, institutions and structures is so widely present, so deeply embedded in societies and, in many ways, it serves us too well, even if it endangers humankind and the planet. What feminist claims for power do, and need to do even more, is inject feminist sequences gradually, yet purposefully and at scale into the present systems. This is almost like unraveling outdated structures and knitting the new structures while using the old, and doing so in a multifaceted, multi-level and multi-issue way. It is hard work and it can be fun.

Feminist power stands for a process of dynamic action and movement. It is by no means a static possession, but the ability to be effective together in the world, in cooperation, complementarity and mutuality. That doesn't mean that everyone has to be the same, equally strong, equally knowledgeable or equally visionary. In her book *La potencia feminista* Verónica Gago uses the term *potencia* to describe this collective, transformative power that emerges from grassroots mobilization and everyday struggles.[14] It's not simply about acquiring power in the traditional sense, but about the collective capacity to reshape societal dynamics, challenge oppression and build alternative futures. *Potencia* is the feminist potential and desire to 'change everything', hence actively building alternative worlds through collective resistance and collaboration.

The collective desire to claim feminist power individually and collectively takes us to the ambiguous concept of *leadership* in the sense of leading transformative change, and as we will see at a later stage, to the process of *stewardship* as the capacity of many different actors, within and outside institutions, within and across countries, to bring about systems change. Let us first stay with the slightly contested term *leadership*, because it traditionally evokes images of heroic, charismatic, visionary and at times authoritarian, predominantly male, only occasionally strong female, actors. But neither the hero nor the dominator needs to be part of a leadership narrative. One of the most prominent examples of an effective combination between individual and collective leadership is the Green Belt Movement in Kenya, initiated in 1977 by the Kenyan politician and professor for veterinary anatomy, Wangari Maathai.[15] Without her courage, vision and perseverance, the movement would not have succeeded. Her claim of power was serving people's future, yet without the collective leadership of thousands of women planting trees in the communities it would not have led to any results. She chose women as the reliable potential amplifiers of her idea, although traditionally tree planting was none of their business, and they needed to learn how to create tree nurseries and tend the small trees. Women took up the tasks, joined women's tree planting groups and became educated in fighting for their rights far beyond environmental issues. Focusing on women was also strategic, as in the beginning, the tree planting activities were not seen as a threat to the government. More than 50 million trees have been planted over the course of four decades, spreading restoration areas like a belt in Kenya. But far beyond the environmental impact Wangari Maathai stood up against the authoritarian government of Arap Moi, exposing brutalities, corruption, land grabbing and unfair wealth concentration. She made a significant contribution to re-establishing democracy in Kenya. In 2004, she received the Nobel Peace Prize for her tireless work against environmental destruction and climate change, and for ecological restoration, human rights, democracy and the empowerment of women.

Feminist transformations, past and current, have come about because women took up leadership, individually and collectively. Leadership and power are intertwined; when we redefine power, we also need to redefine leadership. In envisioning a new narrative of power, we need to find approaches to leadership that match the foundational principles of *collective feminist power practices*. A feminist version of leadership necessitates communicative resonance, mandate and legitimacy; it is subject to checks and balances and aligned with a partnership narrative. It certainly includes self-introspection, but it also aims to build lasting structures for feminist transformations. Above all, feminist leadership is individual and collective, as it moves away from the outdated notion of leader and followers.

The concept of *collective leadership* for a sustainable world refers to the competence of a group of actors who see themselves as jointly responsible and who advance sustainability-related goals in mutual support.[16] This is done on the basis of a cooperative and impact-oriented approach that optimizes one's own contribution, but highlights it in a complementary and flexible manner. It's not just about convincing others to work together, but about a new, collaborative understanding in shaping the future. Leading in partnership means acknowledging that shaping the future takes place in cooperation at eye level instead of in hierarchical or even domination structures. In *collective leadership*, people take on different roles in order to consciously advance initiatives in a goal-oriented manner that complements one another. The contribution of each person is still just as important as before, but the influences are consciously related to one another. Such an approach moves away from competition and towards complementarity and inclusion, away from directives and towards transparent dialogue and cooperation. It's about developing shared capabilities to contribute to the common good. At the heart of *collective leadership* is the human ability for dialogue and to use difference for innovation. This makes it possible to overcome self-centered perspectives – an essential prerequisite for dealing effectively with the challenges of the 21st century. For feminist transformation we need to claim power individually, and that means truly accepting leadership with all the responsibilities and challenges that come with it. Yet, in order to become effective, we need to claim power collectively, and this means developing our abilities for leading feminist transformations collectively.

Major insights for *collective feminist power practices* from redefining power for feminist transformations:

1. The practice of respecting and leveraging difference among women, and feminists, is an art we need to master. Difference can mean inequality in the sense of injustice or it can mean diversity. The latter is a wealth of feminist power; the former needs to be addressed and overcome.
2. Not being aware of hegemonies and privileges is a form of exercising power and perpetuating injustice. Gender equality, female sovereignty and decolonization are deeply interconnected, and one cannot be achieved without the other.
3. A feminist-inspired narrative of power serves life and nurtures the vitality of people and the planet. We need to translate a *feminist reference system* into a framework for *collective feminist power practices* that helps us navigate the complexities and challenges of feminist transformations.
4. Important elements in the process of claiming feminist power are: Disrupting the system, strategic collaboration and networking, creating safe and empowering spaces, (re)-organizing the system and self-attribution and mutual attribution of power.
5. The more connected feminist power claims become, the more will incremental change steps aggregate to systems change. Large-scale transformations are the result of connected feminist actions at scale.
6. In order to become effective in feminist transformations, we need to claim power collectively, and this means developing our strength in collective leadership.

Notes

1 See Mohanty (1984).
2 See Mohanty (2007).
3 This does not mean not to use terms such as global sisterhood, but the call for solidarity needs to be unpacked as a driving force to overcome inequalities and dysfunctional power structures among women.

4 Beyond the pivotal work of Mohanty, the feminist discourse on decolonization continues; for example: Lugones (2007, 2010), Bhambra (2014), Manning, (2018), Pheko (2019), Tamale (2020), Vergès (2022).
5 Suppiah et al. (2022).
6 See *Guardian News* (2020, Youtube Video). Ten years later Gillard gathered feminist authors to write essays about their experiences in seizing power: see Gillard (2022).
7 For a description of the process see Daby & Moseley (2021).
8 It is important to learn from this success story, even if we know that the patriarchal backlash of the election results in 2023 endangers the achievement; see Barber (2024, March 18).
9 See https://umojawomen.or.ke/qinstpckg/index.php
10 See Amnesty International (2003). The report gives a detailed account of structural patriarchal power sanctioning rape as crime and lists the tremendously detrimental effects on the lives of women. All attempts to report the rape cases by village chiefs and victims came to nothing, and even after the report was published, the UK Army, after their own investigation (not an independent investigation), accused the women and village chiefs of having fabricated the rape cases, although the high number of mixed-race children in the area could have been seen as evidence.
11 Already in 1986, feminist activists created the Encuentro Nacional de Mujeres (National Meeting of Women), an annual meeting fostering strategic connections among women's organizations. The meetings are still held annually today. They became the foundation for the development of the campaign (see Anderson, 2022).
12 Starrett (1976).
13 See Kuenkel (2019).
14 See Gago (2019).
15 See Taylor (2013) and the website of the movement: https://www.greenbeltmovement.org/who-we-are/our-history
16 Kuenkel (2016).

References

Amnesty International. (2003). United Kingdom: Decades of impunity: Serious allegations of rape of Kenyan women by UK army personnel. https://www.amnesty.org/en/wp-content/uploads/2021/06/eur450142003en.pdf

Anderson, C.F. (2022). Legalising abortion in Argentina: Social movements and multiparty coalitions. *Journal of Politics in Latin America*, *14*(2), 1866802X2211002. https://doi.org/10.1177/1866802x221100274

Barber, H. (2024, March 18). 'The stigma has returned': Abortion access in turmoil in Javier Milei's Argentina. *The Guardian*. https://www.theguardian.com/global-development/2024/mar/18/argentina-abortion-javier-milei

Bhambra, G.K. (2014). Postcolonial and decolonial dialogues. *Postcolonial Studies, 17*(2), 115–121.

Daby, M., & Moseley, M.W. (2021). Feminist mobilization and the abortion debate in Latin America: Lessons from Argentina. *Politics & Gender, 18*(2), 1–35. https://doi.org/10.1017/s1743923x20000197

Gago, V. (2019). *La potencia feminista: O el deseo de cambiarlo todo.* https://tintalimon.com.ar/public/k3jbhvt08gqeeusq48koqbtjafx7/La%20potencia%20feminista_WEB.pdf

Gillard, J. (2022). *Not Now, Not Ever: Ten Years on from the Misogyny Speech.* Random House Australia.

Guardian News. (2020). Julia Gillard misogyny speech voted most unforgettable Australian TV moment [YouTube Video]. https://www.youtube.com/watch?v=fCNuPcf8L00

Kuenkel, P. (2016). *The Art of Leading Collectively.* Chelsea Green Publishing.

Kuenkel, P. (2019). *Stewarding Sustainability Transformations: An Emerging Theory and Practice of SDG Implementation.* Springer International Publishing.

Lugones, M. (2007). Heterosexualism and the colonial/modern gender system. *Hypatia, 22*(1), 186–219.

Lugones, M. (2010). Toward a decolonial feminism. *Hypatia, 25*(4), 742–759. https://doi.org/10.1111/j.1527-2001.2010.01137.x

Manning, J. (2018). Becoming a decolonial feminist ethnographer: Addressing the complexities of positionality and representation. *Management Learning,* 49(3), 311–326. https://doi.org/10.1177/1350507617745275

Mohanty, C. T. (1984). Under Western eyes: Feminist scholarship and colonial discourses. *Boundary 2, 12(3), on Humanism and the University I: The Discourse of Humanism)*: 333–358. https://www2.kobe-u.ac.jp/~alexroni/IPD%202015%20readings/IPD%202015_5/under-western-eyes.pdf

Mohanty, C.T. (2007). *Feminism Without Borders: Decolonizing Theory, Practicing Solidarity.* Point Par Point.

Pheko, L.L. (2019). Feminist Economics is everything. The revolution is now! Tedx. https://www.ted.com/talks/lebohang_pheko_feminist_economics_is_everything_the_revolution_is_now?subtitle=en

Starrett, B. (1976). *I Dream in Female: The Metaphors of Evolution and the Metaphors of Power.* Gloucester, MA: Cassandra.

Suppiah, S., Chattopadhyay, S., De Nardin, A.C.F., & Couto, L. (2022). Possible Futures. In: Künkel, P., Ragnarsdottir, K.V. (eds) *Transformation Literacy.* Cham: Springer. https://doi.org/10.1007/978-3-030-93254-1_4

Tamale, S. (2020). *Decolonization and Afro-Feminism: An Afro-Feminist-Legal Critique*. Daraja Press.

Taylor, B. (2013). Kenya's green belt movement: Contributions, conflict, contradictions, and complications in a prominent environmental non-governmental organization (ENGO). In: Trägårdh, L., Witoszek, N., & Taylor, B., *Civil Society in the Age of Monitory Democracy*. Berghahn Books. http://www.brontaylor.com/environmental_articles/pdf/Taylor--KenyaGreenBeltMovement.pdf

Vergès, F. (2022). *A Feminist Theory of Violence: A Decolonial Perspective*. Pluto Press.

Part IV
Leading Feminist Transformations

10

Claiming Power for Transformative Change – Towards Collective Feminist Practices

The previous chapters highlighted that for transformative power to be truly effective, it must be actively claimed by feminists. If women and feminists do not claim power, others keep on doing what they are doing. Only if power is claimed will people notice and subsequently attribute power, which they then may support or fight. We have also explored how power can become transformative if it is defined and claimed based on a *feminist reference system*. While this interpretation varies depending on our geography, culture and history, a fundamentally new paradigm of power can help us overcome our ambiguity, because a feminist-inspired narrative of power serves life, nurtures the vitality of both people and the planet, and is firmly rooted in *collective feminist power practice*. What life and vitality mean is open to negotiation, reflection and continuous learning, but it inherently means inclusive and egalitarian approaches. What *collective feminist power practices* can be, we can derive from feminist knowledge and lived experience, yet we cannot determine them once and for all. Instead, such practices emerge from collective co-creation and collective sense-making in a process of enactment and reflection.

We have arrived at the insight that disruptive and revolutionary acts are as important as knitting feminist-inspired concepts of power into the existing patriarchal power structures that are present everywhere. This inevitably means being exposed to complicity traps, inviting us to withstand the temptations of any narcissistic desires for recognition by men. Claiming power in a feminist way requires a culture of *disobedience* and one of *connection*, because only this enables us to stay alert to the patriarchal power pathologies of *gaslighting* and *divide and rule*. Both patriarchal mechanisms isolate women, even feminists, from each other, which we need to prevent by all means. *Disobedience* requires courage and perseverance, which are easier to maintain if we know that we are connected to a circle of feminists supporting us. Particularly, if women move into positions of power in patriarchal institutional structures, it is the *connection* to feminist circles of trust that can help them stay alert to traps while

DOI: 10.4324/9781003508885-14

maintaining their vision. It also helps them stay in tune with the interconnectedness of *individually* and *collectively* claiming power. Because both aspects are important: **We need women to claim power individually, but we need this power to be used for ways of collectively claiming power for feminist transformations.**

There are lots of sustainability initiatives, partnerships, alliances, networks, conferences, books and demonstrations that aim to transform our world and make it a better place. But one detail is often entirely overlooked: Unless patriarchal power structures and pathologies in all their variations get named and dismantled, transitions to a *Good Life for All* will be difficult, if not impossible. There will be no lasting peace with patriarchy in full swing, or with its subtle persistence. Hence, feminist transformation efforts, small and large, which are connected to visions for just and equitable societies and a just and equitable world economic order, have become a necessity rather than an option.

Imagine the following scenario: Every woman who, based on her expertise, is moving into a position of power in politics, corporations or civil society, would be committed to the advancement of feminist transformations. Hence, even if her arrival in a position of power was mediated by men, she would use her influence as an opportunity to consciously strengthen other women and to bring them into power positions. She would also, supported by a feminist circle of trust, begin to collectively rebuild what power and influence means in service of life and planet, and do all she can for this in her particular position with as much disobedience as she can afford. Her feminist circles of trust would serve as a reflective learning space and as checks and balances. Together, the participating feminists would begin to mediate power positions through women. They would individually and collectively create spaces in which a feminist practice of power and influence becomes a reality and where the mutual attribution of power becomes self-evident. Imagine this taking place at all levels and around the globe.

Although this scenario may still seem unrealistic in today's world, I believe it is important as a guiding vision. From such *collective feminist power practices*, a new construction of reality could emerge – one that dismantles the foundation of patriarchal dominance and opens experiential pathways to feminist-inspired futures. Many men would likely follow willingly, but I am convinced that women must take the lead. Slowly, but persistently, the narrative of power would change to serve not a few, but all people and the planet. The destructive trajectories of the world would begin to shift.

At this stage, your comments column may have already remarked that she is dreaming, given the difference among women, the fact that right-wing female power positions are on the rise and feminists are fighting with each other, given the male power structures still in place, the war atrocities becoming normalized and the patriarchal backlash almost in full swing.

We are allowed to dream. Was Wangari Maathai a dreamer? She had tremendous support from grassroots women, friends and political allies. Imagine if she had received active feminist support from all women across her university, from those in parliament, from every single woman in Kenyan institutions, from the entire African feminist community, from the entire feminist world community – would her courageous and persistent claiming of power have achieved even more than her already tremendous impact?

While Wangari Maathai, back from her five years of studies in the United States, began to organize the Green Belt Movement in Kenya, the American journalist, writer and feminist Robin Morgan was in her 20s when she began her feminist activism. In 1984, she published one of her many books and gave it the title *Anatomy of Freedom – Feminism, Physics and Global Politics*.[1] It reads as though she had the ability to see far into the future. At this stage of human development on the planet, she wrote back then, feminism is the call for survival and the next step in human evolution. She pointed out that women constitute more than half of the world's population, and subsequently have billions of different ways of claiming power and developing strategies to overcome patriarchies. Feminist ideas of equality, egalitarian societies, collaboration, mutual respect, freedom of choice, reverence for nature and the interconnectedness of culture and ecology, she reminded us, were aspects that had been explored by quantum physics and systems theory since the beginning of the 20th century, ignored by many scientists, disregarded by politicians and corporations. Yet she suggested that feminist principles align with what many systems scientists predict as a shift in evolutionary consciousness towards a world in balance, between people, and between people and nature.

In the scientific approaches of quantum physics and systems science, the linear world view of cause and effect, in which life is composed of individual parts separate from each other, is nothing more than a very superficial and rather mechanistic view of a much more complex and interwoven reality. In a systems view of life, there is this incomprehensible complexity and constant reciprocal influence.[2] Everything is interdependent and inextricably interconnected. Life, seen through this lens, emerges in dynamic connection; it cannot really be controlled.

In the late 1990s, the American systems scientist Elisabet Sahtouris argued that the understanding of interdependence must be firmly anchored in our worldview. Such a conceptualization of the universe, she thought, would emphasize a deep and inescapable interconnectedness of all things and people would begin to recognize the value and importance of each fragment of the larger whole.[3] They would begin to see the world as open, dynamic, interconnected and full of qualities of life. Systems science shows that the vitality of life emerges in a complex interaction between the many levels of systems, from individual to community to society to world.[4] Does this remind us of matriarchal worldviews, those of the ancient past and those of Indigenous communities today? Have we arrived in science at a point that humankind, long before the rise of patriarchy, was able to know, even though knowing had a different meaning from today's knowledge generation?

Elisabet Sahtouris suggests that the social tensions we have got used to over the last few thousand years can be compared to the body of a person in which individual cells fight and compete.[5] It would make little sense for the health of the entire body. Using the example of living organisms such as the human body and the conditions for its vitality, it is easy to understand that parts only develop in connection with a whole, that no part exists independently of others, and no part merely 'interacts' with others as an individual unit. Moreover, every interaction has many effects. The human species is not at all separate from this complex life system, even if we are able to observe it. We actually do have the ability to look at our own contributions to the complexity of life; we can study the health of systems, be they societies, cities, nations, communities, economies or ecosystems. In a systems view, life is intentional, collaborative, only mildly competitive, always co-creative, communicative and thriving in mutual consistency between the smaller and the larger entities. A new narrative of power needs to be linked to an understanding of *system vitality* at all levels from the individual to society. There needs to be an associated value system that includes aspects that are beyond our narrow sphere of influence and yet still guide the content of our actions. With the global trend towards sustainability, which has taken a long time to establish itself and is certainly not yet as anchored as it should be through all layers of society, humankind has at least made important steps towards creating guardrails for navigating power with a new narrative. But if we take climate change as an example, mechanisms for balancing power have so far only worked to a very limited extent. The numerous climate conferences provide eloquent testimony to the fact that powerful patriarchal actors are using their influence and institutions to not implement the necessary measures to protect our planet. The British lawyer Polly Higgins, who vehemently promoted the concept of *ecocide* as a crime against humanity and the planet in international law, was convinced that only new laws would work as a mechanism for containing power pathologies. Ecocide refers to all actions that result in long-term damage to the environment or the planetary life support system.[6] If ecocide as a crime were entered into international law, it would give the planetary life support system a higher moral authority than it currently has.

We are endowed with reflective consciousness, which allows us to recognize the vitality of both smaller and larger systems, as well as detect when that vitality is at risk. We can understand *system vitality* as the ability of a system to remain vital and resilient as a whole through further development without endangering the vitality of other systems. Out of vitality, new life arises, a future emerges in which entities can continue to unfold, reproduce or regenerate. Today, we can scientifically understand the health or vitality of systems, comprehend the process of its creation and support it positively. Hence, we could learn to contribute to the vitality of systems at all levels, for every human being, for communities, societies, the world. This would not work without partnering with nature, actually with evolution.

The feminist vision of a *Good Life for All* is a translation of systems vitality into the realm of human communities. To achieve transformative change for feminist-inspired futures at scale, we must understand how smaller and larger systems become and remain vital together. A journey through numerous scientific disciplines shows that a lot is already known about the conditions for system vitality, large and small. From such interdisciplinary research trip, six vitality principles can be identified that can inspire us to learn from life for feminist transformation efforts. These principles are non-hierarchically, not distinctly separate, but mutually connected and they operate in conjunction with each other. In their togetherness they create a pattern of conditions for systems vitality.

The **first principle is generativity**. Life unfolds in an intentional way. It expands and creates the future; this includes the capacity to regenerate, replenish and restore in order to stay alive. The **second principle is containment**. Life needs belonging to ensure identity, yet works with permeable boundaries that allow for exchange and energetic inputs. The **third principle is novelty**. Life is generously creative. It is constantly unfolding novel pathways and new identities. This is inextricably linked with invention, adaptation and learning. The **fourth principle is consciousness**. Life emerges from meaning-making cognition that feeds insight into its structures and fosters adaptability.[7] The **fifth principle is interconnectedness**. Life is built on relationality. It requires diversity and grows into complexity in constant adaptive communication, a vast network in contextual interaction. The **sixth principle is wholeness**. Life operates with integrated, nested, complementary and collaborative entities. The functionality of the larger whole and smaller systems is inextricably linked.[8]

Hence, systems science, quantum science and feminism should connect as allies, showing how the egalitarian, just and inclusive futures are not only a feminist vision, but grounded in the insights of modern science. Collaboration, solidarity, navigating different interests and overcoming inequality are not only feminist concerns, but the scientifically predicted next phase of human evolution. This means accepting that this will be a never-ending negotiation between what is good for the whole and what is good for the individual, a continuous navigation of power relations and interests. Contributing to the vitality of systems is continuous work. It means not falling prey to false harmony, but rather accepting accountability for our positive impact on human and planetary integrity.

Has the collective human consciousness already begun to shift? I believe, yes, despite all the rehearsals of power pathologies. The process towards egalitarian, peaceful and life-sustaining civilizations has already begun. Have power relations shifted already in a way that reflects the shift in consciousness? I believe, no.

The insights from transformation research name the paradox: Paradigm shifts happen on their own, but we have to help them come about. The more people start thinking, writing, communicating and acting in a different way, the more likely the paradigm shift will happen. Transformations, which we can understand as adjusted ways of acting, will also happen in self-dynamic and decentralized ways, yet they need to be well organized at all levels. Like life processes, this cannot be centrally steered, managed or controlled; but we need to learn from life's innumerable networks of communicative resonance. Without the stewardship of deliberate networked action, from local to global and transnational, feminist transformative initiatives lose their potential prospects.

We have seen that science has invented the term *Anthropocene* for our age, a period in the process of Earth's evolution in which the actions and influences of humanity significantly influence the course of further evolution on this planet. When, if not now, do we need to claim power as feminists at scale and use our influence to preserve life? Can we take up this responsibility?

For this to happen, we have to unlearn a lot, re-learn a lot and remember a lot. Yet, we need to repeat to ourselves the simple sentence: *Patriarchy is over.* You may experience the existence of patriarchy every day: In the dominance of male management structures, in everyday domestic life, in the loudness of male egos in politics, in monopolistic economic structures, in the addiction to dangerous technologies, in the shift to right-wing thinking in our societies, in authoritarian heads of state, in war – everywhere. How can I say that patriarchy is over?

I would like to invite you to take the first step that will contribute to changing the world, namely to give this idea a place, to nourish it, to nurture it and to care for it. Because *attention energizes, intention transforms*. There is a crucial scientific insight from both quantum physics and cognition theory about the life principle of consciousness: it requires the process of cognition, which is central to the emergence of reality, which then sets a frame for cognition, driving an eternal feedback loop of co-creation.[9] If we take this insight seriously, we are invited into a deeper understanding of the relationship between mind and matter, between thought and manifest reality. Both collectively and individually, thought creates reality beyond the immediately obvious. The American quantum physicist Danah Zohar described this as an undercurrent of our visible reality, a vast and interwoven sea of potentiality, from which we pick out some manifestations, while other possibilities will never manifest.[10] The human mind, many quantum scientists agree, is one of the mediators between potentiality and manifest reality. We could say, as humankind, we collectively *think* ourselves into the future. Acknowledging that there might be a link between thought and manifest reality helps us to see the impact, individually and collectively, in bringing forth the world as we envision it. Hence, it makes sense to focus our attention on all the diverse elements of feminist manifestations of the future.

Do you remember the world map of women's courage and initiatives? Imagine how the islands begin to grow together. I am aware how difficult this intellectual experiment is, as we are trained to perceive the negative, that which bothers us, and which we have to change and fight against. Yet, I would like to invite you to practice attention to feminist transformations no matter how small they might be. The future needs our cooperation, and it starts with cognition as the process underscoring consciousness. Only what we perceive as possible develops traction and power. What receives attention will grow. I am not referring to the fleeting attention span we give to social media posts, but the continuous and thorough attention practiced deliberately. If this is combined with the globally dispersed intentions to overcome patriarchy and work towards feminist transformations, it will have a positive effect. Despite the daily broadcasting of disturbing news, I encourage you to make an extra effort to notice the many signs that patriarchy is over and new, life-sustaining civilizations are emerging. Given the pioneering aspects of the future that already exist around the world, sufficient attention to them will strengthen our intentions to work towards a feminist future, and together this will have a transformative effect. The process of the emergence of future civilizations is a process of becoming in which we can participate. No step is too small to shy away from contributing. For this we need the memory of egalitarian, peaceful societies, because the memory gives us the certainty that a different world is possible. It will strengthen our commitment to do what is necessary, the next small step that is no less important than the next big project. We need the images of the past so that they show us the feasibility of the future, even if this future will look completely different from the ancient past.

When we examine both historic and contemporary feminist writings, the essence of a *feminist reference system* becomes increasingly clear. It operates according to life-serving principles and is grounded in feminist values: Equality as in equal rights and opportunities, justice including distributive justice, inclusivity, self-determination, sustainability, relationality and collaboration, sustainability as care for the well-being of people and planet, peace and participation, good governance, transparency and accountability. We know that, far beyond the feminist movements, these values are shared by many people – they are the foundation of many international declarations, movements, laws and constitutions, even though such a reference system for humanity has not yet made its ways into the mainstream policy and economic practice. If so, it would guide decision-making, policies, economics, power dynamics and social structures, and would be built on agreements that prioritize nurturing life and sustaining the vitality of people and the planet. Ultimately, the goal is to develop such a reference system as the seed for a new global operating system – one that aligns humanity with the principles of aliveness and ensures a *Good Life for All*. As a specifically *feminist reference system* it requires contextualization and adaptation, in order to become the foundation for *collective feminist power practices*. Living these practices means committing to claiming power as a transformative force and it requires collaborative efforts to navigate the complexities of societal change. Power in collective feminist practices is shared and relational, regenerative and life-affirming, rooted in care for people and the planet, and embedded in respect for the interconnectedness of all beings.

Would a compass for such *collective feminist power practices* help us stay on track? Would it help us to integrate our female freedom and our commitment to work for the future of the planet?

The following ideas for such a compass are based on three pillars. The *first* foundation is my thorough research into past and contemporary feminist action and the diverse strategies used, much of which has been incorporated into this book. The previous chapters showed that an individual and *collective feminist practice* is as old as the resistance to patriarchy or the many attempts to build islands of freedom from patriarchal domination. These practices might have had different names, but they showed that claiming power to shape the future has been a female feature throughout the last few thousand years, despite all setbacks.

The *second* foundation is my scientific exploration towards the principles that foster systems vitality. My scientific journey has taken me across many disciplines that all held a piece of a puzzle in understanding what gives life to systems. Feminist transformations cannot be separated from bringing our world and our societies back into a dynamic balance that acknowledges our human entanglement in the overall evolutionary process. Equal rights for all are by far not enough. It means taking responsibility for our human capability to influence evolution and ensure this influence nurtures people and the planet in a positive way. We need to revitalize social and ecological systems, small and large.

The *third* foundation are my decades of practicing, advising on and teaching collective leadership for strategic and transformative change. It made me humbly experience how collaboration and dialogue was suddenly possible across adverse actors, if humanness could pave its way into relationships riddled with mistrust, and if collective future visions invited people to believe in the impossible.

A *compass for a collective feminist power practice* can function like a safety net that we value as a reliable railing on a suspension bridge that takes us over a raging river. It offers support and security for women, ensuring that no one is left behind. It reminds us of the importance of unconditional basic appreciation, because it fosters a culture where women are valued and respected. At other times it can become an encouraging corrective, because it strengthens our ability to reflect, if our actions align with feminist principles and goals. It can serve as a source of female wisdom, because it draws us to the deep well of female knowledge and experiences which can inform our strategies. It helps us keep strategic balance in our efforts, ensuring that they are sustainable and effective. If a *collective feminist power practice* is the conscious and strategic action aimed at accelerating feminist transformations, then a compass is a helpful guide rooted in relationality and mutual support. It can be used to strengthen our collective power while encouraging women to be truly themselves, cherish differences, acknowledge female authority, steward the future collectively and actively drive transformations towards a just and thriving world. A compass is not cast in stone – it is a living tool, dynamic and flexible, growing as we learn together. I invite you to explore the suggested *compass for collective feminist power practices* as a proposal and attempt to navigate the complexity of our feminist endeavors. I also encourage you to take it and run with it, until you might want to adjust it to your context, your focus, your aspirations or your background, or reinvent a completely different one. But keep the idea of a compass as a dynamic support system that helps us not only to claim power in order to shift patriarchal power structures into life-serving structures, but also as a tool nurturing each other's humanness. See it as a way of living a *feminist reference system.*

The compass I suggest comprises of six dimensions of *collective feminist power practices*: **Mutual re-powerment, networked connectivity, courageous discovery, reflective appreciation, dialogic reciprocity and feminist aspiration**. Similar to the vitality principles, these dimensions are not separate or isolated; rather, they interweave and amplify one another. Engaging in any one practice naturally leads to the others, creating a dynamic flow of collective power. Their strength lies in this interconnectedness, where each dimension enriches and supports the others. The order in which they are described is merely a way to explore them individually, but in practice, they operate as a cohesive whole, as Figure 10.1 shows.[11]

Mutual Re-Powerment

Elevating Women's Power and Agency

In light of the previous chapters' insights and the genealogy of female power, it has become clear that we need to reclaim power and shape its meaning within a *feminist reference system*. We can therefore best call this the practice of *mutual re-powerment*. I have not invented this term, but owe it to the Nigerian-Finish feminist author Minna Salami. She critically examined how the term women's 'empowerment' is often used to uphold a destructive economic system. She says: 'If women are truly empowered, we will end patriarchal rule and be able to live our lives free of male dominated structural oppression.'[12] She suggests that the prefix 're' refers to 'undoing' and to 'breathing new life into'. Indeed, the Latin meaning of the prefix is manifold: It can mean 'back to the original', 'undoing', 'anew' or 'return to previous state'. Mutual re-powerment is the cornerstone of claiming a feminist future. It centers on advancing women's access to power and enhancing their capacity to shape the future, both individually and collectively. This practice requires an active, conscious effort to attribute power and grant authority to women and feminists through supporting each other's professional advancement, aiming for leadership roles and leading change from a feminist perspective. *Mutual re-powerment* calls for courage beyond comfort zones and a commitment to challenge the patriarchal status quo. It involves deliberately striving for influence while staying connected to a feminist community for checks and balances, ensuring collective wisdom guides our actions. In this way, *mutual re-powerment* is not just about personal advancement but about fostering collective influence that uplifts all women. Guided by the vision of a *feminist reference system*, this practice offers mutual support in navigating patriarchal power pathologies. It is about strategic positioning, taking responsibility and holding each other accountable for shaping a future that serves life and nurtures the vitality of people and the planet – no matter the

6 – FEMINIST ASPIRATION

Imagining and actively shaping a transformative feminist future towards the *Good Life for All*.

5 – DIALOGIC RECIPROCITY

Fostering structured exchange of strategies, experiences, information and resources for mutual benefit.

4 – REFLECTIVE APPRECIATION

Valuing the diverse lived experiences, contributions and perspectives of women.

1 – MUTUAL RE-POWERMENT

Elevating women's power and agency to shape the future individually and collectively.

2 – NETWORKED CONNECTIVITY

Building supportive feminist structures that sustain women in working towards feminist transformations.

3 – COURAGEOUS DISCOVERY

Leveraging past and present female and feminist wisdom, knowledge and resilience.

Figure 10.1 A compass for collective feminist power practices © by the author

scale of ambition. By practicing *mutual re-powerment*, we build the foundation for transformative feminist power, ensuring that women lead the way toward a just and life-affirming world.

Networked Connectivity

Building Supportive Feminist Structures

Networked connectivity is the lifeblood of a *collective feminist power practice*. It involves creating support structures that elevate, empower and sustain women as they work toward feminist transformations. At its core, this practice is about fostering feminist circles of trust, strengthening transformative networks and building vital and strategic connections among women, including those in positions of power. In a patriarchal system that thrives on division, competition and distrust, we must resist the forces that pit feminists and women against one another. Instead, we need to live pragmatic solidarity by collaborating and driving collective feminist action across issues and interest groups. Although it may not always be easy to determine where pragmatic solidarity is appropriate and where underlying conflicts need to be brought to the surface, it is essential to practice *networked connectivity* to foster trust and cultivate meaningful conversations despite differences. By building connections and nurturing feminist networks, we dismantle the patriarchal divide and rule strategy. *Networked connectivity* allows us to rise above competition, creating a collective power base from which women can lead lasting societal change. Through this practice, we not only support each other but also create the momentum needed to achieve a feminist future, embracing the diverse pathways that lead us there.

Courageous Discovery

Leveraging Feminist Wisdom

Courageous discovery is the regenerative source of collective feminist power. It is about tapping into the vast reservoirs of female and feminist wisdom, knowledge and resilience to chart a path toward a more just and equitable world. This practice encourages us to disrupt the entrenched rules of the game, explicitly drawing inspiration from the strategies and experiences of women, past and present. By elevating women as sources of inspiration and referencing female knowledge, we amplify the expertise needed to create a *Good Life for All*. At the heart of *courageous discovery* is the recognition that feminist knowledge generation and intuitive wisdom provides critical insights for resilience, especially in the face of crises. Learning from female pioneers, acknowledging the lessons of failures and developing persistence are central to this practice. It calls for openness to diverse lived experiences and a reflective understanding of one's own position, rejecting simplistic, one-size-fits-all solutions. *Courageous discovery* requires us to make an intentional effort to elevate women's knowledge and expertise, ensuring that their contributions are at the forefront of shaping the future. By doing so, we utilize the transformative power of feminist wisdom, fueling our collective ability to foster feminist transformations.

Reflective Appreciation

Valuing Diverse Contributions

Reflective appreciation is the commitment to humanness in feminist power aspirations. It is a conscious political practice that honors the diverse lived experiences, contributions and perspectives of women. This practice invites us to extend gratitude toward women, unearth and cherish herstories, and cultivate care and respect for one another. By recognizing the distinct experiences and contributions of women, we foster a culture of acknowledgment that enhances our collective ability to drive feminist transformations. *Reflective appreciation* also strengthens intersectional perspectives, ensuring that women from all walks of life are valued. It is not about avoiding critique or pointing out limitations, but rather engaging in thoughtful, respectful dialogue that takes the efforts of other women seriously – even when we disagree with their approaches. This practice nurtures a space where differences are celebrated without falling into the trap of superficial harmony. It is about the acknowledgment of women's efforts, both large and small, that contribute to our shared journey towards a feminist future.

Dialogic Reciprocity

Fostering Mutual Exchange

Dialogic reciprocity is the knitting and weaving element in collective feminist power. It is about cultivating meaningful conversations and exchanging strategies, experiences and resources to mutually empower women and feminist movements. It goes beyond simple support; it is a deliberate practice of sharing power and influence, where women and feminist organizations transfer privileges or amplify each other's voices to collectively strengthen feminist transformations. This practice is grounded in the principle of fostering egalitarian relationships at eye level, where differences are acknowledged and diversity is leveraged as a source of strength. It requires building feminist learning circles and creating spaces for dialogue where power imbalances are addressed, feminist forms of governance explored and decision-making processes are inclusive. *Dialogic reciprocity* encourages a culture of sharing resources – be they knowledge, networks or financial means – with the aim of expanding women's power where it is most needed. By engaging in this practice, we actively alleviate patriarchal power imbalances, promote diverse representation and ensure that every woman's voice contributes to the feminist transformation effort.

Feminist Aspiration

Shaping a Transformative Future

Feminist aspiration is the driving force behind envisioning and shaping a transformative feminist future, one that is rooted in the feminist values of equality, justice and the *Good Life for All.* This practice is fueled by a deep commitment to imagining a different world, one where patriarchy no longer prevails and where feminist ideals shape every facet of society. Building feminist ecosystems for transformation is essential to this practice, as is connecting local and global feminist initiatives. By analyzing global trends while staying aligned with our feminist vision, we iteratively co-develop strategies that drive collective feminist influence in shaping the future. *Feminist aspirations*, no matter how small, contribute to change, and every milestone – minor or major – serves as a stepping stone toward this shared vision. While patriarchal backlash may attempt to stifle our aspirations, these moments can also deepen our persistence, when we see the connection of different feminist efforts as part of a larger, joint aspiration. It encourages us to seize every opportunity to resist regressive forces. *Feminist aspiration* requires us to imagine and actively shape feminist futures for economies, technologies, democracies and regenerative societies. It is not just about achieving equal participation but redefining the very systems that uphold patriarchy. The global sustainability movement is a crucial ally in this transformative work, but it is not a substitute for our feminist vision. We must take up the challenge of shaping futures, creating institutions and strategies that reflect our feminist ideals and foster long-lasting, systemic change.

As we have seen in the previous chapter, a feminist approach to claiming power necessitates redefining the concept of leadership. Collaboration, co-creation, empathy and communication – once considered soft skills – are now recognized as essential. By examining how feminist leaders cultivate and sustain inclusive, participatory and co-creative leadership models, we can discover how a *feminist reference system* can come alive through *collective feminist leadership* grounded in the many possibilities of *collective feminist power practices*.

Major insights for *collective feminist power practice* from claiming power for feminist transformations:

1. Claiming power in a feminist way necessitates cultivating a culture of disobedience alongside a culture of connection. This dual approach is crucial to remain vigilant against patriarchal mechanisms like gaslighting and divide and rule, which aim to isolate women from each other.
2. While numerous initiatives aim at global transformation and sustainability, they often overlook the critical need to dismantle patriarchal power structures. Without this focus, sustainable transitions will remain difficult, if not impossible.
3. For feminist transformations we can get inspired by a systems view of life: It is collaborative, only mildly competitive, always co-creative, communicative and thriving in mutual consistency between the smaller and the larger entities. A new narrative of power needs to be linked to an understanding of system vitality at all levels from the individual to society.
4. Paradigm shifts are a prerequisite for transformations. The more people start thinking, writing, communicating and acting in a different way, the more likely they will happen. Subsequent transformations happen in self-dynamic and decentralized ways, yet they need to be well organized at all levels in innumerable networks of communicative resonance.
5. As feminists, we need to tune in to the global trend towards co-creation and collaboration, give each other meaning, mutually attribute power and acknowledge the connectedness of our aspirations despite our differences and conflicts.
6. A *feminist reference system* functions like a guiding star for the future we aim to create. A compass for *collective feminist power practices* helps us navigate the complexity of transformative change.

Notes

1 See Morgan (1984).
2 Capra (2014).
3 Sahtouris (2000).
4 Together with a colleague of mine I have reviewed a large body of literature on systems science with the conclusion that it is of utmost importance to understand the systems (not only the biological) conditions for life to thrive. See Waddock & Kuenkel (2019) and Kuenkel (2019).

5 See Sahtouris (2000).
6 See Higgins (2016).
7 I deliberately use the term consciousness, although many people assume this is only a human capacity. But in many variations, it is the capacity of all living beings. Human consciousness might be the most highly developed, but it is also subject to pathologies and degeneration, as evidenced in our civilizational state.
8 An elaborated scientific exploration into these principles can be found in Kuenkel & Waddock (2019) and Kuenkel (2019).
9 See Maturana & Varela (2008).
10 Zohar & Marshall (1994) and Zohar (2021).
11 A previous version of such feminist practice principles, not explicitly related to power, was developed by my colleague Elisabeth Kühn and me as part of the Collective Leadership Institute. See: www.collectiveleadership.com.
12 See Salami (2015).

References

Capra, F., & Luisi, P.L. (2014). *The Systems View of life: A Unifying View*. Cambridge University Press.

Higgins, P. (2016). *Eradicating Ecocide*. Shepard-Walwyn (IPG).

Kuenkel, P. (2019). *Stewarding Sustainability Transformations: An Emerging Theory and Practice of SDG Implementation*. Springer International Publishing.

Kuenkel, P., & Waddock, S. (2019). Stewarding aliveness in a troubled Earth system. *Cadmus Journal*, 4(1), October. http://cadmusjournal.org/article/volume-4/issue-1/stewarding-aliveness-troubled-earth-system

Maturana, H.R., & Varela, F.J. (2008). *The Tree of Knowledge: The Biological Roots of Human Understanding*. Shambhala, MA.

Morgan, R. (1984). *The Anatomy of Freedom*. Doubleday Books.

Sahtouris, E. (2000). *Earthdance: Living Systems in Evolution*. Iuniverse.com, Inc.

Salami, M. (2015, September 7). Repowerment rather than empowerment. MsAfropolitan. Feminism and Social Criticism by Minna Salami. https://msafropolitan.com/2015/09/repowerment.html

Waddock, S., & Kuenkel, P. (2019). What gives life to large system change? *Organization & Environment*, *33*(3), 342–358. https://doi.org/10.1177/1086026619842482

Zohar, D. (2021). What is a quantum society? In: *Zero Distance*, 221–228. https://doi.org/10.1007/978-981-16-7849-3_21

Zohar, D., & Marshall, I. (1994). *Quantum Society: Mind, Physics and a New Social Vision*. Harper Collins.

11

Collective Feminist Leadership – The Driver of Transformative Change

In a small city in southern Tunisia, a local feminist action group initiated a feminist leaders project. The aim was to develop female-led local initiatives for improved living conditions in the city for women. They did not take to the streets and demanded change, but decided on a different approach. The ideas for their approach began in 2020 in a local network among youth civil society organizations. It was formed in response to local sustainability challenges and to malfunctioning governance between administration and citizens. Whereas after the 'Arab Spring', 70% of the population named democracy as the best form of government in 2013, five years later the positive views of democracy went down to 46%.[1] The still existing authoritarian practices were remnants of the old regime, and it was difficult for the newly formed youth organizations to get their voices heard. Over years, a women-led youth NGO engaged the administration in continuous dialogues on a wide range of topics, from improved city management to regenerative agriculture. They had developed good working relationships with the administration and were highly valued for their constructive criticism. Now, it was time to take a step further. The feminist action group identified women's mental health and violence against women as contentious topics in co-creative sessions, and after conversations with many local interest groups. Finally, they brought all interest groups, including the administration, together in a large-scale collaborative dialogue. The aim was to make everybody understand the urgency of the issues around female living conditions and co-develop solutions in a constructive and cooperative manner, acknowledging the expertise of interest groups from the different institutions. The dialogue shifted perspectives and led to tangible commitments for improvements. The feminist action group in southern Tunisia never made it into the news, nobody would have described them as exercising power, but they widened their circle of influence systematically in their own feminist leadership style.[2]

The previous sections of this book have made it unmistakably clear that the challenges lying ahead of feminists are different in content and context, yet

DOI: 10.4324/9781003508885-15

similar in form. Feminist transformations require a delicate balance between the individual commitment and the collective capacity to enact change. This means identifying needed competencies for our own individual leadership capability, yet knowing when and how to let go of individual aspirations, and instead foster the cohesion of a group of collaborating feminists. It also means knowing when to build alliances beyond feminist actors and movements. Success here means making collective contributions to a feminist future, to justice, gender equality, female freedom, a world in balance and sustainability count, no matter how large or small. Claiming feminist power, we concluded, has a clear purpose: It is about collectively shaping the future towards a *Good Life for All.*

However, the relationship between feminism and leadership has been a difficult one. This is unsurprising, given that leadership history has been shaped largely by white American men, who often defined it as a trait of charismatic men convincing others, mostly men, to support their goals. The concept of leadership emerged in the 1970s in the United States as a motivational tool in hierarchical management, offering a softer way of exercising power by enlisting followers rather than forcing obedience. This rise paralleled the growth of democracies as more egalitarian forms of organizing societies. Early research on leadership focused on individual leaders, primarily men in corporations, who guided actions, set structures and achieved goals.[3] However, the complex challenges of the modern world have eroded this male-centered, leader–follower divide. Leadership studies gradually expanded to include public, non-profit and community contexts.[4] The focus shifted to the *how* of leadership, with increased attention to cultural and diversity issues. Concepts like shared or distributed leadership emerged, emphasizing collaboration between leaders. Unsurprisingly, studies found that diverse experiences, collaboration, information exchange and decentralized decision-making improved overall organizational performance.[5]

Inspired by the rise of systems science, the concept of leadership has shifted to reflect a view of the world as interconnected and relational. Insights from quantum physics and systems science introduced a more complex understanding of leadership as both an individual and a collective activity aimed at shaping reality, not only within organizations but also for societal change. The relational nature of leadership became central, and traditional hierarchies – long used to maintain power in patriarchal institutions – were questioned. Flat hierarchies, teamwork and collaboration became popular.[6] Only gradually did the collective nature of leadership by networks of actors working together receive more attention.[7] Although many of these novel approaches were advanced by female leadership experts rooted in systems thinking,[8] men often gained more recognition for suggesting the resulting more egalitarian organizational models like agile teams, holacracy and sociocracy.[9]

For decades, now, female leadership has gained attention, not only because more women have risen to positions of power, but also because the soft skills required in the evolving leadership paradigm – empathy, collaboration, integration and communication – have often been attributed to women. As this *feminine* style of leadership became more popular, women were trained to assert themselves, while men were encouraged to develop soft skills. Though this trend may be unsettling, as it reinforces gender stereotypes, it can also be seen as an early sign of rebalancing power dynamics. Still, we must remain vigilant.

From a feminist point of view, the paradigm shift in conceptualizing leadership reflects an emerging new worldview, from a mechanistic perception of reality to a complex and relational one. Yet, as much as this trend is welcome, we also need to observe it critically. It may be just one of the many ways through which the so long oppressed female traits are integrated into patriarchal structures without fundamentally shifting power imbalances. The mainstream leadership research, despite the gradual paradigm shift towards a different worldview, does not mention feminism or feminist leadership at all. It does refer to feminine styles of leadership, or to women's leadership, or to female leadership, but remains within the normatively accepted female traits of caring and nurturing as an important addition or a better alternative to the competitive male style of leadership.[10] But for feminist transformations, we need a fundamental shift. If we want to claim power, we also need to claim our own understanding of leadership. There have been a number of feminist approaches aiming at redefining leadership while relating it to the paradigm shift in contemporary leadership concepts and, in particular and more recently, to collective leadership.[11] The latter is the ground on which the redefinition of leadership can take shape, if it is conceptualized as *collective feminist leadership*. For approaching such a conceptualization, two of the *collective feminist power practices* are particularly instrumental: *Networked connectivity* and *feminist aspiration*.

The power practice of *networked connectivity* in leadership involves awareness of the underlying complex compositions and dynamics of the systems that require change as well as the dynamics developing in a group of collaborating actors. For feminist transformations, it is crucial to understand how leadership collectives can turn meaningful discussions into forward-thinking collective action. The real potential of these women's circles or networks – whether operating globally on multiple levels or rooted locally – lies in their ability to collaborate and work toward a shared vision of feminist futures.

The power practice of *feminist aspiration* drives collective leadership with a feminist stance. It is purposefully connected to the larger goal of aiming for a *Good Life for All*, even when the change endeavor is small or particular. This means a shift from a self-centered consciousness to awareness of the context and space in which leadership takes place, and ultimately awareness of the global context. Women's individual capacity to lead is of utmost importance, but will inevitably remain less effective, unless leading transformative change becomes the capacity of a collective.

Hence, *collective feminist leadership* requires a collaborative, non-hierarchical approach to leadership that prioritizes shared responsibility, mutual respect and the common good, aiming for transformative change that benefits all, with a focus on rebalancing power towards equality and feminist values. Such leadership often occurs in non-hierarchical, cooperative, often multi-interest group contexts, such as movements or initiatives, where no one actor holds power over others. Yet, even in hierarchical institutions, it operates on the basis of eye-level relationships and a spirit of collective responsibility. While people may differ in experience, expertise or resources, they meet with mutual respect and recognition of contributions. Success is measured by a feminist collective's ability to ensure purpose-driven, future-focused action. The structures in which leadership takes place may vary – ranging from loose networks of actors driving change to collaboratively organized institutions or multi-interest group governance bodies.

For leading feminist transformations there is a lot to learn from cross-sector or multi-interest group sustainability initiatives. It is helpful to be familiar with these change approaches, where collaboration on an issue of common concern takes place between different institutional actors, who often are representatives from different societal sectors such as civil society, the public sector or the business sector. Such multi-interest group initiatives are at the forefront of systems transformation efforts and model a puzzle piece of the future: Participation and collaboration. Helping multiple interest groups achieve a common goal – for example, in developing circular economy strategies, creating sustainable supply chains, setting up ocean ecological governance or developing social policies – requires a sincerely nurturing and integrative approach that rests on a mix of high-quality dialogues and reliable implementation of agreed measures. Not surprisingly, many of the leaders, often not named leaders but instead called process facilitators, in such transformative change processes are women. These experiences are relevant for *collective feminist leadership*, because the purpose of feminist transformations is a system change towards feminist-inspired open and pluriverse societies. Systems change requires approaches and settings that facilitate a shift in the way people perceive each other, work with each other and relate to each other.[12] We can learn a lot from collective leadership in multi-interest group constellations for feminist transformations, but need to delve deeper into what is and could be specific to feminist leadership now and in the future. *Collective feminist leadership*, particularly aimed at transformative change towards overcoming patriarchy, requires increased capacities at three levels.

The *first* is the **self**. This refers to the awareness of one's own potentials and shortcomings. It acknowledges that the individual, even in collective leadership, plays a crucial role regarding her ability to reflect and further develop as a node in a network of influence and power. Self-awareness is an individual commitment, yet greatly advanced through collective reflection and mutual support. The Indian social activist and women's rights advocate Srilatha Batliwala suggests that transforming societies means transforming ourselves first.[13] This also means becoming aware of internalized narratives about women and feminists, our own biases and privileges, our habits and behavior as well as our complicity with power imbalances. The Caribbean researcher and feminist activist Peggy Antrobus insists that feminist leadership requires a process of inner transformation that includes consciousness raising for feminist perspectives on the world.[14] Those of us who are active feminists know that this is a lifelong learning process that would not yield results without personal deep dives into different feminist interpretations of past and present developments, and not without feminist peers who we can reflect with together and get inspired by. Hence, in *collective feminist leadership*, self-awareness is deeply relational. We become who we are and gain courage to lead in exchange with feminist fellow travellers.

The *second* level is the **system**. Most importantly, it is about understanding the dynamics of the patriarchal systems we want to transform with collectives of feminists. Understanding systems means gathering different perspectives, multiple viewpoints, as well as facts and figures. A collective diagnosis through analyzing the context for transformative change will never be perfect, but is far superior to any individual assessment of a situation. While many people in transformative change operate without awareness of patriarchal power pathologies, feminist leaders point to the hidden truth. The American researcher Tracy R. Barton emphasizes this point when she suggests that leadership from a feminist perspective is greatly empowered by this specific feminist lens.[15] It enables feminists to recognize injustice and oppression. It also inspires them to connect micro-level issues with macro-level issues, hence creating analytic connections that are paramount for systems change. Feminist leaders bring a lot of additional and value-based aspects in understanding systems, such as power structures and intersectional linkages between gender identities, race, social class and colonial legacies. Pursuing transformative change, for feminist leaders, is connected to the larger vision of a *Good Life for All*, yet rooted in the lived realities that need to be changed step by step.

The *third* level is **process**. Leading collectively always requires a commonly created goal as well as the design and iterative implementation of dialogic and collaborative processes with multiple interest groups to achieve the goal. This is an art of leading that is often underestimated, because the skills of process facilitation do not feature as brilliant leadership capacities. People tend to focus on tangible results, often staying oblivious to which brilliant processes have been applied to achieve the results. In *collective feminist leadership*, process is never neutral. It is always related to the purpose of abolishing patriarchy, redistributing power and building feminist-inspired societies. This requires attention to two areas simultaneously. Within feminist collectives it is about shared power, collective decision-making, joint responsibility and mutual accountability. This includes taking care of each other's safety and well-being. Externally, *collective feminist leadership* can take vastly different forms. Some feminist leaders focus on advocacy, ensuring transparency, naming challenges, disrupting the status quo and mobilizing movements. They amplify feminist voices, protect marginalized groups and push for legal and procedural change. Others work within institutions, reshaping them from the inside to reflect feminist values in rebuilding power structures. Many engage in multi-interest group initiatives even if they do not have explicitly feminist goals, but contribute to shaping the future by promoting collaboration, dialogue and tangible results.

Collective feminist leadership is a collaborative transformative approach to change, grounded in feminist values, aiming to challenge power imbalances and promote inclusivity, equity and justice. It fosters shared power, encouraging everyone to contribute to change. By connecting global power dynamics with local realities, it operates across diverse contexts, including patriarchal institutions and spaces. It values collective care, accountability and unlearning oppressive norms. Linked to Indigenous knowledge and ecological systems, it promotes system vitality through reciprocity and cooperation. To counter the fragmentation of feminist movements, it calls for unity in pluriversality and recognition of diverse lived experiences. A fundamental prerequisite for *collective feminist leadership* is a shift in women's focus from seeking validation and acknowledgment from the male symbolic order to cultivating mutual support and re-powerment among themselves. The political practice of mutual attribution of power and nurturing alternative modes of recognition and affirmation rooted in women's experiences can pave the way for dismantling patriarchal structures. This requires a critical examination of the ways in which we internalize and perpetuate patriarchal norms, even as we aspire for change.

Against the backdrop of these three levels of capacity – the **self, the system and the process** – let us explore how patterns of lived *collective feminist power practices* can create the conditions for *collective feminist leadership* to become impactful. Each of the six practices invites us to various different and creative forms of leading in a feminist way. The ways to enact the practices are manifold, depending on our experience, our context, our capabilities and whether we can live feminism out in the open or require clandestine strategies. As an invitation, let us unpack each of the six practices to illustrate the possibilities from which we can choose. Beyond my suggestions, I encourage you to add actions you prefer or create your own contextualized menu of practices that enliven *collective feminist leadership*. Pick from the possibilities where you are already active and mark which areas you could improve. Ideally, we implement at least a few deliberate actions for each of the six practices. This would greatly advance our collective feminist potency.

Ways of living the *collective feminist power practice* of **mutual re-powerment** are manifold and depend on who we are and in which context we live. Yet, it always begins with **claiming the space**. Making your voice heard, as well as encouraging other women to speak up, establishes a foundation for feminist visibility. As we navigate female and feminist struggles, we see that **cultivating courage** and persistence are essential to disrupt patriarchy's hold. Collective nurturing strengthens courage, helping us resist exhaustion and negative feedback. **Advancing each other** in professional growth is vital, even if it requires us to operate within structures that don't nurture us. Networks, mentorship, peer-coaching and shared opportunities help women advance professionally while fostering vigilance towards harmful power structures and safeguarding them from falling into the complicity trap of patriarchal cultures. **Granting authority** to women is a very important practice that helps in unlearning ingrained patriarchal habits. It facilitates shifting power away from men and engenders a matrix of female authority that subverts traditional patriarchal expectations. Authority here isn't about hierarchy but about respecting expertise and experience. For feminist perspectives to thrive, we also need to access power positions within patriarchal structures. Structural power allows feminist influence on decisions and policies, while movement power fuels transformation. **Sitting at the table** matters, but we must not sit there alone, because in patriarchal or anti-feminist spaces feminist interventions face resistance, ridicule or hostility. **Taking a feminist stance** with a commitment to change requires connection to support networks or leadership collectives that strengthens feminist influence and representation. Figure 11.1 illustrates these possibilities to enact the practice of **mutual re-powerment**.

At the heart of the *collective feminist power practice* of **networked connectivity** lies confidence in building relationships. It can begin with **creating circles of trust**, protected spaces, where differences can be explored, experiences shared

TAKE A FEMINIST STANCE

Lead intentional change towards feminist futures. Build feminist leadership collectives.

SIT AT THE TABLE

Aim for influence and support other feminists to do the same. Strive for power positions collectively.

GRANT WOMEN AUTHORITY

Attribute leadership capabilities to women and acknowledge your own and other women's expertise and experience.

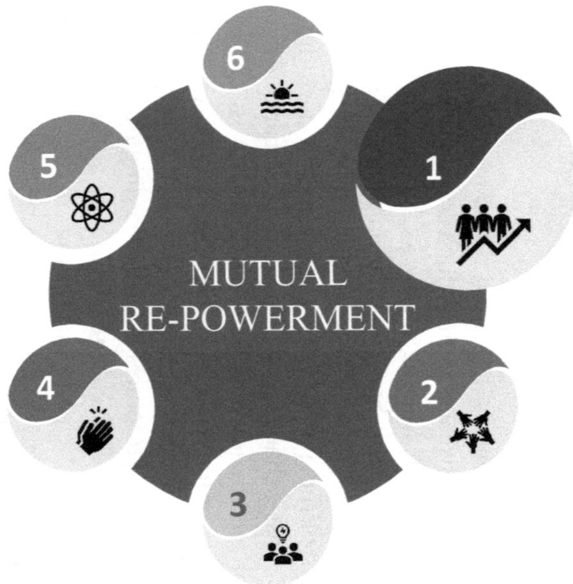

CLAIM THE SPACE

Make your and other women's voices heard and encourage women to speak up.

CULTIVATE COURAGE

Stand together to build resilience and support each other in challenging patriarchal norms.

ADVANCE EACH OTHER

Support your own and other women's professional growth within and beyond patriarchal institutions.

Figure 11.1 Possible practices around mutual re-powerment

and strategies shaped. These spaces foster resilience, offering a sanctuary for reflection and growth as part of feminist collective power practices. Such circles have deep roots in female genealogies, though patriarchy has often fragmented them. Rebuilding inclusive feminist spaces is essential to overcoming the isolation that can stifle activism. The internet and social media have contributed a lot to making networking among women possible across continents. We know that **building networks** is essential for collective re-powerment and amplifying feminist influence. Yet, it is important not only to cultivate like-minded communities, but also to strategically collaborate across networks in order to influence policy, shift institutional structures or create a wider impact. Within these networks, **connecting women in power** is essential, because they are often vulnerable to isolation. Feminists in institutional power positions need connections with both peers and movement-based feminists who operate independently of institutional constraints. Creating dedicated spaces for feminist leaders helps women in positions of influence to shape a feminist future from within traditional institutions. It also fosters an important culture of checks and balances. **Radical collaboration** with an explicit focus on women thrives on working across institutions, movements and networks for advancing feminist goals. It facilitates cross-pollination of ideas and shared strategies, extending the reach and effectiveness of feminist action. In a world that often pits women against each other, **resisting competition** and embracing pragmatic solidarity is a radical act. By supporting one another's achievements, we nurture a culture of mutual respect and collective upliftment, which stands in contrast to the competitive dynamics that we are usually exposed to in patriarchal institutions. **Driving collective action** consolidates such efforts, focusing on coordinated initiatives with clear feminist goals. Celebrating successes together reinforces courage and persistence. Figure 11.2 illustrates some of the possibilities to enact **networked connectivity**.

The *collective feminist power practice* of **courageous discovery** begins by **disrupting the rules**. Without pushing the boundary of the systems that invite us into complicity traps, we won't begin to 'change everything'.[16] By exploring unconventional possibilities, we challenge and redefine existing norms. This requires deliberate acts of disobedience and can be challenging or uncomfortable. While we pay homage to the many brave heroines who have come before us, we must also recognize that disobedience requires collectivity. This amplifies impact and can create a safety net, particularly as these joint efforts rarely take a break. **Favoring female sources** is a deliberate practice to value women's knowledge and their often-untapped resources. When we commit to giving deliberate attention to women's achievements and stories, we begin to rewrite history and shift how reality itself is perceived, because knowledge shapes collective memory and inspires future directions. **Building expertise** in all areas

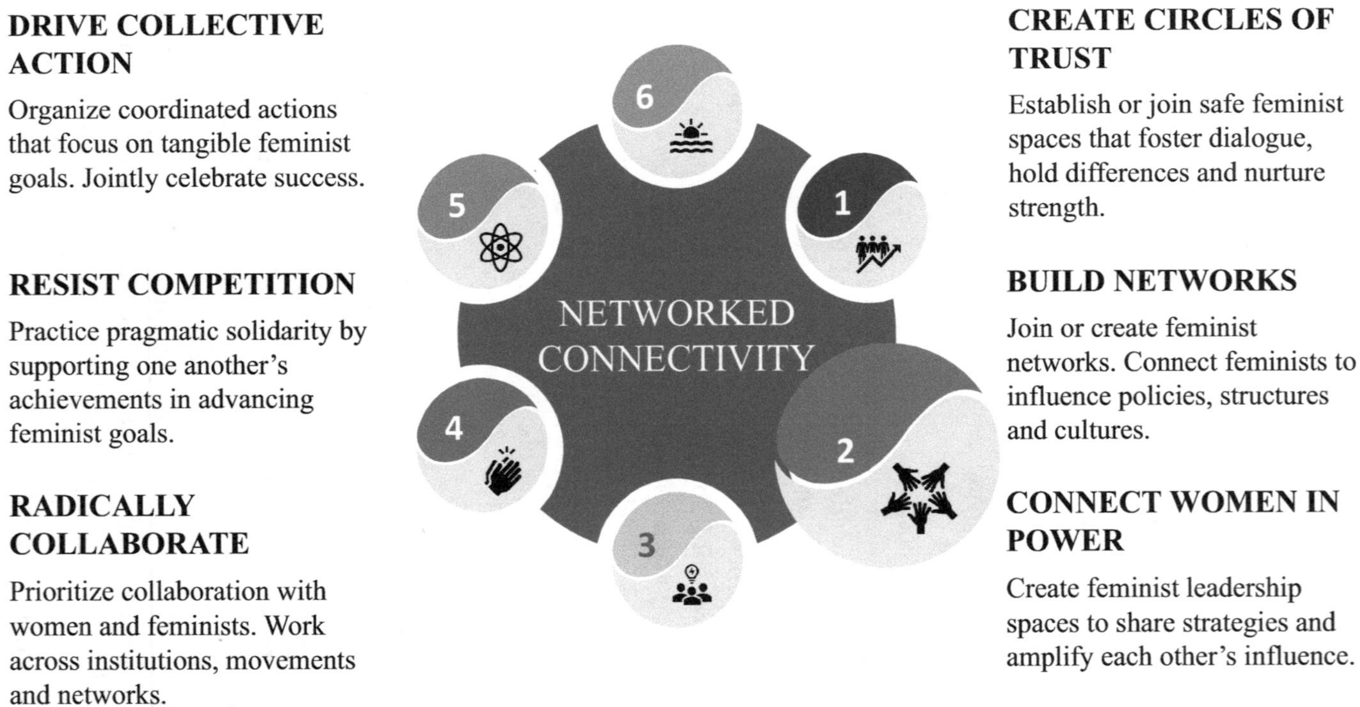

Figure 11.2 Possible practices around networked connectivity

that relate to feminist transformations, such as economics, science and politics, is essential for informed advocacy and for shaping feminist futures. We need to be at the forefront of pathways to feminist-inspired regenerative civilizations. In knowledge building, we need to give us the permission to be biased. The focus on **referencing women** (particularly from the Global South) is a deliberate practice of attributing expertise and power to women in science, politics and the arts. It challenges the hegemony of male-dominated and most often Global North-dominated narratives and ensures the brilliance of female experts and future thinkers emerges from the silencing forces of patriarchal and neocolonial power structures. Similarly, supporting **female pioneers** opens new pathways for feminist discovery. We know that these trailblazers often face more obstacles than men, particularly in technological innovation. Championing women innovators not only acknowledges their contributions but also encourages others to forge new paths in spaces where they've been historically underrepresented. Courageous discovery requires skills and practices in **building resilience** by staying connected to feminist communities, helping us to weather storms together, which will inevitably be part of the journey. Figure 11.3 illustrates some of the possibilities to enact **courageous discovery**.

The *collective feminist power practice* of **reflective appreciation** begins with **acknowledging realities**. By honoring the lived experiences and diverse journeys of women, we build a culture of recognition that values the challenges and achievements each woman encounters on her path. Acknowledgment doesn't mean agreement or following the same path, as women's experiences and strategies for freedom are diverse. Yet, cultivating a culture of acknowledgment significantly strengthens our collective power. Adding gratitude to acknowledgment deepens this practice. **Extending gratitude** becomes an intentional practice, if we actively thank women for their contributions, the battles won or lost before ours, and the pathways they've forged toward feminist transformations that have made our lives easier. **Embracing intersectionality** deepens this appreciation by acknowledging how race, class, sexuality, disability and colonial legacies intersect with patriarchy, shaping women's experiences and influencing their struggles. It reveals privileges we may overlook, making it a necessary step in combating injustice. **Cherishing herstories** honors female genealogies, connecting us to the billions of women who came before, enriching our collective memory and emboldening us for feminist futures. **Taking care** means nurturing our own journey while supporting the growth and well-being of other women. It becomes strategic when we withdraw care from patriarchal expectations and direct it toward ourselves and other feminists. **Cultivating collegiality** emphasizes the importance of professional respect and shared goals. Recognizing the difference between friendship and collegiality is important in feminist transformations. By fostering a supportive, goal-oriented environment,

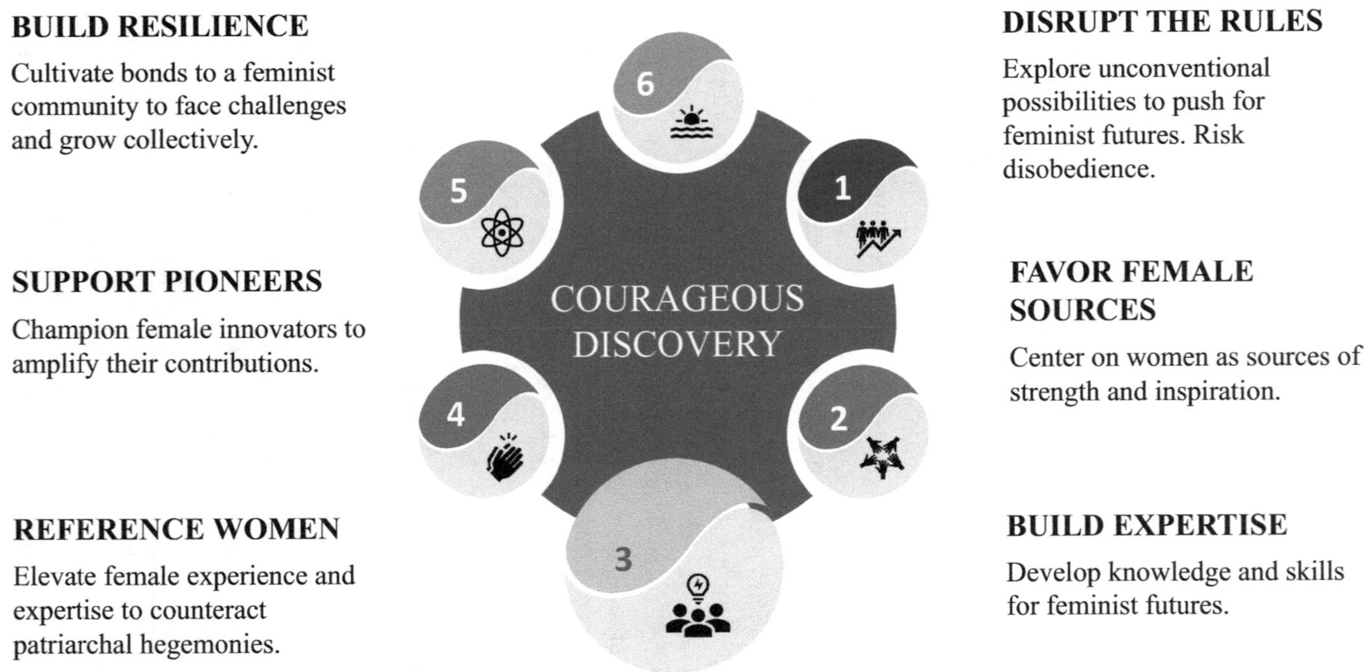

Figure 11.3 Possible practices around courageous discovery

feminists encourage collaboration that strengthens both individual paths and collective feminist transformations.

The *collective feminist power practice* of **dialogic reciprocity** begins by **fostering dialogue** as meaningful and structured conversations. As a feminist practice, this also means refraining from shitstorms, public smear campaigns or bullying, and instead inviting difficult conversations. Respectful criticism and openness to difficult conversations enable us to bridge differences, acknowledge areas of growth and create stronger consensus through honest, constructive engagement. Being vigilant of the patriarchal power pathology of divide and rule is of utmost importance for feminist progress. We need to bear the insight that disagreements precede consensus-building. **Alleviating imbalances** involves promoting inclusive practices and addressing power dynamics. In institutional contexts, this translates to policies that ensure fair treatment and opportunities for all, thus dismantling ingrained hierarchies. **Acknowledging diversity** allows us to agree to disagree, celebrate varied perspectives and invest in finding common ground. Even feminists have hugely different agendas. Beyond acknowledgment, **leveraging difference** transforms varied perspectives into sources of collective strength. Egalitarian relationships do not mean that all are the same, should do the same or carry the same responsibility. Differences in expertise, skills, knowledge, power and experiences among woman can enrich the collective journey to claiming power. Recognizing power in its multiple forms while valuing egalitarian relationships is a crucial aspect of this practice. **Creating learning circles** provides a platform for sharing knowledge and strategic insights. These spaces are dedicated to expanding feminist understanding, building skills and reflecting on collective action. Learning circles support individual growth and strengthen feminist initiatives. **Promoting feminist representation** ensures that feminists are well represented in governance and decision-making structures. Advocating for women in these roles, supporting their advancement and strategically increasing feminist voices in decision-making processes are vital steps in ensuring that feminist perspectives shape the future.

The *collective feminist power practice* of **feminist aspiration** begins with **connecting to vision**, which reminds us to keep the goal of feminist futures ever-present, no matter how far off it may feel. Feminist aspirations are anchored in the belief that every step toward transformation, however incremental, brings society closer to a world rooted in equality, justice and collective well-being. This vision is essential, sustaining us in the challenging work of dismantling patriarchal structures. To support this vision, **understanding trends** is crucial. Staying informed on feminist and other efforts to address sustainability challenges allows us to be responsive and helps us build strategic alliances.

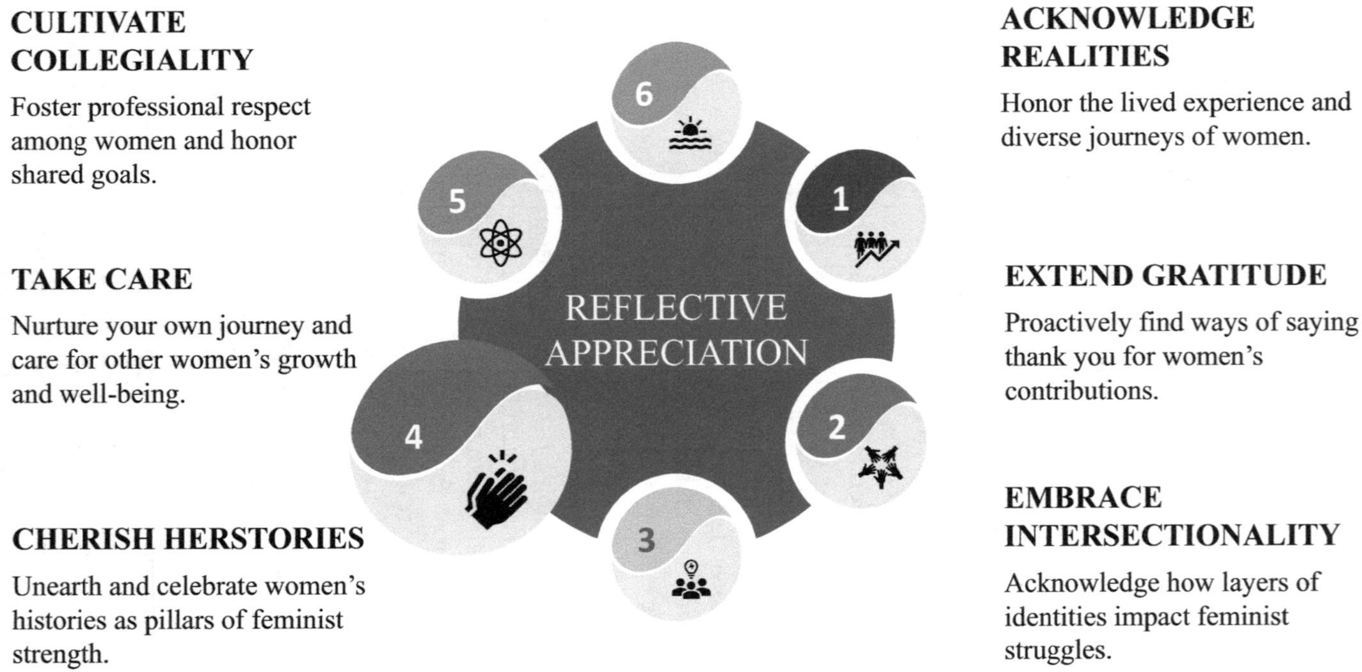

Figure 11.4 Possible practices around reflective appreciation

Connecting with the evolving landscape of feminist activism strengthens our capacity to create and contribute to solutions that are relevant and impactful. **Building feminist ecosystems** means fostering collaboration among feminists across institutions and issue-based initiatives. This can take the form of collaboration between movements and feminists in political or economic institutions; or it can manifest as transnational collaboration between feminist initiatives around certain issues. **Linking feminist initiatives** with other movements, especially those focused on sustainability, creates a multiplier effect for systemic change. Collaborative efforts can address systemic issues like gender-based violence, economic disparity and political underrepresentation, and connect these crucially important issues with economic transformation, regeneration initiatives, social movements or technological development. Institutionalization is an important strategy to build and maintain power. Feminist initiatives need to consolidate their power and influence in the form of institutional power that lasts over a long period of time. Hence, **consolidating power** has two different strategies. One is to establish or strengthen feminist institutions that are pioneers of the future, whether they are housing projects, social institutions, banks, philanthropic organizations, membership organizations or NGOs. The other strategy means establishing feminist rules, procedures or organizational processes within existing institutions that gradually change the institution. This can range from obligatory affirmative action, quotas for female participation, feminist policy development, introducing flat hierarchies and strengthening collaborative teamwork in institutions, to establishing feminist-oriented governance rules, procurement rules or the availability of family-friendly working conditions. Feminist institutionalization is a strategic imperative for long-term influence in shaping societies. **Strategizing impact** means coordinating efforts across borders, institutions and movements for cohesive collective action. Through strategic planning, feminist efforts can become more widespread and create lasting change towards feminist futures

Now I wonder what your comments column says: Is this too complex? Or is it self-evident? Are these practices too general or too specific? Do they already get implemented?

The invitation here is to use them as a compass – or to create your own. This is not about becoming perfect in leading feminist transformations together, or about judging each other. It is about the insight that we need *collective feminist leadership* toward a broadly similar goal on a collective scale if we truly aspire to change power imbalances and shift the detrimental trajectories of patriarchal power pathologies. Small enactments of *collective feminist power practices* add up to reframing power and living power in a feminist way. This is a global collective learning journey that each of us is part of or that we can more

PROMOTE FEMINIST REPRESENTATION

Advocate for feminists in decision-making roles. Actively contribute to shaping institutions.

CREATE LEARNING CIRCLES

Establish feminist learning spaces for knowledge sharing and strategic growth.

LEVERAGE DIFFERENCE

Use varied expertise and experiences as collective strength. Recognize feminist power in its many forms.

FOSTER DIALOGUE

Criticize respectfully, foster structured dialogue and embrace difficult conversations.

ALLEVIATE IMBALANCES

Promote inclusive practices. Address power dynamics within feminist spaces.

ACKNOWLEDGE DIVERSITY

Embrace differences among feminists. Find common ground while celebrating diverse perspectives.

Figure 11.5 Possible practices around dialogic reciprocity

STRATEGIZE IMPACT

Coordinate transformation efforts across countries, regions and continents.

CONSOLIDATE POWER

Build and strengthen feminist institutions. Anchor feminist values in existing institutions, policies and procedures.

LINK FEMINIST INITIATIVES

Seek collaboration between diverse feminist content issues, and connect them with sustainability initiatives.

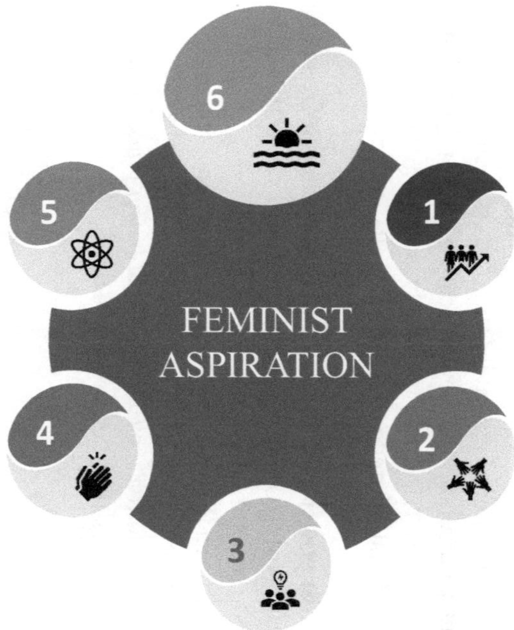

CONNECT TO VISION

Keep the goal of feminist futures clear, no matter how distant it may seem.

UNDERSTAND TRENDS

Stay informed about feminist efforts to overcome global sustainability challenges.

BUILD FEMINIST ECOSYSTEMS

Create issue-based collaboration between feminists across institutions.

Figure 11.6 Possible practices around feminist aspiration

consciously join. It is about finding pathways towards a future in which taking care of a *Good Life for All* becomes the mainstream paradigm, even if each of us will contribute to the journey in different ways. Imagine the impact on people and planet if this way of acting and interacting by women were to expand and flourish. Our task is to make our inherent capacity for *collective feminist leadership* more explicit, to bring it to the surface, to understand how it works, supported by interconnected *collective feminist power practices*.

Major insights for *collective feminist power practices* from *collective feminist leadership*:

1. Feminist transformations necessitate balancing personal commitment and inner transformation with the collective capacity for enacting change.
2. The recent paradigm shift in leadership conceptualization integrates insights from quantum physics and system science, recognizing it as both an individual and a collective activity that fosters societal change.
3. While the shift to a relational view of leadership is positive, it must be critically observed to ensure it genuinely addresses power imbalances rather than superficially integrating female traits into existing patriarchal structures.
4. Claiming feminist power to shape a future that ensures a *Good Life for All* requires adopting interconnected, relational and collective leadership, challenging and redressing power imbalances.
5. *Collective feminist leadership means* expanding our capacities of self-awareness, systems understanding and process *competence*.
6. The manifold enactment of *collective feminist power practices* can help collective feminist leadership to emerge at scale.

Notes

1 Meddeb (2018).
2 See Collective Leadership Institute (2023).
3 The most known male authors were Drucker (1992), Bennis (1994) and Kotter (1996).
4 Ospina et al. (2012).
5 Gronn and Salas (2004).
Boone and Hendricks (2009).
6 See Margaret Wheatley with her highly acclaimed book *Leadership and the New Science*: Wheatley (2006).
7 See Kuenkel (2016) on collective leadership and a more scientific analysis of leadership concepts in Kuenkel (2019).
8 See Helgesen (1995), who emphasized inclusion as a leadership paradigm and early on questioned the male-centered leader–follower paradigm; also Henderson et al.

(2007), who showed how women lead differently, or Hartmann (1999) exploring the leadership style of powerful women.

9 For example, Robertson (2015).

10 A brilliant analysis of this can be found in Batliwala (2019).

11 For a good overview, see Batliwala (2011). She critically reviews both feminine and feminist conceptions of leadership. A thoughtful conception of collective feminist leadership can be found in Ghizzo (2021).

12 For an elaborate open access description of multi-interest group change processes see Kuenkel et al. (2020).

13 See Batliwala (2011).

14 See Antrobus (2000).

15 See Barton (2019).

16 This is a reminder of the inspiration from Verónica Gago. See Gago (2020).

References

Antrobus, P. (2000). Transformational leadership: Advancing the agenda for gender justice. *Gender & Development*, 8(3), 50–56. https://doi.org/10.1080/741923780

Barton, T.R. (2019). Feminist leadership: Building nurturing academic communities. *Advancing Women in Leadership Journal.* https://www.semanticscholar.org/paper/Feminist-Leadership%3A-Building-Nurturing-Academic-Barton/8c5a11a089d2e1c89d9ecbe7467cde3875052c01

Batliwala, S. (2011). *Feminist Leadership for Social Transformation: Clearing the Conceptual Cloud.* CREA. https://Creaworld.org/Wp-Content/Uploads/2020/11/Feminist-Leadership-Clearing-Conceptual-Cloud-Srilatha-Batliwala.pdf

Batliwala, S. (2019). *All About Power: Understanding Social Power and Power Structures*. CREA. https://creaworld.org/wp-content/uploads/2020/07/All-About-Power.pdf

Bennis, W. (1994). *On Becoming a Leader*. Cambridge, Massachusetts: Perseus Books.

Boone, C., & Hendricks, W. (2009). Top management team diversity and firm performance: Moderators of functional-background and locus-of-control diversity. *Management Science*, 55(2), 165–180.

Collective Leadership Institute. (2023). Impact of the Collective Leadership Institute in MENA. https://www.collectiveleadership.de/blog/article/projects-in-mena-region

Drucker, P. (1992). *Managing for the Future*. New York, NY: Truman Talley/E.P. Dutton.

Gago, V. (2020). *Feminist International: How to Change Everything*. Verso.

Ghizzo, E. (2021, October 29). Collective feminist leadership: Unlearning the me, me, me. Heinrich-Boell-Foundation. https://www.boell.de/en/2021/10/29/collective-feminist-leadership-unlearning-me-me-me

Gronn P., & Salas E. (2004). Leadership capacity in teams. *Leadership Quarterly*, *15*(6), 857–880.

Hartman, M.S. (1999). *Talking Leadership: Conversations with Powerful Women*. Rutgers University Press.

Helgesen, S. (1995). *The Web of Inclusion: A New Architecture for Building Great Organizations*. New York: Currency/Doubleday.

Henderson, H., Houston, J., & Marx-Hubbard, B. (2007). *The Power of Yin*. Cosimo, Inc.

Kotter, J. (1996). *Leading Change*. Boston, MA: Harvard Business School Press.

Kuenkel, P. (2016). *The Art of Leading Collectively*. Chelsea Green Publishing.

Kuenkel, P. (2019). *Stewarding Sustainability Transformations: An Emerging Theory and Practice of SDG Implementation*. Springer International Publishing.

Kuenkel, P., Kühn, E., Stucker, D., & Williamson, D.F. (2020). *Leading Transformative Change Collectively: A Practitioner Guide to Realizing the SDGs*. Routledge.

Meddeb, Y. (2018). Support for democracy dwindles in Tunisia amid negative perceptions of economic conditions. Afrobarometer Dispatch No. 232. https://afrobarometer.org/sites/default/files/publications/Dispatches/ab_r7_dispatchno232_support_for_democracy_dwindles_in_tunisia_1.pdf

Ospina, S., Foldy, W., Hadidy, E.I., Dodge, J., Hofmann-Pinilla, A., & Su, C. (2012). Social change leadership as relational leadership. In M. Uhl-Bien, & S. Ospina (Eds.), *Advancing Relational Leadership Research: A Dialogue Among Perspectives*. (Leadership Horizons Series). Greenwich, CT: Information Age.

Robertson, B.J. (2015). *Holacracy: The New Management System that Redefines Management*. Henry Holt & Company.

Wheatley, M.J. (2006). *Leadership and the New Science: Discovering Order in a Chaotic World*. Berrett-Koehler.

12 Feminist Transformation Networks – The Fabric of Future Societies

Imagine the picture of the world map of women's attempts to dismantle patriarchy, equipped with *collective feminist power practices*, working towards feminist futures in movements, institutions, politics and communities. Imagine this not as a two-dimensional map with islands of feminist movements, feminist advocacy and collective action, but as a three-dimensional network. Imagine the hidden strings of communication and exchange between different feminists inside and outside institutions, between different networks, helping and inspiring each other, engaging in communication, learning and discourse about strategies that work, about successes and failures, about ways to support each other. Imagine strings reaching across countries and continents. The picture that might emerge in your mind may look like something the Canadian scientist Suzanne Simard discovered in an entirely different context. In her research, she was able to prove that trees in a forest constantly communicate and cooperate with each other via underground fungal networks. If there is a pest infestation, the affected trees warn other trees. If a tree needs support, nutrients are mobilized. Contrary to popular belief, trees do not compete with each other for nutrients and light, but, according to Suzanne Simard, are downright altruistic. What was laughed at as a research result 20 years ago has now become accepted as scientific knowledge.[1] Research into forest ecosystems shows that mycorrhizal networks create connections between plants and fungi and, as a network in constant communication, are essential for the vitality of the forest. Not everything that nature has to offer can be transferred to human societies, but the similarities between the underground forest communication networks, the structure of our brain, our body's own communication structures, our modern internet technology and the increasing number of feminist networks are striking. Working towards abolishing patriarchy and fostering system vitality in societies and nature requires networks. Feminist networks are crucial for driving social change, addressing misogyny, advocating for policy change and supporting women in power positions as much as women

DOI: 10.4324/9781003508885-16

in grassroots movements. Networks are therefore a core strategy for feminist transformations. They are our pathways into the future.

Neither the existence nor the concept of networks is a new phenomenon. People have always formed networks and acted in networks – in business, in politics, for the enforcement of human rights and for the preservation of the environment.[2] Both quantum physics and systems science have given scientific credentials to what many Indigenous communities know: Life itself is organized in reciprocal relationships. Systems vitality, wherever we find it on our planet in social and ecological systems, thrives on networked communication, iteratively and in mutual support. While we as human beings can consciously decide for or against networks, non-human nature simply lives in networks. In order to understand how much vitality and resilience on our planet are based on functioning networks, we can learn a lot from the natural world: Networks are most effective when they are vital and strengthen all network members. Making use of these insights is important for *collective feminist leadership* and feminist transformations. Human networks thrive when communication flows, when participants support each other and people put the well-being of all at the forefront. This is not just about formal network structures; it is about the purpose of networks as well as the quality of interaction between members of a network; it is about the way women relate to each other in networks that counts. Networks offer a glimpse into a future where citizen engagement and learning societies are the norm. Yet, networks resist hierarchy and centralized decision-making, which can even erode their functionality. Feminist networks are rooted in egalitarian, relational and dialogic approaches, combining strategic purpose with collaborative care.[3]

Today, such networks span a range of purposes and methodologies, from sharing knowledge and providing mutual support to mobilizing for policy change and enacting broad systemic transformation. They represent a vast tapestry of activism, embodying the diversity of feminist agendas worldwide. Whether called alliances, movements or coalitions, feminist networks aim to connect and empower women, influence policies, enable choice and foster collective innovation. Tackling major issues – like preventing femicides, establishing gender-sensitive policies, transitioning to a circular economy, achieving energy shifts or moving to regenerative agriculture – requires coordinated, systemic action across actors and institutions. Internet technologies support connectivity; the pandemic has furthered digital skills, enabling women to harness the internet for feminist networking around the globe.

Recognizing and learning from these networks allows us to build upon their successes, address their challenges and hopefully amplify their transformative potential. Because effective networks connect not only people but also their actions, they can bridge change endeavors of movements and institutional change. Ideally, this connectivity reverberates within organizations, companies and institutions from which the women in the network originate, initiating change in those spaces as well.

Yet, networks have their own dynamics, which are helpful to know. Ideally, they provide enlivenment, the nourishing element that is behind the engagement for a meaningful joint purpose; they support identification and meaning making, making us feel at home in connection to other women on a similar journey, no matter whether the network is local or global. Regarding their purpose, their ambitions, their structure and their effectiveness, feminist networks are very different. They can be legal entities in the form of membership organizations; they can be loosely connected individuals; they can be formalized umbrella structures of a number of organizations; or they can be loose, but regular connections between different feminist networks. It is therefore important to understand the different origins, rationales and purposes that women's and explicitly feminist networks serve. Although their functions can overlap, they can be broadly categorized as exchange and information networks, support networks, advocacy networks, technology and innovation networks, and strategic transformation networks.

Feminist exchange and information networks exist around the globe. They consist of feminist communities with shared interests, primarily aimed at raising feminist knowledge and awareness, exchanging best practices in advancing feminist issues, learning from each other or supporting each other in advancing a certain topic. They contribute to feminist agenda setting, connect feminists with specific professional expertise, or connect feminists working in different institutions. Many of these networks operate as forums that provide women with knowledge resources, best practices and solidarity. One exciting example is the *South Feminist Futures Knowledge Hub*, launched internationally in 2024 and located in Harare, Zimbabwe.[4] Its purpose is to overcome patriarchal and colonial knowledge hegemonies and contribute to decolonizing knowledge. The network of feminist experts provides open access multi-thematic feminist resources, authored or presented by feminists from the Global South. Such networks play a vital role in spreading knowledge, encouraging feminist agenda setting and enabling discourses about feminist topics. They not only give space for women's professional voices and experiences, but specifically amplify intersectional feminist expertise.

Some of these networks center around professional themes and aim to advance feminist thinking in such areas. One such example is *The International Association for Feminist Economists (IAFFE)*, a network in the form of an international membership organization.[5] It was founded in the US in 1992 as an international association. With more than 800 members in over 90 countries, IAFFE fosters global dialogue and resource sharing among feminist economists. Yearly conferences and a scientific journal advance feminist economic inquiry and advocate for feminist perspectives in economic policy and education.

Knowledge and information to support feminist agendas can also include remembrance. Living ancestry refers to the practice of honoring and continuing the legacy of past and present women who have made significant contributions to society. Such practices require networked action to gather both traditional and contemporary knowledge as well as herstories that have been sidelined or deliberately excluded from mainstream history writings. Living ancestry archives feminist transformation work through documenting women-led societal development in order to inform and inspire present and future generations. One example is the *Women's Media Tower* in the German city of Cologne, initiated by the German feminist journalist Alice Schwarzer.[6] It houses 65,000 books and essays, including many out-of-print copies, leaflets, buttons, unpublished documents, feminist magazines and numerous press clippings. A very different, yet also inspiring, example is the *House of African Feminism (HoAF)*, a platform for feminist discourse, resource sharing and enlightenment, focusing on the works of African feminist scholars, artists and thinkers.[7] It promotes cultural exchange, networking and inclusivity, bringing together feminism as an intellectual movement and a daily lived experience.

Feminist support networks can offer emotional, psychological and practical assistance, addressing specific challenges women face in personal, social or professional contexts. These networks are invaluable for marginalized women, survivors of gender-based violence, and others seeking safe spaces for healing and growth. Such acknowledgment inspires, reinforces their sense of potency and empowers women to continue advocating for themselves and others. One example is *Black Women's Blueprint*, a feminist support network in New York, focused on addressing the unique challenges faced by Black women and girls.[8] As an organization founded in 2008 by the feminist activist Farah Tanis, it provides a range of support services, centered on Black feminist thought, including trauma counseling, community healing programs and advocacy on issues like racial justice, gender-based violence and reproductive rights. Beyond these services *Black Women's Blueprint* engages in public advocacy and educational programs, working to amplify Black women's voices and ensure their concerns are included in policy discussions.

There are support networks dedicated to making women visible as powerful agents, promoting stories of women's leadership and success in order to inspire and empower others. One example for this entry point is *TEDWomen*. In 2010 the American journalist and media executive Pat Mitchell suggested dedicating a series of talks to women's advancement. Since then, more than 100 TEDWomen talks have been viewed more than 150 million times in more than 80 languages, while she herself summarized her life conclusions in her own talk, which she called 'Dangerous times call for dangerous women'.[9] One of the most famous talks is the one by Nigerian Chimamanda Ngozi Adichie, 'We should all be feminists', in 2017.[10]

Other support networks are loose and informal, creating personal connections to support the development of collective strength. Such an informal example is the *Soul Sutras*, a loose collaborative initiated by South Asian women.[11] The collaborative creates a safe space for sharing stories, tackling taboos and empowering each other to tackle the daily transformative work.

Some feminist support networks connect women in institutional or government decision-making positions with the aim of furthering women's representation and influence in political, economic and social leadership positions. One example of a network connecting women in power is *Vital Voices Global Partnership*.[12] The network consists of over 20,000 extraordinary women leaders in 185 countries globally. It connects emerging female leaders with established professionals across the globe for mentorship and support. Another example is *Women Political Leaders (WPL)*, founded by Silvana Koch-Mehrin, a former Vice-president of the European Parliament. It is a global network of female politicians – presidents, prime ministers, cabinet ministers, members of parliaments, and mayors – with the aim of increasing the number and influence of women in political leadership.[13] It provides a platform for women leaders to connect, share experiences and advocate for gender equality in politics.

Feminist advocacy networks are mission-driven coalitions that push for policy changes on women's issues like reproductive rights, equal pay, and protection against violence, or connect women around ecofeminist and sustainable development themes. These networks mobilize support, engage in lobbying and work with legislators to create institutional and systemic change. The issues they take on can range from topics such as abortion legalization to female representation at COP meetings, from collective action against femicides to advocating for the introduction of gender budgeting in government planning. Advocacy networks most often consist of representatives of different networks or institutions. They often seek alliances with other topical networks that are not necessarily feminist. Typical outcomes of such platforms include jointly developed statements, open letters or policy recommendations.

One example is the *She Changes Climate* network. It was founded in late 2020 by Antoinette Vermilye, Bianca Pitt and Elise Buckle, aspiring to bring diversity and inclusiveness, transparency and accountability to the COP negotiations on climate change. Its purpose is to ensure women have a leading role in climate decision-making – for example, at the annual COP meetings – driven by the understanding that women, especially those from marginalized communities, are disproportionately affected by climate change and are essential in crafting sustainable solutions.[14] The network links feminist activists from different organizations and provides strategic analysis by highlighting the gendered impacts of climate change.[15] By partnering with other environmental and feminist organizations, She Changes Climate builds a collaborative ecosystem that amplifies women's voices in climate action.

Another example is the *Women's Environment and Development Organization (WEDO)*, founded in 1992 in New York.[16] It is a global feminist advocacy organization for human rights, gender equality and environmental integrity. *WEDO* connects grassroots feminist movements to policy processes, sustainable development and climate justice, particularly in the context of the UN. The organization partners with women's groups around the world to achieve economic, social and environmental justice.

At times, advocacy networks form when feminist organizations recognize a shrinking space for feminist collective action. One example is the Asian *Sangat Network*, created in 1998 in Bangladesh for gender activists and trainers, in response to the realization of difficulties for transformative gender work.[17] Sangat focuses on strengthening regional and cross-border cooperation between women and feminists.

Movement building plays an important role in feminist advocacy. Networked action strengthens civil society influence on policy development. This requires establishing connections between movement activists and feminists and other actors in decision-making positions in institutions, be they public or private. One aim of advocacy is the institutionalization of feminist perspectives in regulations and institutional procedures. An example of a network with this entry point is the *Gender Budget Watchdog Network* connecting countries in south-east Europe that aspire to become part of the European Union.[18] The network includes more than 100 civil society organizations and focuses on the capacity of women's rights organizations to influence climate change policies and finance. The aim is to ensure gender mainstreaming and the implementation of the UN Security Council Resolution 1325 on women, peace and security.

Another example is the recently created *Global Partner Network for Feminist Foreign Policy*, an informal, yet global multi-stakeholder network. Its aim is to push the understanding, the further development, the agenda setting and eventually the establishment of feminist foreign policies in many countries.[19] Such policies prioritize peace, gender equality and the human rights of all, but also seek to overcome colonial, racist, patriarchal and male-dominated power structures. So far, Canada, Mexico, Sweden and Germany have adopted such policies, yet in each of the countries they are subject to changes in government.[20]

Movement–policy connections have long been identified as crucial in bridging the gap between grassroots activism and policy-making. Established in 1988 and located in Nairobi in Kenya, the *African Women's Development and Communication Network (FEMNET)* is a pan-African feminist network with 800 members across 49 African countries. It works to advance women's rights and gender equality in Africa by facilitating and coordinating the exchange of strategies, experiences and information among African women's rights organizations and activists.[21]

Another, global example is the *Indigenous Women's Biodiversity Network (IWBN)*.[22] It was established in 1998 during the fourth Conference of Parties (COP) to the Convention on Biological Diversity (CBD). Its mission is not only to highlight the concerns of Indigenous women in international forums, but also to bring in their expertise and emphasize their crucial role in biodiversity conservation. Its members represent all seven regions of the world.

Feminist technology networks advocate for the development and utilization of technologies that support and empower women and serve the emergence of egalitarian societies. This can relate to the creation of new technologies that address women's needs and to ensuring that existing technologies are used to benefit women and gender equality. One interesting example is the *Feminist AI Research Network*, a consortium of world-class scientists and activists dedicated to reinventing artificial intelligence as an ally for gender equality.[23] Rigorous research cycles ensure that innovation is rooted in robust South–South collaboration and real-world impact. The network is part of the A+ *Alliance*, dedicated to feminist artificial intelligence and algorithmic decision-making that advocates for equality and contributes to dismantling societal barriers for women.[24] Another example is the collective around the *Feminist Internet*.[25] It aims to advance internet technologies to be more inclusive and equitable and promote a feminist approach to innovation and design: It brings feminist innovators together who aspire to re-design the internet as a transformative political space for sustained feminist movement building.

Feminist innovation networks encourage female pioneers who develop solutions to address the societal challenges. This can involve creating new business models, products and services that prioritize women's needs and perspectives. By fostering a culture of innovation, these networks help drive progress toward gender equality in various fields. One example is *Rising Tide Africa*, an investment network situated in Lagos, Nigeria.[26] It focuses on empowering female entrepreneurs across the African continent and aims to increase women's participation in the investment landscape. By providing women with access to capital, mentorship and networking opportunities, the network fosters a more inclusive entrepreneurial ecosystem.

Feminist finance networks focus on funding flows to feminist collective action. Many feminist organizations and networks struggle with financial support, and not all can be financed through membership fees. A lot of funding for feminist issue is channeled as Overseas Development Assistance (ODA). Although a lot of positive programs fund gender equality and women's empowerment in the Global South, the structured power imbalances regarding focus and agenda setting remain untouched. There are countries with feminist ODA policies,[27] but these policies are not fully able to reverse or dismantle ingrained power structures between the Global North as ODA-giver and the Global South as ODA-receiver. The Association for Women's Rights in Development (AWID) states that 99% of the ODA does not reach women directly, and fails to support feminist networks, movements or organizations.[28] The direct funding of feminist transformation efforts is one of the most undervalued leverages for change. It often relies on feminist philanthropy, and even this means that funds usually come from the Global North, in particular from the United States, not always, but sometimes with strings attached, or subject to political changes in the donor countries. One example of a feminist, networked and learning approach to better funding of feminist movements is the *Gender Funders Co_Lab*, founded in 2014.[29] It is a network not of specifically feminist funders, but of private philanthropic foundations that are committed to finding more effective ways to resource gender justice movements and organizations. Together, they fund feminist collective action with more than $200 million annually. The aim is to secure funding for long-lasting feminist movements on the ground. Another networked approach to funding is the *Young Feminist Fund (FRIDA)*, organizationally located in Canada, but networked to grantees in different regions, who received more than $10 million USD in total per year. FRIDA is pioneering a truly feminist participatory approach to grant-making and network grantees.[30] Meanwhile, feminist finance is higher on the agenda, with conferences addressing the topic.

Feminist strategic transformation networks focus on systemic change across institutions, countries and sometimes continents. They work at a high level, often engaging with international bodies to address foundational societal issues towards feminist-inspired practices. These networks operate with long-term goals, aiming to redefine entire systems – such as economic, educational and environmental frameworks – through feminist perspectives. One example is the *Women's Earth and Climate Action Network (WECAN)*.[31] It is a solutions-oriented climate justice organization founded to bring women together globally for policy advocacy, hands-on projects, training and movement building focused on social and ecological justice. It connects women leaders, scientists, allied organizations and activists, emphasizing sustainable practices and equity-focused environmental policies. Its purpose is collective feminist action for pushing systemic reforms that acknowledge women's pivotal roles in achieving climate resilience. Another example is the *Association for Women's Rights in Development (AWID)*, an international, feminist, membership-based organization that serves as an umbrella network for women's rights organizations globally.[32] Founded in 1982, AWID connects over 6000 individual and institutional members worldwide. Its mission is to strengthen the influence, impact and sustainability of feminist movements, particularly in regions where women's rights are under threat. AWID provides resources, convenes global forums, takes up topics such as building feminist economies, and advocates for funding and policy reforms that support women's rights and gender justice.

Feminist strategic transformation networks connect individuals, networks and institutions with the purpose of developing joint strategies, coordinating agenda setting, mobilizing political support or creating pressure for implementation. They do not function as a hierarchical coordination body, but as a space, in which learnings from feminist strategies can be exchanged, adjusted, collectively developed and simultaneously implemented in different contexts. They bring together activities that would otherwise take place in isolation. While exchange networks and advocacy platforms often represent a like-minded community, strategic transformation networks bring diverse groups of feminist stakeholders together. In order to move towards strategic impact, such networks need to work with multiple feminist and non-feminist stakeholders at different levels, and negotiate, and frequently renegotiate, the common goal or interest. Such networks need to deal with differences between feminists, their institutions, movements and networks. **Strategic transformation networks** can only be successful if they are able to navigate these differences constructively. Given the vast variety of feminist collective actions around the world, enhancing their transformative potential requires mutual learning and joint strategy development. Strategic transformation networks organize strategic dialogues in and across feminist networks to develop even more impactful, inclusive and comprehensive strategies. One fascinating example is the *Encuentro Feminista Latinoamericano y del Caribe (EFLAC)*, or the Latin American and Caribbean Feminist Encounters.[33] These are regular and significant feminist gatherings with more than 1000 women that have been convened since 1981. They bring together feminist network activists from various countries in Latin America and the Caribbean into intersectional, intergenerational and intercultural space to discuss, strategize and mobilize around issues of gender justice, women's rights and a feminist future with a *Good Life for All*. The Encuentros have been and are crucial for the development and strengthening of feminist movements in the region.

Such transnational solidarity and collaboration in feminist networks refers to the building of alliances and collaborative efforts across borders to tackle gender injustices and develop strategies to overcome patriarchal pathologies. By connecting activists and organizations from different countries, feminist networks amplify their impact and foster global connections and shared purposes. One famous example of transnational solidarity is the networked action *One Billion Rising*, a global campaign initiated in 2012 by the American artist and feminist activist Eve Ensler.[34] Its mission is to end violence against women and girls, which includes addressing issues such as domestic violence, sexual assault, human trafficking and other forms of gender-based violence. The name refers to the frightening statistics that one in three women will be beaten or raped during her lifetime, amounting to about one billion women worldwide. With a new focus theme every year on February 14, participants in over 200 countries organize events such as marches, rallies, flash mobs, workshops, conferences, dance protests and educational activities to highlight the issue of gender-based violence and to stand in solidarity with survivors.

At times, strategic transformation networks take the form of temporary collaboratives between women of influence, who bring each other on board in order to create systemic change. One interesting example of such an approach to claiming power through a collective of women is the *Council on the Economics of Health for All*, convened by the Director General of the World Health Organization (WHO), Tedros Adhanom Ghebreyesus, in 2020. In a short manifesto, the feminist collective advocates for integrating diverse policy areas – social, economic, financial and innovation – that are inseparable from health. The subsequent report with its 13 recommendations, published in 2023, offers a novel and systemic approach to shaping economies, aiming to create healthy societies that are just, inclusive, equitable and sustainable.[35]

For decades the networked Global South feminist organization *DAWN Feminist (Development Alternatives with Women for a New Era)* has advocated for claiming collective power and for designing alternative development pathways.[36] Its ideas were inspired by early Black power and liberation movements; hence they have brought to the global feminist discourse critical questions about power, racism, colonialism, white privilege and differences between women. They reject the neocolonial, profit-driven resource exploitation that globalization, the world trade system and Overseas Development Assistance caused.

An international network of networks is *Women Engage for a Common Future (WECF)*.[37] With members in over 70 countries, WECF connects grassroots activists, policy-makers and environmentalists, and funds transformative initiatives in gender equality, climate action and health. By advocating for women's rights and amplifying their voices on global platforms, WECF fosters impactful collaborations that bridge local action with global change.

The feminist networks mentioned are just a tiny fraction of the networks that exist around the globe. All of them and the many others not mentioned are important and valuable. We may disagree with some of their focus or approach; we may not feel enticed by all of them or feel strongly connected only to some. Yet, it is important to become aware of these vast numbers of networks, and note that their number has tremendously grown in the past 100 years. Feminists have never been connected the way they are today – across localities, countries, regions and continents. This *networked connectivity* is an asset that could develop into even more intentional and coordinated feminist transformation strategies – a promising pathway to claiming feminist power collectively. For this to happen, we must know and acknowledge the existence of feminist networks, locally and globally, as if we had to acknowledge the underground mycorrhizal communication network that supports the forest, and develop it into a global network supporting all forests. The above selection of feminist networks gives a glimpse into the possibilities of claiming feminist power and leading transformations collectively.

While feminist networks continue to grow, they are often under-recognized in mainstream narratives of social change. Making these networks visible and accessible highlights the range and impact of feminist organizing worldwide. Showing the widespread existence and impact of feminist networks emphasizes that feminist activism is not niche or isolated – it is a global, multifaceted movement addressing complex issues at all levels of society. By looking at how networks operate in different contexts, we can cross-pollinate insights into effective methods for advocacy, support and transformation. When feminist networks avoid competition, and instead draw on one another's resources and support, we are able to increase the overall effect.

Yet, there is more to learn about dismantling patriarchal power pathologies. In one of the International Forums of AWID in 2016, Angelika Arutyunova, a feminist strategist from Usbekistan, emphasized something that is still valid today. The feminist movement, she urges us, is at a crossroads, because given the rising patriarchal backlash there is a need to connect and re-strategize feminist organizing, and work towards even better answers to the question: What does it take to build collective feminist power?

If we take the feminist claim for power seriously, we need more and connected feminist transformation networks that effectively bring *collective feminist leadership* to life and enable women to live the *collective feminist power practices* at scale. The practice of *mutual re-powerment* inspires us to ask how feminist networks *elevate women's power and agency*. The practice of *networked connectivity* lets us look at how feminist networks build transnational *supportive structures*. The practice of *courageous discovery* invites us to assess how feminist networks *leverage feminist wisdom* across times and continents. The practice of *reflective appreciation* lets us ask how we can better leverage the value of the *diverse contributions* of the different networks. The practice of *dialogic reciprocity* helps us check how we can foster *strategic exchange* between different networks and between different geographies. The practice of *feminist aspiration* inspires us to look at how feminist networks can shape *transformative futures* in their togetherness and as strategic alliances. As feminist movements evolve, the importance of strategic, cross-national networking becomes critical. Feminist transformation strategies need to take the network approach to the next level.

Major insights for *collective feminist power practices* from *feminist networks*:

1. Feminist networks are at the core of a collective practice for feminist transformations and the testing ground for *collective feminist leadership*.
2. They are a glimpse into future societies, because they model the way such societies drive progress as learning societies in egalitarian relationships, with dialogue and collaboration.
3. Feminist networks are different and have different valid purposes. We need to understand these differences, because they have different effects on *transforming* structural power in patriarchal systems.
4. Recognizing and showcasing feminist networks is essential to advance feminist *transformations*. By understanding the unique roles that various networks play, from local to global scales, we can learn from their strategies, celebrate their successes and support their ongoing missions.
5. In order to become transformative through *collective feminist leadership* we need to strengthen feminist strategic *alliance across* networks *so that* pioneering movements *link up with* institutional transformation strategies across continents.
6. We need to understand the entire landscape of feminist networks in order to strategize transformative systems change by claiming collective feminist power.

Notes

1 See Simard (2021).
2 It is important to note that patriarchy also functions in exclusionary boys' networks, as does organized crime. However, neither of these is created to enhance the vitality of the whole. We could say both highjack the life principles of networks.

3 There is ample feminist research on networks as a means of mobilization and change. For a selected range of topics covered see Fotopoulou (2016), Moghadam (2000), Calvo (2021), Villesèche (2022).
4 See the South Feminist Future Knowledge Hub, South Feminist Future. (2022, November 22): https://knowledgehub.southfeministfutures.org/data-rights-policy-and-disclaimer
5 See the International Association for Feminist Economists (IAFFE): https://www.iaffe.org. Apart from membership and conference fees, IAFFE funders include the Swedish Development Agency (SIDA), Co-Impact, the William and Flora Hewlett Foundation, and the Friedrich-Ebert-Stiftung, among others.
6 See Frauenmediaturm: https://en.frauenmediaturm.de
7 See House of African Feminism: https://houseofafricanfeminisms.org
8 See Black Women's Blueprint. https://restoreny.org/black-womens-blueprint
9 See Pat Mitchell (2014): https://www.patmitchellmedia.com/tedwomen-dangerous-times-dangerous-women
10 See: the TED Talk, Adichie (2017), available at: https://www.ted.com/talks/chimamanda_ngozi_adichie_we_should_all_be_feminists?subtitle=en. Previously published as a book, Adichie (2014).
11 See Soul Sutras: https://www.soulsutras.co.uk
12 See Vital Voices (2022), available at: https://www.vitalvoices.org/wp-content/uploads/2024/01/2022-Annual-Report.pdf
13 See Women Political Leaders: https://www.womenpoliticalleaders.org
14 See She Changes Climate: https://www.shechangesclimate.org
15 See: She Changes Climate (2023).
16 See WEDO: https://wedo.org
17 See Sangat, A Feminist Network: https://sangatnetwork.org
18 See Gender Budget Watchdog Network: https://gbwn.net/en
19 See Feminist Foreign Policy Collaborative: https://www.ffpcollaborative.org, and Feminist Foreign Policy Collaborative, (2019).
20 See Nylund et al. (2022), Burni & Thissen (2024), Lunz & Bernarden (2019).
21 See FEMNET: https://www.femnet.org
22 See IWBN: https://iwbn-rmibn.org
23 See Women at The Table: https://www.womenatthetable.net/project/fair-network
24 See A+Alliance: https://aplusalliance.org
25 See Feminist Internet: https://feministinternet.org/en
26 See Rising Tide Africa: https://risingtideafrica.com
27 See the case of Germany: The Ministry for Economic Cooperation and Development (BMZ) (2023, March 1). See the case of Canada: Global Affairs Canada (2015).
28 The Association for Women's Rights in Development (AWID) (2021).
29 See Gender Funders Co_Lab: https://www.genderfunderscolab.org
30 See: Djordjevic (2022).
31 See Earth and Climate Action Network (WECAN) https://www.wecaninternational.org
32 See the Association for Women's Rights in Development (AWID): https://www.awid.org

33 See the declaration developed in 2023: Encuentro Feminista Latinoamericano y del Caribe (EFLAC) (2023).
34 See One Billion Rising: https://www.onebillionrising.org. Eve Ensler is known for her play *Vagina Monologues*.
35 See WHO Council on the Economics of Health for All (2023).
36 See Development Alternatives with Women for a New Era (DAWN Feminist): https://www.dawnfeminist.org
37 See Women Engage for a Common Future (WCEF): https://www.wecf.org

References

Adichie, C.N. (2017). We should all be feminists. Ted.com; TED Talks. https://www.ted.com/talks/chimamanda_ngozi_adichie_we_should_all_be_feminists?subtitle=en&lng=de&geo=de

Adichie, C.N. (2014). *We Should All Be Feminists*. Harper Collins.

Burni, A., & Thissen, L. (2024). European feminist foreign policy: The need for a progressive and transformative approach. Policy Brief. Friedrich Ebert Foundation. https://library.fes.de/pdf-files/bueros/bruessel/21143.pdf.

Calvo, D., Campos-Domínguez, E., & Simón-Astudillo, I. (2021). Towards a critical understanding of social networks for the feminist movement: Twitter and the women's strike. *Tripodos*, 50(50), 91–109. https://doi.org/10.51698/tripodos.2021.50 p91–109

Djordjevic, J. (2022, December). A look into FRIDA's participatory grantmaking model. 'Resourcing connections: Reflections on Feminist participatory Grantmaking practice'. FRIDA Young Feminist Fund. https://youngfeministfund.org/a-look-into-fridas-participatory-grantmaking-model-resourcing-connections-reflections-on-feminist-participatory-grantmaking-practice

Encuentro Feminista de Latinoamérica y el Caribe (EFLAC). (2023). Declaratoria del 15 Encuentro Feminista Latinoamericano y del Caribe (EFLAC) Ante la crisis del tejido de la vida: ¡unidas, unides, resistiendo y avanzando! EFLAC 15. https://eflac.org

Feminist Foreign Policy Collaborative. (2019). Feminist foreign policy framework. Global Feminist Foreign Policy Network. https://www.ffpcollaborative.org/ffp-framework

Fotopoulou, A. (2016). *Feminist Activism and Digital Networks: Between Empowerment and Vulnerability*. Palgrave Macmillan. https://doi.org/10.1057/978-1-137-50471-5

Global Affairs Canada. (2015). Canada's feminist international assistance policy. Government of Canada. https://www.international.gc.ca/world-monde/issues_development-enjeux_developpement/priorities-priorites/policy-politique.aspx?lang=eng

Lunz, K., & Bernarden, N. (2019, February 19). Feminist foreign policy: Imperative for a more secure and just world. Heinrich-Böll-Stiftung. https://www.boell.de/en/2019/01/30/feminist-foreign-policy-imperative-more-secure-and-just-world

Mitchell, P. (2014). *Dangerous Times, Dangerous Women.* https://www.patmitchellmedia.com/tedwomen-dangerous-times-dangerous-women

Moghadam, V.M. (2000). Transnational feminist networks: Collective action in an era of globalization. *International Sociology*, *15*(1), 57–85. https://doi.org/10.1177/0268580900015001004

Nylund, M.-L., Håkansson, S., & Bjarnegård, E. (2022). The transformative potential of feminist foreign policy: The case of Sweden. *Journal of Women, Politics & Policy*, *44*(3), 257–273. https://doi.org/10.1080/1554477x.2022.2113662

She Changes Climate. (2023). Women in all their diversity leading on climate. https://static1.squarespace.com/static/5fbd0fcb06ee170e1048dfea/t/6424476e93c18e1413566ce0/1680099250418/UNFCCC+ISSUE+BRIEF.pdf

Simard, S. (2021). *Finding the Mother Tree: Discovering the WISDOM of the Forest.* Penguin.

South Feminist Future. (2022, November 22). South Feminist Futures Knowledge Hub. https://knowledgehub.southfeministfutures.org/data-rights-policy-and-disclaimer

The Association for Women's Rights in Development (AWID). (2021). Where is the money for feminist organizing? https://www.awid.org/sites/default/files/2022-01/AWID_Research_WITM_Brief_ENG.pdf

Villesèche, F., Meliou, E., & Jha, H.K. (2022). Feminism in women's business networks: A freedom-centred perspective. *Human Relations*, *74*(10), 001872672210836. https://doi.org/10.1177/00187267221083665

Vital Voices. (2022). Annual report. https://www.vitalvoices.org/wp-content/uploads/2024/01/2022-Annual-Report.pdf

WHO Council on the Economics of Health for All. (2023). Health for All: Transforming economies to deliver what matters. Geneva: World Health Organization. https://iris.who.int/bitstream/handle/10665/373122/9789240080973-eng.pdf?sequence=1

Part V
Towards Feminist-oriented Civilizations

13 Feminist Transformation Strategies – A Pattern Approach

As we have seen from the vast number of networks already existing, feminist transformation strategies encompass a broad spectrum of approaches: From movement building to establishing feminist organizations and networks, from awareness raising and education to political campaigns, from leadership development to institutionalized policy implementation. These strategies include resistance to patriarchal power manifestations as much as building transnational feminist collectives. They knit feminist rules into existing patriarchal institutions, or take feminist organizing as a testing ground for living a feminist future. It is important to acknowledge this plurality of transformation strategies: Shaped by diverse feminist individuals and collectives, there are different interpretations of what it means to work towards feminist futures, yet they broadly align around the goal of overcoming patriarchy and its pathological effects. No pathway is unimportant, and there are no steps too small. Yet, it has become clear that patriarchal power keeps coming in the way of feminist transformation strategies.

If we take a bird's eye perspective, we can see an almost mythological battle between worldviews. There is a *mechanistic, dissecting worldview* that, in its extreme forms, does not pay reverence to the forces of life on this planet, but considers everything, including human beings, other beings and nature in general as usable or even disposable. There is a *relational or systemic worldview* that pays reverence to all forms and forces of life, acknowledges their interconnectedness and places humankind into this dynamic matrix of life on this planet as an aware, responsible and humble actor.

There is hardly any conversation between these worldviews possible. Yet, in the lived realities, both worldviews intersect and intertwine. Our souls require the enchantment of the world, our minds are trained to operate with utmost rationality. If it comes to power, the mechanistic worldview is so deeply anchored in patriarchal structures, ways of thinking, ways of acting and institutions that we cannot escape it. It determines our being and our reality. The systemic

DOI: 10.4324/9781003508885-18

worldview ensures our survival in a disenchanted world, but is pushed underground, marginalized or used for repair measures. Feminist networks, even though most are anchored in a systemic and relational worldview, must produce their effect in a world whose dominant worldview is still mechanistic. This is an inescapable dilemma, an issue to keep at the forefront of our mind when we strategize feminist transformations. For a feminist claim to redefined power and influence, it is time to take a deep dive into what we know so far about transformative change. The following can only offer a glimpse into the ever-growing systemic transformation knowledge. I will not refer to the vast literature on societal change management, but, in a biased way, focus on a few pioneering female practitioners, thinkers and scientists whose expertise can help us gain insights into crafting feminist transformation strategies.

The aforementioned Margaret Wheatley has left a decisive mark in leadership science, particularly among practitioners. Similar to the scientific insights of Suzanne Simard's forest communication networks, she reminds us that networks are the only way of human organizing that mirrors life processes.[1] They are grounded in self-organization and interdependence, supporting the diversity and resilience of all involved. These networks, according to Wheatley, are the primary incubators of emergence, a process that enables life to adapt, innovate and undergo radical transformation. Mechanistic conceptions of societal change, in her view, are oblivious to the processes in nature, where transformations do not arise from top-down strategies or directives from a single authority. Instead, change starts as local actions that emerge simultaneously in various places. If these actions stay isolated, their impact remains limited. But when they connect, they can coalesce into a powerful system capable of influencing at a larger, more comprehensive scale. Wheatley suggests that the qualities of such emergent systems are not merely the sum of individual parts; through interconnectedness, entirely new properties emerge, which empower individuals within a system in unexpected ways. The concept of *emergence* explains how local actions transform into global systems of influence, providing a pathway for creating needed systemic change. The experiences and insights of these pioneering groups are suddenly valued and amplified, shifting policies and institutional cultures. She suggests that understanding the life cycle of networks – what sustains them, the leadership styles that enable or impede them, and how they transition from loose associations to powerful systems – is critical in order to steward transformative emergence intentionally. Feminist networks can potentially model this process. As they grow into dynamic communities of *collective feminist power practices*, they catalyze emergent systems of thought and action. They lay the ground for feminist mental infrastructures and collective actions within a *feminist reference system*. The transformative systems change, in Wheatley's thinking, is neither sudden nor revolutionary.

It is a non-linear transition from an outdated, malfunctioning system to a new one. This process can be stewarded, but not steered or controlled. As the old system decays, not surprisingly, those invested in it resist change, assuming stability despite widening gaps between belief and reality. Naming the decay of the system and connecting alternatives through networks is a crucial element of stewarding. Supporting the potency of alternatives and highlighting their benefits amplifies their rising power. The tipping point is reached when a majority moves toward the new, and efforts shift to scaling and strengthening it to support broader adoption.[2] The conception of emerging transformations helps us realize that this process is already partly happening in feminist transformation efforts, including the massive resistance to change manifesting as patriarchal backlash combined with the rise of authoritarian regimes.

Feminist networks embody transformative life processes, creating patterns that enhance aliveness and resilience. These life-enhancing patterns, like the harmonious arrangement of mountains and rivers in a landscape or the vibrant interactions in a bustling plaza, inspire connection and vitality. Networks foster collective action, offer support and build strength even in challenging circumstances. As human beings, we thrive on recognizing patterns of life-enhancing moments, structures and experiences. We seek them, can build them and strive for more.

Pattern recognition is as old as humankind, even if it has only recently become the backbone of artificial intelligence (AI). Technological pattern recognition is the basis for automated driving, it is the core of AI-supported medical diagnosis, but it can also be used for spraying harmful substances on agricultural land or it can be abused for warfare. Because, unfortunately, a central question is seldom asked in the technological approach to pattern recognition: Which patterns help systems to become more alive in the sense of individual and collective well-being?[3] This is a central question that we need to ask for feminist transformation strategies. Understanding how to create life-enhancing patterns of structures and human interaction is crucial for feminist transformative change initiatives. This involves identifying patterns that foster individual and collective well-being. This perspective reframes our current patriarchal challenges as dysfunctional patterns of human interaction that can be restructured using design principles promoting aliveness. Transformations are sometimes slow, sometimes radical, often chaotic reconfigurations of dysfunctional patterns to allow new possibilities to emerge. By integrating objective data, collective sense-making and co-creative agency, individuals and groups can consciously design interaction patterns that enhance aliveness at multiple levels. For feminist transformations at scale this also requires understanding how interconnected initiatives and actors form strategic transformation systems, working collaboratively without central coordination to nurture life-enhancing change.

To better understand feminist transformation strategies as life-enhancing patterns of consciousness and collective actions, it is important to note that a pattern is more than a structure or an order. While the latter suggests a state that is fixed and stable, the concept of patterns implies dynamic relational interaction that is permeable, changeable and always in flux. This reflects an Indigenous or matriarchal worldview much more. But it also connects with modern systems theory. Structure is what holds a pattern in a system in place. Order is what patterns aim for – an arrangement, a constellation or composition that influences the degree of aliveness in a certain mental or physical, social or ecological space. Increasingly, expressions such as thrivability, vital social fabrics, economies in service of life, vitality of societies and enlivenment as a societal guide are making their way into the discourse on futuring. Feminist transformations must amplify and support a paradigm shift where equality transcends beyond demanding equal rights within dysfunctional societal patterns, and instead embeds them within a deep reverence for life. We need to learn to become partners of the non-linear and patterned evolutionary process instead of exercising men's will on evolution. At the same time, we need to acknowledge that the linear thinking holds the world in captivity. Hence, for feminist transformation strategies, we need to find ways to connect with the mechanistic worldview without becoming its captives.

If it comes to systemic and transformative change, hardly any professional in this field can ignore the leverage points of Donella Meadows, whom we got to know from her vision of a sustainable world and her co-authorship of the book *Limits to Growth*, published in 1972. She was a systems scientist, familiar with non-linear thinking, yet also thoroughly grounded in linear thinking. At the beginning of her famous article on *Leverage Points – Places to Intervene in a System*, she mocks some (predominantly male) colleagues who on the one hand search for the most important leverage point to change systems, and on the other hand stay oblivious to how interventions may unfold unforeseen self-dynamics.[4] The dream of many feminists may understandably be similar: Finding the leverage point that can finally shift a deathly patriarchal infrastructure. Yet, many feminists, even without explicit skills in systems science, know that the complexity of the global and local systems of interconnected patriarchal dominations requires identifying multiple leverage points.

Donella Meadows was committed to a better world, yet never mentioned patriarchy as forceful element holding an unsustainable world in captivity. But if we take her insights as a learning, we might come closer to understanding how feminist transformation strategies could become successful in a mix between a linear and a pattern approach. Let us take a brief deep dive into her thinking. When she attended a meeting that was about interventions into the world trade systems, she got up to teach her colleagues a system thinking lesson by showing how interventions in complex systems such as ecosystems, societies, organizations or economies, may be less or more effective. These spontaneous ideas she developed further into 12 leverage points, which she ranked according to their effectiveness, from the least to the most powerful effect.

The *first* and lowest leverage point is changing certain *parameters* like taxes and subsidies, or setting standards. They are relatively easy to implement and favored by politicians, but have limited impact on overall system behavior. In feminist transformations these would be, for example, tax cuts for single mothers, or regulations for female representation on corporate boards.

The *second* lowest leverage point is *optimizing buffers and stocks*. This means managing the reserves or capacities within a system to absorb shocks or delays, ensuring stability and resilience. An example of optimizing *buffers* in feminist transformations could be building networks of safe spaces for women, such as shelters, support hubs or digital platforms for solidarity and activism. *Stocks* in this context could include knowledge archives, leadership skills, funding for feminist initiatives, or long-term mentorship programs.

The *third* lowest leverage point is about changing *material and physical infrastructure*, which are more difficult to shift, unless infrastructure gets rebuilt or materials change. An example is to change the infrastructure towards renewable energies and get rid of the infrastructure for fossil fuels. As we all know, this process is extremely slow and riddled with resistance. Yet, once completed, it does have a decisively positive impact on how a system operates.

The fourth leverage point refers to *reducing the delays in measuring or perceiving a system's state*, especially when it is changing, and the *fifth leverage point* is *reducing delays in negative feedback loops* to significantly enhance system responsiveness and quicker adjustments to changes in the system. Negative feedback loops ask for counteraction. If we look at the disastrous effect of climate change on people, the counteractions are still extremely delayed despite the Paris agreement. Commitments to shift towards regenerative societies are extremely hesitant. This leverage point touches issues of information, data evaluation and political readiness to act. An example in feminist transformations would be the speed with which both movements and governments can design countermeasures to prevent patriarchal backlashes and violence against women. We know that these feedbacks and subsequent measures are still far too slow, because patriarchal backlash does not get measured. There is no global index.

Number six on Donella's list is *managing positive feedback loops*, which can amplify changes. A positive feedback loop in feminist transformations could emerge from initiatives that encourage and mediate feminists taking up leadership positions in politics, education or business. This loop amplifies if women in power mediate other women into power, accelerating the breakdown of structural barriers and normalizing women's power in male-dominated spaces. To manage this loop effectively, resources and support must be consistently provided, and the process must remain inclusive to avoid reinforcing existing inequalities.

Leverage point *number seven* is called the *structure of information flows*. This is about who does or does not have access to what kind of information. More informed citizens can make better decisions. In feminist transformations this, for example, refers to the public discourse on overcoming patriarchy and supporting feminist endeavors. The awareness and transparency which the #MeToo campaign created is an interesting example of this leverage point. It also refers to more effective information about the advantages of a feminist future and its alignment with sustainability transformations.[5]

Leverage point *number eight* is about *changing the rules that govern a system*. Here, the leverage increases tremendously and interventions can lead to significant shifts. For example, altering laws and regulations can change how individuals and organizations behave within the system. For feminist transformations, an example would be abortion laws, laws that ensure equal payment for all genders or laws that allow people to self-determine their gender identity. Not surprisingly changing laws is high on the agenda in feminist transformations as well as in sustainability transformations.

Leverage point *number nine* refers to the power to *change how systems self-organize*. Self-organization is the most fascinating aspect of evolution and humankind is no exception regarding people's capability to invent new technologies or transform social systems. Self-organization requires less rules, but more principles and favorable conditions that then can be manifested in billions of different ways, as the evolution of life on Earth has shown. Self-organized systems are resilient. For feminist transformations, examples are feminist networks as well as local and transnational movements on various issues.

Leverage point *number 10* is *shifting the goals of a system*. Shifting the fundamental purpose or goal of a system is more difficult, yet it can lead to profound changes, particularly if new goals are co-created by many. For instance, changing the goal of the economy from sustained growth to maximizing the well-being of citizens could have an impact on how governments, corporations and entrepreneurs act.

Leverage point *number 11* refers to *shifting paradigms* out of which systems arise. Changing the worldviews from which a system operates has a powerful effect on how such a system transforms. Here, we are coming close to the potential power of the worldviews of Indigenous communities and feminist visions for a *Good Life for All*. A new or revived purpose of societies and economies is, according to Donella Meadows, one of the most powerful leverage points. It would gradually shift behaviors, structures and information flows. The most powerful leverage point *number 12* is, according to her, the *power to transcend paradigms*. She refers to a state of not-knowing that realizes that even paradigms are pluriverse and need to adapt. The most effective leverage point, in her view, is the ability to transcend the clinging to paradigms altogether, allowing for a complete rethinking and restructuring of the system. This involves recognizing and understanding multiple paradigms in a pluriverse world and choosing to operate beyond and across them. Although largely embedded in a more mechanistic thinking, Donella's work emphasizes the importance of understanding systems and the leverage points within them. She reminds us that the higher and more effective leverage points are more difficult to manifest.

In her research, the systems scientist Anna Birney took a deep dive into Donella Meadow's leverage points and rearranged them by creating a set of nested circles of interventions.[6] Each circle has its own dynamic and impact, yet fundamentally she follows Donella's insight into increasing effects of higher leverage areas. In her rearrangement nested circles for transformations emerge, in which the *paradigm shifts* still have the biggest impact, followed by what she calls *whole system goals*, which we can also interpret as purpose. The next level in Anna's diagram are the *patterns of relationships and organizing*. The current discourse on decolonization and decolonizing feminism are a move in the right direction. Re-shaping power relationships is an arduous task, but a prerequisite for transformations. The smallest nested circle in Anna's model is the *configuration of system structures and flows*. If we take the economy as a simplified example, the spread of a relational and systemic worldview (*paradigm shifts*) would lay the ground for transforming economic systems with new *whole systems goals* for economies: The well-being of people and planet. This would lead to shifting *patterns of relationships and organizing* economies, such as dismantling power imbalances in capitalist economies, resource exploitation of the Global South and unilateral domination of trade agreements. From this the *configuration of system structures and flows* would follow as equal access to resources, democratized economic policies and funds for re-addressing colonial legacies and the uneven distribution of climate change impacts.

If we bring these insights together, the complexity of feminist transformation strategies becomes clear. Different leverage points, or different layers of nested circles, need to be addressed at the same time across the globe by many feminist change agents. The crucial point is to become more aware of the interaction of different feminist strategies that may not have been planned together, and may seem contradictory or at least incoherent. This is not about centralizing feminist change, but connecting what will ultimately lead to transformative change. This way, we begin to weave a new world into the old. Our memory of a different world before patriarchy can sustain this journey. Again, the prefix 're' as described in Chapter 10 can function as an important re-minder for the underlying current. The leverage areas of feminist transformation strategies are nested layers of going 'back to the original', of 'undoing' and of 'breathing new life into' world-making. If we bring Donella Meadow's and Anna Birney's insights together with feminist aspirations, the picture emerges as layered approaches to feminist transformations. We can call these layers feminist world-making leverage areas that, together, show the hard work that we are doing today and that which still lies in front of us. The following spheres of influence begin with the smallest circle as the leverage area that we can understand as the base. We then work our way up to the largest circle as the leverage that, when implemented, has the greatest impact because it affects all other changes. The leverage areas are captured in Figure 13.1. Focusing only on the smaller circles will not take us into a feminist future. But focusing on the larger circles alone may lack the necessary underpinning.

Re-Allocating Resources is important, because financial and economic power is a decisive factor in societal transformations. This leverage area is about driving the re-allocation of financial and material resources to support feminist goals. This includes funding feminist movements, research, institutions and transformative projects. It advocates for a shift away from resource-depleting systems of concentrated wealth to those that invest in long-term collective, life-affirming purposes.

Re-Organizing Structures seeks to overcome the hierarchical and exclusionary nature of existing governance and institutional structures. It calls for decentralized and participatory systems that empower individuals and communities. People-centered institutions prioritize transparency, accountability and the co-creation of governance mechanisms, fostering a sense of shared responsibility and ownership in societal decision-making.

Re-Shaping Information Flows is not only about challenging patriarchal, colonial and exploitative norms, but replacing them with egalitarian and regenerative narratives. By fostering feminist-informed media, research and education systems, this leverage area amplifies pluriverse knowledge production and democratizes access to knowledge about the potency of feminist futures.

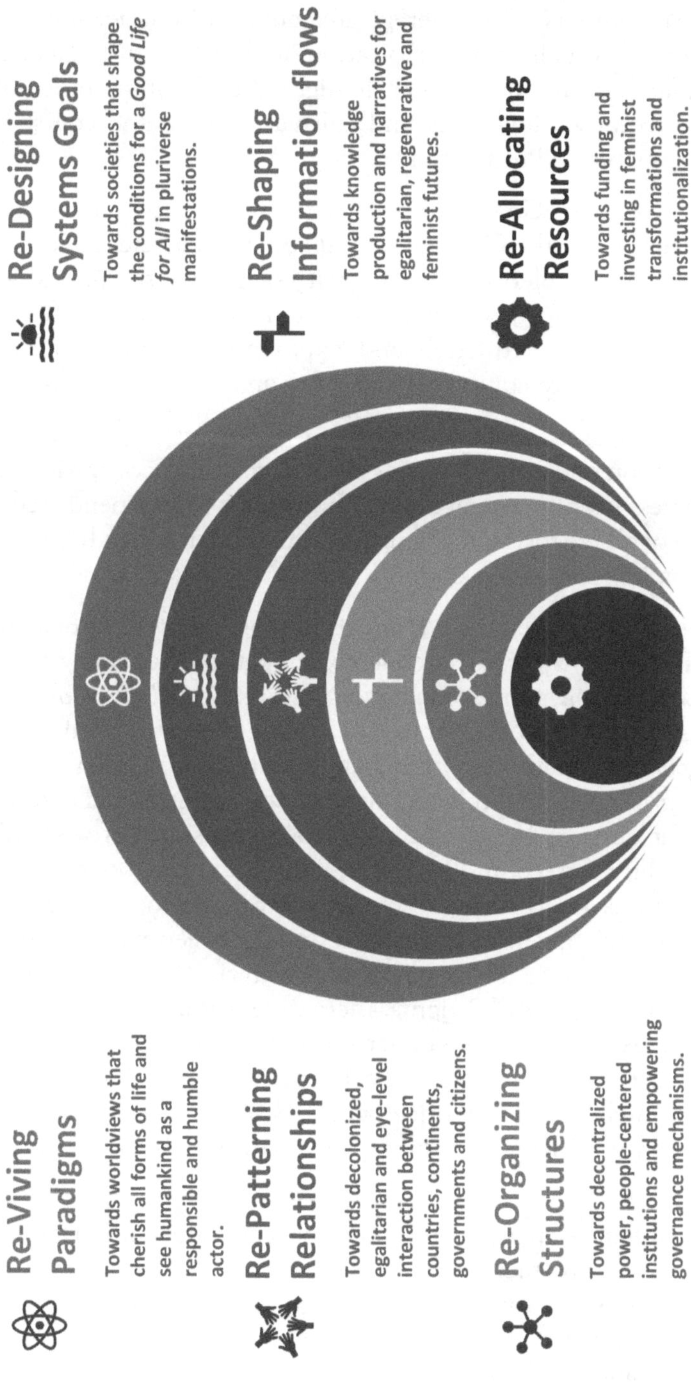

Figure 13.1 Feminist world-making leverage areas

Re-Patterning Relationships means counteracting dynamics of power across global and local contexts. This leverage area envisions relationships free from domination, neo-colonialism or exploitation, and instead fosters partnerships based on equality and mutual respect. It highlights the importance of decolonization, collaborative diplomacy and cultivating trust and equity between citizens, governments and institutions.

Re-Designing Systems Goals is about societal objectives that create the conditions necessary for the *Good Life for All*. Such goals reject one-size-fits-all solutions, and instead celebrate the diversity of pluriverse cultural and ecological contexts. They focus on creating systems that nurture life-sustaining values, moving beyond extractive and exploitative mental frames toward frameworks that prioritize equity, sustainability and collective well-being.

Re-Viving Paradigms is about transforming the underlying worldviews that guide human action and societal norms away from anthropocentric and profit-driven ideologies. It enlivens paradigms that honor interdependence and the intrinsic value of all life forms, recognizing humanity's role as a humble steward within the broader ecological web.

One thing is clear: In feminist strategizing for transformations, we must counteract the four major patriarchal power pathologies and their various manifestations: *coercion*, *institutionalization*, *gaslighting and divide and rule*. The most challenging task is to find strategies against the patriarchal power pathology of *coercion*, the pathology that has accompanied human development for thousands of years. Brutal rule, oppression, state control and extended warfare have so far destroyed even the most courageous acts of women's resistance and struggles for freedom. Patriarchy cannot exist without weapons, and spiraling arms races are the enemy of any attempts to overcome patriarchy. Too little attention is given to the connections between patriarchal backlash in the form of violence against women, authoritarian regimes with state surveillance, diminishing LGBTQ rights, increasing warfare and arms races. The global peace index 2024 could be understood as a patriarchal backlash index.[7] It warns us that the world is at a critical juncture, with 56 military conflicts worldwide, the highest number since World War II. There cannot be lasting peace in patriarchy. There cannot be peace without rising *collective feminist power practices*.

Let us remember female creativity to counteract coercion, both in fantasy and in reality: Rokeya Hossain's mental shield of sunlight that destroyed the aggressor, the naked dance of Cameroon women to frighten and curse exploitative men, or the use of violence against objects and police by the Mexican 'bloc negro'. Demonstrations and strikes have always been part of women's resistance to coercion. On August 9, 1956, in Pretoria, South Africa, approximately 20,000 women of all races marched to protest the Apartheid pass laws introduced for Black women in 1952 and to present a petition to Prime Minister J.G. Strijdom.[8] Organized by the Federation of South African Women, including the ANC Women's League, the march had representatives from each racial group and aimed to amplify the female voice in the anti-Apartheid movement and address issues such as child care, housing, education, equal pay and equal rights in property, marriage and guardianship. One of the songs they sang went: *When you strike the women, you strike a rock, you will be crushed.*

Verónica Gago, the Argentinian feminist activist and scholar, is one of the key figures behind the re-emerging concept of an *International Women's Strike*.[9] This movement is designed to challenge and disrupt the structures of patriarchy and neoliberal capitalism as a form of protest and collective action highlighting intersectional issues such as gender-based violence, economic inequality, reproductive rights and social justice. Gago highlights the importance of solidarity among women and the power of collective action that is not just local or national, but a transnational movement, fostering a sense of unity and shared purpose among women worldwide. The idea of the *International Women's Strike* takes up historic experiences and revives collective actions such as work stoppage, demonstrations and protests, educational campaigns and, importantly, global networking and coordination. Even if difficult to organize under conditions of patriarchal power pathologies, it is a still underutilized route to a really impactful *collective feminist power practice*.

Based on the above insights, let me invite you on a mental journey into possible futures. Imagine, all present and recent past female heads of state (and a few men), including their ministers and allies in parliaments and institutions, were declared feminists. They have claimed power in patriarchal politics and institutions in order to be able to overcome patriarchy. They have been entrusted with institutional power positions, but stay connected to feminist movements and grassroots organizations in a feminist network of networks. Imagine, they all had a feminist agenda, probably not entirely the same, but all committed to a just, fair, ecologically sound and gender-inclusive future. Countries are different, contexts are different, cultures are different and priorities are different. But imagine, these women in power positions exchanged on a regular basis ideas about their joined global feminist transformation agenda: How best to abolish patriarchy? How best to drive their countries towards an egalitarian, peaceful, ecologically sound society? How to reshape global and societal inequalities?

Imagine this happening not only between the most powerful women in politics, but also between other feminists in power: Feminists on corporate boards, feminists in academic institutions, feminist leaders of NGOs, feminist municipality mayors and feminist philanthropists. Most of all, imagine these feminists were connected with each other and feminist movements in a global collective feminist power alliance, open to collective learning and committed to mutual support. They establish a global youth advisory group, connected to youth groups in all countries, and they regularly consult the network of networks of feminists who hold influential positions in civil society organizations. A council of entrusted Indigenous community members regularly provides feedback to the feminist power alliance. What would happen within a few decades? Let's jump into that future and look back from there.

The feminists in political power positions would have used their influence to steward their countries out of crises into still troubled waters, but with a clear direction and a future narrative that resonated with people. They wanted a *Good Life for All*, knowing that the pathways towards life-enhancing civilizations would be riddled with setbacks, mistakes and the need to strategize and re-strategize together. Their clear goal: Transforming the world with a *collective feminist power practice. Power, they would have redefined as the collaborative capacity to steward transformations towards a Good Life for All.* They referred to power as potency, inspired by the Spanish term *potencia* as the *desiring capacity to change everything.*[10] Once a year they came together as a community of practice in a huge offline and online feminist world transformation conference that outnumbered the failing and shrinking COP meetings.

They drove the global feminist and regenerative paradigm shift by all means with narratives of possibilities. A while ago, most governments had been busy reacting to crises caused by eroded social cohesion, catastrophic effects of climate change, right-wing threats, patriarchal backlash, military conflicts and hybrid wars, social disparities and economic vulnerability. Back then, most people believed that a *Good Life for All* would be forever impossible and nobody had time to consult citizens on how a better future could be co-created. Feminists took care of citizens' assemblies and dialogue, and found that despite their commitment to a pluriverse world, the set of values was similar across the globe. In a networked action approach, they introduced herstory into every school curriculum. With all the creative freedom possible the content was adjusted to the specific geographic and cultural context. Everybody began to understand the detrimental effect of patriarchal power pathologies. Students learned not only about female power and women's contributions to history, but about the long period in the evolution of humankind, when rape, wars and violent conflicts did not exist and disagreements had been solved in dialogue and negotiations. Because this remembrance of a different human history was so embedded in cultures, the re-establishment of a peaceful, egalitarian, participatory and regenerative future became a realistic vision for humankind's development, even though people needed to invent myriads of different forms and pathways. Dialogue and peaceful conflict resolution became the norm. Where authoritarian rulers could not abstain from coercive measures, women went on feminist strikes, supported by transnational solidarity.

Towards the year 2035, the Global Sustainable Development Goals became SDGs 4.0, reshaped with a strong feminist lens and supported by artificial intelligence that accelerated collective learning across the globe. Every country put processes in place to adjust the goals to their specific context in dialogues with citizens. Media as well as the arts ensured diverse and equitable representation in media-making and delivery of information. They conveyed so many stories highlighting women's contributions to peaceful societies that the public perception of possibilities shifted. Globally, the momentum grew so drastically that outdated images of femaleness and maleness blurred, and male toxicity had no attraction anymore for boys and men.

Right from the beginning, feminist collectives knew that paradigm shifts would be powerful and were crucially important, yet parallel to an emerging new worldview of interconnectedness and care, outdated structures held the world in captivity, people in conflict and patriarchy in place. They knew they would have to create enlivening structures by knitting the features of feminist networking bit by bit into the existing, most often hierarchical structures of organizations, governments and societies. Hence, they promoted flat hierarchies and new forms of participatory organizing. Citizens assemblies were taken up by districts and municipalities as the new way of bottom-up consensus-building in societies. Yet, the mammoth task that required special attention, and could only be tackled one small step at a time, was the rebuilding of an unjust global economic and financial infrastructure. Collective analysis, with feminist experts from the Global South in the lead, supported by artificial intelligence, revealed so many postcolonial exploitative structures still in place that it was hard to believe they could ever be dismantled. They realized that financing feminist transformations as such was not the issue – in principle, funds were available, but the entire global money flow systematically disadvantaged women, gender-diverse people, young people and in particular feminist movements. Moreover, the global financial system had spiraled out of control by prioritizing financial value over people and the planet, and subsequently making the wealthy even more wealthy, further widening the gap between rich and poor. Its original purpose to facilitate allocation of resources in an economy had long been distorted. Locked in the outdated paradigm, short-term gains outweighed long-term value. This had led to an economic system that supported bubbling finance rather than access to resources for all.[11] Because these structures were so pervasive, several interconnected working groups prepared step-by-step solutions for changing the global finance system in preparation for upcoming feminist world transformation conferences. Feminist collectives frantically searched for small, but pioneering examples of power-shifting financial relations, no matter how small, which could possibly become pioneers for larger, more systemic change.

They focused on feminist funding and an adjusted version of the climate *loss and damage fund.*[12] It was clear that all this would not radically shift the relationships between the Global South and the Global North, but entailed elements that could help fund times of transition, when funding was mainly provided by wealthier nations. Additionally, they worked with circles of feminist philanthropists to channel large amounts of funding into transformative activist collectives and feminist organizations, favoring Global South organizations. Although the feminist alliance considered the so-called Overseas Development Assistance an outdated model of neocolonial control, it picked selected elements from the aforementioned *Feminist Foreign Assistance and Development Policies* that were useful for a transition time such as women's education, economic empowerment and awareness of women's rights. Similarly, they picked up pioneering concepts from *Feminist Foreign Policy* approaches that had been established in some countries before. Together with the long-standing and still ongoing work of the *Women's International League for Peace and Freedom (WILPF)*[13] a feminist working group continued developing a feminist approach to global peace and disarmament. They admitted it was not a revolution, but a way of knitting feminist forms of institutionalization into existing structures.

Members of the feminist power alliance knew that knowledge and its distribution would be at the core of feminist transformations. During the first feminist world transformation conference, some feminists had repeatedly highlighted issues of male biases in technologies, which would, if unattended, reinforce patriarchal mental and physical infrastructures. Heated debates took place in how to guide Silicon Valley's male-biased invention capacity towards innovations in feminist digitization that would serve life rather than reinforcing patriarchy's destructive tendencies. It was clear that many more feminists needed to be spearheading technological development. A global research project on feminist AI became the backbone of reinventing a technology that was meant to take humankind into a new era. A collective of feminists was vigilant enough to know that they needed to get a handle on how artificial intelligence would be further developed and used. They gathered a collective of world-class scientists, economists and activists together to ensure that AI would become a feminist ally and used to nurture the world with a truly social and ecological mission. This was part of an entire network for feminist digital justice.[14] A constitution for the use of artificial intelligence was adopted by many countries and most corporations.[15] Another feminist collective tested and observed the invention and further development of what was called decentralized regenerative finance.[16] The idea was to create access to investments for many people in the Global South who were shut out of financial markets, and to steer finances towards social and ecological investments. A whole financial sector outside the institutionalized finance sector emerged. *Decentralized autonomous organizations* (DAOs), a form of decentralized finance inspired by self-governing capabilities of ecosystems, became important for these regenerative approaches to finance. The intention was to take monetary control back into the hands of communities, particularly those that had been disenfranchised, and enable them to finance activism and social projects, while ensuring tokenized membership and democratized decisions on investments.

All these strands connected in a global discourse that brought together feminist pioneers, visionaries and economists to re-invent the global economic architecture. A global consensus began to emerge that the patriarchal 'take–make–destroy' model in economies was obsolete and considered unethical, while the emerging holistic worldview suggested as the new purpose of economies the well-being of planet and people.

In the beginning, the media ignored the feminist world transformation conferences, but the feminist power alliance was increasingly covered as more feminists promoted other feminists into the media. Already the third conference received more media attention than the yearly COP meeting on climate, and the gathering of patriarchal power protagonists at the outdated World Economic Forum. Both meetings diminished, as women experts intentionally resigned from their work at these institutions, and withdrew their support for these meetings. They had realized how the engagement with outdated patriarchal structures made them complicit with upholding pathological power structures. Instead, they began to work for the feminist world transformation conference. Funding increasingly flowed into conference and preparatory work. The stalling implementation of the bold visions from the Fourth World Conference on Women in Beijing in 1995 meeting had been revived[17] and the ideas from the Generation Equality Forum, which had launched a transformative action plan towards gender equality,[18] were taken up.

Feminists could observe the typical features of a power shift. The more the feminist world transformations conference grew, the more powerful it was perceived to be. Subsequently, more people wanted to be part of such an important meeting and movement. It was then that members of the feminist network on data feminism argued how important it would be to measure the transformative shifts that were under way.[19] People, and in particular girls and women, needed to see the stages of feminist mobilization and its positive effects at their fingertips. Data, they stated and had long been fighting for, should be owned by people, and should be measured in a way that people would participate in. Years ago, they had established a *Patriarchal Backlash Index*, which emerged through feminist participatory data gathering in the majority of countries. It had become necessary to document the rise of authoritarian states, the decline of democracies, the rise in violence against women and the increase in military conflicts. The global index was both shared by and contributed to collaboratively by millions of feminists. Easily accessible on mobile devices, it was linked to apps and digital information on support and mobilization. The index was pivotal in raising the global feminist consciousness, as it clearly showed how patriarchal pathologies impacted not only women, but the world, with detrimental trajectories. In fact, participatory data gathering became an anchor for feminist mobilization. Now, in various areas, feminists, women and finally all others could see how feminist collective power led to realizing new possibilities. With their experiences in previous decentralized data-gathering projects, they began to build similar metrics for different emerging transformative shifts. The most important intention was to make feminists, more and more women, and finally all people see what collective feminist power achieved. A working group of the yearly conference dealt with new measurements of people's and planetary health that would finally substitute the outdated measurement of GDP (Gross Domestic Product). It was hard work to get the siloed experts together, who had for decades worked on alternatives to the GDP.[20] But they finally succeeded.

It was the global erosion of democracies in the early years after the global COVID-19 pandemic that spurred a specific feminist working group on reviving and improving democracies. The debate was fierce, because many feminists from the Global South argued that Western democracies were deeply patriarchal in their multi-party system and models of representation. Even if the share of women in parliaments grew, the typical forms of move–oppose debate as well as the focus on majority vote did not lead to collective intelligence, so they argued. They considered the current models of democracy outdated and searched for traditional and, above all, more suitable and consensus-building forms of societal organization and representation. If democracies, as one could see in Europe in 2024, were capable of abolishing themselves by means of their own rules, and if authoritarian regimes around the world were able to use the cloak of supposedly democratic elections to maintain their power, then, so they argued, it was time to start the great work of radically improving the foundational rules of democracies and participatory societal organizing.

It was both about re-inventing democracies in a feminist way and about renovating existing democratic procedures. The aim was to deepen the participation of all citizens including marginalized groups in democratic governance processes, no matter if the issue was about constitutional reforms, budgeting or policy-making.[21] Such processes, even if implemented in small steps, would model, so their thinking went, the governance in feminist societies of the future. Feminist policies, they were convinced, would lead to feminism implemented by state actors who would become the protagonists in transforming unequal societies towards states that took care of the commons and a *Good Life for All.*[22] They built their strategies on a successful example that had been implemented in Hawai'i. In late 2020, a feminist recovery plan, commissioned by the Hawai'i State Commission on the Status of Women, proposed reevaluating and reorientating government spending and economic policies towards feminist transformations.[23] The plan suggested a move away from those sectors that serve foreign interests, such as military, tourism and luxury development, and instead supported sustainable, equitable and Indigenous livelihoods as well as adopting a universal basic income, raising the minimum wage and improving health care. The feminist power alliance also favored restructuring tax systems towards social and economic justice by, for example, increasing property and corporate taxes. They realized that their feminist future needed to be embedded in existing structures and safeguarded by laws, taxes, regulations, standards, budget allocations and constitutions in order to last. The years of experience in backsliding democracies had sent a clear warning. The constitutional state was considered a backbone of feminist transformations and the rule of law, national and international, the way forward towards feminist civilizations. On the bumpy road to finding humankind's way back to peaceful, egalitarian societies that nurture the Earth, the law had proven to be an achievement. The feminist alliance investigated examples of using and expanding laws to support the paradigm shift. If nature was given rights, they argued, it would change the way people thought about the planet and human actions. Once established, it would safeguard the commons and nobody could simply exploit nature. They were inspired by Ecuador, which, in 2008, as a nation state, recognized nature's own rights in its constitution,[24] and by the legal and governance arrangements for the Whanganui River in Aotearoa (New Zealand), which was particularly interesting as it connected Indigenous law with the establishment of new institutions and shifting power structures towards communities.[25] Another inspiring example came from a court judgment in Hawai'i in 2024. Initiated by 13 Hawaiian youth in June 2022, the first youth-led constitutional climate case addressing transportation sector pollution reached a landmark settlement, forcing the government to invest significantly in clean transportation infrastructure. This historic resolution set a precedent for the crucial role of empowering youth in advocating for climate action.[26] In a feminist future, they insisted, people would take care of nature as much as they would take care of each other. This would also solve the pathologies of short-term thinking, because it would inevitably involve considering the rights of future generations. Soon, the gatherings of the *feminist world transformation conference* had regional and national derivates, for which contextualized strategies were discussed and implemented. Only with feminist transformations, it became clear, would there be a sustainable and regenerative future, and peace on Earth.

I wonder what your comments column has remarked while reading the above scenario imagination. Your intellectual brain may have picked up all the missing strategies: I suggest they could be integrated. The manager in you may have decided this is too complex. I argue, life is complex and so are transformative efforts. The pessimist in you will have probably argued that the patriarchal backlash and the geopolitical trends as well as many national power imbalances are worsening so much that violent resistance towards such feminist strategies would make the entire idea obsolete. I suggest that giving up cannot be our choice. Your heart may have been touched by the pain of longing for our *potencia*, the *collective feminist capacity to change everything*. Is the scenario really utopian? Could it become real? Can we see feminist transformation approaches as patterned and interrelated, even if at the surface they might seem disconnected? Can we, for once, get feminists in power who deliberately collaborate with each other? Can we use the *collective feminist power practices* to combine the insights from transformation knowledge with the leverage areas for feminist world-making and craft patterns of feminist transformation strategies that cut across the different levels and leverage points?

Feminist transformation strategies must be built on the strengths of feminist networking and leverage *collective feminist power practices* across local and global contexts. At the heart of feminist transformation is the deliberate and mutual promotion of women into positions of influence and decision-making. As feminist transformation strategy, the practice of *mutual re-powerment* is about feminists mediating power through one another, ensuring that women's leadership reshapes systems from within. This strategy amplifies feminist voices where they influence. It potentially enables a ripple effect of women in power throughout societies. We know that transformation thrives on collaboration. As feminist transformation strategy, the practice of *networked connectivity* embraces radical collectivity by forging alliances across divides, differences and borders. By connecting local and global feminist movements, this strategy builds a cohesive yet diverse connectivity of thematic alliances that unite feminists across countries and continents. It fosters resilience, solidarity and shared purpose. Feminist expertise is a wellspring of knowledge and innovation. As feminist transformation strategy, the practice of *courageous discovery* leverages this expertise by connecting knowledge and practice around leverage areas for transformative change. Breaking down thematic silos and sharing insights across countries and contexts enables feminists to uncover bold, innovative solutions that disrupt patriarchal systems and show pathways into feminist futures. Acknowledging and valuing diverse contributions are essential to overcoming patriarchy. As feminist transformation strategy, the practice of *reflective appreciation* builds bridges across feminist struggles, recognizing how various strategies intersect and complement one another. By honoring differences and fostering understanding, this strategy strengthens intersectional approaches and creates a richer, more inclusive feminist movement. The future of feminist transformation lies in modelling life-enhancing patterns of interaction. As feminist transformation strategy, the practice of *dialogic reciprocity* creates the conditions for feminists to organize autonomously while linking their struggles within a global spirit of pragmatic solidarity. In a spirit of potency, autonomous initiatives become interconnected and mutually reinforcing strategies. Feminist movements must claim ambitious, transformative visions of future societies. As feminist transformation strategy, the practice of *feminist aspiration* is about collectively stewarding transformative ambitions in transnational collaboration, envisioning societies that prioritize care, equality and sustainability – the *Good Life for All*. By centering feminist values in future-building, this strategy inspires hope, fosters creativity and sets a course for systemic change. Figure 13.2 depicts how, together, these six strategies build on one another. They can guide contextualized feminist movements, initiatives and collective power practices.

What if we were able to take a bird's eye perspective and see the patterned and networked action on our feminist world map? What would we need to do as feminists to make the above scenario real? How could we develop the courage, the clarity and the confidence to collectively claim the power to transform the world, even if it will take several generations?

Major insights for *collective feminist power practices* from insights into feminist transformation strategies:

1. For feminist transformation strategies we need to work with interconnected allies in sustainability, biodiversity, climate movements, human rights and decolonization efforts to overcome harmful societal and economic systems.
2. It is important to recognize and collectively create life-enhancing patterns in transformative change efforts that model vitality of ecological and social systems.

1 – MUTUAL RE-POWERMENT

Mediate power through women: Deliberately and mutually promote feminists into influential and decision-making positions.

2 – NETWORKED CONNECTIVITY

Embrace radical collectivity: Establish local to global feminist thematic alliances across divides, differences, countries and continents.

3 – COURAGEOUS DISCOVERY

Leverage feminist expertise: Connect knowledge and practice on leverage points for transformative change across thematic siloes, countries and continents.

4 – REFLECTIVE APPRECIATION

Build bridges across diverse feminist struggles: Acknowledge how strategies to overcome patriarchy intersect and value different contributions.

5 – DIALOGIC RECIPROCITY

Organize feminist futures: Create life-enhancing patterns of interaction, and embrace autonomous organizing in the spirit of potency.

6 – FEMINIST ASPIRATION

Collectively steward transformative ambitions: Drive transnational collaboration towards future societies that take care of the *Good Life for All*.

Figure 13.2 A pattern of collective power practices in feminist transformation strategies

3. Feminist transformation strategies can get greatly inspired by the knowledge and practice of leverage areas for transformative societal change.
4. Feminist transformation efforts need to value and connect activities in all layered leverage areas of feminist world-making: Re-viving paradigms, re-designing systems goals, re-patterning relationships, re-shaping information flows, re-organizing structures and re-allocating resources.
5. We must realize that finding countermeasures to the power pathology of *coercion* is a real challenge and requires innovative approaches such as the *International Women's Strike*.
6. A pattern approach to feminist transformation strategies means translating *collective feminist power practices* into an overall pluriverse, yet collaborative approach.

Notes

1 Wheatley & Frieze (n.d.) and Simard (2021).
2 See also Otto et al. (2020).
3 See Waddock & Kuenkel (2019); before AI emerged as technology, a voice asking such questions was Gabriel (1996).
4 See Meadows (1999).
5 The current rise of disinformation shows how this leverage point is effectively used to counteract feminist transformations.
6 See Birney (2021).
7 See Vision Of Humanity (2024).
8 See South African History Online (2018).
9 See Gago (2020) and Gago (2019).
10 See Gago (2020).
11 See Jess et al. (2023).
12 See Pill & Hammersley (2024).
13 The emergence of the Women's International League for Peace and Freedom (WILPF) was an outcome of the aforementioned women's peace congress in The Hague in 1915. It was officially launched in 1919. See: https://www.wilpf.org
14 Such initiatives are not utopian. An example can be found here: IT for Change (2017).
15 A suggestion for a constitution particularly for general artificial intelligence has already been published with women in the lead. See: Smitsman (2024).
16 Regenerative finance, DAOs and blockchain are worlds strongly populated by men. A good overview of the potential can be found in Schletz (2023). For DAOs there is an interesting approach by two women authors in Catlow & Rafferty (2022).
17 See United Nations (1995).
18 See the Generation Equality Forum: https://forum.generationequality.org
19 For inspirations see Klein & D'Ignazio (2023).
20 A good overview of approaches to economic and societal progress indicators measuring well-being instead of GDP can be found in Jansen (2024).

21 More inspiration in this topic can be found in Caravantes & Lombardo (2024), Cornwall & Goetz (2005) and Martinez-Palacios (2018).
22 For inspirations on re-enchanting the commons, see Federici (2018) and Elinor Ostrom (1990) for her groundbreaking work on commons.
23 See Hawai'i State Commission on the Status of Women (2020).
24 For example, in the constitution of Ecuador Rights of Nature are embeddded in Title II, fundamental rights Art. 10 and Art. 71. See Ecuador Constitution (2008).
25 See Cribb et al. (2024).
26 See Townsend & Britto (2024).

References

Birney, A. (2021). How do we know where there is potential to intervene and leverage impact in a changing system? The practitioners perspective. *Sustainability Science*, *16*(3), 749–765. https://doi.org/10.1007/s11625-021-00956-5

Caravantes, P., & Lombardo, E. (2024). Feminist democratic innovations in policy and politics. *Policy and Politics*, *52*(2), 177–199. https://doi.org/10.1332/03055736y2023d000000009

Catlow, R., & Rafferty, P. (2022). *Radical Friends: Decentralised Autonomous Organisations & the Arts*. Torque Editions.

Cornwall, A., & Goetz, A.M. (2005). Democratizing democracy: Feminist perspectives. *Democratization*, *12*(5), 783–800. https://doi.org/10.1080/13510340500322181

Cribb, M., Macpherson, E., & Borchgrevink, A. (2024). Beyond legal personhood for the Whanganui River: Collaboration and pluralism in implementing the *Te Awa Tupua Act*. *The International Journal of Human Rights*, *24*, 1–24. https://doi.org/10.1080/13642987.2024.2314532

Ecuador Constitution (2008). Title II, Chapter 1, Fundamental Rights. https://www.garn.org/wp-content/uploads/2021/09/Rights-for-Nature-Articles-in-Ecuadors-Constitution.pdf

Federici, S. (2018). *Re-enchanting the World: Feminism and the Politics of the Commons*. PM Press.

Gabriel, R.P. (1996). *Patterns of Software*. New York: Oxford University Press.

Gago, V. (2019, September 10). *Eight Theses on the Feminist Revolution*. Toward Freedom. https://towardfreedom.org/story/eight-theses-on-the-feminist-revolution

Gago, V. (2020). *Feminist International: How to Change Everything*. Verso.

Hawai'i State Commission on the Status of Women. (2020, April 14). Building bridges, not walking on backs: A feminist economic recovery plan for COVID-19. https://humanservices.hawaii.gov/wp-content/uploads/2020/04/4.13.20-Final-Cover-D2-Feminist-Economic-Recovery-D1.pdf

IT for Change. (2017). Feminist digital justice. https://itforchange.net/feminist-digital-justice-DAWN-ITfC

Jansen, A., Wang, R., Behrens, P., & Hoekstra, R. (2024). Beyond GDP: A review and conceptual framework for measuring sustainable and inclusive wellbeing. *The Lancet Planetary Health*, 8(9), e695–e705. https://doi.org/10.1016/s2542-5196(24)00147-5

Jess, T., Blom, P., & Dixson-Declève, S. (2023). From financing change to changing finance. https://www.clubofrome.org/wp-content/uploads/2023/10/Changing_Finance_2023-3.pdf

Klein, L.F., & D'Ignazio, C. (2023). *Data Feminism*. The Mit Press.

Martinez-Palacios, J. (2018). *Innovaciones democráticas feministas*. Librería Dykinson. https://www.dykinson.com/libros/innovaciones-democraticas-feministas/9788491481843

Meadows, D. (1999). Leverage points: Places to intervene in a system. The Sustainability Institute. https://donellameadows.org/wp-content/userfiles/Leverage_Points.pdf

Ostrom, E. (1990). *Governing the Commons: The Evolution of Institutions for Collective Action*. Cambridge University Press.

Otto, I.M., Donges, J.F., Cremades, R., Bhowmik, A., Hewitt, R.J., Lucht, W., Rockström, J., Allerberger, F., McCaffrey, M., Doe, S.S.P., Lenferna, A., Morán, N., van Vuuren, D.P., & Schellnhuber, H.J. (2020). Social tipping dynamics for stabilizing Earth's climate by 2050. *Proceedings of the National Academy of Sciences*, *117*(5), 2354–2365. https://doi.org/10.1073/pnas.1900577117

Pill, M., & Hammersley, G. (2024). A climate loss and damage fund that works. In *Policy Brief*. Lowy Institute. https://unfccc.int/sites/default/files/resource/PILL-HAMMERSLEY-Climate-loss-and-damage-fund.pdf

Schletz, M., Constant, A., Hsu, A., Simon, J.D., Schillebeeckx, S., Beck, R., & Martín Wainstein. (2023). Blockchain and regenerative finance: Charting a path toward regeneration. *Frontiers in Blockchain*, 6. https://doi.org/10.3389/fbloc.2023.1165133

Simard, S. (2021). *Finding the Mother Tree: Discovering the Wisdom of the Forest*. Penguin.

Smitsman, A., Goertzel, B., Bozesan, M., & George, L. (2024). Participatory framework for a global AGI constitution. *Cadmus Journal*, 5(3), Part 2; World Academy of Arts and Science (WAAS). https://www.cadmusjournal.org/article/volume-5-issue-3-p2/participatory-framework-creating-global-agi-constitution

South African History Online. (2018, August 13). The 1956 Women's March, Pretoria, 9 August. https://www.sahistory.org.za/article/1956-womens-march-pretoria-9-august

Townsend, M., & Britto, H. (2024, June 21). Historic agreement reached in Hawai'i youth-led constitutional climate complaint. Earthjustice. https://earthjustice.org/press/2024/historic-agreement-settles-hawaii-youth-led-constitutional-climate-complaint

United Nations. (1995). Report of the fourth world conference on women. https://www.un.org/womenwatch/daw/beijing/pdf/Beijing%20full%20report%20E.pdf

Vision Of Humanity. (2024). Global peace index. https://www.visionofhumanity.org/maps/#/

Waddock, S., & Kuenkel, P. (2019). What gives life to large system change? *Organization & Environment*, *33*(3), 342–358. https://doi.org/10.1177/1086026619842482

Wheatley, M., & Frieze, D. (n.d.). Using emergence to take social innovation to scale. https://www.margaretwheatley.com/articles/using-emergence.pdf

14
Emerging Civilizations – How Feminist Visions Can Become Possible Futures

If the scenario in the previous chapter became true, feminists would, in collaboration, slowly shift societies towards civilizations that centered around a *Good Life for All*. How long would this take? Perhaps decades, perhaps centuries. It would not just be about fighting or demonstrating, not only about celebrating the power potential of women. It would not be a revolution, but hard and persistent work; and it would require taking power from the current system to shape a different future. Feminists, in all their difference, would need to access the centers of power. They would have to be everywhere and at the same time often invisible. They would have to show, experience and witness how the perception of reality changes when feminists begin to value each other in their differences. This would create a thriving and pluriverse network of powerful connections between feminists within and outside institutions. It would be this pulsating network that would finally make the feminist transformation a growing reality. Anything is possible if we start envisioning the future in our minds, no matter how contradictory reality may seem.

Yet, between our dreams of a different world, our many attempts to tame patriarchy and our aspirations not to renovate but to overcome it, we need to understand a crucial aspect of collective world-making: In the era of the Anthropocene, in which human impact can change the trajectory of the planet, reality is not a given fact out there, to which we react, but a relational occurrence. Insights from quantum physics and cognition theory suggest that our perceptions influence how potentialities are realized into realities, highlighting the interplay between observation, thought and experience. All possibilities of evolution are open to us. It is our thoughts that contribute to creating reality. There is always a choice of apocalypse, or, like the Hopis predict, the ending of our world, before the next begins. Can we do without apocalypse? Can we collectively decide for transformations to another world? The past is always a burden and at the same time an inspiration for the future. Future realities arise from the interaction of collective sense-making and collective co-creation. If

DOI: 10.4324/9781003508885-19

the sense-making changes, co-creation will change. Paradigm shifts happen when people begin to see the current reality differently and when they imagine a different future. Out of this different perception arises different thinking, and new choices and new possibilities emerge that lay the ground for different collective co-creation.

We have learned that the process of life on our planet is always built on life-enhancing patterns. It seeks vitality, and, in principle, as human beings, we are part of this longing for aliveness. The current human trajectories towards wars and armament, social tensions, environmental destruction and increasing planetary emergencies are testimony of collective human folly, manifesting as ignorance towards the run-away dynamics of dysfunctional, destructive patterns. But collective sense-making takes place: Many, not only scientists, have warned of the dangerous trajectories which humankind pursues, but there is not yet a critical mass that is attracted enough to a different future. The current trajectories are caused and maintained by mental and physical infrastructures of normalized patriarchal power pathologies, and this makes them difficult to change. Yet, as humankind, we underestimate the human capacity to recreate life-enhancing patterns. Without this faculty our civilization would not have survived so far. It is a human faculty to gain insight and make different choices. For feminist transformation strategies it is crucial to highlight even more how the destructive patterns of power pathologies poison the collective capabilities of our global humanity and show that different choices are possible, if patriarchy as a mental infrastructure is no longer nourished. The recreation of life-enhancing patterns of interaction is ensuring our survival every day, and many are created and promoted by women. Multiplying them in networked action would let the pulsating network emerge that would finally make feminist transformations a reality.

Here is the conundrum: We need to name the dragon and expose and fight patriarchal power pathologies wherever we identify them. Yet, let us remember: *Attention energizes, intention transforms*. The current patriarchal realities consume a lot of attention. If we focus our perception mainly on fighting what maintains patriarchy, we are supporting it. This is hard to digest, because, in principle, there is nothing wrong with criticizing patriarchal structures. We need to name the culprits and expose the structurally embedded power pathologies. But if we do not intend to make patriarchy adapt to our needs, and instead abolish it, we must focus our attention on possible futures as much as we can. Because only this energizes these possible futures, and it helps our collective intention to work. The rest is the hard work of *collective feminist power practices*. We must focus on what is happening on the world map of feminist collective practice, and on what a civilized future of humanity would look like. This is about making life-serving patterns of thoughts, interactions and structures visible, strengthening them, focusing on them, so that the perception of another reality can begin to co-create this other reality.

One day, when I attended our local choir practice, one of the singers had brought her daughter, approximately seven or eight years old, presumably because she did not have anybody to take care of her at home. The girl sat quietly and listened to our singing practice until we had a ten-minute break. Mother and daughter took the chance to play one round of table football, which was placed outside our practice room. All of a sudden, the girl was wide awake, screaming and trying to beat her mother. For a moment, I looked into the girl's face and it was as if her possible future was flickering in her eyes. A life of freedom, with the choice guaranteed to be exactly who she wanted to be and doing exactly what she intended to do, because she would plan something, she would pursue her goals, she would follow her desire to shape the world. It was a moment frozen in time, because I knew that I was looking into the face of a girl who was not yet constrained by the subtle and overt norms of the patriarchy that would gradually limit her options to choose who she could become. As with this girl, whom I encountered somewhere in the middle of eastern Germany, I often felt the same way in other places: In Tanzania, in Argentina, in Vietnam, in Uzbekistan, in Sweden, in Chile, in Zimbabwe, in India, some girls more privileged, others less privileged. Once, on a business trip, I took a taxi in the early hours of the morning from the airport to the center of Mumbai in India. Countless people were sleeping on the pavements. When the driver stopped briefly at a traffic junction, I saw a girl crouched next to a woman lying down, who was staring into the distance with her eyes open, obviously seriously ill. The girl, aged four or five, with disheveled hair and a dirty brown dress, laid her head on her mother's chest. Then she turned her head towards the waiting taxi with angry, demanding, yet wise and somehow old eyes until the driver handed her a coin, which she greedily collected. Before I could act, the car moved and tears rolled down my cheeks, as I felt helpless and angry at a world that calls itself civilization. They are everywhere, the wild, powerful girls whose souls remember a time when they could be free, who, even if only for a brief moment, believe that they will live into a future that they will own. It is the eyes of these indomitable girls that should remind us that we must fight for possible futures. We must fight for a world that can justifiably call itself a civilization.

You might think, why girls? Are not boys suffering as much as girls? They are and they are not. They are, because some of the world's injustices do not know gender, and boys, everywhere, are captives of patriarchy. Yet, the historic rituals of domination, as we have seen, have always persisted with the divide and rule pathologies, offering boys the many layers of identifications with subtle and overt power over, instead of power for or power with. Of course, to some extent this is true for privileged girls, too, but to a much lesser extent. Our dominant civilization has major flaws. Could it be that the actual process of civilizing our civilization has only just begun?

The term *civilization* is a word we take for granted as fitting into our world. Most people would assume they live in a *civilized* world. Yet, is this really the case, given the inequalities, the colonial past and neocolonial present, the hardships, the past and present wars, the atrocities committed, the femicides? Are we, as a global society ignoring climate change, civilized?

Civilization is usually defined as a complex human society characterized by the development of human settlements, agriculture, urbanization, social stratification and division of labor, symbolic communication forms, and a certain degree of perceived separation from the natural environment. In addition, it includes technology development, which ideally contributes to the overall progress and sustainability of societies. Our current civilization also has increasingly complex institutions such as governments, religious institutions and economic systems. They regulate social relations and ensure societies' continuity and stability. In our dominant civilization, patriarchy with all its power pathologies is still perceived as the foundation of societal living. This includes the justification for regrettable but seemingly unavoidable use of power of some over others, the use of war and exploitation to enforce certain interests.

The story goes like this: The process of civilizing can be seen as the gradual development and transformation of human societies from simpler, less organized forms of social organization to more complex, structured and culturally advanced states. In historic analysis this included a shift from nomadic lifestyles to settled agricultural communities. This allowed for the development of stable food supplies, surplus production and the establishment of permanent settlements. Hence the civilizing process included the domestication of plants and animals, the development of farming techniques that would support larger populations and the growth of cities. Of course, this was followed by the growth of populations and the diversifying of culture, and subsequently more complex economic activities. Urbanization also brought about infrastructure, such as roads, buildings, public spaces, the division of labor and social stratification. Here the power pathology of gaslighting begins to be neatly knitted into patriarchal history. Civilization, so the patriarchal assumption goes, requires the emergence of hierarchical social structures, where individuals or groups have different roles, responsibilities and statuses. Subsequently, the development of classes or castes, with varying degrees of power, wealth and influence gets legitimized as a natural element of the process of civilization. In order to maintain a certain degree of social order, complex institutions facilitate the governance of society, and not surprisingly, in this story, mostly men are the powerful protagonists, and globally, mostly white men. Ethical and moral codes provide guidelines for behavior, ensure justice and promote social cohesion and cooperation. Advanced civilizations place emphasis on arts and culture as well as on education, knowledge creation, personal and intellectual growth. There is the issue of peace: Only stable societies can focus on long-term development and cultural flourishing, so civilized societies make efforts to maintain internal and external peace through conflict resolution, diplomacy and the promotion of social dialogue, participation and various forms of democracy. Of course, the process of civilizing is not linear. It is ongoing, as societies continue to evolve, adapt and develop in response to new challenges and opportunities.

Yet, the previous chapters have made the point clear: Our global society is not civilized and there cannot be lasting peace in patriarchy. As long as patriarchal power pathologies continue to permeate societies, dominate economic activities and persist in societal governance, the foundation for peace is continuously eroded. Male rivalry is an essential ingredient of power pathologies; coupled with modern forms of ubiquitous narcissism and weapons for mass destruction, this makes up a recipe for civilizational decline. Of course, some believers in the natural superiority of patriarchy envision future ecological societies with strong patriarchal leaders and widespread state surveillance.[1] But this is not the future we want. It is not the vision that will inspire feminist transformations, and it is not the dream that lives in the eyes of indomitable girls.

Patriarchal history remains relatively nebulous about ancient civilizations that have failed. But there is a combination of dysfunctional patterns that we can pick up from the many civilizations that disappeared.[2] One of the features is climate change and overuse of resources leading to famine and internal conflicts. The other is the patriarchal invasion of flourishing matriarchal cultures, leading to wars and internal unsolvable conflicts. Again, as we have mentioned, the invasions could have also been a consequence of climate change and subsequent migrations as well as shifts in societal organization under conditions of hardship. None of these extinct civilizations was able either to fully adapt to changed climate conditions or to resist cultural appropriation and subjugation through invasions. People might have found ways to survive, but as we have also seen in previous chapters, particularly the matriarchal societies lost their complex and often thriving civilizational achievements and broke apart with social disparities. Unless we as humankind learn the lessons, we are doomed to repeat history.

Three aspects of today's world are frighteningly similar to the historic decline of civilizations: Climate change, military conflicts and social disparities. One aspect is decisively different: Ancient civilizations were largely localized, whereas our so-called modern and dominant civilization is global, despite all differences. Feminist visions of future civilizations need to elaborate pathways to adapt to climate change, alleviate social disparities and overcome military conflicts. They need to work together globally, yet create their effects locally.

Globalization is a modern term, which has been fiercely criticized for good reasons. It refers to the process by which businesses, cultures and economies become interconnected and interdependent on a global scale. This process involves the exchange of goods, services, information and people across national boundaries. While this sounds neutral, as a matter of fact, the rules of this process have been determined by the few. Globalization has a long history riddled with power pathologies, leading to exploitation of people and natural resources, expropriation of land and assets, modern slavery and a global trade that ridiculously contributes to endangering human security because of increasing CO_2 emissions caused by shipping goods and people around the world. Has it contributed to global solidarity and consciousness about our interconnectedness? To some extent, yes. Transnational feminist collective practices are testimony to this. Yet the awareness about global human connection on this planet is much older than modern globalization. The still existing matriarchies are remnants of a global civilization based on similar principles, yet immensely pluriverse. They probably knew more about each other than we can imagine. The world is interconnected and has always been. The awareness of global interdependence and the recognition of shared global challenges and opportunities is paramount for working towards civilizations that cater for a *Good Life for All*. But we need decisively different terms and different rules than those manifested in the current manifestation of the term globalization. We need to project feminist aspirations into possible futures and turn the harmful process of modern patriarchal globalization into a process of reviving and regenerating human collective intelligence. Can we give each other the permission to dream?

In the future we want to craft, people will all take care of life and each other. Economies will be life-serving. Societies will be learning. Through democratic governance, people will design the future together, no matter which gender, culture, religion or status. They will do so with reverence towards the beauty and intelligence of life. Production and consumption cycles will be regenerative and socially embedded. Economic activities will be adapted to context and strengthen regional cycles. Wealth will be distributed and equal access to resources ensured. Planetary boundaries will be respected. People and governments will take care of the commons and safeguard life support systems. Life-enhancing technological and social innovations will be promoted. Societal progress and economic metrics will create awareness for life-enhancing progress and track the vitality of the respective systems.

How would this dream translate into societal features of future feminist-inspired civilizations?

In feminist-inspired societies, gender equality is paramount. Personal and professional opportunities are accessible to all, irrespective of gender, ensuring that leadership roles and employment are taken up equally by all genders. Policies are intersectional, designed to address the needs of people at the intersection of various identities, such as race, class and sexuality, promoting equity in all facets of life. Resource distribution is equitable, ensuring that healthcare, education and wealth are fairly allocated to all individuals. Non-binary and gender-fluid identities are welcome. Reproductive rights are safeguarded. Family is understood as social or biological kinship connections, and taking care of the upbringing of children is a collective task, strongly supported by social policies. Inclusive policies in healthcare, education and employment ensure that everyone is respected and supported. Tolerance is promoted through education and media representation. Strong measures prevent and respond to gender-based violence, ensuring safety and support for all. Lifelong learning opportunities are available, fostering continuous education and skill development. Curricula are decolonized, integrating Indigenous histories and perspectives, challenging colonial narratives and promoting cultural competency. Art and cultural expressions that promote feminist values are encouraged, fostering a cultural shift towards inclusivity and respect. Robust anti-discrimination laws and gender-sensitive policies are in place across all institutions. Legal systems ensure fairness and equity, with mechanisms to address gender-based injustices. Restorative justice practices focus on repairing harm and rebuilding relationships rather than punitive measures.

Historical injustices caused by colonization, wars, expropriation and exploitation are actively acknowledged and rectified. Indigenous cultures are revitalized, with languages, traditions and governance structures restored. Indigenous communities enjoy autonomy and sovereignty over their lands and resources, allowing them to govern themselves and sustain their cultural heritage. Economic models prioritize sustainability and regeneration. Regional and community-based economies flourish, emphasizing local and cooperative systems that distribute wealth and resources equitably. Global exchange of goods and knowledge is widespread, but the focus is on strengthening regional economies. Economic policies focus on thriving markets with responsible businesses. They prevent poverty and inequality. The purpose of economies is to safeguard life in all its manifestations, and provide a stable and fair economic environment for all citizens. Progress, including economic progress, is measured in the form of context-specific well-being indexes. Citizens participate in the data collection, and give regular feedback. Sustainable practices such as renewable energy, circular economies and low-impact production are the norm. Redistributive policies, including progressive taxation and universal basic income, are implemented to avoid excessive wealth inequality. Environmental justice is a key principle, ensuring marginalized communities are protected from environmental degradation and all people have access to healthy ecosystems. Social policies value care work, and ensure it is fairly compensated.

Collaborative governance models ensure that all voices are integral to decision-making processes and encourage active involvement from all citizens. Deliberative democracy methods, like citizen assemblies, are commonplace, ensuring informed and inclusive decision-making. Transparency and accountability in governance are maintained, with mechanisms in place to hold leaders responsible for their actions. Ecofeminism guides policies, recognizing the interconnectedness of environmental sustainability and gender equality. Practices focus on regenerating natural ecosystems and respecting the intrinsic rights of nature. Legal frameworks protect natural entities, ensuring that ecological health is a central concern in all decision-making processes. Ecocide as a crime against humanity is integrated in constitutions. Power is decentralized and participatory. Local communities have significant autonomy, particularly in environmental and resource management, yet follow overall guidance and contribute their data to measuring progress. Indigenous knowledge and practices are integrated into decision-making, respecting the sovereignty and expertise of Indigenous peoples.

International cooperation addresses gender issues worldwide. Human rights are upheld and advanced on an international scale, with a commitment to supporting equitable development and decolonization efforts globally. Across all societies the paradigm is peace. Mechanisms for resolving conflicts use dialogue, negotiation and legal processes. There is a variety of peaceful means of addressing disputes, from local levels to international levels. There is a global commitment to non-aggression in international relations. It involves diplomacy, participation in international organizations aimed at maintaining peace, and, in the early stages, sanctioning of any threats of military interventions or wars. In later stages, there is no military. The funds are invested into the well-being of societies. Rights of nature and strict implementation of human rights ensure that no actors, be they government, institutional, corporate or individual, will do harm to the members of the societies. Rights of minorities are safeguarded. A culture of peace and non-violent conflict resolution is taught from an early age. Equitable access to technology and digital literacy ensures all genders benefit from advancements. Innovation focuses on sustainability, with green technologies and regenerative design principles guiding development.

How does this sound to you? Would you want to live in such a civilization? Would you thrive? Would it make you feel alive? Or does it feel a bit too smooth, too orderly, too regulated, too perfect?

All of the above is important for future societies and for civilizations that find their way into peaceful, egalitarian and ecologically sound futures. But the future we want must be more than the perfectly regulated post-patriarchal society. The longing for the magical island on which women rule, this deep yearning so many women have and that I have mentioned in the earlier chapters, is less a yearning for a physical place, a form of society or a perfectly regulated country. Rather, it is a spiritual place which holds the intuitive knowledge that a different perception of the world leads to different realities. It is a form of knowledge that knows without asserting, because it reaches down into the vertical axis of time. It connects us synchronously with the existence of times that fundamentally contradict our rationally practiced linearity of historicity. Yet we are not talking about mysticism here, even if much of this island knowledge is hidden in myths, fairy tales and stories, lingering in places in landscapes that we call sacred sites. It is a deeply human faculty to connect with the universe, with nature, with one another. With the discovery of quantum physics, which teaches us that the manifest arises from the space of infinite possibilities and reacts on it in a never-ending spiral dynamic, we begin to understand how perception as a process of cognitive selection creates the world and explains it. We know what the consequences of this are: For thousands of years patriarchal men have monopolized the power of explaining the world, in cleverly reinforcing processes of appropriation and expropriation of knowledge, and of other forms of perceiving the world. Women, and as a result of European colonization also Indigenous peoples, often simply those who thought differently and knew differently, were robbed of their knowledge, banished to a desolate place, forced into spiritual exile, prevented under penalty of law from naming themselves and their access to life. They settled into homelessness, adapted and buried the so-important knowledge that was only accessible to them vertically in their still receptive souls. Today, again, we separate it, and call it traditional knowledge or Indigenous knowledge. What if this vertical knowledge, this connection to times before us and times after us, the essential knowing that we can be at home in a universe without controlling it, became accessible to all?

If many women connect with this knowing, realities will begin to change. The paradigm shift has begun. In the vast multiplicity of life, everything wants to be perceived and everything perceives. Realities emerge from perception. This is a principle of life. That is why *how* we perceive reality is so important. Just as Neolithic women were able to read landscapes in order to strengthen their harmonious effect on people, we can begin to cultivate an ancient, contemporary and future mental infrastructure that cherishes our planet, which, for good reasons, is called Mother Earth in many languages. If we do so, not a few but many, the world will change because we resonate with the possibilities that this different way of thinking promotes.

Do you know anything about mosses? They are millions of years old; they exist all over the world and they are very, very intelligent because they remember. They can be buried under ice for thousands of years or almost completely dry up because of drought. If you take them out from under the ice or give them air and water, they come to life again, grow, spread, multiply. They remember life, develop incredibly beautiful and different species, absorb pollutants and heal the Earth.[3] I am not a biologist, but dare to use the image of mosses. The mental infrastructure in which the Earth is loved and sacred, is like a network of moss. When we remember, and give this form of world perception air and light and water, it will grow. The more it grows, the more networks of knowing will emerge. This is already happening.

In her book *Re-enchanting the World*, Silvia Federici reminds us that modern technological development has contributed to the *disaccumulation* of knowledge through the rise of capitalist exploitation logic. She writes: 'The capacity to read the elements, to discover the medical properties of plants and flowers, to gain sustenance from the Earth, to live in woods and forests, to be guided by the stars and winds on the roads and the seas was and remains a source of "autonomy" that had to be destroyed.'[4] Regaining these forms of autonomy is crucial for the feminist civilizations we envisage. Hence, reclaiming the forests, giving rights to rivers, establishing ecocide as a crime, revitalizing landscapes, creating dark sky reserves that allow people to observe the stars, are not only important for our ecological survival, but essential for the survival of our many ways of human sense-making. In the future we want, there is a farewell to the limitations of patriarchal, male, European and Western rationality. Many feminist and other movements already cultivate the emergence of another, redefined rationality, in which life and vitality are paramount. Reconnecting with nature and humanness helps us to sometimes remember and sometimes re-invent what it means to be human on this planet.[5]

In her book *All About Love: New Visions*, the American feminist bell hooks writes about the transformative power of love and its critical role in the struggle for justice.[6] She describes it as a combination of care, commitment, trust, knowledge, responsibility and respect. This redefinition expands love to encompass a broad, inclusive practice that can transform personal and social relationships. Without love, she suggests, feminist movements for justice lack the necessary compassion and empathy to create lasting change. Moreover, she sees the creation of loving communities as a foundation for social change. These communities should be based on mutual support, care and a shared commitment to justice. They serve as models for the broader society, demonstrating the potential of love to foster genuine solidarity and collaboration. This does not mean that there will be no conflicts, no disagreements, no animosity. But if the genuine acknowledgment of another person as a human being and nature as alive becomes the foundation for future civilizations, violence, psychological or physical, will no longer be an option.

Yet, there is also another radical aspect to the re-enchantment of the world that we need for feminist civilizations. The patriarchal project, as we have seen, was from the beginning a colonial project. It has erased most of the existing Indigenous knowledge, the civilizational matriarchies. In Europe, it completed the project through the institutionalized witch hunts in the medieval age. It was then that European colonizers began to 'discover' other continents, leading to brutal murders, enslavement, appropriation, expropriation and the resource depletion that is still going on today. Colonization is a power pathology, an act that presupposes that violence is legitimate, the claim to dominance seen as justified, and the lives of those defined as 'the others' considered worthless and disposable. Even if we keep in mind that patriarchal history prevailed on all continents even before the European colonization, we must recognize that the colonization of the Global South by Europeans became the project with the most structural and lasting impact. The patriarchal and the colonial project created separation, where there is interconnectedness: In expropriation, in science, in capitalist enclosure, in social tension. Feminist aspirations for future civilizations need to stay aware of this context, which is far from being overcome. Decolonization, including within feminist movements, is a long-term project that will hopefully not take as long as the process of colonization. It is also an ongoing task because the mechanisms of colonization are woven into our societies everywhere, even if they are most visible in the relationship between the Global South and the Global North. This is crucial for the vision of future feminist-inspired civilizations: The dominant Western means of knowledge production can hardly take us into a different future. I agree that, regarding climate change adaptation and mitigation, it is advisable to listen to Western science. But even for dealing with the effects of climate change, we need the recognition and validation of diverse knowledge systems. Decolonial feminism is not just another version of the many feminisms, but at the core of feminist transformations.[7] Decolonial feminism critiques the dominance of Western epistemology, which often marginalizes or devalues the many and pluriverse other ways of knowing that still exist in our world. One of its *collective feminist practices* is to *decenter* Western perspectives, in order to create an inclusive and pluriverse understanding of knowledge. This is more than amplifying voices from the Global South and acknowledging their contributions to global knowledge production. The aim is not to add to the hegemonic knowledge production, but to open minds and hearts to different knowledge systems, and subsequently to a different perception of the world, be it through Indigenous knowledge systems, oral traditions or other epistemologies that have historically been suppressed or ignored.

For the emergence of future feminist-inspired civilizations, knowledge production requires a radical turnaround: From an exclusionary, self-reinforcing system practiced in a more or less universal, yet actually Western-dominated epistemology, to the acknowledgment of pluriverse epistemologies and knowledge production as transformative and empowering processes that lead to insights. This is the prerequisite for transforming collective sense-making and collective co-creation. Yet, insight is more than knowledge. Knowledge is the systematic gathering of facts, observations, experiences and information. It can lead to an overarching understanding of subjects and concepts. Insight is a deep understanding or sudden realization about the nature of a complex situation or problem. It often involves seeing connections or patterns that were not previously apparent. The American scientist Evelyn Fox-Keller suggested long ago that we should no longer separate what belongs together. She advocated for a form of knowledge production that respects the integrity of the world while acknowledging our deeply emotional and empathetic connection with the world. Feminist and pluriverse knowledge production needs to bring issues of power, feelings of love and genuine insight together.[8] Working towards future feminist-inspired peaceful, egalitarian and regenerative civilizations means reclaiming and revitalizing pluriverse knowledge systems, because they are the foundation for creating a *Good Life for All.*

How do we move beyond fighting the current destructive trajectories to focusing our *attention* on the *intentions* we have for future civilizations? There are many different ways of encouraging feminist visioning, from feminist future laboratories to feminist scenario work. We need much more of these practices. Scenario work is an opportunity to inspire imagination by exploring different socio-economic and political futures and analyzing their impact on women. Different scenarios can be inspiring, yet also show limitations, challenges or unintended consequences. This helps us move from dreams to strategizing change. This slowly emerging practice is what can be called *feminist strategic foresight.*[9] The method as such is a very patriarchal one. It emerged from military planning and its general purpose is to enhance long-term planning capacity by analyzing situations, trends and possible development scenarios. Today, it is done in a mix of expert and interest group consultation coupled with data analysis. Done in a participatory way, it can help to create shared visions and collective commitments.

Feminist strategic foresight, however, cannot just be a method to explore possible feminist futures; it must be done in a way that is at the same time modelling this future through creating connections and integrating pluriverse knowledge.[10] As an approach it integrates feminist principles into the practice of strategic foresight, emphasizing inclusivity, equity, questions of power and the consideration of diverse perspectives, particularly those of marginalized and underrepresented groups. Feminist strategic foresight is oriented towards transformative change, aiming not just to adapt to future trends but to actively shape more equitable and inclusive futures. It questions patriarchal norms by critically examining how power dynamics shape future possibilities and working to dismantle oppressive structures. Done in this way, it can bridge the gap between feminist imaginations of future civilizations and the current reality.

Major insights for *collective feminist power practices* from emerging visions of future civilizations:

1. Envisioning feminist civilizations is paramount: We need to not only fight the many manifestations of patriarchy, but also imagine possible futures.
2. Future realities emerge from the interaction between collective sense-making and co-creation. Changing how we perceive current realities can lead to new ways of co-creating the future.
3. Most people would assume they live in a civilized world, but our concept of civilization needs to be questioned in light of global inequalities, historical and ongoing colonialism, wars and atrocities. There cannot be lasting peace in patriarchy.
4. The process of civilization has only begun: We need to project feminist aspirations into possible futures and turn the harmful process of modern patriarchal globalization into a process of reviving and regenerating human collective intelligence.
5. For the emergence of feminist-inspired civilizations, knowledge production needs to acknowledge pluriverse epistemologies and become a transformative and empowering process that leads to insights.
6. Feminist strategic foresight is oriented towards transformative change, aiming not just to adapt to future trends but to actively shape more equitable and inclusive futures. It can bridge the gap between feminist imaginations of future civilizations and the current reality.

Notes

1 For a brief overview of approach and difficulties, see Jiang at al. (2019).
2 An interesting overview of approaches to understanding the decline or transformation of ancient civilizations can be found in Butzer & Endfield (2012).

3 See Eldrigde et al. (2023).
4 Federici (2018, Kindle Version Position 3895).
5 An inspiring publication on re-inventing humanity can be found in Preiser et al. (2020).
6 See hooks (2000).
7 See, for example, Tamale (2020) or Vergès (2022).
8 See Fox-Keller (1995) and a review of her important work in Vicedo (2023).
9 An example of using feminist strategic foresight in a practical way can be found in Kwan (2022), in Mondesir (2024) and in Horn (2025).
10 For examples see International Women's Development Agency (IWDA) (2020) and Feminist Futures Helsinki: https://feministfutureshelsinki.org

References

Butzer, K.W., & Endfield, G.H. (2012). Critical perspectives on historical collapse. *Proceedings of the National Academy of Sciences*, *109*(10), 3628–3631. https://doi.org/10.1073/pnas.1114772109

Eldridge, D.J., Guirado, E., Reich, P.B., Ochoa-Hueso, R., Berdugo, M., Sáez-Sandino, T., Blanco-Pastor, J.L., Tedersoo, L., Plaza, C., Ding, J., Sun, W., Mamet, S., Cui, H., He, J.-Z., Hu, H.-W., Sokoya, B., Abades, S., Alfaro, F., Bamigboye, A.R., & Bastida, F. (2023). The global contribution of soil mosses to ecosystem services. *Nature Geoscience*, *16*(5), 430–438. https://doi.org/10.1038/s41561-023-01170-x

Federici, S. (2018). *Re-enchanting the World: Feminism and the Politics of the Commons*. PM Press.

Fox-Keller, E. (1995). *Reflections on Gender and Science*. Yale University Press.

hooks, bell. (2000). *All About Love: New Visions*. HarperCollins Publishers.

Horn, J. (2025). *African Feminist Praxis: Cartographies of Liberatory Worldmaking (Social Science for Social Justice)*. Sage Publications.

International Women's Development Agency (IWDA). (2020). Imagining feminist futures after COVID-19. https://iwda.org.au/iwda-shorthand/feminist-futures

Jiang, B., Bai, Y., Wong, C.P., Xu, X., & Alatalo, J.M. (2019). China's ecological civilization program – Implementing ecological redline policy. *Land Use Policy*, *81*, 111–114. https://doi.org/10.1016/j.landusepol.2018.10.031

Kwan, S. (2022, September). Feminist visions of the future of women's work: A systemic exploration of the past, present and future of women at work in Canada. *Journal of Futures Studies*, *27*(1). https://jfsdigital.org/2022-2/vol-27-no-1-september-2022/feminist-visions-of-the-future-of-womens-work-a-systemic-exploration-of-the-past-present-and-future-of-women-at-work-in-canada

Mondesir, A. (2024). Embracing feminist foreign policy within EU strategic foresight capabilities. Policy Brief. Foundation for European Progressive Studies. https://library.fes.de/pdf-files/bueros/bruessel/21333.pdf

Preiser, R., Swilling, M., Nnoli-Edozien, N., & Ramphele, M. (2020). Towards new narratives of hope for fostering transformative African futures. https://www.clubofrome.org/wp-content/uploads/2021/01/COR-ENCI_NewNarratives_Dec2020_A4-v1-1.pdf

Tamale, S. (2020). *Decolonization and Afro-Feminism: An Afro-Feminist-Legal Critique*. Daraja Press.

Vergès, F. (2022). *A Feminist Theory of Violence: A Decolonial Perspective*. Pluto Press.

Vicedo, M. (2023). Evelyn Fox Keller (1936–2023): Philosopher who questioned gender roles in science. *Nature*, 624(7990), 31–31. https://doi.org/10.1038/d41586-023-03819-4

15
Transforming Economies – Feminist Strategies to Create a Good Life for All

Wherever feminist strategic foresight is practiced in order to co-develop, plan, coordinate or adjust feminist transformation strategies, we will hear a rhythm of drums in the background, sometimes louder, sometimes more subtle. They remind us that whatever dreams we project into the future, we are captives of the current rules of the system that permeates all our lives: the **economy**. We have seen that, historically, different forms of organizing economies have had different impacts on the lives of women and all people in general. We have also seen that socialist economies did not overcome authoritarian patriarchal rules and that the capitalist way of wealth accumulation works perfectly well with the many forms of patriarchal domination. Together, they have turned our current world into a dangerous place with disastrous effects of climate change, catastrophes, multiple wars, consumerism, an addiction to economic growth and social tensions that will predictably rise. Hence, feminist strategic foresight scenarios will inevitably need to include short-term measures to tame our economic system and long-term measures to transform it. As with patriarchy, taming and renovating alone will not take us into the future. Yet, given the current destructive world trajectories, taming capitalism is a pragmatic start. Transforming economies is the strategy for future feminist-inspired civilizations. Given the fact that there is hardly any escape from the current dominant economic system, this will be another mammoth task.

We are not starting from scratch. There have always been conceptual and practical alternatives to neoliberal capitalism, even though they have been pushed out of the mainstream economic flow. Many alternatives thrive on the fringes of our globalized world, in subsistence farming, in barter trade, in production and consumption cooperatives, in the form of common good companies, in responsible investment and in many others. The paradigm shifts in thinking and acting have already begun. Many women and feminists are frontrunners. It is clear that we must say goodbye to the irrational belief that the extractive and exploitative forms of economic activities as wealth creation for the few

DOI: 10.4324/9781003508885-20

can continue. They will not take us into livable futures, and not at all towards a *Good Life for All*. Without a fundamental change in the global and local operating system called the economy, we will not be able to seize the opportunities to save the climate, restore biodiversity and regenerate land, forests, water and ecosystems. We will not be able to transform our civilization into a truly civilized one. This means that it is time to step out of the niches of our societies and onto the stage with new economic models, with new ideas, concepts and practices. There might be elements we want to keep from the current system, and some we might pick up from socialist ideas. Yet, transforming economies requires fundamental changes.

The emergence of the 17 Sustainable Development Goals in 2015 marked a major turning point in the world. They have contributed to the development of a global consciousness, which in turn paves the way for the awareness that transformations are needed. Yet, the admirable global agreement on the goals obscures two prerequisites for their achievement: One is the abolishment of patriarchy and the other is the transformation of our global economic architecture. If both continue to dominate the world, the chances are slim that the goals can ever be achieved. Let us briefly recap the feminist analyses that have shown the intricate links between capitalist and patriarchal domination to the detriment of women, marginalized people, nature and our planet.

As we have seen in Chapter 5 many feminist writers have in multiples ways analyzed how the capitalist logic of exploitation and appropriation has used women's and marginalized people's bodies, their unpaid work, their reproductive power and their ability to care. They have highlighted how capitalist economies rely on the (today and in the past, often racialized) exploitation of women, the dominated *others* and natural resources, thus not only exacerbating social inequities, but stealing territories that were entrusted to Indigenous people, legitimizing environmental destructions that, again, inevitably further marginalized the marginalized. They argued that the principles and the practices of the colonization of women, nature and the colonies were essential for the initial accumulation of capital. The wealth extracted from bodies and land, particularly in the former colonies of the Global South, but also in contemporary neocolonial practices, made up the foundation of modern capitalism and keeps the wealth accumulation going. Environmental degradation, biodiversity loss, climate change, unsustainable industrial practices and consumerism are and have long been the focus of feminist critique. Moreover, feminists strongly opposed the growing control exerted by multinational corporations, for example, in sectors like agriculture, which affects food security and local economies.[1] Many argue that neoliberal capitalism has begun to commodify all aspects of life, reducing human and ecological well-being to economic transactions.[2] Capitalism, patriarchy and the disenchantment of the world have reinforced each other. Not surprisingly, feminist thinkers advocate for shifting our economic system towards alternative economies.

Feminists are not alone in calling for a change. During the past two decades many proposals for future economies have emerged.[3] In the various different strands of the sustainability movement, there is a general agreement of a need to revamp the way our economies work. Most agree that the growth focus of the prevailing neoliberal economic framework comes at the expense of the integrity of nature and social cohesion, because it is based on extractive mindsets and centuries of exploitation of natural and human resources. This neoliberal economic narrative was introduced in the 1970s, and was gradually anchored in almost all global systems and institutions. It suggests that the only goal of business is to generate financial wealth; that individual (personal or corporate) freedom is the primary societal value; that governments should have little influence on market dynamics and rather protect individuals and private property; and that markets must be free and unfettered, self-organizing for the benefit of all.[4] This narrative assumes that that natural (and social) resources are inexhaustible. Consequently, it ignores planetary boundaries and carefully balanced geo-bio-physical life support systems.[5] The idea of the commons to which all people (and other living beings) should have access, and which are important to people, is entirely missing, as if they did not or should not exist. In the current economic system, the commons can be appropriated and used for individual benefit. Governments that direct or control markets for the sake of the commons are seen as a problem. The doctrine of free markets with constant economic growth is still enshrined as the main goal of good governments and manifests itself in the tyranny of the increase in a Gross Domestic Product as the most important single measure of societal progress. The current economic system is so pervasive that it is hard to question it or frame an alternative. But we may learn from its origins and successful dissemination by taking a detour into recent history.

Neoliberal economies did not emerge naturally – they were created. Some say, by a bunch of white men with initially good intentions. In 1947, after World War II, they came together in the Swiss mountains, at Mont Pelerin, and deliberated about how to free the trashed world (respectively trashed Europe) from National Socialism and Soviet Collectivism.[6] Their intention was to create an economic framework that would prevent state control and totalitarian regimes. So far, so good. They believed that individual sovereignty, small and rather weak governments and free markets were necessary to ensure freedom for all and provide for the needs of a growing world population. The group that stayed connected, known as the Mont Pelerin Society, began to influence institutions and governments to implement the paradigm – for example, through austerity measures. In 1971, in the United States, a confidential memo was written by a corporate lawyer and future Supreme Court Justice to the Chairman of the Education Committee of the US Chamber of Commerce.[7] The content dealt with how to counteract a perceived growing hostility toward the American free enterprise system around the world and how to defend and promote corporate interests. We must remember that it was a period when more and more former colonies became independent and many adopted a communist economy. But the memo was also a response – we could say, a patriarchal backlash – towards social and political, partly left-wing, upheavals in the United States. The civil rights movement, anti-Vietnam War protests, environmental activism and skepticism toward corporate power had risen. Business leaders felt under siege by regulatory measures, public criticism and a perceived anti-business sentiment in academia and media. The memorandum included strategic recommendations such as monitoring criticisms of the free enterprise system, increasing business influence in academia, establishing well-funded think tanks and promoting business-friendly ideas in schools and universities. It galvanized the American conservative movement and reshaped the political landscape in favor of corporate interests. Lobby institutions for shaping public policies towards promoting free-market ideas were established, as were legal advocacy groups to litigate in favor of business interests. Pro-business and conservative policies followed, which implemented significant tax cuts, deregulation and a reduction in the role of government in the economy.[8] There was tremendous support for the growing institutional networks of the Mont Pelerin Society, whose most known protagonist, Milton Friedman, became an advisor to most European governments. We know what followed: The establishment of the World Bank, the International Monetary Fund (IMF), structural adjustment programs, weakened governments who implemented even more austerity measures. For countries in the Global South, it meant extreme hardships and increasing social inequalities.[9] For countries in Europe, it also meant a departure from a different societal narrative that had influenced European state-building after World War II. People may not have noticed it, but it became a farewell to the established welfare state models in many Western countries, which were characterized by strong government intervention in the economy, social safety nets and regulation. Subsequently, economic and social disparities tremendously increased in Europe. The irony of patriarchal history is that some of the neoliberal protagonists became promotors of conservative and neoliberal parties in Europe and the United States, which more recently turned into right-wing parties aiming for authoritarian states. With their populist influence, the danger of totalitarian regimes has now increased.

Why is this story important for feminist economic transformation strategies? For four reasons. *Firstly*, it shows global economic frameworks can change as a result of influential interventions and new narratives. This can give us hope for feminist narratives and intervention strategies. *Secondly*, it is an incredible example of male networking and connectivity across institutions. As indigestible as it may be, we can learn from this and do better in feminist networked connectivity. *Thirdly*, it shows that a mix between outright strategy (influencing politics and academia), coupled with media support, and the establishment of think tanks, foundations and institutions, including their connections, was paramount. We can learn a lot from this process of networked *institutionalization* and massively improve feminist institutionalization strategies. *Fourthly*, incredible amounts of funding went into lasting neoliberal institutions and still do. As feminist transformation strategists we need to get better at obtaining funding and redirecting massive amounts of funding to shift towards life-serving economies. We are far from the amounts of funding we need.

The neoliberal story also shows that for feminist transformations, changing the parameters of our economic system must be extremely high on the agenda. There are two fundamental strategies. **Taming neoliberal capitalism** is a feminist strategy that has many critiques among feminists. It deals with all sorts of measures that ensure women are much better integrated into the economy, care work is more valued, the number of female entrepreneurs increases, more high-level management jobs are held by women, and corporations are regulated in a way that they stop damaging the environment. I do have a sweet spot for these strategies, because economic empowerment is a prerequisite of female freedom and can pave a pragmatic way to gaining more influence and building feminist institutions. Yet, it will not rescue the world from destructive patriarchal trajectories. The second strategy, **transforming our economic architecture**, must be high on the agenda. We need the fundamental change, knowing that it will take time and the courage to survive setbacks. It requires elaborate feminist strategies and strategic alliances. Anybody serious about abolishing patriarchy needs to make the transformation of our economic operating system a priority.[10]

The future needs a global economic architecture that places the living conditions on our planet and the vitality of all living beings – nature and humans alike – as well as our societies at its core. Technological developments must be committed to this goal, and knowledge production must revolve around it. Really well-functioning economies operate within planetary boundaries. This means, first of all, that we need to re-understand the basic principles of how economies work: *Economies must serve life*, and hence benefit *all* people and the planet. Individual and collective well-being, as well as the interaction between humans and nature, must be thought of together. It is about co-creating the conditions for interwoven social, economic and ecological patterns that increase the vitality of local and global systems.

Before we look into feminist future economies, let us have a look at what research says about ancient and contemporary matriarchal economies.[11] This would warrant an entire book, so the following is a daringly broad summary of insights that I consider relevant for our future. It is not about idealizing matriarchal societies, but acknowledging that there may be insights we can learn from.

What are the economic features of matriarchies that are relevant for our feminist transformation strategies today?

The *first* is women's stronghold in *local and regional economies*. There is usually *no private property*, no or little wealth accumulation at an individual level and no land ownership, but land entrusted to tenure and stewardship, often for subsistence farming. The *second* important feature is the role of thriving markets, often strongly in the hands of women, as places to exchange goods for the benefit of all. Hence, albeit different from today's understanding, matriarchal economies are *market economies*. The *third* important feature is the recognition of *the commons* as something to be taken care of collectively. Matriarchal economies are *commons economies*. As the Earth is considered sacred and producing abundance, in matriarchies, economic activities include acts of giving away. Gifts are central to peacekeeping and social cohesion. Those who give most have the highest social recognition. Hence, as a *fourth* feature, we can consider matriarchal economies *gift economies*. At the scale of societies, and this is the *fifth* feature, this develops into what we would today call socially responsible *distribution or care economies*, safeguarding the well-being of the entire community and ensuring that differences in wealth or living standards remain rather small. The driving value is not accumulation, but distribution, in order to create a moderate level of prosperity for all. In addition, and this is the *sixth* feature, matriarchal economies are based on cooperation and community. The production and distribution of goods is done for the benefit of the entire community, not for individual gain. There are strong networks of mutual support where resources are shared and collectively used. We could call this *cooperation economies*. The overall purpose of economies is clear: The well-being of the community or society, hence, they are *purpose or well-being economies*.

From a matriarchal perspective, our current neoliberal economies are completely derailed, serving some very well, pushing others into peril and destroying our planetary life support systems. The above features are much more rational than any of the current neoliberal understandings about the purpose of economies. Let us remember that when we talk today about the *economy*, we can trace the word back to ancient Greek, meaning household account or *household management*. What is meant is the *management of resources in a collective space so that all benefit*. The American architect Jane

Jacobs reminded us long ago that *ecology* means *house knowledge*, while *biology* means *life knowledge*. She suggested that the better term for economy would be *bionomy* as *life management* in a collective space.[12] Hence, if we take the *economy* as part and parcel of *life management*, it is clear that *household knowledge* (*ecology*) and *life knowledge (biology)* are essential foundations to get the household management right, no matter whether at the level of the household, the community, the country or the planet. Economies are part of our lives, nothing separate. This is very much reflected in feminist perspectives on transforming economies.

While no single answer can encompass all needs, feminist thought and practice collectively offer a comprehensive vision for feminist-inspired transformations of economies, recognizing the need for varied approaches to meet humanity's diverse challenges.[13] Across the feminist literature six key features of future economies emerge that can guide us toward the *Good Life for All*. The seeds of change already exist. That is why these features are illustrated by selective examples pioneering their implementation.

Key Feature No 1: Prioritizing People and Planet Over Profit

Feminist-inspired future economies prioritize both people and planetary health, ensuring everyone has access to the resources and opportunities necessary for a dignified life while respecting regional and contextual differences. Governments adopt a mission-driven approach aligned with societal goals for well-being, adapting to varied contexts across nations. Policies focus on reducing income and wealth inequalities, fostering social inclusion and ensuring that economic benefits are broadly shared. This includes progressive, gender-sensitive taxation (shifting resources from the privileged to the marginalized and supporting women's economic engagement), robust social safety nets, universal basic income or dividends[14] and public investment in education and healthcare to achieve distributive justice. It also entails reversing regressive austerity and structural adjustment measures. Nationally, this approach involves proactive policy innovation, state-led investments into the future and sustainable development efforts. Internationally it requires closing economic gaps between countries, compensating for damage caused by wealthier nations and promoting inclusive growth where needed and degrowth where necessary. International frameworks and global governance institutions need to be fundamentally reformed to address historical colonial injustices, redistributing wealth, power and influence to the Global South. While this may sound utopian, fragments of this key feature already exist. They are not enough or widespread enough to achieve the necessary transformations, but serve as examples that can be taken up and expanded.[15]

Progressive taxation policies aim to redistribute wealth more equitably by taxing wealthier individuals and corporations at higher rates, funding social programs that benefit low-income households, particularly women and marginalized communities. Universal basic income (UBI) trials explore the potential to reduce gender disparities and promote financial independence, especially for women and caregivers facing income instability.[16] The Loss and Damage Fund established at the 2022 United Nations Climate Change Conference (COP27) in Sharm El-Sheikh, Egypt, aims to provide financial support from wealthier nations to poorer, climate-vulnerable countries facing severe impacts from climate change, often affecting women disproportionally. It will function as a form of wealth redistribution to address climate justice.[17]

Key Feature No 2: Recognizing Care Work as Essential for Economic Equity

Future economies recognize care work – both paid and unpaid – as essential to economic stability and the functioning of society. This vision acknowledges the fundamental role of social reproduction in sustaining humanity. Policies support caregivers with measures such as paid parental leave, social protections for unpaid caregivers and investments in both public and private care infrastructure. Care work holds high social status and is adequately compensated, with all households – regardless of income, gender or class – having access to professional, equitable care services that transcend racial, regional and gender biases. Caregiving is viewed as a shared societal responsibility, elevating its social significance.[18] Policies are designed to more equitably distribute care work between genders, while labor regulations support work–life balance through flexible working hours. Special attention is given to reducing the burden of unpaid work in rural households, where women and girls often shoulder disproportionate care responsibilities. Investments in effective rural infrastructure significantly ease this load. Macroeconomic policies safeguard job opportunities, allocate resources for social care and enhance physical infrastructure in rural areas.

Again, fragments of this feature are already implemented. Countries like Sweden and Iceland have implemented policies that provide paid parental leave and child-care subsidies, recognizing the value of caregiving and promoting gender equality by encouraging shared responsibilities between parents. The COVID-19 pandemic further emphasized the importance of unpaid care work, leading organizations like UN Women to advocate for social protection measures that support unpaid caregivers, primarily women. Chaired by Mariana Mazzucato, the all-female a WHO Council of ten feminist economists proposed a political economy model based on the concept of 'Health for All'. The Council's 2023 report presents key recommendations under four pillars: Governing health innovation for the common good, rethinking value measurement, financing health as a long-term investment and strengthening public sector capacity for care work.[19] The African Feminist Post-Covid Economic Recovery Statement calls for the recognition of 'the economic, social, political and cultural value of the care economy – where the provisioning of care goods and services to households and the economy'.[20]

Key Feature No 3: Embracing Circularity and Ecological Balance for Long-Term Prosperity

Future economies are guided by both regulations and voluntary standards to uphold ecological boundaries and promote planetary health, addressing and healing the damage caused by extractive capitalist models. These economies embrace regenerative practices to sustain and restore natural resources. Public investment drives research and innovation inspired by nature, prioritizing circularity, conservation and sustainability. Long-term ecological and economic health are paramount, with a focus on community well-being and self-sufficiency. Regenerative agriculture, seed sovereignty and support for diverse small-scale farming are foundational, while circular principles shape product development and supply chains. Renewable energy and circular practices dominate, with land-use policies centering on agroecology, conservation and protection of Indigenous lands. Governments safeguard against corporate and public land grabbing in both the Global South and North.[21] Workforces are respected, safeguarded and fairly compensated, and states ensure a robust social contract. Production and consumption prioritize regional and local economies, while international trade and financial systems are democratically redefined through multipolar leadership rather than dominated by Western powers. Governments recognize arts and culture as vital to societal well-being and regeneration, and technological innovation is guided by ethics and the public interest to address societal challenges. Global collaboration enables shared learning across borders, sectors and cultures, and is genuinely pluralistic, free from colonial legacies.

Efforts to implement this feature can be found around the globe. Women are leading regenerative agriculture initiatives in countries like Kenya and India, promoting sustainable farming and seed sovereignty while restoring ecosystems and empowering women in decision-making and resource management. In 2019 SADC (Southern Africa Development Community) adopted the Regional Multi-Dimensional Women's Economic Empowerment Program

2020–2030 (RMDWEEP) to promote women's economic empowerment and gender-responsive development in order to contribute to social inclusion and justice.[22] It includes developing circular economy models, which prioritize sustainability and address gender disparities. Countries like Rwanda have implemented renewable energy policies that ensure women's participation in decision-making and access to clean energy resources, fostering both ecological sustainability and economic opportunities for women.[23] Mozambique is working with local communities and local government to draw from existing knowledge systems to utilize a system called Improving Local Climate Resilience in Mozambique (MERCIM).

Key Feature No 4: Measuring True Prosperity Through Comprehensive Well-Being Indicators

Future economies will be measured by holistic metrics that encompass social well-being, environmental health and overall quality of life. These progress indicators offer a comprehensive view of economic performance, guiding policies that enhance both human and ecological well-being.[24] In the future, a company's license to operate will be contingent on its positive impact on people and the planet, making 'common good' companies the standard. Product prices will reflect the internalization of social and environmental costs, encouraging companies to avoid these costs through sustainable practices. Transparency and accountability will build trust within economies and societies, with supply chain traceability, corporate reporting standards, and social and environmental impact reporting becoming widely adopted. Societal metrics for progress – such as the Genuine Progress Indicator (GPI), Human Development Index (HDI) and various happiness and sustainability indexes – already signal this shift, though they still incorporate elements of GDP.[25] The rise of common good companies, cooperatives, citizen-owned enterprises, community-owned businesses and locally sourced and consumed products is already under way.

There are many attempts to find economic metrics that can measure what really needs improving: Social and ecological well-being. Feminist well-being economics measures economic wellness within the context of commonality. This means measuring non-financial wellness, including friendship, a community of care, a sense of joy and hope, neighborliness and a life without loneliness, for example. Many non-Western communities measure well-being in mutuality and collective care and there are philosophies like Sankofa and Ujaama that respectively point to reclamation or restoration and communitarian development.[26] In addition there are elements of decolonial well-being economics that recognize the necessity of reparative and restorative economic relations.

Feminist thinking has been integrated in holistic economic metrics and sustainable practices in several notable ways. Although threatened in its continuation, Aotearoa's (New Zealand's) Wellbeing Budget, the first of its kind, integrates well-being indicators into its national budget, emphasizing quality of life, environmental health, prevention of domestic violence, and gender equity over traditional GDP measures.[27] The Māori well-being measurement, particularly through the He Ara Waiora framework, operates by aligning social, economic, environmental and cultural indicators with Māori values. It prioritizes a holistic understanding of well-being, focusing on the interconnectedness of people, communities and the environment. The model integrates both quantitative and qualitative data, emphasizing lived experiences and Indigenous knowledge to measure collective and individual well-being, ultimately promoting a balanced, sustainable future.[28]

Bhutan's Gross National Happiness Index (GNH) measures economic success through sustainable development, cultural preservation and gender equity, highlighting women's empowerment as vital for societal happiness.[29] In the United States, states like Maryland and Vermont utilize the GPI to go beyond GDP, accounting for environmental health, income distribution and unpaid labor, particularly care work typically performed by women.[30] These initiatives showcase how holistic metrics can potentially reshape economies to prioritize human and ecological well-being.

Key Feature No 5: Empowering Citizens and Ensuring Participatory Governance

Future economies will be guided by collaborative, participatory governance and active involvement of the public in decision-making to ensure economic policies align with community needs and values.[31] Democratic and gender-equitable participation in economic planning, alongside transparent governance, fosters policies that are responsive and accountable. Distributive justice supports social equality, well-being and both gender and social justice. Citizens regularly provide feedback on measures for distributive justice and structural equity, while social cohesion is participatively monitored. Decentralized decision-making and community control address local needs while respecting ecological boundaries. Global commons are collectively managed, and local commons are democratically controlled by communities, free from external interference.[32] Nature is recognized as having inherent rights, ecocide is criminalized, and traditional and Indigenous knowledge is valued for ecological insights. Global economic governance structures are reformed to balance power between the Global South and North, with debt relief and fair trade practices supporting equitable development.

There is a long way to go to implement this key feature, but fragments do exist. Gender-inclusive participatory budgeting has emerged as a tool for promoting equity. South Africa pioneered the Women's Budget Initiative after Australia and inspired Tanzania, Rwanda and Uganda. These have resulted in a state-led commitment to gendered fiscal distribution and economic participation. Uganda has now embedded gendered growth, employment and human development in its National Development Plan.[33] South Africa has similarly enacted a National Development Plan that is mandated to dismantle racial and gender inequities across all social, development and economic indicators by 2030.[34] Tanzania was also an early adopter of Gender Budget initiatives in 1997 and the Tanzania Gender Networking Program (TGNP)[35] is a feminist coalition that conducted advocacy and participatory research to monitor the progress by ministries of education, health, agriculture, water, food security, regional administration, gender and children's development. Though episodic, the initiative illustrates that impact is possible with greater long-term government commitment.

Cities like Barcelona have also pioneered this approach, focusing on ensuring that women and marginalized gender groups are integral to discussions about public resource allocation, leading to more inclusive and gender-sensitive outcomes.[36] Participatory budgeting approaches have also been tested and established in cities like Porto Alegre, Brazil, and New York City. They have allowed communities to directly shape how public funds are distributed, reflecting local needs and fostering democratic engagement.[37] In many regions of the Global South women-led community governance initiatives highlight the vital role women play in managing local resources and promoting climate-resilient agricultural practices, while empowering them in economic income and land-use planning.[38] On a global scale, feminist economic reforms are gaining traction, with organizations like the *African Women's Development and Communication Network* (FEMNET) advocating for debt relief and policies that address the unique economic challenges faced by women in the Global South.[39] These feminist approaches are central to ensuring that future economies prioritize gender equity and promote more inclusive, transformative development pathways.

Key Feature No 6: Designing Policies for Transformative Equity and Radical Economic Democracy

In future economies intersectional policies address structural inequalities and promote economic equity. Targeted social programs and affirmative action initiatives work to reduce disparities and foster fairness. Both voluntary and mandatory agreements safeguard common goods, strengthening social and ecological support systems, with fair compensation for communities and individuals who maintain these resources. Legal frameworks – including constitutions, commercial law and land rights – protect the rights of Indigenous peoples, the rights of nature and the interests of future generations. Financial institutions are regulated to prioritize the health of people and the planet, and fiscal policies encourage regenerative agriculture. Tax models incentivize conservation, social transformation and the protection of common goods, with supply chain laws upholding deracialized workers' rights. Green taxation promotes sustainable practices, while governments invest in education and lifelong learning – distinct from profit-driven, neoliberal approaches. Global economic institutions fairly represent the Global South and North, operate democratically and are regularly evaluated for their impact on global well-being. Feminist foreign policies guide multilateral and regional cooperation to prevent military conflicts and support peace.

Again, there is a long way to go implement this key feature, but even here we can find fragments of the future. Countries such as Mexico, Sweden, Germany and Canada adopt feminist foreign policies that prioritize gender equality, human rights and peacebuilding. They integrate feminist perspectives into international relations and development efforts, aiming to create an inclusive and equitable global landscape.[40] How fiscal policies can guide regenerative investments can be seen in Costa Rica's Payment for Environmental Services (PES) program. By offering financial incentives for reforestation, forest conservation and sustainable land use, Costa Rica is fostering environmental regeneration while promoting long-term economic sustainability.[41] Countries like Ecuador and Bolivia have enshrined the rights of nature in their constitutions, granting ecosystems legal recognition.[42] These frameworks not only protect the environment but also involve Indigenous communities in decision-making processes, reinforcing the deep connection between environmental and social justice. The African Feminist Collective on Feminist Informed Policies (AfIP) is a collective that is examining African country positions and global, neoliberal hierarchies. AfIP notes the necessity for Global South countries to have agency and autonomy. These are a key component of radical economic democracy in a multipolar world.

I wonder what your comments columns says about these possibilities for new and feminist-inspired economies. Are they unrealistic? I would argue no, because – as the examples show – fragments and building blocks of each of the principles already exist. It is not that we do not know or that there are no examples of implementation. It cannot be financed? Such economies would not survive? I would argue that if current finances were not invested in wars, fossil fuels and upholding patriarchal power, in tax havens and the overspending of overly wealthy people, it would be no problem to finance both transitions and implementation. If products reflected true environmental and social costs, consumption patterns would change. Are these principles too ideal, failing to consider the negative traits of humans? I would argue that this may be true; however, the negative human traits are exacerbated by patriarchies and accelerated by neo-capitalism. These are power pathologies and it is important to name them as such. Pathologies require treatment. Human nature is inherently cooperative and altruistic, otherwise humanity would not have survived the past 6000 years of patriarchy. If it seems to be so easy, why is it not happening? Because the current power arrangements prioritize monopolized profits over people's and the planet's collective well-being, and they secure patriarchal power pathologies to continue.

There will be no transformations toward future feminist-inspired economies without feminists collectively claiming power: From entering corporate boards to strengthening feminist movements; from participating in local community councils to aiming for presidency; from resisting land grabbing to organizing women's strikes; from strengthening feminist academia to influencing international treaties; from advocating for collective responsibility in social reproduction to ensuring feminists sit at the table of decision-making in global institutions. At the same time, the transformations towards future economies are about the re-enchantment of a pluriverse world with plural knowledge systems; the acknowledgment of a living world in its utmost variety and beauty. Although the above key features sound thoroughly anchored in rational Western language, they will not emerge without the situated knowledge and the radical feminist work on decolonization and relational ontologies that are powerfully emerging from feminists in the Global South.[43] If we go back to the interlinked leverage areas of feminist world-making in Chapter 13 we know that the most powerful leverage will come from shifting and *re-viving paradigms*. The feminist anti-racist, anti-patriarchal, decolonial, ecological, Indigenous and social justice movements around the world are paramount for this paradigm shift. *Re-designing systems* goals can only be based on these shifted worldviews, no matter whether the terms chosen are well-being of planet and people or life-serving economies. All other elements of the key features above deal with *re-patterning relationships*, *re-shaping information flows*, *re-organizing structures* and *re-allocating resources*.

Even with new ways of thinking, strategic collaboration, feminist alliances and alliances with other actors pursuing economic system change, the transformation of the global economic operating system is not an easy task. It must also take place much faster than most people think. It is time to come together, acknowledge and respect feminist differences, yet collaborate between feminists with institutional power and feminists with movement power to create a broad *feminist transformation ecosystem* addressing the required change in a *collective stewardship* approach, as shown in Figure 15.1.

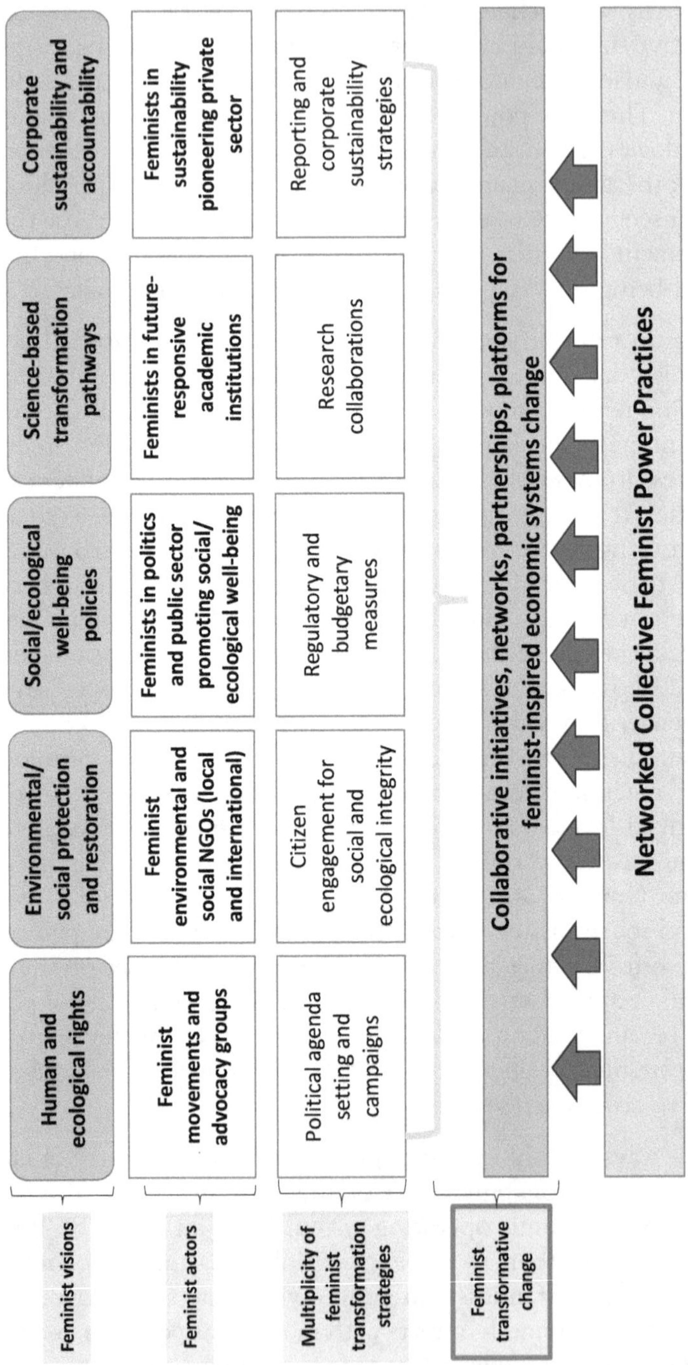

Figure 15.1 A collective stewardship approach in feminist transformation ecosystems

For the exponential acceleration that we need, there is a lot to learn from the innovative transformations that are already taking place at the fringes of the core economic process: Responsible value chains, circular economic cycles, regional bioeconomies, regenerative innovation, the sharing economy, value-based banking, regenerative communities or decentralized renewable energies – and much more. In other words: The restructuring of our economic system has basically already begun. As dedicated feminists, we need to make sure that in the current efforts to transform economies, patriarchal power pathologies are not maintained and do not resurge. To achieve this, it is essential to organize *collective stewardship* within the *feminist transformation ecosystem*, while forging alliances and collaborating with other initiatives – whether explicitly feminist or not – that aim to shift societies and transform economies. Feminists must go beyond supporting transformations; they need to step into the driver's seat of transformative change through *collective feminist power practices.*

Such collective feminist transformation strategies need to be radical and pragmatic. It is about the growing ability to gradually introduce new forms of economic thinking and acting into the outdated structures in order to change them step by step. For better or worse, the reorientation of our economies means building the new while the old is still in operation. Prototypes of the new must be integrated into existing structures, organizations and processes. This does not mean renovating the old and saving the neoliberal doctrine of capitalism together with patriarchal power pathologies. It means taking the transformation of economies seriously by connecting and scaling the new economic approaches so that they work together to regenerate, maintain and protect ecological and social vitality on Earth. Most importantly, it is about listening to each other and connecting feminist transformation efforts; it is about networked *collective feminist power practices.*

While there is agreement on the need for fundamental change, future economies need a variety of different approaches. They must leave room for different forms of implementation, as long as they serve the principle of regeneration and the maintenance of ecological and social vitality; and as long as they are based on the idea that humans and nature are inextricably linked.

This transformation in thinking and acting will require major decisions (such as changes to constitutions, business law, tax policy or financial regulations) and at the same time many small steps in spreading emotionally convincing narratives of the feminist future, or the strategic networking of movements, projects and initiatives on new economic practices. The time for implementing transformations towards future life-serving economies has begun. Whether climate change, social and planetary challenges will plunge us into chaos in the coming decades or whether the current patchwork of promising changes will lead us to a positive turning point of transformative change cannot yet be answered today. But we must start with these transformative changes and, together, make them the priority of our *feminist collective power practice.*

Major insights for *collective feminist power practices* from feminist approaches to transforming economies:

1. Feminist strategic foresight scenarios will inevitably need to include collaborative strategies to transform our economic system. It is time to step out of the niches of our societies and onto the stage with new economic approaches.
2. A future feminist-oriented civilization needs a global economic architecture that focuses on the living conditions of our planet and the vitality of all living entities, including nature, humans, our societies, our technologies and our pluriverse knowledge.
3. Matriarchal economies with their focus on well-being of communities, distribution of wealth and absence of private accumulation can inspire the economic paradigm shift.
4. Future economic systems must prioritize inclusivity and equity, ensuring access to opportunities and resources for all. This involves balancing wealth disparities, ensuring social inclusion, addressing colonial legacies, adopting regenerative practices and operating within ecological limits.
5. We must highlight efforts to transform economies and, together, make them the priority of our *feminist collective power practice.*
6. Feminist transformation strategists need to take the lead in bringing visionaries and practitioners of new economies together, while respecting feminist differences, and create *feminist transformation ecosystems.*

Notes

1 Among the strongest voices were Vandana Shiva and Maria Mies; see: Shiva & Mies (1993) and more recently Gago & Mason-Dreese (2017).
2 For a good description of how laws create such developments, see Pistor (2020).
3 These include the Economy of Common Good (Felber 2018), an Economy in Service to Life (Lovins et al. 2018), the Mindful Economy (Magnuson 2007), the Sufficiency Economy (Bergsteiner and Dharmapiya 2016), the Caring Economy (Folbre 1995, 2006) and Eisler (2007), the Wellbeing Economy (Fioramonti 2017), the Feminist Economy (Jacobsen 2020 and D'Allessandro 2017), the Circular Economy (Ellen MacArthur Foundation 2013), the Doughnut Economy (Raworth 2017), Economics of Arrival (Trebeck and Williams 2019), Mission Economy (Mazzucato 2021), Live Economies (Kuenkel 2022).
4 An overview of the historic development and major narratives can be found in Peters (2010).

5 The concept of the planetary boundaries can be found at Stockholm Resilience Centre (2023) and a recent update of transgressions is in Richardsen et al. (2023).
6 See Peters (2010).
7 See Powell (1971, August 23).
8 Early on the influence went far beyond the United States. The US-supported military coup that brought one of the most brutal dictators, Pinochet, into power in 1973 made Chile into a laboratory for implementing neoliberal concepts. A textbook example of combined patriarchal backlash and neoliberal extractiveness worked hand in hand with disastrous consequences for human lives. See Pryluka (2022).
9 See Campbell (2010).
10 More inspiration can be found in Kelleher (2019).
11 See Göttner-Abendroth (2013).
12 Jacobs (2000: Position 175, Kindle).
13 The ideas of the following have inspired a paper that I have written together with my Club of Rome colleague Liepollo Lebohang Pheko; see Kuenkel & Pheko (2025). In turn, the paper has then greatly influenced the revision of this chapter.
14 See Ramphele (2022); Webster (2022).
15 Feminist inspiration can be found in Shiva (2005), Eisler (2007), D'Alessandro (2017).
16 An example of such a pilot project is evaluated in Ghuman (2022).
17 See UNFCCC (2024).
18 Inspiration can be found in Folbre (2006).
19 See WHO Council on the Economics of Health for All (2023).
20 See FEMNET (2020, July 7).
21 See Chomba &Belay (2024, June 3).
22 For more information, see SADC (2020).
23 See Oluoch et al. (2022).
24 An example can be found in Berik (2020).
25 For an overview of alternative sustainability progress indexes, see Jansen et al. (2024).
26 This was attempted in Tanzania under Mwalimu Julius Nyerere.
27 See Mintrom (2019).
28 For an overview, see Durie (2006).
29 The reality seems that women are still less happy, meaning there is a long way to go. See Verma & Ura (2022).
30 Berik (2020).
31 Inspiration can be found in Shiva (2005).
32 See Ostrom (1990).
33 See National Planning Authority Uganda (2020).
34 See National Planning Commission South Africa (2012).
35 See Tanzania Gender Networking Program (TGNP): https://tgnp.or.tz
36 See Castaño (2023, June 9).

37 Such efforts can be found in different areas of the world, often based on international agreements, such as the *UN Convention on the Elimination of All Forms of Discrimination against Women (CEDAW)*; see: UN Women (2009).
38 Bryan et al. (2024) and Amoak et al. (2022).
39 An overview of an Africa-based feminist approach to debt relief can be found in FEMNET (2021).
40 Kristina Lunz offers a very comprehensive overview of the history and contemporary approaches to feminist foreign policies in her book *The Future of Foreign Policy Is Feminist*. See Lunz (2023).
41 For more information, see UNFCCC (2021).
42 See Berros (2021).
43 A brilliant overview article about Feminist Ecologies can be found in Ojeda et al. (2022).

References

Amoak, D., Najjar, D., & Kyle, J. (2022). *Gender and Climate-relevant Agri-Food Systems Governance: A Strategic Evidence Review*. Beirut, Lebanon: International Center for Agricultural Research in the Dry Areas (ICARDA).

Bergsteiner H., and Dharmapiya P. (2016) The sufficiency economy philosophy process. In Avery, G.C. & Bergsteiner, H. (Eds.). *Sufficiency Thinking. Thailand's Gift to an Unsustainable World*. Sydney, Australia: Allen and Unwin.

Berik, G. (2020, March). Measuring what matters and guiding policy: An evaluation of the Genuine Progress Indicator. *Special Issue: Future of work (Part II): Rethinking institutions for social justice*, *159*(1), 71–94.

Berros, M.V. (2021). Challenges for the implementation of the rights of nature: Ecuador and Bolivia as the first instances of an expanding movement. *Latin American Perspectives*, 48(3), 192–205. https://doi.org/10.1177/0094582x211004898

Bryan, E., Alvi, M., Huyer, S. & Ringler, C. (2024). Addressing gender inequalities and strengthening women's agency to create more climate resilient and sustainable food systems. *Global Food Security*, 40: 100731. https://doi.org/10.1016/j.gfs.2023.100731, https://www.sciencedirect.com/science/article/pii/S2211912423000615

Campbell, H. (2010). Structural adjustment policies: A feminist critique. *Journal of Political and International Studies Sigma: Journal of Political and International Studies*, *27*(2), 1–1. https://scholarsarchive.byu.edu/cgi/viewcontent.cgi?article=1184&context=sigma

Castaño, L.P. (2023, June 9). *Barcelona: A Feminist Municipalism Now at Risk*. Social Europe. https://www.socialeurope.eu/barcelona-a-feminist-municipalism-now-at-risk

Chomba, S., & Belay, M. (2024, June 3). *Land Squeeze: The Hidden Battle for Africa's Soils*. African Arguments. https://africanarguments.org/2024/06/land-squeeze-green-grabs-hidden-battle-for-africas-soils

D'Alessandro, M. (2017). *Economía feminista: Cómo construir una sociedad igualitaria (sin perder el glamour)*. Sudamericana.

Durie, M. (2006). *Measuring Māori Wellbeing*. New Zealand Treasury Guest Lecture. https://www.treasury.govt.nz/sites/default/files/2007-09/tgls-durie.pdf

Eisler, R. (2007). *The Real Wealth of Nations: Creating a Caring Economics*. San Francisco, CA: Berrett-Koehler Publishers, Inc.

Ellen MacArthur Foundation (2013). *Towards the Circular Economy*. Isle of White, UK.

Felber, C. (2018). *Gemeinwohl-Ökonomie*. Piper.

FEMNET. (2020, July 7). African feminist post-Covid-19 economic recovery statement – FEMNET. https://www.femnet.org/2020/07/african-feminist-post-covid-19-economic-recovery-statement

FEMNET (2021). Debt & Women's Rights: A Pan African Feminist Perspective. African Feminist Macroeconomic Academy. https://femnet.org/wp-content/uploads/2022/10/AFMA-Report-2022_Optimised.pdf

Fioramonti, L. (2017). *Wellbeing Economy*. Pan Macmillan South Africa.

Folbre, N.(1995). Holding hands at midnight: The paradox of caring labor. *Feminist Economics, 1*(1), 73–92.

Folbre, N. (2006). Measuring care: Gender, empowerment, and the care economy. *Journal of Human Development, 7*(2), 183–199. https://doi.org/10.1080/14649880600768512

Gago, V., & Mason-Deese, L. (2017). *Neoliberalism From Below: Popular Pragmatics and Baroque Economies*. Duke University Press.

Ghuman, U. (2022). A Policy Review of the SEED (Stockton Economic Empowerment Demonstration) Project: Is the Devil in the Details? *Int Journal of Community Wellbeing*, 5(4), 819–830. doi: 10.1007/s42413-021-00145-3. Epub 2022 Sep 13. PMID: 36118591; PMCID: PMC9469043. https://www.ncbi.nlm.nih.gov/pmc/articles/PMC9469043

Göttner-Abendroth, H. (2013). *Matriarchal Societies: Studies on Indigenous Cultures Across the Globe*. Peter Lang.

Jacobs, J. (2000). *The Nature of Economies*. Random House Digital, Inc.

Jacobsen, J.P. (2020) *Advanced Introduction to Feminist Economics*. Elgar Advanced Introductions series. Hobart and William Smith Colleges, US.

Jansen, A., Wang, R., Behrens, P., & Hoekstra, R. (2024). Beyond GDP: A review and conceptual framework for measuring sustainable and inclusive well-being. *The Lancet Planetary Health*, 8(9), e695–e705. https://doi.org/10.1016/s2542-5196(24)00147-5

Kelleher, F. (2019). Disrupting Orthodoxies in Economic Development – An African Feminist Perspective. *Feminist Africa*, 22, 128–138. https://feministafrica.net/wp-content/uploads/2019/05/fa22_critical_reflection_3.pdf

Kuenkel, P. (2022). Collective stewardship towards life economies. In: Künkel, P., Ragnarsdottir, K.V. (eds). *Transformation Literacy*. Cham: Springer. https://doi.org/10.1007/978-3-030-93254-1_21

Kuenkel, P., & Pheko, L.L. (2025). Feminist perspectives on transforming economies. *Earth4All Deep Dive Paper*. The Club of Rome. Available at: forthcoming.

Lovins H.L., Wallis S., Wijkman A. & Fullerton J. (2018) *A Finer Future. Creating an Economy in Service to Life*. Gabriola Island, British Colombia, Canada: New Society Publishers.

Lunz, K. (2023). *The Future of Foreign Policy Is Feminist*. John Wiley & Sons.

Magnuson J. (2007). *Mindful Economics. How the U.S. Economy Works, Why it Matters, and How it could be Different*. New York: Seven Stories Press.

Mazzucato M. (2021). *Mission Economy. A Moonshot Guide to Changing Capitalism*. HarperCollins.

Mintrom, M. (2019). New Zealand's Wellbeing Budget invests in population health. *The Milbank Quarterly*, 97(4), 893–896. https://doi.org/10.1111/1468-0009.12409

National Planning Authority Uganda. (2020). *Third National Development Plan (NDPIII) 2020/21 – 2024/25*. https://www.npa.go.ug/wp-content/uploads/2023/03/NDPIII-Finale_Compressed.pdf

National Planning Commission South Africa. (2012). Our future – make it work: National Development Plan, 2030. Nhttps://www.gov.za/sites/default/files/gcis_document/201409/ndp-2030-our-future-make-it-workr.pdf

Ojeda, D., Nirmal, P., Rocheleau, D., & Emel, J. (2022). Feminist Ecologies. *Annual Review of Environment and Resources*, 47(1), 149–171. https://doi.org/10.1146/annurev-environ-112320-092246

Oluoch, S., Lal, P., Susaeta, A., Mugabo, R., Masozera, M., & Aridi, J. (2022). Public Preferences for Renewable Energy Options: A choice experiment in Rwanda. *Frontiers in Climate*, 4. https://doi.org/10.3389/fclim.2022.874753 https://www.frontiersin.org/journals/climate/articles/10.3389/fclim.2022.874753

Ostrom, E. (1990). *Governing the Commons: The Evolution of Institutions for Collective Action*. Cambridge University Press.

Peters, M.A. (2010). Neoliberalism, the market and performativity. *International Encyclopedia of Education*, 11–16. https://doi.org/10.1016/b978-0-08-044894-7.00543-1

Pistor, K. (2020). *The Code of Capital: How the Law Creates Wealth and Inequality*. Princeton University Press.

Powell, L.F. (1971, August 23). Memorandum: Attack on American free enterprise system. Scholarlycommons.law.wlu.edu. https://scholarlycommons.law.wlu.edu/powellmemo

Pryluka, P. (2022). Advertising Pinochet: The Cold War limits to a neoliberal crusade. *International History Review*, *45*(2), 1–15. https://doi.org/10.1080/07075332.2022.2139283

Ramphele, M. (2022). A living systems approach to achieving global equity for a healthy planet. *Earth4All Deep Dive Paper*. https://www.clubofrome.org/wp-content/uploads/2022/06/Earth4All_Deep_Dive_Ramphele.pdf

Raworth, K. (2017). *Doughnut Economics: Seven ways to Think like a 21st Century Economist*. Chelsea Green Publishing.

Richardson, K., Steffen, W., Lucht, W., Bendtsen, J., Cornell, S., Donges, J.F., Drüke, M., Fetzer, I., Bala, G., Werner von Bloh, Feulner, G., Fiedler, S., Gerten, D., Gleeson, T., Hofmann, M., Willem Huiskamp, Matti Kummu, Mohan, C., Bravo, D., & Petri, S. (2023). Earth beyond Six of Nine Planetary Boundaries. *Science Advances*, 9(37). https://doi.org/10.1126/sciadv.adh2458

SADC. (2020). Women Economic Empowerment Programme. https://www.sadc.int/pillars/women-economic-empowerment-programme

Shiva, V. (2005). *Earth Democracy: Justice, Sustainability, and Peace*. Zed Books.

Shiva, V., & Mies, M. (1993). *Ecofeminism*. Zed Books.

Stockholm Resilience Centre. (2023). Planetary Boundaries. https://www.stockholmresilience.org/research/planetary-boundaries.html

Trebeck K. and Williams J. (2019). *The Economics of Arrival. Ideas for a Grown Up Economy*. Bristol, UK: Policy Press.

UN Women. (2009). *Convention on the Elimination of All Forms of Discrimination against Women*. https://www.un.org/womenwatch/daw/cedaw

UNFCCC. (2021). Payments for Environmental Services Program | Costa Rica. https://unfccc.int/climate-action/momentum-for-change/financing-for-climate-friendly-investment/payments-for-environmental-services-program

UNFCCC. (2024). Fund for responding to loss and damage. https://unfccc.int/loss-and-damage-fund-joint-interim-secretariat

Verma, R., & Ura, K. (2022). Gender differences in gross national happiness: Analysis of the first nationwide wellbeing survey in Bhutan. *World Development*, 150, 105714. ISSN 0305-750X, https://doi.org/10.1016/j.worlddev.2021.105714. https://www.sciencedirect.com/science/article/pii/S0305750X21003296

Webster, K. (2022). The long road to a social dividend. *Earth4All Deep Dive Paper*. https://www.clubofrome.org/wp-content/uploads/2022/06/Earth4All_Deep_Dive_Webster.pdf

WHO Council on the Economics of Health for All. (2023). *Health for All: Transforming economies to deliver what matters*. Geneva: World Health Organization. https://iris.who.int/bitstream/handle/10665/373122/9789240080973-eng.pdf?sequence=1

The Way Forward

When writing this book, at times I felt like an astronaut who, returning from the moon, gazes at our fragile blue planet with all its beauty, which ought to be loved, cherished and cared for. Like the astronaut, from a distance, I could not see borders, not the brutal, yet absurd wars that for minor reasons, for an additional dose of power during a life time of a pathological man, destroy souls, people, civilizational achievements, love and the beauty of nature. The magic glasses that I wore let me see *collective feminist power practices* around the world, today and since ancient times. My heart leaped. Wherever I landed – be it a geography, a feminist discourse, a place of female longing, a sacred site, a crowd of women who took to the streets, a home in which women were suffering – I saw how women who made a decisive contribution to world development, small or large, disappeared from knowledge production and memory. I felt the tension between my landings in reality and my bird's eye perspectives that clearly revealed the potency of feminist transformations. I believe we need both the immersion in female suffering, feminist anger, feminist aspirations and the conviction that recreating and co-creating a different world is possible.

We need to give credit to the many waves of feminist movements that have enhanced our ability to see, observe and name patriarchy, as well as analyze the mechanisms of its self-preservation – from different perspectives and in great detail. In order to overcome patriarchy, we have devised, argued about and implemented strategies, of which there are almost as many as there are women in the world. We have disputed our choice of strategy, accused each other of complicity and succumbed to the lure of a share in power. It is time to move beyond the arguments, to cherish contentious discourses while embracing the bigger picture. What unites us is the desire to change everything – toward future civilizations where women realize their potential, because everyone does, and where caring for life on this planet is the essence of freedom.

We know that, before patriarchy, there were societies all over the world that used a different symbolic order, one in which creating, maintaining and protecting life was sacred. We have seen that all major monotheistic religions have made use of this sacredness of a female creation myth by twisting, turning and abusing it, so that the potency to create life was glorified as unattainable and paradisiacal, while the mandate to destroy life was established as the right of the strongest. Many people, men and women, fought against this dominant order. Eventually, more and more mechanisms were created to curb its out-of-control dynamics. Our imperfect democracies, human rights, laws, constitutions and governance mechanisms are such attempts. But globally, the right of the strongest has repeatedly prevailed in its life-destroying form. It is time we change these trajectories and take our power back.

Patriarchy is in decay. No matter how severe patriarchal resurgence occurs, the process towards egalitarian, peaceful and life-sustaining civilizations has begun. It is the process to rehabilitate life on this planet. Our attention must go to these manifestations of the future. They exist worldwide, though the strongest moves so far come from the Global South. World-making can no longer be delegated to men with severe power pathologies. We need to invest our ability to care into places that are pioneers of feminist transformations and we need to take on political and economic decision-making responsibility in order to transform patriarchal spaces from within into feminist ones. We need to do more than demand that those who uphold the system act differently. We need to get to the centers of power.

In view of the many crises that we as humanity will face in the coming decades, we need the decentralization of power, in other words a high level of competence in involving everyone in decision-making processes in such a way that consensus is more likely and conflict is avoided. Feminists can and will be the pioneers of distributive power, knowing that many of our global crises can only be solved locally. Our power will grow with our ability to access power, and in doing so we will realize how important it is not to squander our energy on institutions that maintain the world of the past, but to transform them – together. To do this we need pragmatic feminists in positions of influence. Not a few feminists, but many. Not individual women who despair of the future and ultimately bow to the social realities of patriarchy. We need feminists who exercise power collectively and share responsibility among themselves – as they have done since ancient times all around the world. In English and many other languages, the term responsibility entails both *responsiveness* and *ability*. This is the skill we must re-acquire. Exercising power responsibly as women, with women and among women. *Collective feminist power practices* are part of our path into the future. Not abusing power is an art that women must also learn. But today we have few places, forms, rules or training for this. Instead, we have countless examples of abuse of power. Power needs control mechanisms.

They existed in ancient times. They exist today, but need to be tremendously improved.

In order to improve the mechanisms for controlling power, we must free ourselves from the demons of our limited thinking instilled in us from childhood. We learned it in every school lesson and still breathe it in every day. It whispers mercilessly that world-making, decision-making power by and among women is morally unacceptable. It feeds the belief that power, when it grows, can only have a destructive effect, an idea rooted in our collective experience, shaped by centuries, by millennia of patriarchal history. Deep in our hearts, we encounter the thought that we must always share power with men, and that women having more power than men will inevitably lead to violent backlashes. This is not about denying slightly less than half of the world's population the power of world-making. Collaboration with all egalitarian futurists is the route to take. But we must not reject the collective power of women because we have learned that the collective power of men is destructive. One day we will begin to notice that power is more than asserting interests against others, more than claiming an area of influence at any cost, more than translating aspirations into clear goals. We will remember that power is the generative potency to create the future together. It is our potency. It emerges when we help each other achieve meaningful impact. When we reach this crucial crossroads on our shared path, the responsibility that comes with power may at first feel like a burden. And yes, responsibility is a burden – but collective responsibility can also be a source of joy.

Do I want to look into the future, knowing that scientists predict a bleak outcome due to climate change? Do I want to arm myself against the storms that destroy houses, the floods that sweep away cities, the fires that turn entire regions into lifeless grey, and the droughts that wither grain in the fields? Do I want to witness men starting endless wars and, when one ends, new ones beginning elsewhere? All because of nothing but their addiction to power, disguised as freedom, protection or salvation? No, I do not want to look into the future.

But when I look into the past, a question arises on the horizon: Who, if not us women, has forfeited our power? What if there were an awareness of our potency for world-making that spanned the globe like an invisible net? What if what has survived for so long on islands of feminist future-makers was now coming together – intertwined, connected – so that these islands begin to bloom, shine and speak? Each in her own beauty, her own clarity? What if this old and new consciousness were growing stronger, emerging across female territories?

The visionaries of feminist futures – the pioneers of peaceful, egalitarian societies who honor and care for people and the planet – have always existed and are here today. What if we became aware of our majority? How will we learn to hear the choir, multi-voiced in both harmony and disharmony?

Most ancient and contemporary cultures across the globe know a variation of the practice of *Ubuntu.* This is a South African term that stands for an understanding of 'I am because you are', suggesting a deep interconnectedness, meaning that world-making is a co-creative, collaborative and collective act. Life is a dynamic matrix, influenced by every single act. The dominant patriarchal, often western, capitalist and surely neoliberal doctrine, however, is 'I can only be, if you are not.' This globally sanctioned mental state that is actually an aberration of human consciousness, has determined patriarchal history and present. It is enacted in the many variations we know, from colonization, genocide and war atrocities to declaring the lives of people disposable to monopolist wealth supremacy.

Yet the days of patriarchy are numbered. Women will take over the spheres of influence in the world. This is the only chance for future civilizations to shape the many worlds within one world. Periods of peace have always been those in which women experienced strong recognition. During these times, humanity developed culturally, embracing social diversity, participation and flourishing art and culture. All advanced social cultures have been built on peaceful eras. War has always cost human lives and brutalized people, leading to long phases of cultural regression. There will be future wars – not instigated or led by the protagonists of the new, ancient consciousness, but by those determined to preserve the current order at all costs. The signs of a resurgence of violent addiction to dominating power are visible at every corner.

But never again – really, never again – should we lose ourselves in the traps of complicity or become targets of patriarchal divide and rule pathologies. Never again should our vision of the *Good Life for All* be forgotten in the fog of daily struggles. We must act here and now.

It starts with a culture of disobedience in thinking. This means boldly and courageously identifying positions of power and influence where feminists could make important decisions. Then it is a matter of finding possible candidates from a feminist network and paving the way for them to take up these positions. This network will develop dynamically and decentrally as mutual support from circles of women who feel committed to the basic principles of a feminist future. The prerequisite for assuming positions of power is that women are prepared to relate to one another radically and to perceive and assume power through women. This will give rise to three positive obligations that the women being supported by other women would have to accept. Firstly, to ensure that other women in the network also come into positions of power and influence. Secondly, to use their influence in such a way that the building blocks of a future society are put together step by step – i.e. to transform the respective organizations or policy areas in a feminist way. Thirdly, that women in influential positions recognize that they have become influential through women and therefore expose themselves to feedback from a dedicated circle of feminists. Although crucially important, simply redefining power and building it up as female power outside of dominator structures is not enough for our feminist transformation project. Patriarchal structures have their own dynamics and resilience. To erode these structures, a global network of feminists, diverse in their identities and approaches, is absolutely essential. But this alone is not enough. Feminists must also take up positions of power within patriarchal structures, as these structures uphold the system. Only by being at the center of these structures can feminists transform them, and they must do this in collaboration with women working outside patriarchal institutions. This will create a dynamic network, a powerful connection between feminists, alive, learning from consensus as much as from disagreements. It will be such pulsating networks that will make feminist transformations one day a reality.

We have developed feminist knowledge, forged strategic plans and drawn up blueprints for feminist futures. We have accused the culprits of life-destructive patriarchy. We have made our presence known, shouted loud, given speeches and written open letters. We will continue to do so. But all of this remains only a hope of exerting influence, if we do not take power ourselves, and that can only happen step by step. Power must be claimed; only then will it be attributed. It depends on how this claim takes place, because we must weave a feminist-defined concept of power into patriarchal power structures everywhere. We must resist all modern temptations of narcissistic greed. We must do everything we can to change the patriarchal order without succumbing to its temptations. Where participation in power leads to social privileges that others do not have, and this is neither reflected upon nor criticized nor changed, we are complicit with the patriarchal culture of dominance. Female freedom, or more precisely, sovereignty, cannot be realized in equality as an adaptation to the symbolic order of patriarchy, nor in the successful struggle for recognition within the limited constructs of society that patriarchy offers and with which it maintains itself. Female freedom, the possibility of choosing how to shape one's life, arises where women create relationships of mutual attribution of power and recognition and rebuild patriarchal structures. What we need when we take up positions of power in order to change power structures is a *feminist reference system*, one that redefines power in terms of its impact on positive social change towards a *Good Life for All*. Such a *feminist reference system* would then be the underlying symbolic order of the future, one that strengthens us and guides our actions. It would be the basis of our actions, of our *collective feminist power practice*.

Feminist transformations are both revolution and evolution. We do not seek to renovate patriarchy; we aim to abolish it.

Thus, we are on our way. The feminist vision is neither a rigid rule nor a fixed code of conduct. It is not a single recipe for a universal solution, politically, economically or culturally. It represents many solutions, many worlds within one world. It is a process of transformation in which the patterns of future societies must be embedded in the present – pattern by pattern, step by step, activity by activity, dream by dream, organization by organization. This is how the vision of peaceful coexistence, a balance between human cultures built on social generosity, and harmony with nature takes root. It recognizes and appreciates the diversity of peoples, cultures, ways of life, languages, religions and philosophies. Groundbreaking changes – those that are truly transformative – happen slowly. They require time and repetition in countless variations to become effective through a network of change agents. They must take root to anchor themselves deeply, growing many branches into the air. Success will prevail gradually. Setbacks are not proof of failure.

Our planet is asking for humanity to change, even though it can exist without us. Even if we want to help shape the change, the future cannot be unraveled. But maps of our feminist futures need to be written in its many forms. This is the challenge: In view of the current political and ecological situation, the question arises whether we have already lost the future. The rivers are crying, the seas are shedding tears on their shores, wars are not diminishing, patriarchal imperialism is booming, the staging of pathological masculinity in fascism is once again becoming socially acceptable, militarization is stirring up trouble with rearmament, and nuclear war is silently looming.

Understanding the possible patterns of future feminist-inspired civilizations is crucial for our departure into utopia that can became real. The future feminist-inspired civilizations we envisage do not prescribe behavior. They do not have a fixed framework like communism, socialism, capitalism or anarchism, but take up those elements that further a *Good Life for All*. This vision is to be understood as a process, a global learning process, based on understanding life in its ability to generate, learning from it, protecting it, expanding it. When we begin to remember a world before this world, then we know that the path to future civilizations requires peaceful coexistence, that only balance and generosity will keep us on the path.

The certainty of the impending patriarchal catastrophe can be projected linearly into the future. Will we be able to stop this projection in a non-linear way? When we begin to live feminist futures, time takes on a new dimension. We will begin to think in centuries, possibly millennia. The present becomes more important, somehow fuller, more alive. Some things lose importance, others gain.

What if we are truly approaching a turning point that will change the entire system? What if many elements of our transformative work – networks, initiatives and connections between feminists in positions of power and influence – are already beginning to converge, step by step? What if the many changes taking place in so many parts of the world are already the foundational building blocks of new civilizations? What if it is simply a matter of connecting the nodes to create the future? What if women have already taken power long ago, but it remains dispersed, and we need to ensure they connect so they can exercise power in countless places simultaneously?

We can take two paths. One is a radical return to humanity – an immersion in our capacity to love: Life, people and Mother Earth. As bell hooks taught us, this is the only road that leads to freedom.[1] The other is a radical claim to collective feminist power – a commitment to taking humanity's fate into our collective hands. Can we recognize that these paths are not in conflict, but rather loving siblings?

Note

1 hooks (1999).

Reference

hooks, bell. (1999). *All About Love: New Visions*. Harper Perennial.

Annex 1: Glossary

Anthropocene The current geological age, characterized by humanity's significant influence on Earth's ecosystems and evolutionary processes.

Attention Economy A concept in information management that views people's attention as a scarce, valuable and sellable commodity.

Capitalist Enclosure The process by which common resources, land or social goods are privatized or commodified, restricting access and concentrating power within capitalist systems.

Collective Feminist Leadership A non-hierarchical approach to leadership that prioritizes shared responsibility, mutual respect and feminist values, aiming for transformative change.

Collective Feminist Power Practice A collaborative approach to claiming power grounded in feminist practices of mutual re-powerment, networked connectivity, courageous discovery, reflective appreciation, dialogic reciprocity and future aspirations.

Collective Intelligence The shared or group intelligence that emerges from collaboration and collective efforts, enabling effective problem-solving and decision-making.

Collective Stewardship The collective capacity of diverse actors to bring about systems change for a sustainable and equitable future, spanning institutions, countries and communities.

Commodification of Nature The process of assigning monetary value to ecosystems or natural resources, often leading to exploitation within a capitalist framework.

Complicity The unconscious or tacit support of oppressive systems, particularly patriarchy, through subtle or invisible actions and inactions.

Corporate Capture The process by which economic elites exert undue influence over public institutions, laws and policies, undermining human rights and environmental protections for personal or corporate gain.

Ecocide A term used to describe actions that cause significant and lasting damage to the environment or the planet's life support systems, considered a crime against humanity and the planet by legal frameworks.

Ecofeminism A movement or perspective linking ecological preservation with feminism, emphasizing the interconnectedness of environmental and gender justice.

Feminist Power The collective capability to shape futures centered on equality, justice and the well-being of all, creating the conditions for a *Good Life for All*.

Feminist Reference System A framework guiding decisions, values and social structures based on feminist principles, emphasizing equality, justice and inclusivity while centering the well-being of people and the planet.

Feminist Transformation Ecosystem A dynamic, interconnected, collaborating, cross-sectoral and loosely coordinated network of institutions, individuals in institutions and initiatives dedicated to fostering feminist transformations across societal, cultural and economic systems.

Gender Equality The state in which individuals of all genders have equal rights, responsibilities and opportunities in all aspects of life.

Globalization The process by which businesses, cultures and economies become interconnected and interdependent on a global scale.

Good Life for All An inclusive, life-serving vision centered on achieving well-being, justice and vitality for all people and the planet. It emphasizes feminist values such as equality, interdependence and sustainability, creating the conditions for everyone to thrive.

Intersectional Feminism A framework acknowledging how different forms of discrimination – such as sexism, racism and classism – intersect, aiming to address these interconnected oppressions.

Intersectionality A concept highlighting how various forms of discrimination and privilege intertwine, such as those based on gender, race, class, sexuality or ability, shaping individuals' experiences and opportunities.

Matriarchy A societal arrangement that demonstrates a balance between the sexes, with female spiritual, social and economic power playing a central role.

Mental Infrastructure The collective cognitive and emotional frameworks, beliefs and norms that shape individual and societal understanding, decision-making and behavior. It reflects deeply ingrained cultural narratives and values that influence how societies operate and evolve.

Nuclear Family A family unit consisting of two parents and their children, viewed as a foundational social structure of patriarchal societies.

Patriarchal Backlash The reactionary resistance against feminist progress and gender equality, often characterized by attempts to reinforce traditional patriarchal norms and structures. It manifests through policies, cultural narratives or violence aimed at suppressing feminist advances.

Patriarchal Power Pathology Dysfunctional or harmful expressions of power that perpetuate oppression, inequality or environmental harm.

Planetary Boundaries Thresholds within which humanity can safely operate, ensuring that Earth's critical systems remain stable and sustainable for future generations.

Policy and Regulatory Capture The undue influence of private or elite interests on public regulatory bodies and policy-making, often resulting in decisions that prioritize profits over public welfare.

Polycrisis A situation where multiple, interconnected crises (e.g., climate change, economic inequality, political instability) reinforce and exacerbate one another, creating complex challenges that require systemic, holistic solutions.

Potencia A form of collective, transformative power emerging from grassroots mobilization and everyday struggles, embodying feminist agency that confronts patriarchy and builds alternative futures.

Potency The inherent power or capacity to create, influence and transform. In feminist contexts, potency refers to the generative force of collective and individual actions that drive transformative change and world-making.

Realization Power A form of individual and collective capacity to create futures that have meaningful impact, whether on a small or large scale.

Reproductive Enclosure The restriction or control of reproductive rights and labor through systems of patriarchy and capitalism, limiting women's autonomy over their bodies and choices.

Soft Authoritarianism A form of governance that maintains control through subtle, indirect means, such as media manipulation, cultural influence or the erosion of democratic norms, rather than overt force.

State Capture The manipulation of government laws, policies or institutions by private interests, leading to systemic inequality and harm to public welfare.

Symbolic Order The system of cultural symbols, norms and structures through which meaning is constructed and maintained in a society. It shapes identities, relationships and power dynamics, often reinforcing dominant ideologies such as patriarchy unless it is challenged and transformed.

System Vitality The ability of a system to remain resilient and develop sustainably without compromising the vitality of interconnected systems.

Transversality A concept describing dynamics or relationships that intersect and traverse across domains, fostering interconnected and inclusive approaches.

Wealth Concentration The accumulation of wealth in the hands of a small elite, often leading to systemic inequality and a concentration of power.

Women's Strike A global movement challenging patriarchy and neoliberal capitalism through collective protest, addressing intersectional issues like gender-based violence, economic inequality and social justice.

Index

Kolibri 360 GmbH
Ferdinand-Jühlke-Straße 7
99095 Erfurt, Deutschland
produktsicherheit@kolibri360.de